KNOWING THE

Historians have traditionally seen domestic service as an obsolete or redundant sector from the middle of the twentieth century. *Knowing Their Place* challenges this by linking the early twentieth-century employment of maids and cooks to later practices of employing au pairs, mothers' helps, and cleaners. Lucy Delap tells the story of lives and labour within British homes, from great houses to suburbs and slums, and charts the interactions of servants and employers along with the intense controversies and emotions they inspired.

Knowing Their Place also examines the employment of men and migrant workers, as well as the role of laughter and erotic desire in shaping domestic service. The memory of domestic service and the role of the past in shaping and mediating the present is examined through heritage and televisual sources, from *Upstairs, Downstairs* to *The 1900 House*. Drawing from advice manuals, magazines, novels, cinema, memoirs, feminist tracts, and photographs, this fascinating book points to new directions in cultural history through its engagement in innovative areas such as the history of emotions and cultural memory. Through its attention to the contemporary rise in the employment of domestic workers, *Knowing Their Place* sets modern Britain in a new and compelling historical context.

Lucy Delap is a social and cultural historian with research interests in feminism, class, religion, and gender. Her book *The Feminist Avant-Garde: Transatlantic Encounters of the Early Twentieth Century* was published in 2007 and won the 2008 Women's History Network Prize. She co-edited *The Politics of Domestic Authority in Britain since 1800* (2009), contributed to *Feminist Media History* (2010), and has published widely on British and American feminism. She was educated in London, Swaziland and Cambridge, and has taught at the University of Cambridge and King's College London.

Knowing Their Place

Domestic Service in Twentieth-Century Britain

LUCY DELAP

OXFORD
UNIVERSITY PRESS

OXFORD
UNIVERSITY PRESS

Great Clarendon Street, Oxford OX2 6DP

Oxford University Press is a department of the University of Oxford.
It furthers the University's objective of excellence in research, scholarship,
and education by publishing worldwide.

Oxford is a registered trade mark of Oxford University Press
in the UK and in certain other countries

© Lucy Delap 2011

The moral rights of the author have been asserted

First published 2011
First published in paperback 2014

All rights reserved. No part of this publication may be reproduced,
stored in a retrieval system, or transmitted, in any form or by any means,
without the prior permission in writing of Oxford University Press,
or as expressly permitted by law, by licence or under terms agreed with the appropriate
reprographics rights organization. Enquiries concerning reproduction
outside the scope of the above should be sent to the Rights Department,
Oxford University Press, at the address above

You must not circulate this work in any other form
and you must impose this same condition on any acquirer

Published in the United States of America by Oxford University Press
198 Madison Avenue, New York, NY 10016, United States of America

British Library Cataloguing in Publication Data
Data available

Library of Congress Cataloging in Publication Data
Data available

ISBN 978–0–19–957294–6 (Hbk)
ISBN 978–0–19–871824–6 (Pbk)

Each agent has a practical, bodily knowledge of her present and potential position in the social space, a 'sense of one's place', as Goffman puts it, converted into a sense of placement which governs her experience of the place occupied, defined absolutely and above all relationally as a rank, and the way to behave in order to keep it ('pulling rank') and to keep within it ('knowing one's place', etc.). The practical knowledge conferred by this sense of position takes the form of emotion (the unease of someone who is out of place, or the ease that comes from being in one's place)... It is this practical knowledge that orients interventions in the symbolic struggles of everyday life which contribute to the construction of the social world.

Bourdieu, *Pascalian Meditations*, 184

I dedicate this book with love to Clive Lawson, who has shared in its long genesis, and provided all kinds of support, domestic, emotional, and intellectual.

Preface

During my years of schooling in Swaziland, I learnt some basic siSwati from a booklet issued to me, which seemed squarely aimed at giving the employers of domestic servants the ability to issue orders to their staff. I learnt how to conjugate all my verbs in the imperative, alongside the more useful insults and endearments learnt from my school friends. I was the beneficiary of the labour of a 'cleaning lady' during my London childhood, of Swazi domestic workers while a teenager at school, and since then, of bedmakers, gardeners, and kitchen staff in the Cambridge colleges that have hosted me as a student and lecturer. And during my years of study, I myself worked as a cleaner, in hospitals and homes for the elderly. It was during these years that my mother showed me a note received from her long-term cleaner, employed throughout most of my childhood, which reminded her: 'Did you know it'll be 22 years I've worked for you on Tuesday and can I have some more cream cleaner next week please.' I still exchange birthday cards with her. The world of paid domestic labour and its complex, insistent emotional ties has never seemed particularly distant. Though British public opinion widely considers domestic service to be safely confined to the past, it is in reality integrally, if unevenly, present in contemporary Britain. When journalist Martin Kettle assessed the impact of David Cameron during his early days as Prime Minister, he looked to the manner in which Cameron treated the staff at Chequers, compared to the lack of appreciation shown them by Gordon Brown.[1] The treatment of servants by patrician figures is still a yardstick of good breeding and suitability to govern.

During the writing of this book and as my two children were born, I myself hired my first of a series of domestic workers to help in my own home. I have been acutely conscious of the emotions and ambiguities of my own relationships to these domestic workers, male and female, migrant and local. My own intersections with domestic labour and domestic workers has deeply informed the writing of this book, and I acknowledge my indebtedness to these sometimes transient, sometimes cherished domestic workers.

This project was given initial direction and substance through the generosity of Leonore Davidoff, who bequeathed me many of her research notes and sources examining twentieth-century domestic service, and discussed chapters and ideas with me—I am hugely grateful and indebted to her. Special thanks are due to Mary Chapman and the Centre for Women's and Gender Studies at the University of British Columbia, for hosting me for two indispensable periods of leave and providing such wonderful intellectual stimulation. I also thank the eagle eyes and critical interventions of Maria Dicenzo, who sustains me in so many dimensions, always accompanied by so much laughter. Other colleagues and friends have read

---

[1] Kettle, 'A Man of Grace', *Guardian*, July 9, 2010, 31.

drafts and generously suggested directions and leads, and I thank Sarah Roberts, Andrew Urban, Michael Epp, Jan Ruger, Deborah Thom, John Davis, Barbara Taylor, Kath Holden, Ben Griffin, Jane Hamlett, Selina Todd, Laura Schwarz, Carol Dyhouse, Liz Delap, Glen Cavaliero, and Rebecca Empson. My archival work has been greatly helped by John Southall of Qualidata, University of Essex, and John Sargent of the City of Westminster Archives Centre. King's College and St Catharine's College, Cambridge, have both provided funds and wonderful spaces of collegiality that have sustained this research; the Centre for Research in the Arts, Social Sciences and Humanities of the University of Cambridge gave me a term's leave that enabled the final threads to be tied together.

I have interviewed and consulted many individuals during this research, and am grateful to the willingness of numbers of former servants and employers to share their memories, and to Ursula Holden for generously giving me access to her unpublished memoirs. Andrew Hann of English Heritage, Wall to Wall Productions Ltd, Helen Johnson of the Shugborough Estate, Bob Carter, Colin MacConnachie of the National Trust in Scotland, and Sophie Brown, Frances Bailey, Mike Sutherill, and Anna Forrest of the National Trust have also generously and insightfully discussed servant-keeping and its historic interpretation with me on various occasions. My thanks go to the Trustees of the Mass Observation Archive, University of Sussex, and to the Essex Record Office and Age Concern Essex for permission to quote from their archives, to the editors of the *Journal of British Studies*, for their supportive engagement with my work, and permission to reproduce parts of a journal article based on Chapter 4 of this study, and to the Trades Union Congress for permission to reproduce material from the Domestic Workers' Union. I'm also grateful to the editors of *Home Cultures* for permission to reproduce parts of a journal article in Chapter 3.

Contents

List of Illustrations	xiii
List of Abbreviations	xiv
Archives and Datasets Consulted	xv

Introduction	**1**
Emotional history	9
Employment trends	11
Sources	22
1. Twentieth-Century Servants	**26**
Entering service	31
Living-out servants, charwomen, and cleaners	35
Aspirations	41
Conditions in work	48
Wages and contracts	51
Mothers	56
Conclusions	59
2. Servant-Keepers and the Management of Servants	**63**
Victorian mistresshood	67
Variations in patterns of authority	77
Men, masculinity, and service	83
Legal constraints, philanthropy, and servants in combination	87
Children	93
Conclusions	96
3. 'Doing for Oneself': The Servantless Home	**98**
Varieties of servantless homes	100
Etiquette	102
Lady helps and nannies	105
Labour-saving homes and households	110
Interwar domesticity	115
Kitchens and cooking	121
Post-war 'servantless homes'	127
Conclusions	137
4. Kitchen-Sink Laughter: Domestic Service Humour	**140**
The laughter of employers	156
The laughter of servants	160
Shared jokes	166
Conclusions	168

5. 'The Good, the Bad, and the Spicy': Servants in Pornography and Erotica	**173**
Transformations of the erotic imaginary	177
'Public women'	181
Courting and comic Edwardian servants	183
Continuities and change	189
Domestic service re-eroticized	194
Periodization	199
Counter-narratives	201
Conclusions	204
6. **Heritage Nostalgia: Domestic Service Remembered and Performed**	**206**
Heritage and memory	207
Memoirs, dramas, and comedies	211
'Below stairs' in the 'great house'	220
Nostalgia and 'untold stories'	228
Conclusions	231
Conclusion	**236**
Bibliography	244
Primary Sources	244
Secondary Sources	247
Index	259

List of Illustrations

1. Daisy Noakes, courtesy of QueenSpark Books — 54
2. Front Cover Image from *The Town Bee Hive* by Daisy Noakes, courtesy of QueenSpark Books — 55
3. W. K. Haselden, 'Lady Domestic', *Daily Mirror*, Feb 24, 1921 (Mirrorpix) — 107
4. Our Susan, *Daily Mail Ideal Labour-Saving Home*, 1920, plate xxxiv, by permission of the National Library of Scotland — 113
5. 'The Hard Hit Middle Classes', British Commercial Gas Association advertisement, *The Times*, Mar 19, 1924, 18, by permission of Cambridge University Library — 114
6. W. K. Haselden, 'The Electric Kitchen', *Daily Mirror*, Sept 26, 1905 (Mirrorpix) — 119
7. Mrs Peel, *The Labour Saving House*, 1917, plate xiii, by permission of the National Library of Scotland — 122
8. 'How to Live Your Life Without Servants—and Enjoy It', advertisement, *The Times* Sept 18, 1959, 9, by permission of Cambridge University Library and courtesy of the BP/Castrol Archive, ARC203554 — 132
9. Pansy Pancake, *Comic Cuts*, Feb 22, 1913, 4–5, © The British Library Board, LON NT141 — 151
10. Mrs Sudds the Charlady, *Picture Fun*, Feb 11, 1913, 8 © The British Library Board, LON NT181 — 152
11. 'Spread of The Servant-Girl Graduate Idea', *Punch*, vol. 146, Jan 14, 1914, 36, by permission of Cambridge University Library — 153
12. W. K. Haselden, 'When Jack Tar takes Mary Ann's place', *Daily Mirror*, July 22, 1914 (Mirrorpix) — 162
13. H. M. Bateman, 'The Maid who was but Human', *Punch*, Dec 13, 1922, The Fitzwilliam Museum — 167
14. 'The Treasure', *Housewife*, Nov 1956, 185, by permission of Cambridge University Library — 171
15. 'Through the Opera-Glass', *Pick-me-up*, Feb 8, 1902, 311, by permission of Cambridge University Library — 187
16. 'Maid to Measure', *Parade*, June 30, 1962, 12, courtesy of Goldstar Publications, © The British Library Board, Cup.806.ee.5 — 196
17. *Curious*, May 1973, no. 39, 50, by permission of Cambridge University Library — 198
18. Union-Castle Safmarine advertisement, *Sunday Times Magazine*, Feb 25, 1968, 38, courtesy of Safmarine — 214
19. Ironing, Audley End House, English Heritage — 223
20. National Union of Domestic Workers pamphlet, 'Something Nice', 1938, courtesy of the Trades Union Congress — 241

List of Abbreviations

AC—Age Concern essay competitions
DWU—Domestic Workers Union
ERO—Essex Records Office
MRC—Modern Records Centre
NIH—National Institute of Houseworkers
TUC—Trades Union Congress

Archives and Datasets Consulted

- Blickling Hall Oral History Archive, Norfolk
- Birmingham Libraries and Archive Services
- British Film Institute
- British Library Sound Archive
- City of Westminster Archives Centre
- Edward Carpenter Papers, Sheffield City Council, Libraries Archives and Information
- The Edwardians: Family Life and Work Experience before 1918, Middle and Upper Class Families in the Early 20th Century, 1870–1977, Families: Families, Social Mobility and Ageing, an Intergenerational Approach, Qualidata/The National Social Policy and Social Change Archive, Albert Sloman Library, University of Essex
- Essex Records Office and Age Concern, Essex
- Exmoor Oral History Archive
- Imperial War Museum
- Mass Observation Archive, University of Sussex
- Modern Records Centre, University of Warwick
- The Women's Library, London Metropolitan University

Introduction

Throughout the twentieth century, domestic service had a compelling presence in British economic, social, and cultural life. For the first half of the twentieth century, it employed the largest numbers of women of any labour market sector in Britain. Households at all social levels employed domestic help. 'Servant problems' were painstakingly analysed in the periodical and daily presses, parliamentary investigations, and philanthropic reports, as well as featuring very prominently in comics, music hall, cinema and radio, drama and novels. Complaints and observations about employing servants were a staple of middle-class conversation; as Vera Brittain noted during World War I, 'The universal topics of maids and ration-cards... completely dominated the conversation in every household.'[1] 'The servant question' also influenced state policies, of housing, welfare, immigration, training, and education, and played out in courtrooms. Domestic service was extraordinarily prominent, as a socio-cultural and policy problem, as a widely experienced institution, and as a symbolic resource for social criticism and nostalgia. It formed a uniquely significant site in which individuals of different classes, generations, and migrant origin encountered each other and negotiated their social boundaries and identities.

Being employed or employing a servant had been a widely shared experience for large numbers of women at the start of the century, and though this was not so for the generations working after World War II, there seems to have been no corresponding diminution of cultural interest in domestic service. During the 1950s, when service has been judged by most historians to be definitively 'over' for Britons, the organization of domestic spaces and tasks was still permeated by talk of servants and how to live without them. In 1960, Katharine Whitehorn reviewed a book of reminiscences about domestic service in *The Spectator*, and admonished readers not to:

think of having maids simply in terms of having someone else to make the beds and chop the spinach. A book like this is a reminder that the very existence of servants imposed a way of life. It was a life without privacy; weaknesses, deviations from the social norm were all instantly remarked; *pas devant les domestiques* became an unconscious code affecting people's ideas of behaviour in everything.[2]

---

[1] Vera Brittain, *Testament of Youth: An Autobiographical Study of the Years 1900–1925* (London: V. Gollancz, 1933), 404.
[2] Katharine Whitehorn, 'Service Hatch', *The Spectator*, Sept 16, 1960, 416.

There is little sign, however, that her contemporaries ever took service to be just the sum of domestic duties. Domestic service had, and has, a high cultural profile in post-war Britain, in family history, light comedy, reality television, nostalgia cinema, and Britain's heritage industry. Its discomforts and encounters have been taken to stand in for much wider horizons—the 'spirit of the times' or social change in general. Simply put, domestic service has served as a foundational narrative amongst the stories British people tell about the twentieth century and its changes—about the formation of classes, about intimacy and individualization, about homes and housework, about 'modernity' and gender. This book sets out to explore why and how domestic service has had this powerful, continuing role in narrating the twentieth century and shaping our sense of the past.

Doing so requires a rethinking of the 'when' of domestic service. The underpinning 'rise and fall' domestic service narrative, ending variously at the death of Queen Victoria, or either of the World Wars, has been a convenient shorthand for talk of an 'end of an era', or the final demise of social relationships or forms of labour variously imagined as old, traditional, Victorian, or feudal. An 1890 'servant problem' article by Ellen Darwin (the wife of Francis Darwin and daughter-in-law of Charles Darwin), for example, noted the 'stale odour of feudalism' around domestic service, which had not kept pace with the 'modern spirit of human relations'.[3] Edwardians sometimes used domestic service as providing an index to the development of civilization or modernity in a society, in ways that paralleled attention to the condition of women. Amy Bulley, a suffragist writing in the *Westminster Review*, argued in 1891 that 'Domestic service, as it has existed hitherto, is a survival from a social state of things which has passed away, and, being now an anomaly, it is disappearing with as much rapidity as may be.'[4] The feminist Charlotte Perkins Gilman declared in 1903, 'As fast as industrial evolution progresses we find men less and less content to do [household labour] in this way; or, for that matter, women either.'[5] In 1927, J. B. Priestley termed domestic service 'as obsolete as the horse'.[6] Domestic service has been counterposed to ideas of modern living or 'modernity', which came to be articulated not simply through ideas of industrialization or post-industrialization, but also through new forms of domestic organization—'servantless' or 'labour-saving'—and associated material objects such as the long-handled floor polisher or the washing machine.[7]

---

[3] Mrs Francis (Ellen) Darwin, 'Domestic Service', *The Nineteenth Century*, Aug 1890, 287.
[4] Amy Bulley, 'Domestic Service', *Westminster Review*, 1891, 182.
[5] Charlotte Perkins Gilman, *The Home: It's Work and Influence* (New York, 1903), 107.
[6] J. B. Priestley, 'Servants', *Saturday Review*, Mar 19, 1927, 430.
[7] The prism of 'modernity' has proved productive, though historically slippery. Traditionally, modernity has been associated with the growth of an urban, middle-class 'public sphere', and thus with masculine worlds, though recent historical accounts of women's participation in civic, philanthropic, and professional activity has allowed more inclusive versions of modernity to emerge. 'Modernity' has been redefined as bound up with the emergence of suburban, working-class, or lower-middle-class lifestyles, suggesting its plurality (Judy Giles, *The Parlour and the Suburb: Domestic Identities, Class, Femininity and Modernity* (Oxford: Berg, 2004)). And in a significant extension to the Habermasian concept of the public sphere, attention to consumption amongst historians has expanded the realms in which modernity and its associated gender and class identities can be traced (Alan Kidd and David Nicholls, *Gender, Civic Culture and Consumerism: Middle-Class Identity in*

'Modernity' as an analytical concept tends to stress discontinuity with the past, and thus has lent itself to narratives of the decline or obsolescence of domestic service. 'Modernity' has, however, been too blunt a tool to uncover the ongoing ways in which servant-keeping was *reworked* rather than discarded in the twentieth century. It proves unhelpful to recognize the very contingent factors that have led to the fluctuating employment of domestic workers, and to discern the ways in which servant-keeping might be understood as modern, or amenable to modernization. The continuing use of cleaners, chars, and au pairs after World War II, as well as the rise in new forms of private domestic employment from the 1980s, has made the post-war decline in domestic service unconvincing as a necessary feature of a modernizing or post-industrial society. From an early-twenty-first-century perspective, there is nothing inevitable about the demise of servant-keeping; it no longer looks like a 'feudal', anachronistic institution that is obsolete in a modern, individualistic, secular democratic society, as many argued in the 1970s.[8] Instead, servant-keeping must be related to contingent factors of availability, affordability, and social acceptability; the 1980s and 1990s witnessed a conjunction of factors that allowed for a large expansion of domestic employment in some private homes.[9]

This book explores the evolution and reception of a number of competing discourses of 'modern living'. In doing so, it offers an alternative periodization of service, which reconnects the early, mid-, and late twentieth century, setting them within a single analytic frame. It traces the stories of three loosely defined generations. The first group are those entering adulthood during the Edwardian years, during whose childhoods domestic service had seemed a secure institution, but who were beginning to debate its discomforts, look for alternative jobs, and might somewhat jokingly envisage alternative domestic arrangements. Many began to experiment with, or were forced to tolerate, alternative domestic circumstances during World War I. Second, there are those entering adulthood during or after World War I, who variously felt domestic service to be insecure, intolerable, or anachronistic as a social institution, but nonetheless still widely experienced it. Provincial elementary schools in the interwar decades were still routinely aspiring for nothing more than domestic service for their female pupils, and were teaching a domestic science curriculum to that end. Middle-class households complained of, but did not widely experience, 'these servantless days'.[10] This is the generation

---

Britain, 1800–1940 (Manchester: Manchester University Press, 1999)), 19–24; Mica Nava, 'Modernity's Disavowal: Women, the City and the Department Store', in Mica Nava and Alan O'Shea (eds), *Modern Times: Reflections on a Century of English Modernity* (London: Routledge, 1996), 38–76. Indeed, it has proved productive to envisage diverse forms of modernity being marshalled against each other in the twentieth century, in contests to gain social and cultural capital and to stabilize class or gender identities in the twentieth century.

[8] Lewis A. Coser, 'Servants: The Obsolescence of an Occupational Role', *Social Forces*, 52 1 (1973), 31–40.

[9] N. Gregson and M. Lowe, *Servicing the Middle Classes: Class, Gender and Waged Domestic Labour in Contemporary Britain* (London: Routledge, 1994); Rosie Cox, *The Servant Problem: Domestic Employment in a Global Economy* (London: I. B. Tauris, 2006).

[10] Selina Todd, 'Poverty and Aspiration: Young Women's Entry to Employment in Inter-war England', *Twentieth Century British History*, 15 2 (2004), 119–42.

identified by J. B. Priestley as peculiarly shaped by domestic service: 'Their mothers were frankly servile, and their daughters will probably be frankly independent, but their generation, as oddly placed as this generation of masters and mistresses, will neither abandon itself to servility nor cut itself loose from it.'[11] And third, the generation born in the interwar years but entering adulthood during and after World War II is examined, for many of whom domestic service was still deeply influential upon their sense of self and family history, their expectations of home and working life, but who were increasingly likely to take alternative jobs, or manage their homes without residential servants. Many, however, still worked informally as cleaners, nannies, or home helps, or relied on au pairs and 'dailies' to clean their houses and mind their children. Finally, the book also places the late twentieth and early twenty-first centuries into the frame, periods when 'domestic service' became a site of nostalgia or fantasy, but which also witnessed a resurgence of paid private domestic work.

A focus on the twentieth century prompts revised historiographical approaches, new kinds of sources, and attention to diverse categories of domestic workers and employers. Carolyn Steedman has argued that a nineteenth-century frame is often inappropriately deployed to understand eighteenth-century domestic service, assuming low status, vulnerability, and sexual exploitation for which there is little historical evidence.[12] A similar comment might be made for the twentieth century, in which the melodramatic account of nineteenth-century service as a site of victimhood has persisted. Historians of domestic service have tended to situate it as an illustration of the lives of the poorest, most marginal, and most degraded workers. They have stressed the indignities of the lives of 'skivvies'; service has been represented as a dead end job that led at best to marriage or at worst, to a life of monotonous labour and economic insecurity. Though some domestic workers did lead marginalized lives and experienced exploitation, marginality is not the most revealing of historical frameworks. This book outlines a far more diverse setting for domestic service than the monotony of drudgery that has predominated in historical accounts.

In the twentieth century, new ways of thinking about service were offered by feminism and trade unionism; new scripts and aspirations for working-class young women were offered by the radio or cinema, and the organization, rituals, and material contents of British homes were transformed. Domestic service was shaped by the interventions of the state in labour markets, family life, and fiscal and welfare policies, though politicians were always unwilling to intervene in the conditions of work for private servants. Perhaps most significantly, alternative work, new forms of leisure, and better access to education for young women became widespread. Servants and other domestic workers had more labour-market choices, as well as opportunities to speak and write and became more culturally visible. 'Knowing

---

[11] J. B. Priestley, 'Servants', *Saturday Review*, Mar 19, 1927, 430.
[12] Carolyn Steedman, *Master and Servant: Love and Labour in the English Industrial Age* (Cambridge: Cambridge University Press, 2007), 14. Eighteenth- and early-nineteenth-century servants were, as Steedman has stressed, governed by a historically specific legal context of fiscal policies, competing bodies of law, and the development of ideas about slavery and political economy.

their place' was no longer simply a form of knowledge generated by the middle classes, but a form of self-fashioning and reflection on the part of servants. This book departs from an account of economic and social marginality and will explore domestic service through an account of the cultural and emotional centrality of service in British society. The familiar account of service as a location for the establishment of class will be re-assessed, and set alongside attention to other features of social experience—generational divides, regional and local diversity, gender, migration and ethnicity.

This study will use an inclusive definition of domestic work, prompted by a critical awareness that in the twentieth century, certain kinds of domestic service have been over-represented in historical narratives. 'Great house' service, for example, was the most valorized and recorded of the experiences of servants, despite being highly unrepresentative. There was a declining role for live-in servants in the twentieth century, and also for large staffs with specialized tasks assigned to individuals. Great houses formed a small minority of servant-keeping households, as did institutional service in nursing homes, hotels, and boarding houses. Yet the existence of working- or middle-class servant-keeping was made relatively invisible. The photographer Bill Brandt aimed to record the intense social contrasts of 1930s Britain in his collection of images *The English at Home*, first published in 1936. He foregrounded the domestic servants of the upper classes, set against images of deprivation within poor working-class households, and a comfortable servantless formality of the middle-class suburban home. The 'frowsy servant' working in a slum house acknowledged in Jack London's *The People of the Abyss* was never portrayed, nor the incorporation of servants' bells and rooms into newly built interwar suburban villas. Brandt's images dwelt instead on the formal spotless caps and aprons of parlourmaids and nannies, and didactically juxtaposed images of tired servants kept in late-night kitchens to their upper-class employers, in evening dress, laughing and socializing.[13]

This study will predominantly discuss the more typical single- or two-servant households, though the divide between institutional, great house, and small private house service became more fluid in the twentieth century. Institutional service lost much of its stigma as being 'not respectable' and very hard work in the twentieth century. It became a job of choice for larger numbers of young women, since it offered less surveillance of behaviour and fewer rituals of deference and servility.[14]

---

[13] Bill Brandt, *The English at Home* (London: B. T. Batsford, 1936). Brandt published many images of upper-class servant-keeping, including the *Picture Post* series 'The Perfect Parlourmaid', featuring the sinister 'Pratt', 'the stately parlourmaid of England': 'Pratt directs the other maids like a general in charge of an army. Nothing escapes her dark and inscrutable eyes. Everything about her is impeccably correct. Grown-ups are frightened to misbehave in front of her.' *Picture Post*, July 29, 1939, 43–7. Jack London, *The People of the Abyss* (London: Isbister, 1903), 18.

[14] By 1931, only 30 per cent of servants worked in houses employing more than one servant. Violet Markham and Florence Hancock, *Report on the Organisation of Private Domestic Employment* (London: HMSO, 1944), Table II. On great house service, see Pamela Sambrook, *Keeping Their Place: Domestic Service in the Country House* (Stroud: Sutton, 2005). For a valuable case study of institutional service, see the chapter on Oxford college scouts in Laura Schwarz, *A Serious Endeavour: Gender, Education and Community at St Hugh's 1886–2011* (London: Profile Books, 2011).

Since workers moved more freely between institutional and private house service, the chapters that follow will investigate both kinds of setting, though inevitably the much larger sector of employment in relatively small private houses predominates. Farm servants will also be discussed, though their experiences were fairly distinct from those of private indoor domestic servants, and their labour and conditions were much more closely connected to the agricultural workforce.[15]

Private house service varied dramatically in its conditions. It can loosely be divided into two sectors. On the one hand, there were the 'older', higher status servant-keeping establishments, in central London or amongst the elites of smaller provincial towns and cities. On the other, servant-keeping was found in the newer suburban households on the outskirts of London, Birmingham, Manchester, and other larger cities. It is in these latter households that the really intense antagonism seems to have been felt between mistress and servant. In the widespread invective against suburban living that characterized Edwardian commentaries, it was the 'villa mistress' who came in for the deepest dislike. Judy Giles has argued that the denigration of suburbia for much of the twentieth century has been an attempt to feminize this space and exclude it from any narratives about modernity. The figure of the 'villa mistress' specifically connoted the petty snobbery and empty tedium imagined in characterizing the subjectivities of suburbia.[16]

These suburban homes often employed married women working as chars or young servants still living at home; their experiences have been largely written out of historical narratives. Through these kinds of casual 'helps', 'servant-keeping' extended to some quite impoverished households. Mrs Chambers, who entered service in 1908, recalled her own mother in London employing a washerwoman, a char three days a week, and a sewing woman, who were all treated as social equals and referred to as 'Mrs'.[17] The perspectives of these domestic workers and their working-class or lower-middle-class employers are rarely integrated into what it was to be a servant. Their relative absence from both historical narratives and sources is one of the things that allows for domestic service to be seen as over by the mid-twentieth century. In what follows, they are where possible re-integrated into the history of domestic service.

Domestic service in twentieth-century Britain was overdetermined and 'meaning-drenched', largely through its presentation in 'culture'. What is meant by this? 'Culture' can be understood as a realm of symbolic meanings and representations, formed through material artefacts, written and visual texts, social institutions and practices.[18] Cultural history has been richly productive in recent decades, and

[15] On farm service, see Alun Howkins and Nicola Verdon, 'Adaptable and Sustainable? Male Farm Service and the Agricultural Labour Force in Midland and Southern England, c.1850–1925', *Economic History Review*, 61 2 (2008), 467–95.

[16] Giles, *The Parlour and the Suburb*, 29–39.

[17] Mrs Chambers (b. 1892), Interview 141, in P. Thompson and T. Lummis, *Family Life and Work Experience before 1918, 1870–1973* [computer file], 7th edn, Colchester, Essex: UK Data Archive (distributor), May 2009, SN: 2000, henceforth cited as *Edwardians*.

[18] T. G. Ashplant and Gerry Smyth, *Explorations in Cultural History* (London: Pluto, 2001), 5–6; Peter Burke, *What Is Cultural History?* (Cambridge: Polity, 2004); Kidd and Nicholls, *Gender, Civic Culture and Consumerism*, 6–7.

through its close association with social history, has suggested new ways of looking at topics that were previously approached as belonging to 'the social'.[19] The cultural dimension has been neglected in the social history literature on domestic service, which has predominantly focused on the experiences of servants, their pay, status, and conditions. Social history has seemed to provide the basis for explaining the establishment and then decline of domestic service, weaving it into larger narratives of class and gender identities, industrialization, migration, urbanization, and technological change. However, these factors only tell part of the story, and personal experience was also mediated by the ways in which domestic service was encountered in the field of culture. *Knowing Their Place* is organized around the ways in which popular, polemical, and elite cultural productions envisioned servants and servant-keeping, and traces the ways in which these texts influenced and were influenced by changing social, demographic, and technological contexts. Such discourses had emotional power and were sometimes incorporated into the subjectivities and feelings of individuals, though, of course, they sometime lacked resonance and failure to gain purchase. This study remains alert to the 'space between social reality and its representation' that Dror Wahrman has stressed.[20] Historical actors were far from determined by culture, but could reinterpret or make choices between the symbolic meanings domestic service conveyed. In the twentieth century, a range of competing meanings were available, and few moments of closure or consensus can be found.

Servants themselves were well aware of the centrality of culture and its resources. One of the advantages of offering a cultural history of domestic service lies in taking seriously the idea that cultural representations were of active concern to late-nineteenth- and twentieth-century servants. When Mrs Sturgeon, a teenage general servant in Suffolk, managed to leave an exploitative job and took a housemaid's job in a wealthy bohemian London household in the 1920s, she described the novelty of being addressed 'as though you could read and write.'[21] The cultural metaphor is revealing, and it was the power of servants to intervene in print media and other cultural spaces that changed the terms of 'the servant problem'. These forms of cultural consumption by servants were problematized, policed, and mocked, making culture an important terrain of the servant problem, and a realm in which servants sought dignity and agency.

Twentieth-century servants experienced more years in education before taking up their jobs. They also gained increasing amounts of time off work once in employment, and reductions in the social isolation and surveillance that went with service during the twentieth century. This enabled servants to interact with

---

[19] Significant social histories of twentieth-century domestic service include Leonore Davidoff, *Worlds between: Historical Perspectives on Class and Gender* (New York: Routledge, 1995); Pamela Horn, *Life below Stairs in the Twentieth Century* (Stroud: Sutton, 2001); Theresa McBride, *The Domestic Revolution* (London: Croom Helm, 1976).
[20] Dror Wahrman, *Imagining the Middle Class: The Political Representation of Class in Britain, c.1780–1840* (Cambridge: Cambridge University Press, 1995), 6–8.
[21] Interview with Mrs Sturgeon (née Powley, b.1917), George Ewart Evans collection, British Library Sound Archive ref. T1434WR. Alison Light gives a fuller account of her experiences in her *Mrs Woolf and the Servants: The Hidden Heart of Domestic Service* (London: Penguin, 2007), 297–300.

print culture of all kinds, and to experience the mass leisure offered by the cinema, public dancing, bicycles, and radio; they gained in confidence and authority through this. Mrs Hadley, a servant in the 1940s, commented that her employer 'Mrs C. showed me how to wait on tables, but I had my own ideas because I read a lot of books about how things were done years ago. My mother's mother had servants and so I had a sort of background in this. I already knew how to place the things.'[22] The authority of her own reading and sense of the past were used directly to resist her mistress's authority. Mrs Hadley's sense of her own family's servant-keeping also reminds us of the greater mobility of the twentieth century. Servant-keeping could no longer be seen as an uncrossable dividing line of social class, as Seebohm Rowntree had assumed in his 1899 study of poverty and social status in York. Nonetheless, as the chapters that follow make clear, structural inequalities persisted in this employment relationship.[23]

Twentieth-century servants were not a silent class, but were articulate, vocal, and active participants in the presentation of service. As literacy became more widespread from the 1860s, there were enhanced possibilities for servants to read and comment on the 'servant problem' literature aimed primarily at mistresses, and to gain cultural authority to write and publish.[24] The influence of the women's movement was also felt, and empowered some servants to read and contribute to feminist periodicals. In the face of numerous diatribes from suffragist mistresses about their servants in the suffragist paper *The Common Cause*, one Edwardian servant wrote to the editor to remind her pointedly that 'This servant agitation belongs to the feminist movement.'[25] Domestic servants were variously interpreted by feminists as 'sweated' female workers, or as key to enabling public contributions by middle-class women. This ambivalence was never resolved, but the feminist movement nonetheless provided resources for imagining and debating utopian or reformed domestic arrangements, and for servants to articulate their aspirations and concerns.

Attention to the cultural representations of domestic affairs was found not only amongst live-in servants in the earlier part of the century, but also by the later domestic workers (sometimes the same individuals) who worked as cleaners and chars after marriage. In 1952, the *South London Press* headlined: 'Women cleaners say they won't be called Mrs Mopp'. Mrs Mopp was the iconic-comic char from the wartime radio show *It's That Man Again*, and she was quickly incorporated into the ongoing disputes about status and dignity at local levels. Like servants of the earlier twentieth century, post-war domestic workers were fighting 'culture wars',

---

[22] Mrs Hadley, Birmingham Libraries and Archive Services, Library Services at Home, Upstairs, Downstairs Oral History Project, http://www.birmingham.gov.uk/libraryservicesathome; henceforth Birmingham, *Upstairs, Downstairs*

[23] Seebohm Rowntree, *Poverty: A Study of Town Life* (London: Macmillan, 1902), 14, 31.

[24] Carolyn Steedman's work reminds us of the eighteenth-century traditions of servants deploying cultural and legal resources to 'answer back' and reverse the class and gender polarities of cultural authority. Carolyn Steedman, 'Poetical Maids and Cooks Who Wrote', *Eighteenth-Century Studies*, 39 9 (2005), 1–17.

[25] Kathlyn Oliver, *Common Cause*, December 7, 1911, 622.

determined to gain for their work 'the respect it deserves' and to efface the demeaning cultural representation of themselves as 'Mrs Mopps'.[26] Later in the century, the television series *Upstairs, Downstairs* began to provide a cultural counterpoint that helped to organize and give meaning to the stories of service being recorded within the oral history movement at a shared historical moment.

A cultural history can help to make sense of the intensity of the servant question, its significance beyond the personal experiences of servants and employers, and its persistence in cultural life beyond the sharp decline in numbers of the late 1940s.[27] It does not imply that cultural, social, material, or economic factors belong to different 'worlds', and reflects a methodological approach rather than an ontological claim. This understanding of cultural history remains attentive to the structural and material context in which texts are produced and interpreted.[28]

EMOTIONAL HISTORY

Alongside the insights of cultural history, another field of historical research, the history of emotions, has also suggested new and productive ways of understanding domestic service. As defined in 1913, the home was 'the abiding place of the affections, especially of the domestic affections'. It hosted and generated deep emotional investments; as Bourdieu has argued, forms of practical knowledge are experienced emotionally and arise from an embodied 'sense of one's place'.[29] Domestic service, in particular, stimulated powerful emotions; looking at Bill Brandt's photographs of aristocratic servant-keeping published in the 1930s, art critic Raymond Mortimer asked rhetorically, 'Is there any English man or woman who can look at these without a profound feeling of shame?' The 'emotional work' of service has been recently highlighted by Carolyn Steedman, Judy Giles, and Alison Light, and the historiography of emotions provides powerful new ways of investigating the links between socio-cultural discourses and personal subjectivities.[30]

---

[26] *South London Press*, February 8, 1952.

[27] An important aspect of this cultural historiography has been an exploration of the literary depictions of servants, most notably in Giles, *The Parlour and the Suburb*; Bruce Robbins, *The Servant's Hand: English Fiction from Below* (New York: Columbia University Press, 1986); Kristina Straub, *Domestic Affairs: Intimacy, Eroticism, and Violence between Servants and Masters in Eighteenth-Century Britain* (Baltimore: Johns Hopkins University Press, 2009). This study draws on their work, and occasionally cites literary works, but mainly works within a broader cultural context.

[28] On recent debates in cultural history, see Victoria E. Bonnell, Lynn Avery Hunt, and Richard Biernacki, *Beyond the Cultural Turn: New Directions in the Study of Society and Culture* (Berkeley: University of California Press, 1999); M. A. Cabrera, *Postsocial History: An Introduction* (Lanham, MD: Lexington Books, 2004); Peter Mandler, 'Problems in Cultural History', *Cultural and Social History*, 1 (2004), 94–117.

[29] N. Porter, *Webster's Revised Unabridged Dictionary* (Springfield, MA: Merriam, 1913). Pierre Bourdieu, *Pascalian Meditations* (Stanford, CA: Stanford University Press, 1997), 184.

[30] Mortimer, introduction to Brandt, *The English at Home*; Light, *Mrs Woolf and the Servants*; Judy Giles, 'Authority, Dependence and Power in Accounts of Twentieth Century Domestic Service', in Lucy Delap, Abigail Wills, and Ben Griffin (eds), *The Politics of Domestic Authority in Britain since 1800* (Basingstoke: Palgrave Macmillan, 2009); Carolyn Steedman, *Labours Lost: Domestic Service and the Making of Modern England* (Cambridge: Cambridge University Press, 2009).

This is an important extension to the writing of cultural history. As Michael Roper has argued, an account of the cultural representations of a social institution or identity does not by itself tell us about what purchase such representations had at the level of individuals. In other words, the study of culture must be supplemented by attention to a separate but related 'psychic' realm where meanings are internalized and interpreted.[31] One cannot assume, for example, that the low socio-cultural status of being a servant was transcribed directly onto individual subjectivity. Attention to how individuals inhabit cultural imaginaries suggests a more diverse emotional economy for domestic service. The relationships between servants and employers were complexly formed through the power play surrounding emotions of dependency, shame, guilt, and intimacy, yet 'servant' was also understood as a workplace identity, and might, as Selina Todd has recently argued, also be organized around emotional detachment.[32] This book investigates the emotional component of the encounters and daily tasks of domestic service, and asks how such emotions were represented in and shaped by culture.

The history of emotions must sometimes be a tentative and speculative project, and the relationships of domestic service were sometimes opaque or intensely private. The emotional aspect to being a servant sometimes went beyond the power of words to name. Rosina Harrison, in service as a lady's maid in the 1920s, wrote: 'My relationship with Miss Patricia isn't easy for me to describe. We weren't friends, though if she was asked today she might well deny this. We weren't even acquaintances. We never exchanged confidences, never discussed people, nothing we said brought us closer.'[33] Yet this nameless relationship between 'distant companions' was a profound keystone of the psychic stability of servant-keeping classes.[34] As one mistress wrote of her servants after World War I: 'Always there. The phrase seems to me to sum up the true worth of such people as Flora, Annie, Hobbs and this Emily. The war seemed endless, and the post-war world hardly less tumultuous and agonising, but as long as they were *there*, doing their normal work through thick and thin, some sense of security remained.'[35] These sentiments were often even more heightened when associated with the emotional care servants provided for children. Nannies were described by a contributor to *Good Housekeeping* in 1935 as 'a curiously stable factor in a world apparently increasingly distracted. Nursery tea remains a rite long after late dinner has become a post-cocktail snack'.[36] Yet this sense of security and comfort was in

---

[31] Michael Roper, 'Slipping out of View: Subjectivity and Emotion in Gender History', *History Workshop Journal*, 59 (2005), 57–72. Roper discusses the emotional relationships of domestic service with great insight in *The Secret Battle: Emotional Survival in the Great War* (Manchester: Manchester University Press, 2009).
[32] Selina Todd, 'Domestic Service and Class Relations in Britain 1900–1950', *Past and Present*, 203 (2009), 181–204.
[33] Rosina Harrison, *Rose: My Life in Service* (London: Cassell, 1975), 20.
[34] I adopt 'distant companions' from Karen Tranberg Hansen, *Distant Companions: Servants and Employers in Zambia, 1900–1985* (Ithaca, NY: Cornell University Press, 1989).
[35] M. C. Scott Moncrieff, *Yes Ma'am! Glimpses of Domestic Service, 1901–51* (Edinburgh: Albyn Press, 1984), 70.
[36] Joan Woollcombe, 'Nannies—Old Style and New', *Good Housekeeping*, Jan. 1935, 52.

no sense a symmetrical one, and for employers was threatened by other emotions, of suspicion, guilt, shame, and acute self-consciousness.

For all its nameless qualities, domestic service could also stand in for apparently unsayable strong emotions in both personal experiences and cultural depictions. At the most intense emotional point of Vera Brittain's memoir of the First World War, for example, following the death of her fiancée, her friends, and finally her beloved brother, Brittain recorded, not her own reaction to her brother's death, but the behaviour of her maid, who, she felt, had used the chaos surrounding the death to enjoy 'a few hours' freedom': 'She had not even finished the household handkerchiefs, which I had washed that morning and intended to iron after tea; when I went into the kitchen I found them still hanging, stiff as boards, over the clothes-horse near the fire where I had left them to dry.'[37] Her maid's absence served as a metaphor for her bereft emotional state, with the marks of the maid's undone domestic work figured as corpses. Servant-keeping operated within a vivid emotional landscape, and indeed, as Leonore Davidoff has argued, the work of domestic servants was emotional as much as material. Yet in many of the cultural sources examined here, servants emerge as flat characters, without emotional depth. We have many records of the feelings felt for nannies by their charges, but less is known about how nannies felt about the families they cared for.[38] This book aims to explore the emotional landscape of domestic service in ways that are attentive to both sides of the relationship, and to chart the asymmetrical relationships and emotional investments that resulted.

EMPLOYMENT TRENDS

Domestic service had a fluctuating rather than declining place within British labour markets over the twentieth century. It has widely been read as residual and anachronistic in the twentieth century, yet it still employed very large numbers. Census records and other evidence reveal that a very wide range of households were employing servants between 1890 and the World War II, though there was a declining role for live-in servants. The census figures are unreliable, and fluctuate according to the various definitions of a domestic servant adopted by enumerators. They also fail to include the casual jobs that predominated, especially for married women, and girls still living at home. Nonetheless, the 1891 census suggested that 41 per cent of the female labour force in England and Wales worked in domestic service, and nearly half of these women were under 20 years old.[39] The numbers of women entering service varied according to regional labour markets. Rural areas such as North Wales, districts with a concentration of middle-class households such

---

[37] Brittain, *Testament of Youth*, 438.
[38] See, however, Katherine Holden, *The Shadow of Marriage: Singleness in England, 1914–60* (Manchester: Manchester University Press, 2007).
[39] Judy Giles, 'Help for Housewives: Domestic Service and the Reconstruction of Domesticity in Britain, 1940–50', *Women's History Review*, 10 2 (2001), 299–323.

as parts of Sussex and London, or regions with little other employment available to women had particularly high numbers going into service throughout this period. In 1881, one in nine of the entire workforce in Bath, both male and female, was employed in service. In London, the equivalent ratio was one in fifteen, whereas only one in thirty was a servant in textile-dominated Lancashire. Regions such as West Yorkshire, Northern Ireland, and South Wales saw low levels of servant-keeping.[40] In Scotland, Edinburgh was home to large numbers of professional families, and therefore had a disproportionately large domestic service sector. Cities such as Dundee were far more likely to generate industrial employment for working-class women, and the overall balance of female employment in Scotland slowly shifted away from domestic service and agriculture, towards industrial work. By 1914, 45 per cent of Edinburgh female workers were in industry, while 40 per cent remained in domestic service.[41]

World War I, saw domestic upheavals, as servants were directed into war work, and as some who would previously have been looked after by servants took on menial service jobs. Ursula Bloom, brought up in a servant-keeping family, joined the Voluntary Aid Detachment (VAD) during the war, and became a parlourmaid within a convalescent home: 'I myself became a servant,' she declared in dramatic terms. Violet Butler of the Women's Industrial Council noted, 'A considerable number of the servant-keeping classes have in the last eighteen months done strenuous manual work in hospitals and canteens; they may have revised their previous views as to domestic service.' Her report quoted 'a London general' who announced that she hoped 'at the end of this year to be in a position to keep a maid of my own'.[42] Anecdotes circulated widely about the 'topsy-turvy' days of war, symbolized by changes in servant-keeping; Bloom recalled that their housemaid married a major. This class-crossing was largely greeted with ironic laughter; Bloom commented that it 'showed the new spirit, and I meditated, did I now have to call Alice "ma'am"?'[43] The end of the war marked a particularly potent period of discontent with domestic service, and of intense middle-class anxiety as to whether women would willingly return to domestic service. The fear that they would not resulted in two government inquiries, a 1919 Ministry of Reconstruction report and a 1923 report to the Minister of Labour. Each report generated widespread media coverage on the topic of service, and both warned of the trend towards the balkanization of social class.[44] Nonetheless, there was a widespread assumption that private domestic service would continue, perhaps reworked as a contribution to

[40] *Sell to Britain through 'The Daily Mail'* (1929), reproduced in Alan Jackson, *The Middle Classes 1900–1950* (Nairn: David St John Thomas, 1991), 344–5.
[41] A. J. McIvor, 'Women and Work in 20th century Scotland', in Tony Dickson and James H. Treble (eds), *People and Society in Scotland*, vol. 3: *1914–1990* (Edinburgh: John Donald, 1992).
[42] C. V. Butler, *Domestic Service: An Enquiry by the Women's Industrial Council* (London: Bell, 1916), 5, 28.
[43] Ursula Bloom, *Mrs Bunthorpe's Respects: A Chronicle of Cooks* (London: Hutchinson, 1963), 23.
[44] Gertrude Emmott, *Report of the Women's Advisory Committee of the Ministry of Reconstruction on the Domestic Service Problem* (London: HMSO Cmd. 67, 1919); E. M. Wood, *Report to the Committee Appointed to Enquire into the Present Conditions as to the Supply of Female Domestic Servants by the Ministry of Labour* (London: HMSO, 1923), 8.

national efficiency, but substantively along pre-war lines.[45] The 1923 government report spoke of service as 'the highest privilege of life'. Another contemporary claimed, 'Domestic service requires a re-statement which will chiefly and among other things re-establish its goodness as of infinite worth, not only to the individual, nor to the particular family in question, but to the nation as a whole.'[46]

Despite such sentiments, domestic service employed a declining number of women in England and Wales immediately after World War I. Its numbers recovered during the 1920s, with rises of 29 per cent for men (discussed below), and 16 per cent for women. By 1931, it employed around 24 per cent of women in work and about 8 per cent of the entire workforce. This amounted to around 1.6 million servants—as opposed to, for example, 0.8 million mostly female shop assistants. Around 60 per cent of these female servants lived in.[47] These figures mask considerable regional variations. Young women's labour-market aspirations were expanding in the twentieth century, through the availability of new kinds of paid employment in some localities—clerical, retail, or light manufacturing—as well as the growth in secondary education after the Fisher Education Act of 1918.[48] They therefore had increasing psychic, economic, and social resources to resist or opt out of the indignities of service. In addition, the supply of young women to work in private homes was falling because the average age of marriage was decreasing after World War I, and the age at which women left school had risen to 14, leaving fewer years between school leaving and marriage in which to work. Moreover, many interwar employers struggled to afford servants, as rising rents, wages, and food prices compromised middle-class budgets. Nonetheless, the feminist writer Ray Strachey characterized the 1930s as a period in which domestic service was more popular than in the 1920s, and had 'gained in profitableness and in the leisure time offered'.[49] Strachey was therefore confident that domestic service could be rejuvenated and sustained in British society. It was in reality the economic downturn and the coercive nature of the unemployment benefits system that returned some women to service. The proportion of women employed as servants continued to be much higher in some 'distressed' regions, despite the further expansion in clerical and 'clean' factory work for young women during the 1930s.[50] A disproportionately large number of refugees and migrants also began to be employed as servants during this decade, with census figures in 1951 showing Austrian and other alien workers employed alongside the long-standing Irish, Welsh, and Scottish migrant workers.[51]

---

[45] See for example Marchioness of Londonderry, 'A New Phase of Domestic Service', Nov 1922, *Good Housekeeping*, 17.
[46] Wood, *Ministry of Labour Report*, 17; K. Dewan, *The Girl* (London: Bell, 1921), 178.
[47] Census of England and Wales 1931, *General Report* (London: HMSO, 1950), 152.
[48] Gregory Anderson, *The White Blouse Revolution: Female Office Workers since 1870* (Manchester: Manchester University Press, 1988); Mirriam Glucksmann, *Women Assemble: Women Workers and the New Industries in Inter-war Britain* (London: Routledge, 1990); Selina Todd, *Young Women, Work and Family in England, 1918–1950* (Oxford: Oxford University Press, 2005).
[49] Ray Strachey, *Our Freedom and Its Results* (London: Hogarth Press, 1936), 146.
[50] Todd, 'Poverty and Aspiration', 131.
[51] Census of England and Wales 1951, *Occupation Tables* (London: HMSO, 1956); Census of Scotland 1951, *Occupations and Industries* (IV; Edinburgh: HMSO, 1956).

Domestic service remained the most common of all entry-level jobs available to young women until World War II. But the range of households employing servants in the interwar years had narrowed. By 1931, only around 5 per cent of households were employing indoor servants that were recognized by the Census of England and Wales.[52] Many more, however, were still employing casual help or charwomen, and continued to do so throughout the interwar and post-war periods.

During World War II, the idea of 'doing for oneself' became more acceptable amongst upper- and middle-class households, bolstered by the rising status of what was often celebrated as a class-neutral 'housewife' identity during the years before and during the war. Many middle-class housewives, however, had continued to rely on a single maid or non-residential help of various kinds. A state system of home helps continued to allocate domestic workers to households deemed as suffering hardship, though the Ministry of Labour and National Service reported 'extreme difficulty' in finding women willing to take on this role.[53] After the war, the school-leaving age rose to 15, and the servants who remained in the following decades tended to be older and to take on less specialized roles, as the separate functions of nanny, cook, parlourmaid, and housemaid were rolled into one. The 1951 census of England and Wales showed 13 per cent of all occupied women aged 20–24 worked as servants, and in Scotland, similar numbers of women were employed in charring and indoor domestic service as worked as typists and clerks.[54] However, the 1950s seemed to mark a terminal decline for domestic service, and 'these servantless days' became a common cultural cliché, despite the continuing reliance on chars and cleaners. Yet there was a startling resurgence of private domestic service during the 1980s, with an estimated £524 million being spent on cooks, cleaners, gardeners, and child-carers by the mid-1980s. This had risen to an estimated £4 billion by 1997, with agencies reporting that demand for such workers outstripped supply.[55] Some had become qualified and relatively secure workers in the late-twentieth-century phase of domestic service, though many cleaners continued to be marginalized and casually employed. Differences of ethnicity became a more significant feature of these domestic relationships, while gender became less significant, as agencies and the continuing flow of migrants from Eastern Europe changed the conditions of domestic service and partially opened it up to male workers.

The employment of men in indoor and outdoor domestic service was not large in the early to mid-twentieth century; it employed around 1 per cent of the male workforce in urban areas and 4–5 per cent of the rural workforce from 1900 to 1911. The long-standing tax on male servants, which stood at 15 shillings annually per male servant in 1930, had perhaps discouraged the employment of men, or led to the disguise of the domestic tasks that some men may have carried out. As many as 214,388 men were employed in domestic service in 1904, mostly in gardening, care of horses,

---

[52] Census of England and Wales 1931, *General Report*, at 152.
[53] *Hansard*, HC Deb, Mar 2, 1943, vol. 387, cc 475–6.
[54] Census of England and Wales 1951, *General Report* (London: HMSO, 1958) at 168; Census of Scotland 1951, *Occupations and Industries*, at Table 1, 143.
[55] Andrew Adonis and Stephen Pollard, *A Class Act: The Myth of Britain's Classless Society* (London: Penguin, 1998, 1997), 101; Gregson and Lowe, *Servicing the Middle Classes*.

and as drivers. World War I saw a precipitous fall in this number, though numbers recovered to 173,363 in 1924; this number remained stable until 1937, when the tax was abolished.[56] Only in Ireland, where male servants were not specifically taxed, did men continue to undertake domestic work, and even there, they were frequently working fluidly across the boundaries of agricultural work and domestic work.[57] In England and Wales, the numbers of men employed as indoor domestic servants rose between 1921 and 1931, but more than 99 per cent of these men worked in institutional service in hotels, schools, and so on.[58]

There had been discussion amongst policymakers of encouraging more men, particularly ex-servicemen and the disabled, into private domestic service after World War I.[59] Increasing numbers of men did indeed temporarily enter service, but the sector was so firmly feminized that most employers found the prospect of male servants alarming or ridiculous. In the nineteenth century, *Fraser's Magazine* had conducted a campaign against the pretensions of male flunkeys, chiefly footmen, with the character of 'Charles Yellowplush' invented by William Thackeray, who also created the snobbish 'Jeames' for *Punch*. The ridicule was pervasive, and few working-class men considered domestic service an option in later decades. One agent of a domestic employment bureau noted the large numbers of men answering domestic help adverts in the early 1920s, but felt that this was only motivated by 'their anxiety to obtain employment'. He considered it very unlikely 'that many of these men will elect to remain domestic workers when occupations in other directions are less difficult to obtain,' and only expected the disabled to continue in this role.[60]

One couple who worked respectively as cook and gardener for a household in Surrey after World War I were disconcerted when their employers moved to a house with a smaller garden in Golders Green. As the wife recalled, it was then that 'trouble began. There was only a small garden and my husband was expected to help with the housework and he just hated it.' Despite their deep concerns about unemployment, they resigned and the husband took lower paid temporary work as a tram-conductor, while she worked as a char.[61] The government had intended the abolition of the licence duty on male servants to promote their employment, but this was unsuccessful. The attributes that John Tosh argues had become associated

---

[56] Diane Aiken, *The Central Committee on Women's Training and Employment: Tackling the Servant Problem, 1914–1945* (Oxford: Oxford Brookes University, 2002), 69. English and Welsh local authorities were compensated for the abolition of the tax on male servants in 1937 by an annual payment of £115,000 in the Exchequer block grant. The Scottish Exchequer was estimated to have foregone £11,000, suggesting the presence of just under 15,000 male domestic servants in Scotland. *Hansard*, HC Deb, June 9, 1937, vol. 324, cc 1871–2.

[57] Mona Hearn, *Below Stairs: Domestic Service Remembered in Dublin and Beyond, 1880–1922* (Dublin: Lilliput Press, 1993).

[58] Census of England and Wales 1931, *General Report*, at 151.

[59] *Hansard*, HL Deb, June 25, 1930, vol. 78, cc 119–26.

[60] An Old-Established Domestic Employment Agent, *The Servant Problem: Can It Be Solved? Why Not?* (London: E. R. Alexander, 1922), 12–13.

[61] Mrs D. Presland (b. 1895), Essay contributed for the Age Concern competition [AC], 'My First Job' (1961), Essex Record Office (ERO), T/Z 25/784. This and all subsequent quotes from this source are reproduced by courtesy of Essex Record Office and Age Concern Essex.

with idealized forms of 'modern' masculinity by the twentieth century, such as an attachment to one's home, an entrepreneurial and individualistic outlook, and a commitment to self-improvement, seemed incompatible with the feminized and child-like identities established through domestic service.[62] The men employed in indoor domestic service by the 1951 census showed a strong presence of foreigners—Polish and Italian men featured prominently in England, and foreign workers made up around 15 per cent of male domestic servants in Scotland, far outweighing Irish servants.[63] This suggests that vulnerable male workers were still being transiently employed in domestic service, but few stayed in this sector during the full employment conditions of the 1950s.

The role of employer of servants was also feminized. Male employers were mostly uninvested in the role of 'master', and there is little historical evidence to show their encounters with servants. Masters were subject to much less criticism than mistresses. Their involvement in the management of servants was sporadic and sometimes read as comic. While men feature in this book, its focus will be predominantly on the experiences of female servants and employers, whose numbers were far greater than those of their male counterparts and who dominated in cultural and social representations of domestic service.

How unique are these trends to Britain? There were similar debates around various 'servant problems' in other servant-keeping economies, though few are directly comparable to Britain. In Zambia, for example, female domestic servants were deeply eroticized, as in Britain, but in this labour market, male servants remained the preferred worker, and women were excluded from many middle-class and white colonial households.[64] In India, a major servant-keeping society, men also continued to be employed, but divides of caste and ethnicity were as significant as those of gender.[65] In the United States, racial and ethnic differentiation predominated, and by the twentieth century, few native-born white Americans served as servants.[66] Only Australia shows anything like a similar profile for domestic service to Britain, though even here, the emigration process was deeply

---

[62] John Tosh, *Manliness and Masculinities in Nineteenth-Century Britain: Essays on Gender, Family, and Empire* (Harlow: Pearson Longman, 2005).

[63] Census of England and Wales 1951, *Occupation Tables*; Census of Scotland 1951, *Occupations and Industries*.

[64] Hansen, *Distant Companions*.

[65] Swapna M. Banerjee, *Men, Women, and Domestics: Articulating Middle-Class Identity in Colonial Bengal* (New Delhi/Oxford: Oxford University Press, 2004).

[66] Faye Dudden, 'Experts and Servants: The National Council on Household Employment and the Decline of Domestic Service in the Twentieth Century', *Journal of Social History*, 20 (1986), 269–89; David M. Katzman, *Seven Days a Week: Women and Domestic Service in Industrializing America* (New York: Oxford University Press, 1978); Phyllis Palmer, *Domesticity and Dirt: Housewives and Domestic Servants in the United States, 1920–1945* (Philadelphia: Temple University Press, 1989); Evelyn Nakano Glenn, *Issei, Nisei, War Bride: Three Generations of Japanese American Women in Domestic Service* (Philadelphia: Temple University Press, 1986); Daniel E. Sutherland, *Americans and Their Servants: Domestic Service in the United States from 1800 to 1920* (Baton Rouge/London: Louisiana State University Press, 1981).

influential. Moreover, Australia was frequently regarded as an egalitarian society, in which being 'servantless' was more socially acceptable than in Britain.[67]

Transnational influences shaped ideas about service and the home in Britain—many of the cultural products discussed in this book (music hall, pornography, periodicals, cinema) travelled easily, and were part of an international network of trade and export. As Andrew Urban has recently argued, Britain was held up as an example in other nations of how servants were to be managed.[68] The British were widely perceived as being at home with their past, and able to sustain institutions seen as anachronistic elsewhere. British people sometimes celebrated this, describing the nanny, for example, as 'the famous product of Britain, and until recently, one of our most sought-after exports'.[69] Others, however, held up their servants or homes to unfavourable comparison with other countries, and looked overseas to copy what was done elsewhere. The well-known domestic reformer, novelist, and journalist, Mrs Peel, for example, compared her own servants with those she encountered in France, where 'everything was as well done as it would have been in an English house where double the number of servants were employed.'[70] The many Britons who had lived in British imperial possessions wrote of their experiences of servants as a means of conveying other ways of life and forms of hierarchy, often in nostalgic terms. Nonetheless, the servant problem explored in this study was regarded largely as a British problem, or as pertaining to specific localities or regional labour markets. The practices of other countries or import of foreign servants were rarely proposed, and the presence of divides of race, caste, and ethnicity in other servant-keeping economies were seen as making the comparison invidious.

Despite the many transnational and imperial exchanges that underlay the British economy and society, domestic service remained mostly a sector employing internal migrants, except during the late 1930s when Jewish refugees became briefly visible in this sector.[71] During the period of high immigration after 1948, Afro-Caribbean women predominantly took service jobs in the public sector; though they may have been scrubbing and cooking, they rarely did so in private homes. Indeed, many black migrant women, some of whom had been raised with servants in their countries of origin, refused to take such jobs, resenting the menial connotations and fearing the loss of status if their relatives should hear of it. As Wendy Webster points out, British householders were reluctant to employ them, fearing that they were 'dirty' workers who could not be associated with private domesticity.[72] South Asian immigrants tended to take assembly line manufacturing employment, and

---

[67] B. W. Higman, *Domestic Service in Australia* (Melbourne: Melbourne University Press, 2002); 'Architecture: Some Modern Tendencies', *The Times*, Monday, May 9, 1927, xxiii.
[68] Andrew Urban, 'Irish Domestic Servants, "Biddy" and Rebellion in the American Home, 1850–1900', *Gender and History*, 21 2 (2009), 263–86.
[69] Joan Woollcombe, 'Nannies—Old Style and New,' *Good Housekeeping*, Jan 1935, 52.
[70] Mrs C. S. Peel, *Life's Enchanted Cup: An Autobiography (1872–1933)* (London: Lane, 1933), 117.
[71] Tony Kushner, 'An Alien Occupation—Jewish Refugees and Domestic Service in Britain, 1933–1948', in Werner E. Mosse (ed.), *Second Chance: Two Generations of German-Speaking Jews in the United Kingdom* (Tubingen: JCB Mohr, 1991), 553–78.
[72] Wendy Webster, *Imagining Home* (London: UCL Press, 1998).

few entered domestic service. The Irish came closest to supplying a migrant class, but only formed a substantial minority in the London labour market. Irish women did not dominate representations of the servant problem as they did in the United States. They tended to be older workers, and were more likely to work in institutional domestic service, or later in the century as casually employed chars.[73] Nicky Gregson and Michelle Lowe have argued, 'in post-war Britain . . . it is class and the life-cycle rather than ethnicity, which play critical roles in the production and reproduction of the private domestic cleaning labour force.' This conclusion, however, underestimates the significance of ethnicity in shaping the encounters of domestic service.[74] Metaphors of ethnicity flourished, and British servants and employers were quite frequently described as 'foreign' to each other; *Cassell's Household Guide* described in 1912 the way in which the servant 'regards her mistress as her natural enemy, who knows no more of her real character and circumstances than she does of the domestic arrangements of a Chinese house'. The interwar novelist Lettice Cooper characterized servants in the minds of their employers as exotic: 'The life lived so near to them and so far apart from them was a dark continent, full of unexplored mystery.'[75] But this was a means of dramatizing what was understood to be a peculiarly British phenomenon: the organization of society around divides of social class.

Domestic servants were a recurrent reference point for the establishment of class differences, and for many early-twentieth-century Britons, contact between servant and employer might be the only encounter they had with individuals of another class. For some the servant question was a vivid means of bringing home the 'social question' of poverty and inequality in society. One commentator (paraphrasing George Eliot) wrote in 1890,

One has a head knowledge that thousands of lives, by no fault of their own, are limited, and dulled and spiritually starved compared to ours. This we bear with equanimity: indeed, if we did not it would be like hearing the grass grow and we should perish under the burden of our sensibilities. But this fact stares one in the face, and meets one at every turn, in one's relations with the servants with whom one lives side by side.[76]

---

[73] On Irish domestic servants, see Bronwen Walter, 'Irish Domestic Servants and English National Identity', in A. Fauve-Chamoux and R. Sarti (eds), *Domestic Service and the Formation of European Identity: Understanding the Globalization of Domestic Work 16th–21st Centuries* (Bern: Peter Lang, 2004), 471–88; Bronwen Walter, 'Strangers on the Inside: Irish Women Servants in England, 1881', *Immigrants and Minorities*, 27 2 (2009), 279–99.

[74] Gregson and Lowe, *Servicing the Middle Classes*, 126. Ethnicity is understood in what follows as a category that, as Amalia Sa'ar has argued, 'is almost always intertwined with additional exclusionary mechanisms, notably race, religion, and nationalism.' Following Wendy Webster (1998), I use the concept of 'indigenous' identity to delineate the mostly 'white' individuals who self-defined as English, Scottish, or Welsh, against migrants and refugees. Amalia Sa'ar, 'Postcolonial Feminism, the Politics of Identification, and the Liberal Bargain', *Gender and Society*, 19 5 (2005), 680–700, esp. 683.

[75] Mrs Stuart Macrae, *Cassell's Household Guide: A Complete Cyclopaedia of Domestic Economy* (London: Waverly Books, 1912), 842.; Lettice Cooper, *The New House* (London: Virago, 1987 [1936]), 100.

[76] Mrs Francis (Ellen) Darwin, 'Domestic Service', *The Nineteenth Century*, Aug 1890, 296.

As the most everyday and intimate realm in which individuals of different social classes confronted each other, domestic service seemed central to the ongoing enactment of class. A writer in the *Nineteenth Century* noted in 1900, 'of all classes of women the only ones who are addressed without the prefix of *Miss* are servants.... it is interesting and instructive to note that this is actually the only clear dividing line of social class that is left among us in the present day.'[77] For an elderly Mrs Peel, a journalist of domestic affairs, her servants were the canvas on which class divisions continued to be painted, and she went into extraordinary detail in describing her encounters with maids and chars in her 1933 autobiography. The much younger Celia Fremlin, a socialist social investigator and popular writer, also understood the servant problem as an illustration of the 'bedrock of class society' that she believed underlay all social interactions in Britain. In domestic service, she argued, 'class distinctions are most forced into prominence.'[78]

Historians have thus seen class as that which gave the servant problem its unique purchase and prominence in Britain. As one historian put it in 1971, servant-keeping 'went to the very heart of the idea of class itself,' and specifically, 'played an essential part in defining the identity of the [middle classes].'[79] For historians interested in working-class identities, the significance of domestic service has been complex. When social historians began to make new claims about history 'from below' from around the 1960s, they tended to focus initially on strikes and other forms of collective organization, situated within apparently cohesive, traditional communities.[80] Domestic service seemed anomalous; Standish Meacham, for example, described domestic servants as illustrating 'how complex this business of class can be.' He struggled to identify a cook in class terms, and concluded: 'Where do *we* put her? Marriage to a London tradesman or to a mill hand from her native town would solve the problem for us. Until then, we shall be forced to leave her in limbo.'[81] The problem resided in the apparent deference and adoption of middle-class values by servants, which divorced them from any kind of working-class identity, at least until an association with a working-class male could re-establish it.

Occasionally, servants were taken to stand in for the broader working class—as chapter 5 argues, Edwardians found that servant girls came to mind when asked to think about working-class sexuality. However, the class identity most actively

---

[77] Major, *Nineteenth Century*, Aug 1900, 277.
[78] Celia Fremlin, *The Seven Chars of Chelsea* (London: Methuen, 1940), vi, 7.
[79] J. F. C. Harrison, *The Early Victorians* (London, 1971), 110, quoted in Patricia Branca, *Silent Sisterhood: Middle Class Women in the Victorian Home* (London: Croom Helm, 1975), 54.
[80] On the failure of E. P. Thompson to include domestic service in his *Making of the English Working Class*, see Steedman, *Master and Servant*, 26; Hue-Tam Ho Tai, 'Remembered Realms: Pierre Nora and French National Memory', *American Historical Review*, 106 3 (June 2001), 906–22. Chris Waters traces this nostalgic evocation of class through 'industrial heritage', charting the fascination in British culture from as early as the 1950s with the working-class communities of the industrial north: 'Representations of Everyday Life: L. S. Lowry and the Landscape of Memory in Postwar Britain', *Representations*, 6 (1999), 121–50.
[81] Standish Meacham, *A Life Apart: The English Working Class 1890–1914* (London: Thames and Hudson, 1977), 23.

formed in reference to servant-keeping was that of the 'middle'. Servant-keeping facilitated the achievement of the leisured lifestyles needed to participate in cultural or civic activities that have translated into middle-class identities since the early nineteenth century. Its rituals and deferences were of symbolic as well as practical significance. It has thus been commonly seen as an arbiter of middle-class identity, despite the diversities of domestic organization in less wealthy middle-class homes. Servants provided the social 'other' that allowed middle classness to be thrown into focus. Their bodies, clothes, laughter, taste, smell, courtship, and language were all evoked as sites of class differentiation.

The servant question thus provided a vehicle for discussions of class that were quite tangential to the relations of production or political or civic activism with which class has traditionally been associated. Domestic service was organized around systems of differentiation that made meaningful areas of social experience as diverse as jokes, labour markets, generational differences, and sexual desire. Class is read in this study as a 'structure of feeling', a means of organizing knowledge and positioning individuals that pre-exists agency, but to which historical actors could contribute in its reproduction and reformulation.[82] Class frames but does not determine any single subject position. Class hierarchies sometimes conjured a sense of exclusion and injustice, but not always.[83] Karen Hansen has argued that domestic service is always marked by asymmetrical encounters, and cannot function without devices through which difference can be established. Class was one such device, and though it has sometimes been seen as an 'Archimedean point', historical actors often used it as a shorthand for the positioning created by multiple axes of social difference, including age, gender, rurality or urbanity, ethnicity, and occupation.[84] While class tensions are commonly found in or projected into the relationships of domestic service, they do not sum up its sense of 'place' in individual subjectivities and British society; as Bourdieu reminds us, a sense of 'place' within a social world is not synonymous with class consciousness. Instead, servant-keeping emerges as a loose social grouping that spanned the divides that historians have conventionally drawn between different income and occupational groups, classes, and lifestyles.[85]

Chapter 1 explores the experiences of young women who became domestic servants, with a particular focus upon the ways in which they joined the labour market, and the kin and neighbourhood relationships that mediated this. Divides of generation will be highlighted as particularly significant in this context, and social class emerges as opaque to many of those who participated in surveys, or who recalled former experiences as servants or employers in the oral histories collected during and

---

[82] Joan W. Scott, 'The "Class" We Have Lost', *International Labor and Working-Class History*, 57 (Spring 2000), 69–75; Beverley Skeggs, *Formations of Class and Gender: Becoming Respectable* (London: Sage, 1997), 94; Beverley Skeggs, *Class, Self, Culture* (London: Routledge, 2004).

[83] I depart here from Beverley Skeggs' account, which categorically positions working-class femininity as experienced as exclusion and deprivation. Skeggs, *Formations of Class and Gender*, 74.

[84] Geoff Eley and Keith Nield, *The Future of Class in History: What's Left of the Social?* (Ann Arbor: University of Michigan Press, 2007); Hansen, *Distant Companions*, 7.

[85] Bourdieu, *Pascalian Meditations*, 185.

after the 1970s. This chapter sets out the broad range of emotional investment that servants had in their occupation, and critically examines the prism of exploitation and subalternity that has shaped existing histories of domestic service.

Chapter 2 examines the fashioning of servant-keeping identities amongst those employing servants, with a particular focus on the deep tensions found in being a 'mistress'. It is readily imagined that the nineteenth- and twentieth-century servant question was a litany of complaints against servants on the part of employers; in actual fact, the servant question amounted to a very critical examination of the role that employers, and particularly mistresses, played in exacerbating social unrest and misunderstanding between the classes. It was a long-running and widespread complaint among commentators of all levels that the servant problem had been created by mistresses, who were accused of vices ranging from timidity and fear of servants to ignorance and snobbery. This chapter examines the changing authority strategies deployed by mistresses, the role of children in the relationships between employers and servants, and the ways in which the management of servants was also structured by legal contexts and the labour movement. Though there was growing informality in mid-twentieth-century relationships between servants and employers, it proved extraordinarily difficult to stabilize servant-keeping in a viable new form. Failures of authority over servants carried symbolic meaning that went beyond domestic practicalities, and few alternative roles for servant-keeping women emerged that could stand in for 'mistresshood'.

In Chapter 3, the establishment of the 'servantless home' is traced, in the flood of new advice aimed at labour-saving for the women variously termed housemistress, hostess, or housewife. The material and symbolic reworking of twentieth-century kitchens, cooking, and domestic intimacy are examined, alongside the introduction or imagining of alternative domestic workers such as lady helps and au pairs. Yet the transformation of the home is argued to be partial, and the continuing power that the 'structuring absence' of servants had to influence the organization of middle-class homes and identities is observed into the 1960s.

Many servantless home texts aimed to be funny, and Chapter 4 argues that laughter was one of the most important means of managing and negotiating domestic service. This laughter is traced out in both cultural and quotidian interactions, with particular attention to its physical enactment. The persistent power of domestic service humour in the later twentieth century, as some aspects of service became remembered rather than directly experienced, is discussed. Attention to laughter adds another element to the reperiodization suggested by earlier chapters, and demonstrates the significance of service well beyond World War II. Chapter 5 examines another related set of emotions associated with the erotic appeal of domestic service; I discuss the processes of sexual objectification available to both employers and servants. Servant and employer were profoundly sexed subject positions; sexual difference, sometimes queer and always historically mobile, pervaded their interactions. The changing nature of what was erotic about domestic service is mapped out, with early-twentieth-century voyeurism and ideas of the 'natural' giving way to later fantasies of sexually charismatic male servants and cross-class seduction. The ability of servants to reverse and satirize the discourses of sexual degradation is outlined; there was no simple internalization by servants of the eroticization of dirt.

Finally, in Chapter 6, the late-twentieth-century popular memory of domestic service is investigated, in the realms of television and cinema, and in the heritage performances located within stately homes. Domestic service has had a central place in imagining the past through popular history, and serves to illustrate both exploitation and past certainties of belonging. It has provided a compelling and entertaining narrative of class, an alternative to that of the 'communities of class' represented by the industrial north, conveying to audiences and participants something of the everyday 'texture' and 'taste' of class inequalities. Influenced by James Young's call to 'reinvest the monument with our memory of its coming into being', this chapter aims to write into the memory of domestic service a history of how we come to remember it on those terms. In its late-twentieth-century expressions, domestic service can be termed a 'public dream'—a shared story, or 'collected memory' that is dreamlike in its contradictory, ambiguous nature, tending to be narrated by the powerful, yet historically contingent and mutable.[86] In the face of the late-twentieth-century rise of paid domestic employment, however, British audiences are commonly invited to perceive domestic service as an institution of the past rather than as a feature of contemporary society.

Knowing Their Place is organized around a broad definition of 'place' that encompasses places of privilege as well as of deprivation. This study pays particular attention to the ways in which place is formed from cultural as well as social, material, and economic resources. Place is also related to locality and spatiality, elements that have often been neglected in its more familiar association with social class. 'Knowing one's place' has long been imagined as a form of working-class subjectivity, built on exclusion and exploitation. Histories of servants of earlier periods have usefully emphasized alternative understandings of place.[87] This research explores the distinctive twentieth-century constructions of place in relation to domestic service, as an active form of self-fashioning, a site of popular knowledge, entertainment, and memory, as well as an externally imposed set of constraints.

SOURCES

In this study, I draw on a number of oral history collections, including interviews conducted by Paul Thompson and Thea Vigne (with a national focus) and George Ewart Evans (focused on East Anglia), as well as collections made in the East Midlands, Birmingham, Essex, Exmoor, Norfolk, and Westminster. I have also conducted my own interviews with both employers and former domestic workers.

---

[86] James E. Young, *The Texture of Memory: Holocaust Memorials and Meaning* (New Haven, CT: Yale University Press, 1993), 14. I'm grateful to Barbara Taylor for sharing her work on 'public dreams' with me.

[87] See, for example, Steedman's account of the importance of a settlement under the Poor Law as creating a servant's sense of 'place'; Carolyn Steedman, 'Lord Mansfield's Women', *Past and Present*, 176 1 (2002), 105–43.

I do not claim to offer complete national coverage, but my account of domestic service does foreground place and space, and highlights the diverse regional and local labour markets for domestic service.

Oral history sources relating to domestic service are frequently revealing of the experiences of those not in formal work, the married chars and teenage day servants. These kinds of workers were least likely to leave historical traces, but their work did become increasingly prevalent in the twentieth century and is reflected in the oral accounts they have left. The census showed a tenfold increase in chars between 1901 and 1951, though this is probably an underestimation of the real numbers.[88] Oral histories also reveal a different range of emotions from the other 'historical footprints' of twentieth-century servants, found in autobiographies or memoirs. Subjects being interviewed may discuss service as simply one part of a varied life story. Servants offered typical comments such as 'I didn't mind the work', or 'we had a lot of fun', often seemingly integrated with less positive judgements of the indignities of service. Some of the positive comments may have been motivated by a need to dignify experiences retrospectively.[89] Commonly, there are unresolved tensions within their interviews as contentment or happy memories contend with a sense of ill-use. Narratives of domestic service tend to be ambiguous, expressing complex emotions. The most revealing moments are sometimes found to be silences, or the offering of answers to questions not asked. In what follows, I seek to make sense of the full range of these comments.

Memoirs and autobiographies are also heavily drawn upon in what follows. Some of those written by servants were elicited by the oral history movement and its associated community publishing ventures that flourished in the 1970s. Employers had long felt comfortable with the publication of memoirs recording their domestic dramas, or offered textual portraits of their servants, sometimes fond, usually described in sensationalist or 'othered' terms. Servants began to write their own narratives for diverse reasons—to record a passing way of life for posterity, to warn others, to make money, to confront emotions of conflict and bitterness. As Regina Gagnier reminds us, memoirs and autobiographies are shaped by 'socio-economic status, rhetorical purpose, status of labour, and geography' and must be read with attention to these factors.[90] These kinds of sources offer similar

---

[88] On the ubiquity of chars in eighteenth-century domestic service and onwards, see Leonard Schwarz, 'English Servants and Their Employers during the Eighteenth and Nineteenth Centuries', *Economic History Review*, 52 2 (1999), 236–56, esp. 254; Steedman, *Master and Servant*, 16, 77. In 1901, 25,378 worked as chars, while in 1911, it was 126,061. Employment of chars had reached 215,336 in 1951. Census figures, quoted in Aiken, *The Central Committee on Women's Training and Employment*, 162.

[89] Oral histories must also be read with critical attention to their tendency to follow formulaic patterns and seek retrospective emotional closure, though such 'formulae' may be less prevalent within women's oral histories. Todd, *Young Women, Work and Family in England, 1918–1950*, 17. On the gendered nature of closure/composure issues in oral history, see Penny Summerfield, 'Culture and Composure: Creating Narratives of the Gendered Self in Oral History Interviews', *Cultural and Social History*, 1 1 (2004), 65–93.

[90] Regina Gagnier, 'The Literary Standard, Working Class Autobiography and Gender', in Sidonie Smith and Julia Watson (eds), *Women, Autobiography, Theory: A Reader* (Madison: University of Wisconsin Press, 1998), 267.

challenges to oral histories—the need to be attentive to retrospective memory and the search for composure. Novels have also been important to capturing the contested ground of domestic service, and give important insights into its cultural trajectory, which sometimes diverged quite significantly from the social presence of servants. Few servants, however, have opted for this cultural form, and it is mostly middle-class women for whom domestic service has provided the makings of literary plots and encounters.

Neither oral histories nor memoirs and novels are produced within a cultural vacuum, and the extensive attention given to domestic service within British cultural life (cinema, television, autobiographies of all kinds, discussed in Chapter 6) has clearly influenced the memories of domestic servants. Some respondents were motivated to counter the negative depictions of service that circulated throughout the twentieth century—though others were also concerned to re-narrate service away from the jolly, convivial mode of *Upstairs Downstairs*. Former servants reflect on their memories using phrases such as 'You know that "Upstairs, Downstairs" was nothing to what I remember it being like.'[91] One former Edwardian servant reflected in the 1970s:

I was very lucky in service...I don't think I had one bad place....I was really lucky because—I'd read books, I don't know if they were true you know, those weekly books and that was all about service and all sorts, they brought it in you know. And some awful places some of them. Some ladies they were awful you know to live with.[92]

She recognized that the cultural depiction of service was negative, but found this hard to square with her own positive experiences. It seems realistic to assume that the wide circulation in the mid- to late twentieth century of depictions of service in 'former times' may be reflected in the oral histories of domestic service, or may have provided a script for its narration and assessment, just as the oral histories and memoirs have themselves proved influential in constructing popular memory.

In their turn, interviewers have also been influenced by the cultural profile of service, and by their sense that this was a key realm in which 'class happened'. Paul Thompson's directions to interviewers in the early 1970s in the 'Edwardians' project were prescriptive in noting that interviews with servants or servant-keepers 'will be more complicated and longer than most other interviews'. Special attention was therefore paid to recording and to some degree privileging these memories of service, even though most subjects experienced service not as an all embracing experience, isolated from the rest of working-class experiences, but as one part of a lifelong negotiation of the labour market and home life. The oral histories of service, produced through the interaction of memory, contemporary context, and the concerns of interviewer and interviewee, should be read as heavily shaped by the historical moment and theoretical context in which they were collected; they do,

---

[91] Mrs Millie Milgate, in Samuel Mullins and Gareth Griffiths, *Cap and Apron: An Oral History of Domestic Service in the Shires, 1880–1950* (Leicester: Leicestershire Museums Publications, 1986).
[92] Mrs Edith Green (b. 1890, Yorkshire), Interview 268, *Edwardians*.

however, offer a rich set of sources for the construction of a revised narrative of domestic service.

In what follows, retrospectively produced sources are set alongside other more contemporary sources, including surveys, advice manuals, government reports, personal letters, court cases, trade union records, and the periodical and newspaper presses. I have particularly focused on those periodicals for which domestic service was a recurrent interest—*Good Housekeeping*, *The Lady*, *The Queen*, *The Spectator*, and amongst the daily papers, *The Times*, *The Telegraph*, and *The Daily Express*. These are set alongside smaller circulation feminist, labour, church, or domestic periodicals. They offer a rich set of visual and textual sources, and indicate the centrality and contested nature of service as it was used to sell products, generate moral panic and moaning, to titillate and inspire laughter. Alongside memoirs and novels, these sources have helped to trace the experiences of the employers of servants, which are much less prominent in oral histories. The interactive genre of the periodical also uniquely offers sources in which servants and employers confronted and addressed each other, and discussions of domestic service were acknowledged by editors to add greatly to their postbag. Other forms of popular media such as pornography, cinema, radio, and television are also examined, giving insight into the construction of the servant question in the broadest spheres of socio-cultural experiences.

1

Twentieth-Century Servants

Aspirations and Emotions

Daisy Noakes became a live-in dormitory maid in 1922, aged 14, at a school near Brighton, after her sister had 'spoken for' her. She had worked as a casual cleaner from age 12, and had also delivered washing and served tea to shopkeepers, aiming to save enough to buy her uniform for entering live-in service. Other jobs were available—she might have become a shop assistant, but 'Their pay was not large, they were always expected to look smart, so new clothes were almost a must, and walking to and from work daily must have worn their shoes more than ours.' Domestic service seemed a better option, despite the hours—in her first job, 5.30am to 10.30pm—which must have taken a toll on her shoe leather. Her mother made her up some dresses, renovated a tin trunk, and told her to 'always add "Ma'm" to every answer, and stand up when spoken to.' She also made it clear that her daughter could not come home if she disliked the job. Indeed, her mother charged for Daisy's upkeep when she came home on holiday. When Daisy brought her fiancé home for the first time, she was charged a shilling for his tea by her mother. She had mixed experiences of service for the next twelve years; she was happy, and had plenty of fun, but resented being made to work so hard.[1]

Kathlyn Oliver was an Edwardian servant in London from around 1905. Her background was middle class—her father had 'a good position in the Civil Service.' But unfortunately, 'he did not think it necessary that his daughter should have more than a very secondary education.' When he died, Kathlyn was left without options to support herself, and in a letter to the homosexual radical Edward Carpenter, she commented on her intense frustration at her lack of choices: 'I took up domestic work—the conditions and spirit of which I loathe. I am by nature something of a revolutionist and as may be supposed I have not felt in my element with employers who (as so many still do) possess the feudal spirit towards those who serve them.'[2] She was active in setting up a servants' trade union in London, and also described herself as a feminist and of the 'intermediate sex'.[3]

---

[1] Daisy Noakes, *The Town Bee-Hive: A Young Girl's Lot in Brighton, 1910–1934* (Brighton: QueenSpark Books, 1975), 86, 47.

[2] Kathlyn Oliver to Edward Carpenter, Oct 25, 1915, Edward Carpenter Papers, Sheffield City Council, Libraries Archives and Information

[3] Kathlyn Oliver, *Domestic Servants and Citizenship* (London: People's Suffrage Federation, 1911); letter to the editor, *The Freewoman*, June 20, 1912, 98.

Rosina Harrison, born into an artisan family in 1899, by contrast, saw her entrance into service in around 1917 as a career, though she acknowledged that there were in fact few other options—service was an inevitability for working-class girls in her part of rural Yorkshire. Nonetheless, she was 'very close' to her mother, and confided that she desperately wanted to travel. Her mother arranged for her to stay on at school, and have extra French lessons, so that she could be a ladies' maid. 'I did suggest that I could go into service as a housemaid or kitchen-maid and then transfer, but Mum wouldn't hear of that.'[4] She ended up working for the super-rich Astor family, and did indeed become a career servant. Her nine-year engagement to be married was eventually broken off because she had no time and inclination to marry, or even maintain her own social life. Instead, she preferred to pursue her complex relationship with Lady Astor, in which Rosina spoke her mind and openly contested the low status of servants, but was also subject to petty tricks. They continued to spar throughout their eighteen-year relationship, which lasted until World War II.

Each of these servants entered service in very contrasting ways, with different kinds of emotions and aspirations. Each was situated within a web of familial and social relations that helped shape their experiences of service. Unusually, they each left an account of their experiences as servants, in oral histories, published memoirs, or letters to friends and to periodicals. Twentieth-century servants were a marginalized and hard-worked group who, by and large, had little time or inclination to write of their lives. However, their higher standards of literacy, improving work conditions, and broader social horizons meant that we have far more evidence of how they thought and felt about their lives than for their nineteenth-century equivalents. Servants were increasingly likely to be articulate, and to engage with that long-standing set of social controversies, 'the servant problem'. Later in the century, their experiences were actively solicited by the oral history movement.

The inclusion of the voices and experiences of servants enriches and nuances our understanding of British social history. Nonetheless, the historiography has also been powerfully shaped by the assumption that service was a 'total institution' in which working-class women were exploited by the unlimited demands placed on them. Becoming a servant has been seen as a powerful moment of anomie and self-alienation. Even in more recent histories, service has been portrayed as the lowest status occupation, an aspiration-free zone, in which sullen workers were patronized and talked down to by overbearing mistresses: 'there were few jobs in which the reality and sensation of exploitation was so great.'[5] As one historian put it, the servant was so stigmatized that putting on a cap was 'a tacit admission that one no longer existed as a person.'[6] But such a belief seems likely to efface the actual

---

[4] Rosina Harrison, *Rose: My Life in Service* (London: Cassell, 1975), 15–16.

[5] Callum Brown and Jayne Stephenson, 'The View from the Workplace: Women's Memories of Work in Stirling c. 1910–c. 1950', in E. Breitenbach (ed.), *The World Is Ill-Divided: Women's Work in Scotland in the Nineteenth and Early Twentieth Centuries* (Edinburgh: Edinburgh University Press, 1990), 14.

[6] Standish Meacham, *A Life Apart: The English Working Class 1890–1914* (London: Thames and Hudson, 1977), 184–5.

historical presence of servants, who were far from deferential and acquiescent. The mostly oral testimonies of domestic servants discussed in this chapter make clear the dangers of what Carolyn Steedman has memorably termed the 'subordinating gaze of sympathy'.[7] A revised narrative of domestic service is needed to make sense of the servant who, when asked whether she would have preferred another job, answered: 'No I don't think so. I loved me job you see. You see, at school I was very interested and passed with honours at Domestic Science. The cooking and all that sort of thing attracted me.'[8] Pleasure and satisfaction, a sense of skill and accomplishment are found alongside sentiments of bitterness and resentment.

The narrative of exploitation has proposed that servants became outsiders to their own communities, 'declassed' in their personal subjectivities, and deferential to their employers. There is evidence that service gave some women a life-long commitment to a middle- or upper-class lifestyle: 'there was a certain enforcement of discipline and general manners which was something perhaps my mother had never been taught, herself. She'd picked it up from being in service and what was done in nice households and she tried to introduce it into her own.'[9] Some former servants adopted starched white tablecloths for their own tables, even if made from cotton sheets, and used serving dishes, as they had done in grander homes. As one Scottish maid said of her mother-in law: 'she was well spoken, and been in a good place. She still retained that. She'd a sort of superior air about her.'[10] This effect was celebrated by employers and campaigners on domestic service questions—they insisted that service provided a good training for women in their roles as mothers and wives, imparting the habits of social superiors, and making the transition of the children of servants into domestic service more comfortable. As the son of a cook put it: 'When I went into service it was easier for me as we applied the same standards at home as they did.'[11] Carolyn Bridger experienced similar influences when she went into private domestic service in 1979 after her marriage had broken down. Her mother and other relatives had been in 'good service', and it felt very natural for her to become a live-in cook-housekeeper in private houses between 1979 and 1985, accompanied by her two young children. She mostly worked alongside daily cleaners, but found the provision of accommodation helpful as a single parent. The wages compared well with other jobs, and she drew on her experiences as a school cook and matron on a cruise ship before her marriage. Private domestic service was easily integrated with these other roles, and as a woman in her thirties, she found the relationship with her employers to be mutually respectful.[12]

---

[7] Carolyn Steedman, *Master and Servant: Love and Labour in the English Industrial Age* (Cambridge: Cambridge University Press, 2007), 178.
[8] Mrs Florence Thompson (b. 1893), Interview 117, in P. Thompson and T. Lummis, *Family Life and Work Experience before 1918, 1870–1973* [computer file], 7th edn, Colchester, Essex: UK Data Archive (distributor), May 2009, SN: 2000; henceforth cited as *Edwardians*.
[9] Paul Thompson, *The Edwardians: The Remaking of British Society* (London: Routledge, 1992), 84.
[10] Mrs Winifred Sturgeon (b. 1885), interview 363, *Edwardians*.
[11] Samuel Mullins and Gareth Griffiths, *Cap and Apron: An Oral History of Domestic Service in the Shires, 1880–1950* (Leicester: Leicestershire Museums Publications, 1986), 38.
[12] Carolyn Bridger, interview with the author, Sept 3, 2010.

Historians and sociologists have seen such traditions within families as the construction of a deferential worker, or a 'class apart', aspiring to their employer's lifestyle and unable to identify with fellow workers. As David Lockwood described it, 'the typical work role of the deferential traditionalist will be one that brings him into direct association with his employer or other middle-class influentials and hinders him from forming strong attachments to workers in a similar market situation to his own.' Servants could be seen as socially isolated, deferential workers who were 'socially acquiescent and conservative'.[13] For Standish Meacham, writing in 1977, service was hard and monotonous, and left the female servant 'in a kind of limbo, rejecting the values of employers . . . while discontented and distressed' by working-class lifestyles.[14]

Other historians, more sensitive to the nuances of gender and kinship, looked to working-class familial relationships to explain deference and acquiescence.[15] Pam Taylor in the late 1970s focused upon the much earlier and deeper internalization of social norms, in the relationships of working-class mothers and daughters. The strict authority of working-class mothers over daughters going into service was seen as analogous and complementary to that exerted by mistresses. Working-class mothers played a key role in arranging and attending interviews and, motivated by poverty, sometimes gave their children no other option but to enter and stay in domestic service. Pam Taylor concluded, 'There is a sense in which mothers were contributing to the exploitation of their daughters.'[16] Leonore Davidoff elaborated,

This kind of gradual introduction to the authority system of service in which discipline was enforced first through the mother and then often through female teachers, relations or friends is one of the factors which made it possible to maintain the institution of domestic service for so long and make it seem so 'natural' even to those who were subordinated and who gained very little in real terms from their positions.[17]

Historians have thus tried to make sense of what has been seen as the 'surprising' finding from oral histories, that domestic service was remembered in a positive

---

[13] David Lockwood, 'Sources of Variation in Working Class Images of Society', *Sociological Review*, 14 (1966) 252–3.

[14] Meacham, *A Life Apart*, 188–9.

[15] See Lynn Jamieson, 'Rural and Urban Women in Domestic Service', in Breitenbach, *The World Is Ill-Divided*; Jane Hegstrom, 'Reminiscences of Below Stairs: English Female Domestic Servants between the Two World Wars', *Women's Studies*, 36 1 (2007), 15–33; E. Roberts, *A Woman's Place: An Oral History of Working-Class Women 1890–1940* (Oxford: Blackwell, 1995), 11.

[16] Pam Taylor, 'Daughters and Mothers–Maids and Mistresses: Domestic Service between the Wars', in Chas Crichter, Richard Johnson, and John Clark (eds), *Working Class Culture: Studies in History and Theory* (London: Hutchinson, 1979), 121–39. Taylor's research was based in the Birmingham Centre for Contemporary Cultural Studies alongside that of Paul Willis, whose classic text *Learning to Labour* attempted to explain 'how working-class kids [let themselves] get working-class jobs' (*Learning to Labour: How Working Class Kids Get Working Class Jobs* (Farnborough: Saxon House, 1978)). Both reach similar conclusions—that working-class culture creates and sustains patterns of socialization that encourage workers into taking 'appropriate' jobs—ones that do not encourage social mobility or aspirations.

[17] Leonore Davidoff, *Worlds between: Historical Perspectives on Class and Gender* (New York: Routledge, 1995), 119.

light. One oral history interviewer of the late 1980s, Mary Harrison, argued that the enjoyment of housework expressed by the former servants she'd interviewed was 'a survival mechanism'. She believed that dislike and resentment were latent within these women, but remained unexpressed, because 'in the agricultural economy in which they grew up working-class men were also severely exploited and this tended to mask women's additional and particular exploitation.' Harrison acknowledged that she was offering her subjects a threatening set of 'consciousness raising views on housework from a feminist perspective'.[18] This made for a highly directive set of questions which failed to give voice to the emotions her subjects expressed. More recently, Jane Hegstrom similarly believed that servants' 'relatively positive recollections of their time in service may well be the internalization of a working-class ideology of acceptance of their status in society.'[19] She adopts David Lockwood's idea of the 'deferential worker' and Howard Newby's concept of working-class ideology, to account for why servants accepted poor and stigmatizing working conditions, attributing 'false consciousness *par excellence*' to explain their acquiescence.[20]

However, there is little evidence that domestic service was predominantly experienced as a 'total institution', under the authority of mothers and immune from the changes in women's work in the twentieth century. Indeed, workers often moved fluidly in and out of service and other occupations or roles, according to their circumstances. Individuals other than mothers were often equally significant in shaping attitudes to employment. Nor was service always experienced as exploitative. A wider range of experiences and a more complex emotional landscape can be traced for those women who became servants. Theories of deferential workers and false consciousness don't easily lend themselves to making sense of the subjectivities of service. Instead, one might usefully ask the same kinds of questions of domestic servants that Joanna Bourke has asked of housewives—in what way did servants try to gain symbolic authority through their experiences? What forms of dignity and satisfaction did domestic service provide, both retrospectively and at the moment of employment? And in what ways might servants 'acquiesce yet protest, reproduce yet seek to transform their predicament'?[21] The historical evidence includes mothers such as Rosina Harrison's, with aspirations for their children and who worked extremely hard to position their children to expect more from the labour market than exploitation. Young workers emerge with their own preferences, aspirations and sense of 'career' progression. The experience of 'becoming a servant' was neither of a total and overwhelming identity, nor 'just a job'. As the biographies at the start of this chapter indicate, domestic service was so diverse that generalizations can only cautiously be made about it. It was mediated by

---

[18] Mary Harrison, 'Domestic Service between the Wars: The Experiences of Two Rural Women', *Oral History*, 16 1 (1988), 48–54, esp. 54.
[19] Hegstrom, 'Reminiscences of Below Stairs', 22.
[20] Ibid. 29; Lockwood, 'Sources of Variation in Working Class Images of Society'; Howard Newby, *The Deferential Worker* (London: Allen Lane, 1977).
[21] Joanna Bourke, 'Housewifery in Working-Class England, 1860–1914', in Pamela Sharpe (ed.), *Women's Work: The English Experience, 1650–1914* (London: Arnold, 1998), 332–58 334.

individual preferences, family circumstances, geographical location, labour market trends, cultural context, and the intervention of the state, all of which were historically specific. Its stories cannot be told in isolation from this bigger picture. This is not to suggest that service was not exploitative—in some situations, it certainly was. But this study aims to move on from the somewhat sterile debate about whether service was a good or a bad thing, and whether servants suffered from false consciousness. As James Scott has noted, there is an 'immense political terrain that lies between quiescence and revolt', and in this chapter I examine how we might chart such a territory and represent the subjectivities and emotional investments which emerge from it.[22]

ENTERING SERVICE

Entering service is often imagined to be a very abrupt shift, as depicted for example by the 1974 autobiography of Winifred Foley (1914–2009), a former servant who was active in Communist politics in later life. She wrote: 'The bony finger of poverty was pushing me out into an alien world' when she turned 14, to 'earn a living in a stranger's house'.[23] Foley came from the Forest of Dean, typical of the less economically buoyant regions such as Wales, the Scottish Highlands, or Lincolnshire, from which servants were more likely to migrate for work. These servants often took jobs in areas of high demand—London, and seaside or spa towns such as Liverpool, Brighton, and Bath—and were more likely to use formal channels of recruitment such as adverts in a newspaper, rather than word of mouth, preferred in urban areas.[24] They reported experiences of abrupt transition and dislocation in becoming a servant. However, they were a minority, and this is important because the sense of service as a total institution, removing young women from all that was familiar and placing them in vulnerable and isolated homes, is not borne out by the evidence. Entering service was typically much more gradual. Many girls had already taken casual jobs cleaning doorsteps or minding neighbours' children before going into a more formal domestic job after leaving school at around 14 years of age. Even then, many took daily or very casual jobs initially, perhaps covering the evenings that a maid had out, or helping out after house decorating. As one Liverpool-born housemaid put it, after some years spent caring for her mother, 'then I went to—sort of—help out with these people that mother had been a children's nurse with.' After her marriage in 1911, she again experienced a gradual entry into the labour market: 'I had a friend who was a sort of school room maid and she used to come and visit me and one time they had

---

[22] J. C. Scott, *Domination and the Arts of Resistance: Hidden Transcripts* (New Haven, CT: Yale University Press, 1990), 199.
[23] Winifred Foley, *A Child in the Forest* (London: Futura, 1974), 146.
[24] Diane Aiken, *The Central Committee on Women's Training and Employment: Tackling the Servant Problem, 1914–1945* (Oxford: Oxford Brookes University, 2002), 63.

some—missionary stayed in the house and I went along there just to sort of give a hand with the fires up at the top.'[25]

Many servants experienced a gradual entry to service, and also sometimes gradual exit or multiple re-entries. There is an assumption that service ended upon marriage, but in fact the reality was more complex. Mrs Myers, for example, worked as a servant in a number of different households in and around Leicester. She then tried factory work and disliked it, returned to service, and then helped a working-class mother with a large family and lodgers, on an informal basis. It was there that she met her husband. After marriage, she undertook domestic work in canteens and as a dormitory maid, while raising her family.[26] Overall, servants were quite likely to experience both non-domestic work and domestic work, and thus likely to negotiate a number of transitions in the labour market—one might 'become a servant' on multiple occasions. Servants were thus not 'a class apart' from the rest of the working class, and did not always choose domestic service as a last resort. Becoming a servant might be a gradual process, within which young women like Daisy Noakes exercised choice and agency within the constraints of poverty and family expectations.

The employers of servants in their first jobs were often kin, godparents, or family friends. Siân Pooley's recent research on Lancaster has suggested that fewer servants were rural–urban migrants than has previously been thought; these more locally based servants were more likely to share cultural and social norms with their employers.[27] Day servants often described employers as 'just poor like us', and sometimes called them 'Mr' and 'Missus' rather than 'Sir' and 'Madam'.[28] There were some who experienced relatively formal and distant relationships with their 'masters' and 'mistresses', but many did not. One farm servant in Cornwall recalled spending her time off playing in the garden with her employer's children. She related to her employer as a mother, and 'felt I could stay there for always'.[29] Employers sometimes treated their younger servants as children, and such relationships were more common in rural areas, where the average age of servants was younger and where older traditions of farm service persisted.[30] Being treated as a child did not necessarily entail paternalism and high levels of control, but might also mean informality and some tolerance of 'childish' behaviour such as not liking to eat all kinds of food.

Most servants found their first few jobs through their mother's intervention, though other contacts might also be involved particularly for second and subsequent jobs. For Winifred Foley, when she wanted to leave her first job,

---

[25] Mrs Annie Banks (b. 1884, Liverpool), Interview 119, *Edwardians*.
[26] Mrs Myers (b. 1901, Essex), Interview 315, *Edwardians*.
[27] Siân Pooley, 'Domestic Servants and Their Urban Employers: A Case Study of Lancaster, 1880–1914', *Economic History Review*, 62 2 (2009), 405–29.
[28] Mrs Laura Macafferty (b.1904), Interview 210, *Edwardians*.
[29] Mrs Norah Blewett (b. 1897), Interview 408, *Edwardians*.
[30] In rural areas in 1901, 66% of servants were under 20, contrasted with less than half under 20 in urban areas. Census of England and Wales 1901.

I wrote home and told them... Mam told a neighbour, and the neighbour put this item of news in a letter to her daughter who was working in London. By this means, before I had left the farm, I had a letter from my neighbour's daughter telling me she could get me a job any time.[31]

Many recalled joint decisions made about their futures with their mothers; a few went against their mother's wishes. Some, however, were not consulted in the process of finding work, and might be 'talked over' without much possibility of intervention. A girl born in South Wales in 1905 reported that: 'They would never think of letting me go to a factory. My mother thought that was awful... She had a bit of silly pride; the girls all swore and were rather common, she had that idea.'[32] As Selina Todd has argued, mothers had an investment in household status, which would be affected by a daughter's place of work. One servant recalled that her mother had taken her for an interview as a servant and when asked 'Will she work hard?' answered with brutal honesty, 'She won't for me, but she might for a stranger.'[33]

Others bypassed their mothers, and obtained work independently through their friends, neighbours, or sisters. Less often, fathers and schoolteachers were mentioned as conduits to work. The numbers using formal registry offices or even newspaper adverts were relatively few, though for those seeking work in 'great house' service, such channels were more important.[34] On entering service, most young women were interviewed for local jobs in middle-class households, providing 'characters' from school teachers or clergy, and had someone at the interview, usually a mother, to 'speak for' family background. Those of illegitimate birth often found jobs closed to them, even during the servant shortages of the 1930s. Non-Anglicans and those of non-European ethnic origins or non-Anglican religions also found obstacles to employment. Mothers might be quizzed about their own background and work experiences. One daughter recalled having her biceps felt. However, where jobs were obtained with kin or family friends, the process was often less formal, and strong links were maintained with the servant's home through regular visiting.

The lack of consultation over employment was particularly true of girls in institutional care, who were routinely placed in domestic service by the committees in charge of their welfare, and seem to have been rarely consulted. Those who were under the care of orphanages, homes for unmarried mothers, or workhouses did mostly experience the transition to such a job as an abrupt ejection, though often they had faced very similar conditions of hard work and strict discipline in their

---

[31] Foley, *A Child in the Forest*, 210.
[32] Mullins and Griffiths, *Cap and Apron*, 1.
[33] Frank V. Dawes, *Not in Front of the Servants: Domestic Service in England 1850–1939* (London: Wayland, 1973), 118; Selina Todd, 'Poverty and Aspiration: Young Women's Entry to Employment in Inter-war England', *Twentieth Century British History*, 15 2 (2004), 119–42.
[34] Though advertisements are revealing of some of the social assumptions underpinning domestic service, the tendency for historians to base their research on quantitative surveys of them is problematic, since so few servants used this medium.

former institutional life, and so may not have felt it to be materially very different.[35] These institutions might be said to provide what I argue most twentieth-century mothers did not—a socialization that induced deference or acquiescence. Nonetheless, orphans sometimes resisted what other servants regarded as normal, because they had not come across it before. One orphan, Mrs Myers, recalled that she would not wear a cap with streamers, because she had never seen one before:

I wouldn't wear one. I said, I don't want those—one of those, I'm not wearing one of those,' cos I'd never worn anything like it at the orphanage, naturally. I had one of those little—like a nurses cap. Oh well, that'll do me, I said. And I wouldn't have one of the aprons crossed over at the back with lace.

When the mistress asked why she wouldn't wear the cap, 'I said, cos I don't like the stuff on my hair.'[36] We should not understand workers from institutions as particularly passive or deferential workers, despite their previous institutionalization. Some orphans did, however, report that they could not quit their jobs, or even take the holiday time they were offered, because they had no other home to return to, or no suitable clothes to wear beyond their servant's uniform.

Orphans who became servants were well aware that they were more vulnerable in the labour market. One who became a farm servant in Essex in 1898 recalled, 'I had no mother or she would not have let me stay.'[37] This comment makes clear the degree of protection that mothers offered even in the late nineteenth century, when historians have assumed that mothers were unable or unwilling to protect their daughters in service. And even for those young workers coming from institutions, siblings might continue to provide a degree of protection, by visiting and policing conditions of work. Furthermore, the institutions themselves, harsh though they were in many senses, sometimes offered protection beyond that which parents might be able to afford. Miss Bailey, an orphan born in 1890, was raised in the Tendring Union in Essex, and later by a foster family. Even when fostered out, she continued to receive occasional gifts from the workhouse, which she remembered as leavening the grim environment of her foster home.[38] She was placed by her foster mother as a general servant at 14 years old, for a family who had no running water. The Board of Guardians, however, realizing that she was too physically frail for the work, sent her back to school for a further two years, and continued to pay an allowance for her upkeep. Mrs Myers was prevented from leaving an orphanage in

---

[35] Pamela Horn, *Life below Stairs in the Twentieth Century* (Stroud: Sutton, 2001), 106–12. Servants raised in institutions did, however, suffer greatly from the isolation of many domestic service jobs, having become used to being always in the company of others. Mrs Newman, raised in a London Parish School, recalled being literally paralysed when her employers first left her alone in the house, unable to leave the window for hours until they returned. She was also emotionally bereft at leaving her institutional home: 'on being recalled to the room to bid the officer goodbye I flung myself into her arms and begged her to take me back with her, this after stating at the school how glad I would be to leave it all. Yet remember it was the only home I had ever known.' Mrs E. Newman, AC, 'My First Job' (1961), ERO T/Z 25/337.
[36] Mrs Myers, Interview 315, *Edwardians*.
[37] Mrs Shearman, AC, 'My First Job' (1961), ERO T/Z 25/222-405.
[38] Interview 19, *Edwardians*.

Leicester to go into domestic service because they did not release girls until their periods started—hers did not start until she was nearly seventeen, and thus the move into service was delayed for nearly three years. As she put it, 'They didn't let you out to service until you were—become a woman.'[39] The shift to domestic service was experienced as a physical shift to adulthood, and the orphanage, in keeping with the policies of other institutions such as Parish Schools, provided an unexpected degree of protection against child labour. Relations with the state or public institutions were thus not all of constraint, but might also carry connotations of entitlement or protection, even before the changes in the relationship between citizen and state after World War II.[40] Nonetheless, young women cared for by institutions suffered higher levels of exploitation because of their stigmatized origins, and because they lacked the depth of social networks that might protect them from 'bad places'. There was strong demand for such girls, and it was not until the late 1940s that institutions such as Dr Barnardos or the Church of England Children's Society became willing to imagine other kinds of employment for the girls they looked after.

LIVING-OUT SERVANTS, CHARWOMEN, AND CLEANERS

Charwomen and 'dailies' were ubiquitous figures in nineteenth- and twentieth-century homes. To see living-out as an achievement brought by more assertive servants after World War I obscures its prevalence in earlier years. Casual work was very commonly a part of domestic workers' experiences at various stages in the lifecycle, and many homes employing live-in servants also had a char or daily 'help'. It is particularly hard to trace the extent and conditions of charring, since such economic activity often does not show up in census records, though a sharp rise was recorded between 1901 and 1911, and again after World War II.[41] Chars predominated in the poorer areas of cities—in Bethnal Green, for example, there were 57 chars in formal employment to every 50 domestic servants in the 1920s, and probably many more who worked informally.[42] Where accounts of domestic service have been solicited by oral historians, experiences of 'live-out' service tend to be skipped over as incidental to the 'real thing'. Similarly, char work or cleaning

---

[39] Mrs Myers, Interview 315, *Edwardians*.
[40] See Abigail Wills, 'Delinquency, Masculinity and Citizenship in England 1950–1970', *Past and Present*, 187 (2005), 157–85, and the much-quoted statement on the empowerment of school milk and meals by Carolyn Steedman, *Landscape for a Good Woman: A Story of Two Lives* (London: Virago, 1986), 121–2.
[41] Aiken, *The Central Committee on Women's Training and Employment*, 62; Roberts, *A Woman's Place*, 54–8, 139; Bronwen Walter, 'Irish Domestic Servants and English National Identity', in A. Fauve-Chamoux and R. Sarti (eds), *Domestic Service and the Formation of European Identity: Understanding the Globalization of Domestic Work 16th–21st Centuries* (Bern: Peter Lang, 2004), 471–88.
[42] Cicely Hamilton, 'Women Workers', in Arthur St John Adcock (ed.), *Wonderful London* (London: Amalgamated Press, 1926), 190.

after marriage is usually regarded by historians as an ad hoc strategy to make ends meet that did not result in any particular social identity or meaning-laden encounter. However, it was clearly economically important to family budgets, and was often regarded as an integrated part of a working life that might also include other forms of making money such as casual agricultural work or taking in lodgers. Its prevalence continued into the mid- to late twentieth century. One Mass Observation correspondent who was brought up in Blackpool after World War I described her mother's aspirations and work:

My mother had one burning ambition—to own her house, so everything was sacrificed to it. She worked as a 'char' with no such dignity as Home Help. The work was exhausting chiefly because she made it so. It was badly paid and I know she was cheated by two sets of people. She arrived home tired out and usually in a temper. In the summer she took in visitors.

The 'burning ambition' of this woman to be a homeowner is suggestive of the mass affluence of postwar Britain, but also reminds us that this did not always go hand in hand with the attainment of housewife status for working-class women. Many continued to work in low-paid cleaning jobs, in order to realize a vision of domestic security, or simply to get by. Another correspondent described her mother's exhausting work as a cleaner in the 1950s, and the desire of her children, acutely conscious of the family's shortness of income, to help her by running errands.[43]

No hard and fast distinction can be made between 'the daily', 'the help', 'the char', and 'the cleaner'. An extra pair of hands, paid by the hour, might be brought in to help a housewife, or equally, to help servants by undertaking those tasks named 'the rough'. Casual employment was sometimes organized around a particular task such as knife and boot cleaning, undertaken by boys, or laundry and step cleaning by girls and women. Vera Frith recalled the washerwoman, Mrs Rear, hired by her mother in Edmonton in the 1890s, and paid 2s 6d per week: 'Oh, you should have seen that woman—great fat arms and a man's—thick coat. She was very civil—very civil. She was pleased to get this half a crown. You see out of the workhouse, she—she was in the workhouse and mum rented her from the workhouse.... She was so—always so pleased to come.'[44] Casual domestic service was one of the few jobs that could be undertaken while in the stigmatized location of the workhouse, and Frith recalls being encouraged not to mix with the washerwoman, who was described in objectifying terms as 'rented'.

The individuals who undertook 'the rough', through their proximity to 'dirt', were portrayed as uncouth and sometimes threatening. One child of a servant-keeping family described in the 1920s the girls who cleaned the steps of suburban houses in South London:

The step-girls were a band apart. Lucy [the maid] regarded them as 'poor things'; when we saw them trailing down the streets with their buckets and cloths, she would point out in an

---

[43] A022 and A002, Mass Observation Archive (University of Sussex), replies to summer 1983 Directive on Work, Leisure and Unemployment.
[44] Vera Frith (nee Potts, b. 1883, Edmonton), Interview 85, *Edwardians*.

undertone of prim pity that one of them had 'a great big potato in her heel.' This meant a hole in her black stocking; Lucy also told me they were dirty, and rough, and *really* 'common.' Compared with them, Lucy regarded herself as a lady. The step-girls were as low as you could get. We used to see them coming down the road in a straggly bunch; they never seemed to have coats, even in the winter; their sleeves were always rolled up, and they wore big dirty aprons all the time... I could hear them coughing and cackling and yelling to each other in the raw Brockley evening. I couldn't understand anything they said; they were going home, I supposed—yet... I couldn't imagine them even having a home.[45]

This sense of otherness and association with dirt allowed workers at the lowest levels of domestic service to be eroticized, as Chapter 5 discusses, and sometimes led to abuse. Mrs Betsy Miller, a charlady in interwar Salford, reported that her master 'said something filthy to me one day and I nearly knocked him over with the brush. He thought that because I was there as the cleaner he could say anything he liked.'[46]

Char work was often denigrated as only attracting women of the lowest skill and intelligence. *Cassell's Book of the Household* described chars as gossiping, ignorant, and greedy, their work marred by the customary provision of beer or gin alongside their wages.[47] The psychologist Violet Firth talked of charring as 'a danger to national life' because it encouraged married women to limit their fertility.[48] Occasional attempts were made to formalize and improve the status of this kind of work, as in the founding of the Association of Trained Charwomen, in 1898. This body aimed to act as an employment agency, but also to guarantee the moral character of those seeking employment. Its relatively high joining fee of 10 shillings would have excluded most women, and it only touched the more privileged end of this group of workers. Most such workers found their work informally—the social investigator Ada Chesterton simply knocked on doors asking for charring work when she was impersonating a 'down and out' in 1920s London. Others found work through contacts made when they had lived-in as servants, or were placed by bodies such as the Poor Law Guardians into casual, live-out domestic work.[49] In some regions, the char or daily achieved a higher degree of social status as an autonomous, reliable worker; Bernard Thornley, for example, described how the residential maids of his childhood in the textile town of Bolton, Lancashire, were ephemeral: 'There's so much other attraction in a place like Bolton. In the way of work... we relied chiefly on the—daily people who were stable.' His family employed an Irish woman, always addressed as Mrs Butchings, who called the children by their Christian names.

---

[45] Jenifer Wayne, *Brown Bread and Butter in the Basement: A Twenties Childhood* (London: Victor Gollancz, 1973), 10.

[46] N. Gray, *The Worst of Times: An Oral History of the Great Depression in Britain* (London: Wildwood House, 1985), 118.

[47] 'Servants of the House: XII, Occasional Help', *Cassell's Household Guide*, new and rev edn (c.1880s [no date]), 3: 26.

[48] Violet M. Firth, *The Psychology of the Servant Problem: A Study in Social Relationships* (London: Daniel, 1925), 52.

[49] Association for Trained Charwomen, 'Annual Report 1904–5' (London: Women's Industrial Council, 1905); Ada Chesterton, *Women of the Underworld* (London: Stanley Paul, 1928).

As a married woman, she had more freedom than the residential servants: 'She was left to her own initiative. Because she was a capable housewife.'[50]

Irish domestic workers were over-represented in these sorts of jobs, and were more likely to be older, married, living-out workers than their English counterparts. Many female Irish migrants to England and Scotland at the beginning of the twentieth century went into institutional domestic service because they were less acceptable within private houses. One mistress commented on her Irish cook, 'her religion was a nuisance and caused quarrels in the kitchen.' She believed that Irish servants filled their employers' houses with unemployed relatives, and always avoided employing them.[51] There was widespread discrimination against Roman Catholics. One woman, herself an unpaid companion to a 'lady', wrote to the National Union of Domestic Workers in 1938 asking for help in finding a 'good, honest woman': 'We should be glad if she were a Protestant. We don't mind whether she is a Nazi, Austrian or Pole but we would rather not have a Roman Catholic, as our experience with them has been disappointing.'[52] Irish-born servants formed around 4 per cent of interwar indoor domestic servants (3 per cent in Scotland), but made up 19 per cent of the servants surveyed in the *New Survey of London Life and Labour*. Welsh servants made up another 8 per cent.[53] Domestic service continued to be the largest single sector employing Welsh women until 1939, and though some worked locally, most migrated to jobs in England, where they were more acceptable in private homes than Irish women.[54] Towards the middle of the century, as Bronwen Walter has argued, Irish migrants became depicted as less racially 'other', as race became more about skin colour than ethnicity. They therefore became more acceptable within English homes, and were actively encouraged into cleaning and charring jobs by the Catholic Church.[55]

The status of casual worker often led to exploitation, and this was particularly true of those who, like many married Irish domestic workers, had other care responsibilities. Some simply took their children with them to cleaning jobs, where they might play with the children of the household. But having children certainly limited the jobs that could be taken. One married cleaner commented of her work in the 1930s:

---

[50] Bernard Thornley (b. 1894), Interview 33, *Edwardians*.
[51] Mary Wylde, *A Housewife in Kensington* (London: Longmans, Green, 1937), 44, 146.
[52] Report of Our First Year's Work, from Household Service League and National Union of Domestic Workers, 1938, MRC 292/54.76/8 [53.3].
[53] Census of England and Wales 1951, *Occupation Tables* (London: HMSO, 1956), at Table 26; Census of Scotland 1921 (Edinburgh: HMSO, 1923), at vol II; Census of Scotland 1951, *Occupations and Industries* (Edinburgh: HMSO, 1956); Census of England and Wales 1951, *General Report* (London: HMSO, 1958); H. Llewellyn Smith, *The New Survey of London Life and Labour* (London: King, 1929), 2: 467.
[54] Deirdre Beddoe, 'Munitionettes, Maids and Mams: Women in Wales, 1914–1939', in Angela John (ed.), *Our Mother's Land: Chapters in Welsh Women's History, 1830–1939* (Cardiff: University of Wales Press, 1991), 189–209, esp. 190.
[55] Enda Delaney, *The Irish in Post-War Britain* (Oxford: Oxford University Press, 2007); Walter, 'Irish Domestic Servants'.

When you've got children, you're in a terribly awkward position as regards getting jobs. Moreover, if Dad [her husband] had known I was working, he would have deducted my wages off the housekeeping. We were desperately poor. I had to get a few hours work and know the money would be mine. The only job really available was cleaning. In those days we were given 1s 9d an hour, and we had to clean a whole house from top to bottom in three hours.... there were no labour saving devices. You were lucky if you got a hoover. Everything was done on your hands and knees. You had to polish the floor, a whole parquet flooring, on your hands and knees.... Then there were coal fires. You had to lug the coal from bunkers in all weathers and clean the fire places out. Very heavy work. And the lady of the house would walk around watching you as you did it all, the corners you know. You really worked very hard for which you got the princely sum of six shillings for a morning's work. You'd often stay after your three hours, doing extra jobs. She'd say, 'you don't mind washing the breakfast things do you?' They'd leave everything for you to do.[56]

However, many 'helps' worked for relatively poor families, and some found friendship and warmth in this role, often working alongside their employers. Though casual or daily work had the lowest status of all domestic work, it did offer a degree of freedom, as the cackling gang of step-girls suggests. Servants themselves were very aware of the status hierarchy involved in particular kinds of domestic tasks, but even the casual cleaner was vocal in defending her dignity in work. After the salacious comments of her Salford employer, Betsy Miller went on, 'I just took the brush and ran into him. I knocked him spinning. I never spoke to him again and he used to lift his hat to me when I passed him. I didn't tell his wife.'[57] Very occasionally, cleaners and chars took collective action. In 1952, for example, a group of women cleaners, all married with children, formed a branch of the National Union of Domestic Workers. They invited employers to join alongside them, and sought social respect and greater status for their work.[58]

The work of cleaners and chars overlapped with, but is distinguishable from, the work of 'live-out' servants who became increasingly common in interwar Britain. The *New Survey of London Life and Labour* conducted in 1929 showed that day servants formed a third of those in private service.[59] Most chars did not wear uniforms, and were paid by the hour or task. Day servants, however, took on the more traditionally defined roles of 'housemaid' or 'cook', and their jobs only differed from live-in servants by their slightly shorter hours. Though this gave opportunities for freedom, there were also material disadvantages to living-out. One servant told Ada Chesterton in the early 1920s: 'I don't hold with girls doing daily work; by the time you've paid for your room and had a bit of fun it doesn't leave enough for food. If you live in you get your nourishment. There's a lot said against service nowadays, but there's a lot to be said for it.'[60]

[56] Liz, 'Lucy', *Spare Rib*, Jan 31, 1975, 9.
[57] Gray, *The Worst of Times*, 118.
[58] *South London Press*, Feb 8, 1952.
[59] Smith, *New Survey of London*, 3: 452, and 2: 27–31.
[60] Chesterton, *Women of the Underworld*, 28.

By the middle decades of the twentieth century, more young women began to resist living-in. The union organizer E. P. Harries noted: 'Whenever I have found a domestic workers' meeting to be stodgy and apathetic, I have led up to the point of abolition of the living-in system. It works like magic.'[61] Good food and one's own bedroom, which had been such a luxury even in the 1920s were no longer so attractive, as working-class living standards increased in the economically prosperous Midlands and South-East. One former live-in servant, Alice Harrison, took up daily work in interwar London because: 'I think I was getting tired of being stuck in of a night... having to be there, in all day sort of thing and I begin to feel me feet, me wings, I wanted to get out and meet the lads.'[62] She acknowledged, though, that what she termed this 'char-lady' or 'Char-woman' work was seen as 'not very nice'. Nonetheless, she continued to work after marriage, as a part-time 'home help' for Hounslow Council, as was typical of many former servants. Mrs Harrison had been born in London, and with her mother's support, was able to assert her need for leisure and courting opportunities in a way that was rarely open to migrant domestic workers from poorer, depressed areas.

Despite Alice Harrison's sense of her social needs, leisure opportunities in the interwar decades were not evenly or widely distributed for young women.[63] Domestic workers recognized that living-out gave them some autonomy from the control of employers, but most lived out primarily because they had other care responsibilities. Mrs Hadley, who went into service in Worcester in 1942, recalled her resistance to living-in, which her mistress would have preferred: 'I could have had the bedroom, which was off the maids' sitting room. It was so small it was like a tin box. Just enough room in there to have a small bed and a washbasin and a small wardrobe with a chest of just two drawers.' For Mrs Hadley, working 9am to 5 or 6pm as a live-out servant, her hours were better than those of many live-in contemporaries, though she was expected to run errands on her way home, and went back to more work at home: 'I said no [to living-in] because I thought that would mean more work and also I had to look after my mum at home and do things in the house that mum couldn't do.'[64] For all the talk of a new generation of hedonistic, modern young women in the interwar decades, most working-class girls were still expecting to take on very significant care responsibilities within the family, and the illness or bereavements of their kin continually interrupted their experiences of paid work.

The shift to living-out has been taken by some historians to be the historic moment at which the balance of power in domestic service shifted irrevocably to

---

[61] Notes on organizations of mistresses, from E. P. Harries to Walter Citrine, June 28, 1938, Modern Records Centre at the University of Warwick, 292/54.76/1.

[62] Alice Harrison, born 1908 in Fulham, City of Westminster Archives Centre, *Upstairs Downstairs* Collection, henceforth cited as Westminster, *Upstairs, Downstairs*.

[63] Claire Langhamer, *Women's Leisure in England 1920–1960* (Manchester: Manchester University Press, 2000).

[64] Mrs Hadley, Birmingham Libraries and Archive Services, Library Services at Home, Upstairs, Downstairs Oral History Project, http://www.birmingham.gov.uk/libraryservicesathome, henceforth Birmingham, *Upstairs, Downstairs*.

the employee. However, living-out did not prove to be the revolution that would modernize and perpetuate domestic service as many reformers had hoped. A day servant of the early 1940s, Mrs Aulton, found that she was too exhausted at the end of her working day to go out, and so the freedoms of living-out were unavailable to her.[65] In fact, her working day was remarkably similar in the 1940s to what the previous generation of Edwardian live-in house parlourmaids might have expected. She was still expected to cook and scrub, blacklead the grate, fetch coal, sweep the carpet after it had been sprinkled with damp tea leaves, clean the silver, and receive callers. Mrs Aulton worked seven days a week, including Christmas Day, from 8am to 6pm. As a live-out maid, she did not get the traditional every other Sunday off because her hours were seen as short. She also did all the household's washing, using a copper, a dolly, and a mangle. Though some appliances such as kettles, irons, and vacuum cleaners were available between the wars, many servant-keeping homes did not feel they were needed. Appliances were thought of and marketed as replacements for servants, rather than for use by servants, and where they were present, servants were sometimes forbidden to use them. Larger objects such as fridges, water heaters, and cookers were still semi-luxuries and mostly confined to more prosperous areas.[66]

Though World War II has often been held to have finally dissipated domestic service in Britain, in the short term it had little impact in Mrs Aulton's workplace. The war meant that food was in short supply, and as a result, her mistress weighed all Mrs Aulton's purchases as she returned from shopping to check that nothing had been stolen. Such treatment and conditions generated deep resentment, and made the long-term continuation of service unlikely. Mrs Aulton was far less willing to defer to her mistress than her mother's generation would have been, and in the end she quit, aged 20, after three years' service, triggered by her mistress's insistence that she call her 'madam'.

ASPIRATIONS

Mrs Aulton found her aspirations to be thwarted by being treated, as she put it, 'like a lackey' in her job. But this does not capture the wide range of aspirations that might be felt by servants. Indeed, the aspirations of young women entering service is a dimension normally neglected from historical accounts because service has been historically scripted as a 'last resort' job. Some workers did indeed report that

---

[65] Mrs Aulton, Birmingham, *Upstairs, Downstairs*.
[66] Suzette Worden, 'Powerful Women: Electricity in the Home, 1919–40', in Judy Attfield and Pat Kirkham (eds), *A View from the Interior: Feminism, Women and Design History* (London: Women's Press, 1989), 140; Sue M. Bowden, 'The Consumer Durables Revolution in England 1932–1938: A Regional Analysis', *Explorations in Economic History*, 25 1 (1988), 42–59; Sue Bowden and Paul Turner, 'The Demand for Consumer Durables in the United Kingdom in the Interwar Period', *Journal of Economic History*, 53 2 (1993), 244–58; Caroline Davidson, *A Woman's Work Is Never Done: A History of Housework in the British Isles, 1650–1950* (London: Chatto and Windus, 1982); Christine Hardyment, *From Mangle to Microwave: The Mechanisation of Household Work* (Cambridge: Polity Press, 1988), 30–9.

domestic service 'was the only thing going really because we lived in a very isolated place'. Others had aspirations to get other jobs such as millinery, nursing, dressmaking—but pragmatically concluded, 'there were too many of us at home and I was forced to go out.'[67] Poverty constrained career choices and forced some young women into service. It clearly underlay the rise in numbers of servants recorded by the 1931 census (of 16 and 29 per cent for women and men, respectively), though the role of the interwar state in denying unemployment benefits to women in the 1920s who refused domestic service jobs also played a part. Employment Exchanges in the interwar period directed a third to two-thirds of all women into domestic service—a far greater proportion than into any other employment.[68] Diane Aiken has argued that coercion to enter service was widely practiced by the officials involved in unemployment assistance and state-led employment and training initiatives throughout the interwar period. The enactment of the 1925 Widows, Orphans and Old Age Contributory Pensions Act also gave older women a reason to seek employment as domestic servants, since by doing so they would be able to enter an insurance society and gain pension rights.[69] In 1938, private domestic service became an insurable occupation under the National Insurance provisions, giving rights to medical and unemployment benefits and lifting an institutionally generated stigmatization of domestic workers.

Service was experienced in some regional or local labour markets as an option for the unqualified, those who were 'simple' or 'feeble-minded', or the least well off. A typical comment was made by the Tyneside-born Mrs Panter, who went into service in 1929 after working in a factory and a bakery beforehand: 'It was the poorer class that had to go into service, people with no money, people that were having a hard time.' One family in early-twentieth-century Stockport had been servantless, but then employed a residential servant

really because no one else would employ her—I think she had been in the local lunatic asylum once or twice. She was a big strong hefty woman. I remember quite well, one big tooth sticking out of her mouth. Not at all intelligent, she used to do the most appalling things sometimes through lack of intelligence, very willing and very loyal and she could carry big packets of coal and keep the kitchen clean, do the washing up and things like that. And we paid her, I suppose, very, very little probably. I think for a woman in her position she was thankful to get a home. She was kept warm and comfortable and mother paid for her uniform . . . I think she realised the rest of the world was a bit harsh.[70]

Many other sources comment on the prevalance of the 'simple' as domestic workers; some such posts were a place of refuge, but these workers were vulnerable to

---

[67] Mrs Edith Green, Interview 268, *Edwardians*.
[68] In 1921–2, for example, the Ministry of Labour was declared to have placed two-thirds of its successful female job applicants into domestic service. Dr Macnamara, *Hansard*, HC Deb, July 19, 1922, vol 156, cc 2057–8.
[69] Aiken, *The Central Committee on Women's Training and Employment*, 56, 129.
[70] Mr. Geoffrey Hampson (b. 1898), Interview 194, *Edwardians*. On 'simple-minded' servants, see Dorothy Burnham, *Through Dooms of Love* (London: Chatto and Windus, 1969), 180; Foley, *A Child in the Forest*, 117; Wayne, *Brown Bread and Butter*, 11.

exploitation. Particularly after World War II, when servants were in short supply, the 'simple' were chosen for their lack of knowledge of employment conditions and norms. Nella Last, a housewife and Mass Observation correspondent in Barrow-in-Furness, recounted her efforts to obtain domestic help for a neighbour, Mrs Jones, a 'spoilt' woman prone to tantrums. Last described Elsie, the woman she recommended, as 'very slow, in fact somewhat "mental," but someone who had her said she is very clean and trustworthy.' The neighbour was horrified to learn that Elsie had had two illegitimate children, and refused to employ her. However, Nella Last concluded, 'I doubt if a normal girl or woman would allow anyone to speak to her as Mrs Jones apparently does, or work for so little money.'[71] Ursula Bloom noted of the 1960s, 'the ones you could employ were the peculiars, the chuck-outs, or the dotties.'[72]

Service served as a fallback occupation in times of unemployment, and this was clear not only in early decades of the twentieth century, but right into the 1980s. The survey project Mass Observation recorded numbers of women who employed other women as cleaners or 'help' because their husbands had been made unemployed, and who commented on the desperation for such work in their localities.[73] But even in the 1930s, service could still be seen as an option for the brightest, with teachers in some areas still sending their most able pupils for 'choice' domestic service jobs. Service therefore had a varying or ambiguous status nationally. Most servants were aware that domestic service and charring was viewed as 'low class' in some areas, though in rural districts with few other options, or those bordering on London, a job in service even in the 1920s was so much the norm that it was not regarded as low status. As a general servant from rural Lincolnshire recalled, 'It all depended where you came from. If you came from the villages and you got a good place, they were pleased for you and that was good. But if you came from the towns you used to be looked down a bit if you were in service.'[74] For the generations working between 1890 and World War II, there is strong evidence of choices made within constraints, which enabled a sense of agency to be associated with joining the labour market even for those with apparently fewest options. Winifred Foley, born into a mining community in 1914, may have had few options when she went to work in 1928, but recalled: 'Since I had no choice about leaving [school], at least I was determined to be mistress of my own fate. I had heard about domestic service in Bristol or Cheltenham from older girls in the village. I was going to go to London.'[75] However, the taint of compulsion continued across the century, and when Annette Dobson worked as a cleaner in southeast London in the 1990s, she found that friends and acquaintances assumed that she had no other options. Some treated her as set apart by her work: 'Working as a cleaner was almost like belonging to a different caste, not just a lower class.' She later worked as a cleaner in

---

[71] Nella Last, Patricia E. Malcolmson, and Robert W. Malcolmson, *Nella Last's Peace: The Post-War Diaries of Housewife, 49* (London: Profile, 2008), 264–7.
[72] Ursula Bloom, *Mrs Bunthorpe's Respects: A Chronicle of Cooks* (London: Hutchinson, 1963), 190.
[73] Mass Observation, summer 1983 Directive on Work, Leisure and Unemployment.
[74] Mullins and Griffiths, *Cap and Apron*, 32, 44.
[75] Foley, *A Child in the Forest*, 146.

Edinburgh schools, and noted an implicit hierarchy set up through naming. The teachers were addressed by the cleaners using formal titles, though this was not reciprocated. As one of her co-workers noted, 'we're just scum to them, we're the lowest of the low.'[76]

There was no easy internalization or taking for granted of the low status of domestic service in the twentieth century. This was true even where alternative jobs were available. Some of those who became servants in the 1910s and 1920s commented: 'I could have worked in a shop but I didn't want to do that,' or 'I never did work in a factory, never; no, I shouldn't have wanted to.' Factory work was still largely regarded as dirty and 'not nice', while service offered security and lodgings, and could be entered with little training. Narratives of choosing service and obtaining employment are as frequently about autonomous actions on the part of the young woman, or about the intervention of older sisters, friends, and neighbours as they are about prescriptions of mothers, despite the historiographical stress on mothers as agents of oppressive socialization.

Indeed, some young women made a positive choice to enter service. One London girl, Millie Milgate, who entered service in 1922 aged 14, said of her decision:

It was all caused through a film. . . . There was only one thing in that cinema that took my fancy and that was one of those French maids gracefully walking down a beautiful staircase—marble staircase—with a frilly apron on, long streamers down the back. I thought 'that's what I'd like to do, that's what I'd like to be!'

The idea of service as necessarily exploitative and entered into as a last resort seems in part to be a projection of our current evaluation of service onto the past. We cannot dismiss the positive reasons for entering domestic service as 'false consciousness'. The cinema-influenced sense of domestic service as glamorous problematizes the 'hated' cap and apron—signals of servitude to some, but described by others as 'lovely'.[77] There was no single cultural depiction of domestic service, which was both feted and mocked within films, books and magazines. Though Millie Milgate's cinematic fantasies were probably not fulfilled by her subsequent job as a scullery maid, the sense of service as glamorous was quite widely commented on by twentieth-century servants. One housemaid for a well-travelled and sociable Admiral's wife in Suffolk in the 1920s said of her job that though she never left Suffolk, 'I went round the globe.' Another South Wales servant saw service in London as 'going from the pigsty into the palace'.[78]

The range of emotions felt by young women becoming servants was broad. Some young women entered service with reluctance, others with pragmatism, and still others with expectancy and optimism. Many reported loneliness, missing their families and overwhelmed by a new environment. Some ran away, and recalled the humiliation of a family member publicly collecting their tin trunk. Others felt

---

[76] Annette Dobson, interview with the author, Sept 3, 2010.
[77] Mrs Millie Milgate and Mrs Goodman, quoted in Mullins and Griffiths, *Cap and Apron*, 40, 29.
[78] Grace Cooper, George Ewart Evans collection, British Library Sound Archive ref. T1436R; ibid. 4.

positive emotions, and these need careful reading. Some were pleased to get away from home. Mrs Laflin, born in 1896 in Essex, went into service in 1910. She was given a tin box, new clothes, and a sack apron, and recalled 'Never in my life had I been given so much before.' She enjoyed seeing the novelties of a middle-class home, and especially liked cleaning the taps above the sink and bath, having never seen such things before. Another young woman working as a ward maid at a convalescent home in Felixstowe found the bathroom a delight: 'the joy of my life was the bathroom and lovely hot water without boiling saucepans, and a bath without lighting the copper.'[79]

Even though scrubbing the front steps in public was often seen as a form of public humiliation, some found satisfaction in it; one maid recalled scrubbing the steps at 5.45am: '[the step] was lovely, it was green and white marble, it was really lovely.'[80] Another was even more effusive:

Steps? Well they were my pride. Every Weds. and Sat. weather permitting of course, I had to clean them thoroughly with hearthstone, and there were quite a lot together with the side-pieces, but I took a real pleasure in doing them and was very often complimented on them. Sometimes now I pass that house and see those steps all green and as if they're never cleaned and it makes my heart ache and wish I could get down to them again.[81]

Servants had powerful relationships to the material objects they encountered, and found both pleasure and self-endorsement in them. This relationship to material objects can be read as a tacit claim to ownership, and a challenge to the income and property-based hierarchies of servant-keeping homes. The novelist R. C. Sherriff imagined this subtle form of resistance in his novel *Greengates* (1935), depicting a domestic servant's refusal to relinquish 'her' broom to her master:

'That's my broom! Put it down!' she shouted. 'It happens to be *my* broom,' he said—and shame rushed over him. It was not his broom; every inch of it was Ada's—two dark patches on the handle worn by Ada's hands, the bristles worn diagonally across from the patient motion of her hands. It was steeped in her personality as his old, favourite razor was steeped in his.[82]

Annette Dobson commented on her work as a cleaner: 'if you're cleaning someone's house, you do own it for that short period of time.' She remained, however, acutely conscious of the inequity built into the perceived worth of her work, which meant that her income as a cleaner would never allow her to purchase a three-bedroom South London suburban home of the type that she cleaned.[83]

Other domestic workers mention their pleasure in aspects of service such as cooking or using the 'domestic science' they had learnt at school. Miss Bailey felt

---

[79] Mrs Laflin (b. 1886), Kate Brooker (b. 1909), AC 'My First Job' (1970 and 1991), ERO T/Z 25/1139 and T/Z 25/2493.
[80] Mrs Winifred Cooper née Brown (b. 1919), Westminster, *Upstairs Downstairs*.
[81] Mrs Bainbridge, AC 'My First Job' (1970), ERO T/Z 25/222.
[82] R. C. Sherriff, *Greengates*, excerpted in *Good Housekeeping*, Nov 1935, 164.
[83] Dobson, interview with the author.

quite positive emotions on entering service with a shopkeeper in 1904, though she was well aware of her exploitation. She had been pleased to leave school at 14 because 'I wanted to go and do something'. Though the work was overwhelmingly hard, 'I liked it very very much. I was very happy... and I was so proud.' Compared to living at home with her foster mother, domestic service was a life of independence, and a shift to a more adult status. She enjoyed the sense of her own space: 'I used to get up at 5 o'clock in the morning and sit on a summer morning up in the attic. It was lovely up there, early morning.'[84] Many twentieth-century servants mention their pleasure in having a bedroom to themselves.

The emotional range included those who found friendship and deeper intimacies. Some saw employers as 'pals', or as offering the emotional sustenance they had not got at home. Mistresses might sometimes be caring 'as though she was me own mother'. One unmarried servant, asked by an interviewer whether she had wanted to get married, answered that 'I lived with Miss Biggs [her employer], and we were very happy together.'[85] A sense of almost conjugal or sisterly happiness underlies this dignified comment. Others felt pride in their work, and vicariously enjoyed their employers' achievements. Florence White worked for priests between 1916 and 1921 in a Scottish Girls' Friendly Society lodge:

I honestly felt that in looking after them I was not merely attending to the fire in the kitchen, but that I had a share in the sermons they preached, the parish work they did, and the comfort they gave to the sick and sorrowful. It is true that my work was like the seed sown in the earth, hidden and unnoticed, but it was very well worth doing.[86]

Most servants, however, reflect with ambiguous emotions, conveying their simultaneous sense of compulsion and some positive appreciation for the shift towards adult or independent status; one former housemaid, asked whether she had liked her job, answered 'Well I must have liked it or else I had to like it, see.'[87]

Though service has been labelled a life-cycle job, filling the years between school and marriage, surprisingly large numbers of young women had a clear sense of career progression, which might span several occupations, or operate within the different branches of service. Mrs Clarke, born in Glasgow in 1917, had various aspirations, and clearly shared her decision-making with her mother. When it came to finding work, 'There were options to get a job in a shop in the town but we lived

---

[84] Miss Catherine Bailey (b. 1890), Interview 19, *Edwardians*.
[85] Interview with Miss Spence (b.1891), George Ewart Evans collection, British Library Sound Archive ref. T1442R. On the various factors that led many European servants to remain celibate, see Raffaella Sarti, 'All Masters Discourage the Marrying of Their Male Servants, and Admit Not by Any Means the Marriage of the Female: Domestic Service and Celibacy in Western Europe from the Sixteenth to the Nineteenth Century', *European History Quarterly*, 38 3 (2008), 417–49. On the ways in which the unmarried sought to dignify and locate their relationships, see Leonore Davidoff et al., *The Family Story: Blood, Contract and Intimacy, 1830–1960* (London: Longman, 1999), 223–6.
[86] Florence White, *A Fire in the Kitchen: The Autobiography of a Cook* (London, 1938), 277.
[87] Mrs Edith Green, Interview 268, *Edwardians*.

perhaps two miles out of town. We thought the next best thing was into service but the idea at first, when I got into the nursery, was to work my way up and get to be a lady's maid.'[88] Joint decision-making was not always harmonious. Mrs Boyce recounts how her mother had arranged for her training and placement as a lady's maid in the early 1920s, near to her home in rural Northamptonshire. However, Mrs Boyce recalled,

> My time at Lady Palmer's won me to London. My parents were very upset at me going... When I got [the job in London], Mum really broke up. Naturally I wanted some clothes and extra things to go with and some money. 'Well,' mother said, 'I shan't let her have anything. She's not to go. She's not ready to go to London, she's too gay, she's not ready for London.' I could hear my mother crying every night.[89]

Nonetheless, with her father's support she persisted, and saw this move to London as furthering her career.

It was not only the higher rungs of domestic service that could sustain a sense of career. Mrs Hadley was a live-out maid-of-all-work in the 1940s. On realizing that she had few chances of promotion in her household, she gained a job in the laundry to which the household's clothes had been sent, and regarded this as an advancement.[90] Service was not regarded as a monolithic occupation, but as highly variable, with possibilities for progression and satisfaction through changing jobs. One housemaid who made a point of moving every two years commented: 'I never left without I was improved. Me wages always went up whenever I left you know.'[91] Service might be combined with non-service jobs to form a career progression; a job as an upper servant such as a footman or lady's maid could follow from an apprenticeship to a dressmaker or tailor. Service itself could be an 'apprenticeship' to other trades; Mrs Thompson became a Liverpool kitchenmaid in 1907, aged fourteen. Service was the only job her mother, a widow, envisaged for her daughters (similarly, all her sons were sent to sea). Her daughter, however, was waiting to go into 'the licensed trade' when she was sixteen, and transferred to the kitchens of a restaurant. She later ran public houses, as her father had done, and viewed her two and a half years in service as an apprenticeship to her later roles. Historians have stressed the loss of caste servants suffered, and the strong preference for non-service work if it was available, but this example suggests that at least in the more buoyant urban labour markets there was fluidity between types of job, and service might be regarded as a form of skilled apprenticeship or a career building-block.

---

[88] Mullins and Griffiths, *Cap and Apron*, 46–7. Perhaps aware that the lady's maid would need certain accomplishments, Mrs Clarke went on a three-month training course in Edinburgh at the Royal School of Domestic Science—paid for through her mother's work as a caretaker on a Perthshire estate. In the end, she became a nursery maid, gaining her jobs through job adverts in the paper.
[89] Ibid. 46.
[90] Mrs Hadley, Birmingham, *Upstairs, Downstairs*.
[91] Mrs Edith Green, Interview 268, *Edwardians*.

CONDITIONS IN WORK

The conditions under which servants worked were variable, but for those working in typical one- or two-servant households, the hours were long and the physical labour was intense. Servants' oral histories dwell on the loneliness of domestic service, and the very hard work. Mrs Happy Sturgeon went into service aged 14 in 1931, as cook-housemaid to a provincial auctioneer in her local town in Suffolk. Only two maids were kept, both aged 14, and the work was intensely exploitative. She recalled being 'worried all the time' because the work could never be finished; her employers were aggressively authoritarian. The irony was that she had been placed in this 'good job' by her school teacher, as a reward for being top of the class. In the local or day jobs in which young women were often placed, mothers could play a relatively active part in determining work conditions, though other family members were also significant. However, for those who, before World War I, had travelled long distances to gain employment, travel was not yet cheap enough to allow parents to make a personal visit, and daughters had to rely on writing home to gain permission, as well as psychic and material support, to leave a job. Even where they were local, mothers were not always willing to intervene: 'I had the kindest mother,' Mrs Sturgeon commented, but during her year of impossibly hard labour, her mother, living in the same town, had simply stated that 'this is what it is to work for a living.'[92] Siblings sometimes provided alternative perspectives of support, particularly sisters, who may have been better acquainted than mothers with the norms of domestic service conditions. It was Happy Sturgeon's sister who encouraged her to leave her first job, and helped place her in London.

There is strong evidence that servants looked to those in their age cohort for support, and saw themselves as pitted against older generations, sometimes to the extent that generation trumped the class divides that are usually seen as so central to domestic service. Edna Forder commented of her time in service in the Midlands from 1925:

I found the work very hard ... the most difficult aspect of the job was the fact that the other maids were all so much older. I had to sit quietly at the table with them after lunch while they had a snooze; I couldn't go and wash because that would be noisy, so I read or did sewing or made up poetry.[93]

Margaret Cox, an orphan born in 1922, worked as a domestic servant in the late 1930s. She remembered the head parlourmaid, who was called 'Oliphant': 'we never called her anything else. Actually I imagine she was a retainer because to me, at that age, she seemed very very old.' After a dispute with Oliphant, Cox was dismissed and simply ejected from the house where she had been employed; as an orphan, she had nowhere else to go, and found the lack of care shown by older

---

[92] Interview with Mrs Sturgeon (b.1917), George Ewart Evans collection, British Library Sound Archive ref. T1434WR.
[93] Mrs Edna Forder (b. 1910), Westminster, *Upstairs Downstairs*.

servants towards the young very disturbing. What she called 'the disparagement between older servants and younger servants' was for her the worse aspect of service: 'You couldn't talk to the older people.' Mrs. Cox perceived the intergenerational conflicts as 'like a class system that we get in society today'. Class, for her, was formed through a combination of age and employment status.[94]

The policing role performed by siblings of servants may have reinforced this sense of generation gap. One orphaned servant reported that when her brother visited her in one household, he said, 'you're not stopping there... you'll go silly if you stop there with those two elderly people to live with all the time.'[95] He was referring, in this case, to the mistress and an elderly parlourmaid, who could be seen as united by age rather than divided by class. And other servants talked of their sense of generational disorientation; Elizabeth Young commented that when she left her first 'between maid' job, 'I was only 14. I felt a hundred.'[96] Age and generation have been historically neglected, but formed an important part of the subjectivity of being a servant.[97]

For many the hard work was acceptable, but the hierarchical social relations of domestic service were strongly resented. Social hierarchies were established through rituals of naming, uniforms, and segregations of space and material culture that persisted into the middle of the twentieth century. Many servants still reported having their name changed on entering a household, and being forbidden to use the same toilets and washing facilities as their employers. They might be offered different grades of soap and toilet paper, or inferior forms of food. Servants were sometimes expected to perform symbolic rituals of servility, in curtseying, making formal greetings, and handling objects using tongs or gloves. In a deliberate breaking of pollution taboos, Lady Astor made a habit of offering her maid Rosina Harrison a chocolate, but only after biting into it herself, to establish whether it was a flavour she liked. Her maid would simply throw it into the wastepaper basket. Such habits were not limited to aristocratic service; one Edwardian housemaid remembered that when she worked for a coal merchant in Barnsley, 'I even had to take his shoes off and put them on—had these—outdoor shoes to take off and put his slippers on. And I thought that was a dreadful thing to do.'[98]

These kinds of rituals and humiliations, often revolving around concepts of pollution, did not seem natural to young women born in the 1890s, despite the historiographical stress on the deference that mothers tried to inculcate in their daughters. The account given here of twentieth-century domestic service is not one of a slow increase of resistance to such practices, because one can see well-developed

---

[94] Mrs Margaret Cox (b. 1922), ibid.
[95] Mrs Myers, Interview 315, *Edwardians*. See Leonore Davidoff, 'Where the Stranger Begins: The Question of Siblings in Historical Analysis', in *Worlds between: Historical Perspectives on Gender and Class* (New York: Routledge, 1995).
[96] Elizabeth Young, *Bessie Remembers* (Braunton: Merlin, 1989), 11.
[97] See Krista Cowman and Louise Jackson, 'Introduction: Women's Work, a Cultural History', in Krista Cowman and Louise Jackson (eds), *Women and Work Culture: Britain c.1850–1950* (Aldershot: Ashgate, 2005), 1–23, esp. 12–13; Selina Todd, *Young Women, Work and Family in England, 1918–1950* (Oxford: Oxford University Press, 2005).
[98] Mrs Edith Green, Interview 268, *Edwardians*.

attitudes and strategies of resistance amongst late Victorian and Edwardian as much as interwar servants. Some of these were tacit strategies; as Margaret Powell (1907–84), an interwar kitchenmaid and later a cook, observed, 'Servants that feel they're being put upon can make it hard in the house in various ways like not rushing to answer bells, looking sullen, dumb insolence and petty irritations to make up for what you're not getting.' But servants were also able to articulate overt defiance. One Edwardian maid, in service in Warwickshire, had been made to pay for a replacement tea set after she had dropped a tray. She paid, but on the condition as she put it, that 'the matter was closed'. The mistress's authority to 'close' subjects was usurped by the servant. When the maid asked for the chipped plates from the original tea set, her mistress refused. However, the mistress's authority was insufficient; the maid explained: 'I went to see her and I told her, I said, I shall take that, I said, that is mine, I've replaced yours at my own expense. Oh, she couldn't say much—she let me have it.'[99]

This anecdote helps capture the sense of entitlement and 'rights' that might be a pervasive part of the subjectivity of being a twentieth-century servant, though as the next chapter discusses, this was usually informally expressed rather than cashed out in legal terms compared to the litigious servants of earlier centuries.[100] Such a sense of entitlement and the confrontations that might accompany it led to a softening of authority on the part of twentieth-century employers, who were becoming aware that they could not retain servants if their orders were unjust or arbitrary. While some were lonely and overworked, others recall working alongside their mistresses, eating the same food, and being given significant freedoms. As one Edwardian servant said of her farming employer: 'She didn't make no difference.... You didn't think you were a maid, you just lived with them you see.' Another remembered: 'I used to love being with my mistress there in the daytime... She used to chat away as though she were my mother to me.' Friendship between mistress and servant had long been unconvincingly claimed by mistresses and reformers, but it did occasionally flourish even outside of the more informal conditions of farm service.[101] However, inequalities of power and attachment pervaded the relationship. One Edwardian mistress claimed that 'some of my best life-long friends are domestic servants,' but it was clear that the relationship she had in mind was not particularly reciprocal; her 'friends', she noted, 'still write to me often thanking me for all they learned while in my service.' The 'friendship' recorded between an employer and her cleaner in a memoir published in 1962, *Jam Tomorrow: Portrait of a Daily Help*, records the gratitude and admiration of the employer, tempered with voyeuristic fascination. Their failure to achieve a friendship or even a stable relationship is revealed in their initial inability to successfully exchange gifts.[102]

In many households, servants' needs for a social life or cultural experience were still squashed or ridiculed, as Chapter 4 discusses. One servant, caught listening to

---

[99] Mrs Florence Davis (b.1892), Interview 40, *Edwardians*.
[100] On the legal rights of eighteenth-century servants, see Steedman, *Master and Servant*, Chapter 1.
[101] Interviews 268, 408, *Edwardians*.
[102] Emma Randall Vickers, letter to the editor, *Common Cause*, Dec 7, 1911, 622; Margaret Norton, *Jam Tomorrow: Portrait of a Daily Help* (London: Victor Gollancz, 1962).

her employer playing the piano during the First World War years, was told 'that's nothing to do with you, you go into your own place. That's very rude.' Servants were often forbidden to form friendships, or to read books and magazines. Many could only take walks, knit, or visit the cinema for leisure, though the bicycle did start to give rural servants more freedoms in the interwar years.[103] The level of supervision did, however, become less intense in a growing proportion of homes. While perhaps the majority of mistresses still sought to regulate dress, reading matter, hair style, bedtime, and even 'lights out', a significant minority were uninterested in these details, and levels of supervision varied dramatically. Many interwar servants recall their mistresses as being indifferent to their comings and goings, their dress, and their demeanour, as long as the domestic work was done promptly. However, in relation to their care for children, the surveillance of nursemaids, nannies, and au pairs continued to be high, with many employers commenting on their guilt at delegating childcare. The practices of intense surveillance culminated in the spread of the 'nanny cam', first available in the 1990s, and supplemented in more recent years by the use of GPS technology to locate the exact whereabouts of children and their carers, and blogs that invite readers to report negligent child carers.[104]

Nonetheless, the psychic resources invested in 'being a mistress' had diminished in many interwar households. Many 'hands-off' mistresses simply had other interests—leisure pursuits, or their own work—and where they could, took a functional, contractual view of domestic service. Of course, such a relationship wasn't easy to establish. Virginia Woolf notoriously wrote in 1929 of her longing for a servant, 'who had her baby in Kentish town; and treated me as an employer, not friend,' but as Alison Light has sensitively charted, she remained deeply emotionally entangled in her relationship with her servants.[105]

WAGES AND CONTRACTS

The increasing willingness amongst mistresses to let their servants determine their own schedules was partly founded on the wider circulation of the idea of domestic service as a simple contract, in which wages were paid for carrying out specified tasks, without further impositions of social or moral constraint, deference rituals, or implication of a deeper relationship. Social reform organizations, feminists, and trades unionists insisted that contracts were the solution to the 'servant problem', and many different versions of trial contracts were circulated and discussed. Woolf's

---

[103] Mrs Myers, Interview 315, *Edwardians*. On the reading, social lives, and entertainments of servants, see Horn, *Life below Stairs*, Chap. 5; Margaret Beetham, 'Domestic Servants as Poachers of Print: Reading, Authority and Resistance in late Victorian Britain', in Lucy Delap, Abigail Wills, and Ben Griffin (eds), *The Politics of Domestic Authority in Britain since 1800* (Basingstoke: Palgrave Macmillan, 2009).

[104] Margaret K. Nelson, '"I Saw Your Nanny": Gossip and Shame in the Surveillance of Child Care', in Nelson (ed.), *Who's Watching?: Daily Practices of Surveillance among Contemporary Families* (Nashville: Vanderbilt University Press, 2009).

[105] Woolf, quoted in Judy Giles, *The Parlour and the Suburb: Domestic Identities, Class, Femininity and Modernity* (Oxford: Berg, 2004), 72.

impossible longing for a simple contractual arrangement reminds us of the limits of the reach of these utopian ideas, and many structural and customary features of domestic service prevented the contractual mode from ever being realized. The reference system—the written testimonial servants could receive from employers on leaving their post—still skewed the balance of any employment contract in domestic service to favour employers; a reference was not legally compulsory and might be withheld on whim, leaving a servant extremely compromised in the labour market. Furthermore, the wages of servants had long had a manipulative function. Payment of wages in service was a highly variable social institution, dependent upon the traditions of families and localities, and the choices of individuals. Wages at the start of the twentieth century were often paid annually or quarterly, though were more commonly weekly after World War I. Nonetheless, young women going into service from institutional care found their wages withheld for up to a year, even in the interwar period. Barnardos insisted that those they placed in domestic service should have their wages paid directly to the directors of their 'Village Homes', who would pay it into a Savings Bank and only release it after twelve months. Barnardos girls would also be liable to pay back the £3–5 spent on their uniforms if they left their employment at any time in the first nine months.[106] Infrequent or indirectly paid wages left servants with very little cash in their pockets, especially after deductions had been made by some mistresses for buying articles of uniform or travel expenses. Many of the benefits of service were provided in kind rather than in cash, and employers often tried to lay down restrictions on what could be bought by their servants, forbidding fashionable clothes and hats, or magazines and novels. In the earlier years of the century, wages therefore did not lead directly to consumption power.

Moreover, some servants had a very tenuous relationship to their wages, since they may have handed the entire amount to their mothers. Mothers were sometimes paid directly by employers. One Yorkshire servant said of her first wages: 'I used to take it home you see. And I don't—I don't think they ever gave me anything back, so I don't know whether I ever spent anything. I can't—I—I—gave it all to me mother.'[107] Most received some money back from their pay packet, as spending money, or to save for clothing or their marriages. In a reminder of how young some servants were, many recalled spending their portion on sweets. But the institution of handing wages over to mothers did vary according to personal practices, locality, and over time, and shouldn't necessarily be read as indicating maternal control or exploitation of daughters. One mother offered to buy her daughter a bicycle if she stayed at her service job for a year, suggesting a sense of reciprocity and negotiation over the daughter's contribution to the household, which was clearly not taken for granted.[108] There was a complex calculation of when and how much of wages would be remitted to mothers, with

---

[106] See, for example, the Memorandum of Second-Class Agreement issued by the Barnardo Village Home for Destitute Girls, Barkingside, still in use in 1918.
[107] Mrs Edith Green, Interview 268, *Edwardians*.
[108] Interview with Mrs Drewery (b.1917), George Ewart Evans collection, British Library Sound Archive ref. T1419W C6.

much local variation. Most young women expected to pay their mothers back for the clothes they had been bought when entering service, but might then regard the debt as closed. Others offered wages in return for housing, or occasionally for other assistance, at moments of illness, or even after marriage. There was certainly no open-ended dependence or continuing direct authority of mothers, but rather a flexible and regionally variable set of mutual obligations.

Practices of handing over wages to mothers were gendered, with girls more likely to do so than their male siblings. However, such arrangements have been over-emphasized in the historiography, obscuring other more diverse practices. Traditions of autonomous saving were also strong; Daisy Noakes in Brighton banked all her earnings at the Co-operative Penny Bank, and many other servants also took advantage of the 'Penny Banks' or Cooperative-run 'small savings funds'.[109] One servant commented: 'Mother trained me to put it in the post office each week. I saved all me life. I was trained to save, put money away. But I used to buy a little box of chocolates now and again on the way home. I loved buying things for [Mother], otherwise she said, "stick it in the post office, I don't need it."'[110] Another reported a conversation on getting her first job in the 1920s: 'Mother... remarked "You had better let me have your wages and I will give you money to spend." "No. I will keep my money, I will give you some willingly, but I will control my own money." There was no argument. I had been coping with my 6d a week pocket money plus any earnings from shopping for neighbours or minding babies since I was ten.'[111] Mrs Laura Macafferty recalled her mother in Wales treating the pennies she earned and handed over to her mother as loans, and refusing to take any of her wages once she had a live-in service job.[112]

Despite the restrictions imposed by employers, many servants mention a sense of independence that was very firmly linked to earning and spending. Servants talked of their pleasure in lending friends who were not in service small sums of money, or bringing extensive gifts home for their families: 'I remember buying small presents for my two little stepbrothers with my first wages. I enjoyed playing "lady Bountiful" in that way for a few weeks until I was reminded that my one and only pair of shoes would one day need replacing.'[113] Some recalled feeling superior to factory girls, gaining in independence and individuality through service.[114] Material independence, or the ability to provide for their families through earning, was an important aspiration for most servants, as was saving for marriage or old age. But

---

[109] Paul Johnson, *Saving and Spending: The Working-Class Economy in Britain 1870–1939* (Oxford: Clarendon Press, 1985); Duncan M. Ross, '"Penny Banks" In Glasgow, 1850–1914', *Financial History Review*, 9 1 (2002), 21–39.
[110] Dora Holtom (b. London, 1914), Westminster, *Upstairs Downstairs*.
[111] Edna Forder, ibid.
[112] Mrs Macafferty (b. 1904), Interview 210, *Edwardians*. On the limits of mothers' authority over their daughters, see Lynn Jamieson, 'Limited Resources and Limiting Conventions: Working-Class Mothers and Daughters in Urban Scotland, c. 1890–1925', in Jane Lewis (ed.), *Labour and Love: Women's Experience of Home and Family, 1850–1940* (Oxford: Blackwell, 1986).
[113] B58, Mass Observation Archive (University of Sussex), reply to Summer 1983 directive on Work, Leisure and Unemployment.
[114] Mrs Kemp, AC 'My First Job', (1961), ERO T/Z 25/265.

consumption of clothes was for many the most direct satisfaction. 'You'd put up with [service], you felt really independent. I know I did the first time I went down to Leicester and bought myself a tweed suit; I can see it now.' Mrs Newman, an orphan who had been put out to service from a Lambeth Parish School at aged 15 (a comparatively late age) recalled:

My first month's wages bought me twelve yards of unbleached calico at 6¾ a yard, total cost 6/9, which I made into underclothes, and joy of joys trimmed with lace. Such luxury I had never dreamed of until now, I had begun to live. The surplus was banked... next month I bough a pink French sailor hat for 4/11 which was most unsuitable but which I thought glorious.[115]

Daisy Noakes described in detail the joy of purchasing her own hat and coat, the first that had ever fitted her, after 13 months in service. She had a formal photograph taken wearing these items (Figure 1), a form of self-fashioning that usurped the long British tradition of servants' portraiture commissioned by

Figure 1. Daisy Noakes. courtesy of QueenSpark Books.

[115] Mullins and Griffiths, *Cap and Apron*, 4; Mrs E. Newman, AC 'My First Job' (1961), ERO T/Z 25/222-405.

Figure 2. Daisy Noakes. Front cover image of *The Town Bee Hive*, courtesy of QueenSpark Books.

employers. Noakes' autobiography is illustrated by a number of group portraits of servants and a more formal one of her posing in a traditional dairymaid yoke (Figure 2), which probably was taken or commissioned by employers.[116] However, commissioning a portrait was no longer solely in the keeping of employers, and was available to servants as a defiant assertion of adult selfhood that went with wage-earning. For those working in the later years of the century, the wages for some areas of domestic service improved. *Guardian* journalist Betty Jerman recorded paying her 'daily nurse' £1.5s a day in 1959, in return for charge of two children, washing, shopping, and cooking. These wages compared well with those of nurses and shop assistants, but reflected the higher wages that could be commanded by those with nannying qualifications. 'Full-time' au pairs were paid less than half this amount, at £3 for a six-day week.[117]

---

[116] Noakes, *The Town Bee-Hive*, 72–3; Giles Waterfield, *Below Stairs: 400 Years of Servants' Portraits* (London: National Portrait Gallery, 2004); Merlin Waterson, *The Servants' Hall: A Domestic History of Erdigg* (London: Routledge, 1980).

[117] Betty Jerman, quoted in Obituary, *Guardian*, July 26, 2010, 39; Sheila Williams and F. D. Flower, *Foreign Girls in Hendon: A Survey* (London: Hendon Overseas Friendship Association, 1961), 16.

Wages had a powerful emotional and symbolic dimension. Some servants clearly experienced becoming a servant as a move into adulthood, sometimes signified by their material acquisitions, away from the direct influence of their mothers and from the recapitulation of their mothers' life choices. Some servants were young teenagers, and might still regard themselves as children, subject to their parents' authority. However, the question of to what extent servants continued to feel childlike and dependent in their employment requires a nuanced answer. The growth into adulthood historians have associated with waged work was not a series of steady steps for servants, but a fluctuating process that might see periods of dependency increase or decrease according to health, shifts in the labour market, and familial circumstances. Parents continued to have a great deal of influence and moral authority, but relationships were often reciprocal and supportive of children's choices. The narrative of exploitation that accompanies the 'subordinating gaze of sympathy' does not adequately capture the nuances of these relationships.

MOTHERS

Mothers remained the emotional lynchpin around which the memories of servants were organized. They were frequently the reference point around which daughters organized their aspirations, the individual to which they turned to achieve their goals, and to whom they might send their wages. The relationship between young women in domestic service and their mothers was often close in practical and emotional terms. Mothers provided an enduring motive for their choices. As one pantry maid put it, 'the reason I went into service was that I just had no money. You thought, at least your mother won't have to feed you.' Mothers might not only receive wages and have one less mouth to feed, but other practical benefits might stem from their daughters' work. Many mistresses used to send butter or dripping, cast-off clothes, or other supplies home to their servants' mothers, and sometimes servants pilfered these things on their mothers' behalf. One child of a servant-keeping household recalled that during the Depression years in Derbyshire, 'it was an understood thing that, on their weekly day off, [servants] always took a little case with them containing their "tea." This, of course, meant a few pounds of butter, sugar, etc for their families.' In this case, the pilfering seems to have been condoned by an employer keen to relieve economic distress, but in many cases, it was done more covertly.[118]

Mothers could have close participation in every sense in their daughter's workplace. Selina Todd has argued in broader terms for the interwar period that mothers were an important 'gatekeeper' for children entering employment, shaping their aspirations and their job search, though Todd also points to the increasing influence of other relations and friends, and state agencies.[119] Mothers

---

[118] Gray, *The Worst of Times*, 194.
[119] I'm indebted to the work of Selina Todd and Carol Dyhouse in exploring the relationship between mothers and daughters. C. Dyhouse, 'Graduates, Mothers and Graduate Mothers: Family

accompanied daughters to and from the workplace, and sometimes would sleep in the house when employers were absent. They offered advice about when to leave, or sometimes compelled their daughters to give notice.[120] For some mothers, this involvement created vicarious pleasure; one Welsh housemaid from the 1920s reported that 'Mother used to like to hear everything; dinner parties, "Oh fancy all that food," she used to say.' Another commented, 'Mother was interested in it all. She got to know the households through me, you see, she used to love to hear every detail.'[121] However, this closeness should not lead us to project emotional intimacy onto all such relationships; some went into service to get away from their mothers, and experienced service as independence, or as a realm of unexpected emotional intimacy with employers.

Young women themselves sometimes experienced strong feelings of not wanting to repeat their mother's experiences of marriage, and the crushing domestic work of raising a family. Domestic service, providing mobility and an independent wage, could be conceived of as a way out of their mother's lifestyle and authority. In 1922 one young woman from a South Wales mining family, fascinated with the lifestyle of the employers of her sister, a lady's maid, became 'determined I was going to leave, and I was determined I was never going to marry a miner.' A general servant who left her home in Redcar in the 1930s wanted privacy and independence in service: 'Before I left home I was at everyone's beck and call; "do this, go there, do that, look after him"—you can imagine. I never had a life of me own.... when I got into service, I know you were restricted then, but you still hadn't got the kids around you and your mother.'[122]

Jean Rennie's account of sixteen years of domestic service in the 1920s and 1930s continually refers to the financial and emotional links between herself and her mother, and this relationship acts to make sense of her years in service. Her mother, who had been a servant herself, was devastated that her daughter's secondary education had not led her to anything more than a job as a housemaid. Rennie (b. 1906) wrote in 1955, 'I can only vaguely imagine what my mother must have felt. All that time, and all those books, and all my education.'[123] Pam Taylor reads this relationship as one of instilling a deep-rooted obedience in Jean Rennie's character, and thus adding to her exploitation; but it can also be read as one of both mother and daughter cultivating a vision of a life not structured by servility and drudgery.[124] The picture of mothers with limited aspirations, placing children in service because they knew nothing else themselves is not borne out by the oral histories and autobiographies examined here. Twentieth-century mothers

---

Investment in Higher Education in Twentieth-Century England', *Gender and Education*, 14 4 (2002), 325–36; Todd, 'Poverty and Aspiration', 131.

[120] Mrs Florence Davis (b. 1892), Interview 40, and Gwendolen Mary Whitlam (born 1899), Interview 359, *Edwardians*.
[121] Mullins and Griffiths, *Cap and Apron*, 17; Dora Holtom, Westminster, *Upstairs Downstairs*.
[122] Ibid. 4.
[123] Jean Rennie, *Every Other Sunday: The Autobiography of a Kitchenmaid* (London: Barker, [1955] 1978), 18.
[124] Taylor, 'Daughters and Mothers', 128.

increasingly worked hard to secure the best conditions for their daughters in domestic service. Memories of becoming a servant are full of comments such as 'My mother was reluctant, because she thought I'd end up a little drudge'; 'My mother didn't want me to go into service, because it was such a hard life.' Mothers were well aware of the negative side of service. One cook reported to the 1916 inquiry by the Women's Industrial Council: 'a girl's life is crushed directly she enters service... I think that is why so many mothers keep their girls from it; they have either experienced it themselves, or see what their relations and friends have to contend with.'[125] For young servants in the 1920s and 1930s, parents were often active, perhaps because travel was becoming more feasible, and time off work more available for all parties. One maid-of-all-work from the rural Midlands, who had attended a grammar school, reported that in her first post in 1932, 'my mother came over to see me and said oh no you're not stopping there.' Another said of her first job as a 'general' in the early 1930s, 'My parents came down to see me and I wasn't very happy there and they weren't satisfied so I left.'[126] As Carol Dyhouse's survey of entrants to universities in the 1930s and 1940s has shown, mothers had a role in facilitating intergenerational mobility during this period, and this was true of mothers who had been in service or still were in casual domestic work as much as any other—service did not necessarily create a 'deferential' subjectivity that limited social aspirations.[127]

The role of mothers was clearly not simply socializing daughters to endure exploitative conditions, though mothers across the social spectrum before World War I tended to establish high levels of control over their children.[128] Particularly in the late Victorian and Edwardian years, and during times of economic hardships later in the twentieth century, parents enforced compliance with the norms of domestic service because they were anxious about unemployment. However, in broader terms, there seems to have been less certainty about the scope of the authority of mothers in the post-World War I period. One mistress in Cumberland, for example, wrote to her servant's mother in 1920 asking for permission for her to join a confirmation class. The mother wrote back to say that it was her daughter's decision—and despite her isolation and low status within the household, this between-stairs servant refused to join.[129] There are many examples of

---

[125] A cook, quoted in C. V. Butler, *Domestic Service: An Enquiry by the Women's Industrial Council* (London: Bell, 1916), 28–9.

[126] Mullins and Griffiths, *Cap and Apron*, 27, 32, 28, 43.

[127] Carol Dyhouse has catalogued the mothers who undertook cooking, charring, laundry, and other casual work in order to give their children the chance to attend university in the 1930s and 1940s in 'Graduates, Mothers and Graduate Mothers: Family Investment in Higher Education in Twentieth-Century England'. An alternative discourse of motherhood can therefore be seen as operating in the interwar years, of aspiration, sacrifice, and support. Dyhouse's work reminds us that domestic service did not create deferential workers who could envisage little else for their own children—indeed, Dyhouse suggests that it was working-class mothers, more aware of the drudgery of low-paid jobs, who nurtured ambitions for their children, to a greater extent than fathers.

[128] Anna Davin, *Growing up Poor: Home, House and Street in London* (London: Rivers Oram Press, 1996); Thea Vigne, 'Parents and Children 1890–1918: Distance and Dependence', *Oral History*, 3 1 (1975), 5–13.

[129] Mollie Prendergast papers, 7MOP, The Women's Library, London Metropolitan University.

uncertainty amongst mistresses and mothers over who should take decisions, and in most cases, the servant or daughter began to be awarded more powers of choice and decision.

The role of mothers of servants from the 1890s to World War II shows a range of strategies, from vicarious involvement in their daughters' work, to strong aspirational support, to the ongoing imposition of authority. Mothers might be taken into account in negotiating the labour market, but they did not have such a dominant nor such an exploitative role as has been suggested. Other figures were also important—the siblings, fathers, friends, and neighbours of young women in domestic service. Some daughters entered exploitative service jobs on their mother's advice, and some mothers refused to take back daughters who complained of exploitation. However, mothers in the twentieth century were by and large supportive of their daughter's aspirations, and this was true of mothers who were in service or casual domestic work as much as any other.

The authority of mothers, just as that of mistresses, was changing over these decades, and looking at service is revealing of the powerful links and increasing intergenerational reciprocity between young workers and their mothers. Most mothers did not try to impose a fatalistic acceptance of poor conditions on their daughters. Where mothers did fail to acknowledge exploitation or aspirations for a better life, there is evidence that this was actively rejected by daughters. Mrs Sturgeon, who felt that her mother had 'conditioned' her to accept a servant's job, reported her resistance and unease at experiences as a servant. She told an interviewer: 'When you were in service, you'd think, why am I doing this? Why should I do this?' The power of mothers was only one factor for young women workers, and siblings or friends might offer other worldviews. One cannot assume that a social attitude (such as deference) was unproblematically transmitted by mothers to daughters, just as it was not directly transmitted by employers to servants. Daughters did not passively internalize any fatalistic messages received from some mothers about duty and deference.

CONCLUSIONS

The memories of servants reveal a fluid and diverse set of experiences and emotions associated with domestic service. Exploitation is an unnecessarily limiting framework for describing servants' relationship to work, to their employers, and to their mothers. A close reading of the descriptions and assessments of servants problematizes the idea that in taking a domestic service job, young women somehow took on a fixed identity that settled their 'mentality', or their attitude to social class. Servants did internalize something of the norms of service, and sometimes carried them into their own later lives or imposed them on their children. However, this did not make them 'deferential workers', and could coexist with a lack of acquiescence in their experiences, as well as feelings of bitterness, of thwarted aspiration, of 'them and us'. Elizabeth Roberts found that the women of the North West who had been servants and absorbed some of the habits of middle-class lifestyle did not aspire to send their own children into service.[130] There was little submission to the indignities of service—rather, a wide range of strategies of resistance that make accusations of false consciousness unconvincing accounts of what it was to be a servant. Deference and class disorientation does not characterize the historical sources discussed above.

So if acquiescence and deference are not predominant, what impact did domestic service have on servants, in terms of subjectivities and lifestyles? Resistance, bitterness, and a rejection of the symbolic hierarchies of service do emerge. Equally challenging to the deferential worker thesis is the sense of intimacy, friendship, and emotional co-dependency that emerges in accounts of twentieth-century service. Often the positive emotions of domestic servants are in relation to the privacy and independence that could be found within it, despite its appearance of confinement and discipline. However, surprisingly high numbers of servants found also pleasure in their work (at least retrospectively), and intimacy with their employers.

Young women became servants for a wide variety of reasons, and constructed very different subjectivities around this experience. As Selina Todd has recently argued, the categories of social class that have attempted to capture the subjectivities of servants have been somewhat crude, portraying servants either as deferential workers or as an alienated and exploited class who were likely to have an aggressive 'them and us' attitude that could be mapped on to 'above' and 'below stairs'. Yet servants themselves understood service as part of a working life, made up of periods in paid work and periods undertaking care responsibilities. As Todd points out, this allowed some servants to stay detached from their work and construct their sense of self through other areas of their lives.[131] In both a practical sense and as a part of personal identity, home life continued to feature large for servants whose jobs neither left them 'declassed' or 'in limbo'.

Domestic service can perhaps be better seen as a site of 'double consciousness' rather than class consciousness—a sense of always looking at the self through the eyes of another, that was available to servants *and* their employers.[132] The irresolvable tensions of domestic service stem from this shared sense of gaze, surveillance, and judgement that all parties felt subject to, though employers had greater opportunities to ignore or minimize its effects. This chapter has, however, argued that it was not only the employer who provided the real or imagined gaze to which servants were subject, but also their kin and friends. Servants were not locked in to an exclusive relationship with their employers, and situated in a single 'place' of exclusion, for all their sometime economic marginalization and isolation. This, however, is not to imply that servants could freely choose from a variety of

---

[130] Roberts, *A Woman's Place*, 56.
[131] Selina Todd, 'Domestic Service and Class Relations in Britain 1900–1950', *Past and Present*, 203 (2009), 181–204.
[132] I draw here on the work of theorists of ethnicity, including W. E. B. Du Bois, *The Souls of Black Folk* (Oxford: Oxford University Press, 2008 [1897]); Gemma Romain, *Connecting Histories: A Comparative Exploration of African-Caribbean and Jewish History and Memory in Modern Britain* (London: Kegan Paul, 2006), and Paul Gilroy, *The Black Atlantic: Modernity and Double Consciousness* (London: Verso, 1993).

subjectivities. Servants were positioned by class, gender, and ethnicity, and were subject to what Beverley Skeggs describes as a 'double movement of being made to feel invisible and under scrutiny' in ways that employers were not.[133] Yet employers were not only practically dependent upon servants' labour, but also emotionally dependent upon their regard. This could sometimes be refused. As the Edwardian housemaid Edith Hanran recalled, 'What they did never—never interested us—we had to wait on them and—er—that was that.... I was paid to—to do the work for them and that was all there was to it.'[134]

While Todd's formulation of detachment captures Mrs. Hanran's refusal to 'know the place' of her employers, and is a useful addition to the range of subjectivities associated with class, this study has pointed to a far wider spectrum of responses amongst servants. A wariness in front of employers was commonly reported, but respect and friendship might also mark the relationship. Social class has been rehabilitated in recent historical narratives, but must not eclipse other ways of organizing the social world. 'Class' seemed opaque to many former servants interviewed in the 1970s, or at least marginal to their social identity, though this may have been due to the late-twentieth-century political context of labour conflict and perceived hostilities of class. One woman who had worked as a housemaid before World War I, when asked what class she thought her employers were, answered: 'well, I don't know what they would call themselves—they definitely wouldn't call themselves working class I suppose those days. Well they couldn't call themselves upper class could they [sic]. The middle class maybe—something like that, yes.' She went on, 'they were just like ordinary people. Bit stand-offish you know.' Status differences, she hazarded, were 'with the men more than the women'.[135] Another servant who came from a poor mining family in Stoke-on-Trent described her widowed mother, who took in washing and claimed Poor Law support as 'just middle class, a decent—decent woman'. When pressed by the interviewer, she elaborated that middle classness in her opinion stemmed from having high standards of respectability and decency, though she acknowledged that her family 'hadn't any education'.[136]

Other respondents questioned about class offered answers that indicated its locally specific nature, and integration with alternative languages of status and difference. One child of a marine engineer, whose mother employed a general servant with whom she shared the housework, preferred the language of high and low, though she reluctantly identified herself as working class. Having grown up in Bootle, Lancashire, a site of Irish immigration, she identified ethnicity as a major factor of social differentiation within this schema, with the Irish described as 'the very low you see.... the lower ones nearly all tended to be Catholics.' Specifically,

---

[133] Beverley Skeggs, *Formations of Class and Gender: Becoming Respectable* (London: Sage, 1997), 93.
[134] Mrs Edith Hanran (b. 1894), Interview 53, *Edwardians*.
[135] Interview 119, *Edwardians*.
[136] Mrs Elsie Thompson (b. 1894), Interview 213, ibid., was labelled by the interviewer as charlady, though this was not a term she used herself.

she placed her Irish servant Mary in the group lower than herself, and the step-girls one grade lower.[137]

Servants talked of their employers as 'average', 'ordinary', 'toffs', 'middling', or 'high class', alongside the vocabulary of middle, upper, and working class. However, there was little correspondence between the two sets of terms—'toffs' might refer to snooty working-class employers, while 'ordinary' might mean moneyed professional people. Large numbers of servants recalled that 'there was no difference between us'. This may be read as a projected disavowal from a late-twentieth-century perspective of a denigrated working-class subject position.[138] However, this runs the risk of giving class too much a priori prominence, refusing alternative frames of reference that may have been more meaningful in certain historical contexts. The comments of former servants suggest that service was a site neither of monolithic class antagonisms or of passive deference. As David Cannadine has argued, there were many possible ways of formulating and expressing social differences and identities in twentieth-century Britain.[139] Servants were just as likely to construct an identity based on gender and generation than class, frequently pitting an older mistress and female servants against the young of the household, including the employer's children. Thinking about the experiences of domestic servants enables us to think about class as a complex, processual category, not straightforwardly antagonistic, nor formed solely through workplace culture, but shaped also through families, wider social relationships, cultural influences, and necessarily co-constituted by the equally fundamental categories of gender, ethnicity, and generation.

---

[137] Mrs Annie Tulloch (b. 1894), Interview 80, *Edwardians*.

[138] This is the reading offered by Beverley Skeggs, of class as a 'structuring absence' that is at play even when it is refused by subjects. Skeggs, *Formations of Class and Gender*, 74.

[139] David Cannadine, *Class in Britain* (New Haven, CT: Yale University Press, 1998), 21.

2
Servant-Keepers and the Management of Servants

Mrs Dorothy Peel (1872–1934) was an English servant-keeping middle-class woman, who had established herself as an authority on the home during her long career as a journalist, writer, and editor of cheap domestic papers such as *Myra's Journal*, *Woman*, and *Hearth and Home*. She was also a suffragist, and advised progressive treatment of servants, such as adequate leisure time, labour-saving devices, and social freedoms. Nonetheless, she found her authority as a mistress harder to sustain as the twentieth century progressed. Her autobiography dwelt on her deteriorating relationship with servants in the 1930s:

Having occasion to engage a new maid I was told that a young girl was waiting to see me. I went downstairs, entered the room, and bade her good morning. The young girl was lolling back in an armchair; she continued to loll and made no reply to my salutation. 'Good morning,' I said again. The young girl still lolled and said nothing. I felt my temper rising, but I subdued it. 'Don't you think it would be pleasant if you stood up and said good morning to *me*?' I suggested.

'I see no necessity to do so,' replied the young girl in a loud, sharp voice.

You could have knocked me down with the proverbial feather. At last I recovered sufficiently to remark that I thought our interview might end and to bid her another good morning. Now what maggot had that girl in her brain? Did she wish to infer, 'I am as good as you?' I have no objection to her being as good as me, in fact I should like her to be considerably better. But in what way does such an exhibition of bad manners and unfriendliness help her or anyone else to achieve anything? I am sorry now that I did not still further strangle my wrath, loll in another chair and in the course of a little friendly conversation try to elucidate her point of view.[1]

We cannot know how the young woman experienced this interaction. She emerges in 'flattened', stereotypical terms in this story, as was typical of many of the representations of servants in British cultural life.[2] However, this anecdote illustrates the nagging suspicion that affected Mrs Peel and many other mistresses (but not, in the main, their male equivalents): that servants were asserting their social equality in all interactions with their employers, sometimes angrily and explicitly,

---

[1] Mrs C. S. Peel, *Life's Enchanted Cup: An Autobiography (1872–1933)* (London: Lane, 1933), 260.
[2] Karen Hansen notes this flattened form of presentation as also typical of colonial presentations of servants, in *Distant Companions: Servants and Employers in Zambia, 1900–1985* (Ithaca, NY: Cornell University Press, 1989), xii.

other times in their 'lolling' and disguised or 'off-stage' laughter. The inability of servant-keeping women to manage their servants and sustain their self-identities as 'good' (liberal, firm, caring, knowledgeable) mistresses was a pressing domestic concern that dwarfed concerns over the dwindling supply of domestic workers. It was also understood as symbolic of wider social changes: the servant question provided a means to talk about the variety of ways in which authority was exercised in society. Servant-keeping gained in significance through being a political metaphor. In an age tending painfully towards mass democracy, the concepts of political authority and exercise of power were high profile and contested, particularly in the troubled Edwardian years. Spaces where different classes, generations, or ethnic/religious groups encountered each other tended to be overshadowed by the wider questions of power and authority in society. The relationships of domestic service were inevitably implicated in this, as Mrs Peel's anecdote suggests.

Authority of all kinds was fragile and under scrutiny in early- to mid-twentieth-century Britain. There was a growing uncertainty about the right of the old to govern the young, of elites to dictate to the masses, and of men to command the affairs of women. Religious certainties became less compelling to many, and the idea of social hierarchies, cultural 'taste', and political authority seemed to lack the secure foundations that had underpinned them in earlier decades. As one interwar female politician noted nostalgically, the Edwardian period had been marked by certainties of 'place': 'There was no more doubt about how a lady ought to behave than about the hat and pelisse she ought to wear. *She knew, precisely, where she was.*' But in 1936, it had become impossible to tell the social origins of young women: 'No guessing from face or clothes what kind of work she does; she may be a civil servant or a shop assistant, a typist or a factory hand, or the mother of young children: they look much alike nowadays.'[3]

Both these projections—of Edwardian certainty and modern democratic anonymity—were polemical constructions. The identity of 'lady' had long been subject to fears of blurring, but was still a recognizable and useable identity through much of the twentieth century. This privileged position was formed from many components of social standing, material resources, and bodily comportment, and this chapter will explore the ways in which many axes of social difference were implicated in the unstable and ongoing 'classing process'. While the main focus here is on mistresshood as a middle-class identity, class is understood as a multifaceted organization of social and cultural hierarchies. To be 'middle-class' had long been established relationally, lacked clear content, and was vulnerable to re-evaluation. Roland Barthes coyly defined the middle class as 'the social class which does not want to be named'. Alison Light has described it as an unstable identity, depending 'on an extremely anxious production of endless discriminations between people who are constantly assessing each other's standing.'[4] It was an internally diverse

---

[3] Mary Agnes Hamilton, 'Changes in Social Life', in Ray Strachey, *Our Freedom and Its Results* (London: Hogarth Press, 1936), 281, 38, emphasis added.

[4] R. Barthes, 'The Bourgeoisie as a Joint-Stock Company', in Roland Barthes, *Mythologies*, trans. Annette Lavers (London: Cape, 1972); Alan Kidd and David Nicholls, *Gender, Civic Culture and*

pecking order of taste, consumption, ethnicity, and geography. Historians are divided as to when, if ever, it achieved stability and a recognizable set of core values. Some suggest the late nineteenth century as its apogee, when demographic and material distinctions began to make smaller families, professional identities, and suburban homes the hallmarks of middle-class identities.[5] In Charles Masterman's words, being middle class represented being able to 'stand for England'.[6] But this was also a period of rapid occupational change that blurred social boundaries. Since the late nineteenth century, the British middle classes had undergone expansion, in the fields of science, engineering and management. No longer epitomized by the clergy and a narrow range of professions centred on the law and medicine, a lower middle-class strata developed, made up of white collar employees such as clerks, 'petit bourgeois' shopkeepers, and small businessmen.[7] The coherence of the middle-class identity was challenged by the growing presence and confidence of the lower middle-classes, and for women, by the diminishing salience and practicality of concepts of leisured, cultured lifestyles.

There were also persistent political, religious, and regional divides amongst 'middling' Edwardian groups, and many historians prefer to see the interwar period as the historical moment when class identities seemed to coalesce. After World War I, the middle classes arguably became a more cohesive, homogenous group. Understood in the rough shorthand used by contemporaries as those earning an annual salary of £250–£500, they became more unified around the Conservative Party and the Anglican Church.[8] Many more owned their own homes, as the interwar building boom supplied the market with semi-detached suburban houses that epitomized the core middle-class values of comfort and privacy.[9] Deborah Cohen describes an ethic of 'safety first', a slogan chosen by the Conservative leader Stanley Baldwin for his 1929 election campaign, which conveyed the atmosphere of conformity and anxiety within interwar middle-class households.[10] The interwar middle classes suffered acute fears of their loss of social and political authority and affluence. Anxiety arose from the threat of a more cohesive and politically influential labour movement, and many dramatic fluctuations associated with war, economic slumps, food prices, and changes in taxation, which greatly affected

Consumerism: Middle-Class Identity in Britain, 1800–1940 (Manchester: Manchester University Press, 1999); Alison Light, *Forever England: Femininity, Literature and Conservatism between the Wars* (London: Routledge, 1991), 13.

[5] Harold Perkin, *The Rise of Professional Society: England since 1880* (London: Routledge, 1989), 266–73.
[6] C. F. G. Masterman, *The Condition of England* (London: Methuen, 1960 [1909]), 21.
[7] See Geoffrey Crossick, *The Lower Middle Class in Britain* (London: Croom Helm, 1977).
[8] See Ross Mckibbin, *Classes and Cultures: England 1918–1951* (Oxford: Oxford University Press, 1998), 46–9.
[9] Alan Jackson, *The Middle Classes 1900–1950* (Nairn: David St John Thomas, 1991). The values of comfort and privacy were not entirely compatible. Comfort required the employment of servants in one's home, but this contravened privacy ideals, creating a constitutive tension at the heart of middle-class identity.
[10] Deborah Cohen, *Household Gods: The British and Their Possessions* (New Haven, CT: Yale University Press, 2006), 187.

middle-class budgets and led to their powerful sense of being the 'new poor'.[11] Servant-keeping was the canvas on which these changes were vividly illustrated.

The interwar novelist Lettice Cooper captured this middle-class anxiety and sense of defeat in her fictional description of a 1930s removal to a smaller, suburban house where only one maid would be kept:

> In the new house, Rhoda perceived, there would be no unexplored dark continent. There would be Ivy living at close quarters with them, talking to them about her own affairs because she would have no one else to talk to in between her days out. When Ivy came in at ten o'clock and bounced into the drawing room to show them her new Marks & Spencer jumper, Mrs Powell said that she did not know her place. Ivy was nineteen, and belonged to a generation for whom this mysterious place hardly existed. Her complete unconsciousness of it was defeating Mrs Powell, and would defeat her still more as time went on.[12]

The department store jumper confidently displayed by a youthful servant epitomized the interwar sensation of the erosion of certainties of 'place'.

Domestic assistance was central to enabling the more public or civic elements of middle-class identities, which for married women were mostly organized around philanthropic and voluntary activities. Yet with fewer or more truculent servants, it became much harder for middle-class women to self-identify as 'busy, useful women' until paid employment became more common for married women after World War II.[13] Prior to this, the way in which they managed their servants proved their ability to establish themselves, as one journalist put it, as 'a class that is essentially modern..., a most important class because it is forward-looking and is giving the cue to oncoming generations.'[14] Middle-class women were deeply invested in this 'modernizing' and trend-setting identity to which mistresshood was both practically and symbolically linked. Yet this chapter traces the ways in which mistresshood became devalued in the early to mid-twentieth century. Lettice Cooper's character Rhoda, an unmarried middle-class woman, captured this self-doubt: 'It's absurd, thought Rhoda, to envy this child [Ivy], but I believe I do. She's independent. She's a servant in our house, but she can go whenever she wants. She has her good times and enjoys them. She's out in the world, at grips with it, working and keeping herself, not just a parasite.'[15] Viewed as the employers of 'sweated' labour, or as parasites, mistresses found it hard to gain the moral authority to represent and shape public opinion and establish themselves as 'essentially modern'.

---

[11] Charles Frederick Masterman, *England after War: A Study* (London: Hodder and Stoughton, 1922).

[12] Lettice Cooper, *The New House* (London: Virago, 1987 [1936]), 101–2.

[13] Winifred Peck, *House-Bound* (London: Persephone Books, 2007); Caitriona Beaumont, 'Citizens Not Feminists: The Boundary Negotiated between Citizenship and Feminism by Mainstream Women's Organisations in England, 1928–39', *Women's History Review*, 9 2 (2000); James Hinton, *Women, Social Leadership, and the Second World War: Continuities of Class* (Oxford: Oxford University Press, 2002); Cordelia Moyse, *A History of the Mothers' Union Women, Anglicanism and Globalisation, 1876–2008* (Woodbridge: Boydell Press, 2009).

[14] Constance Eaton, 'The Gordian Knot of Domestic Service', *Good Housekeeping* (Feb 1930), 48–9, esp. 48.

[15] Cooper, *The New House*, 103.

VICTORIAN MISTRESSHOOD

A domestic manual in 1841 advised that 'A well-governed family is an invaluable branch of the great family of the kingdom, and a treasure to the state; while one that is neglected, becomes a curse to the land.'[16] The author placed the relationship between mistress and servant as the centrepiece of domestic authority and a model for wider social relations. She believed that women could satisfactorily exercise authority, if they put their emotions aside and 'dare[d] to be masters and judges'. The domestic service relationship was perhaps the last one to be cast as an absolutist relationship within British society. An 1870 etiquette manual similarly maintained in comforting terms, 'Every mistress of a house is a minor sovereign, upon whose bounty the comfort and happiness and refinement of her little court depend.'[17]

Queenship was one metaphor that portrayed in positive terms the 'unwomanly' role of the authority figure amongst Victorian domestic advice writers. Other metaphors used to describe the authority of women are revealing of how difficult it was to convey the figure of a woman in command. A common one was that of the mistress as the captain of a ship—carrying implications of tight discipline, and extreme levels of order and precision in household management. Others examples were that of the mistress as a 'king on his throne, [a] cleric in his pulpit'.[18] These masculine roles were, however, uncomfortably linked to mistresshood, and the metaphor that emerged as most successful in the nineteenth century was one of the mistress as a foster-mother, exercising authority with a loving paternalism. An 1885 editorial in *The Lady*, for example, portrayed servants as children—silly, and easy to deal with if treated with a firm hand.[19] While the mistress might look like a tyrant, another writer acknowledged in 1894 that this was actually the exacting conscientiousness of a guardian towards a ward.[20]

Conscientious care was not, however, to be confused with kindness or friendship. Nineteenth-century mistresses were frequently excoriated as overly kind and sentimental in their relations with their servants. In the mid-nineteenth century, being a mistress was presented in exacting terms. 'A Mother' in 1841 wrote that the 'chief barriers to the proper development of authority in superiors' was to be found *'within ourselves'*. Kindness and charity had a 'paralysing effect' on mistresses. It was appropriate that women should feel these sentiments, but they should only be felt

---

[16] Adelaide Sophia Kilvert, *Home Discipline; or, Thoughts on the Origin and Exercise of Domestic Authority. By a Mother, and Mistress of a Family* (London, 1841), ii.
[17] Right Hon. The Countess of *******, *Mixing in Society: A Complete Manual of Manners* (London/New York: Routledge, 1870), 14.
[18] A Mistress and a Mother, *At Home* (London: Macintosh, 1874), at 7. On the metaphors American mistresses deployed, see Andrew Urban, 'Irish Domestic Servants, "Biddy" and Rebellion in the American Home, 1850–1900', *Gender and History*, 21 2 (2009), 263–86.
[19] *The Lady*, Feb 19, 1885.
[20] Lady Laura Ridding, 'The Conditions of Domestic Service from the Mistress's Point of View', in Women Workers, Conference Report, Glasgow, Oct 1894 (National Union of Women Workers and the Glasgow Union for the Care and Help of Girls and Women).

in the heart, while retaining a stern, reproving exterior.[21] Other mid-Victorian writers were similarly sceptical about the kinds of relationships that could be established with servants. The *British Mother's Family Magazine* argued in 1864:

Be just to your servants, and expect obedience from them, but anything that you may do for them beyond their 'rights,' any concession you make to them is simply thrown away. Perhaps it does positive harm by weakening your authority and lessening the distance between you. Friends in servants, indeed!...I have tried, but it cannot be. It is not in their nature to soften or yield to kindness.[22]

The authority of mistresses might be bolstered through devices such as norms of naming that indicated social status. Most Victorian servants were called by their Christian names, while employers were either 'Sir' and 'Madam' or 'Mr' and 'Mrs'. Some servants, particularly in great house service, were given generic names that related to their post: 'In the places I lived there was always a general name for footmen. In one house they were William and another Henry, and where there were three the first was John, the second William and the third was always Henry. We maids were called by our own christian [*sic*] names.'[23] If servants' names were inconvenient—being the same as one of the family members—the servant's name was usually changed.

The segregation and distribution of physical space also allowed mistresses to exert their authority in the home, as Jane Hamlett's work has suggested.[24] 'Knowing one's place' had a literal spatial element, and household manuals paid close attention to the spatial elements of domestic authority—several advised the mistress who needed to give a dressing down to a servant to go to her own sitting room, where she would gain more authority by being in her own, secure space.[25] Another advised taking a flat rather than a house, since in such a layout 'Followers are practically an impossibility, or at any rate the opportunities for receiving kitchen visitors are few.'[26] Servants were frequently confined to certain rooms and routes within the house, while theoretically, employers were free to move throughout the house. Victorian mistresses were advised to personally inspect servants' rooms

---

[21] The exercise of authority was, for this author, women's 'absolute duty', built into the nature of her 'station'; to employ and manage servants did not bring ease or indolence—quite the reverse. She believed that a mistress who commands 'can know no real ease'. Nonetheless, 'we must surrender our indolence for the good of the whole' (Kilvert, *Home Discipline*, 35).

[22] *British Mother's Family Magazine* for 1864, 270, quoted in Patricia Branca, *Silent Sisterhood: Middle Class Women in the Victorian Home* (London: Croom Helm, 1975), 34.

[23] Margaret Thomas, 'Behind the Green Baize Door', in Noel Streatfeild (ed.), *The Day before Yesterday: Firsthand Stores of Fifty Years Ago* (London: Collins, 1956), 88. It should also be remembered that re-naming was not simply an imposition by the middle classes onto working people; Winifred Foley recalled that on going out to service, her mother wanted her to abandon her nickname and thus take on the status of an adult: 'Mam was very concerned that I should be aware of my own status. "You'll be a young 'oman," she said, "now you be goin' into service, and you'll 'ave to start bein' called by your proper name, Winifred."...I did not want to be a young 'oman, a Winifred, I just wanted to stay a Polly' (*A Child in the Forest* (London: Futura, 1974), 148).

[24] See Jane Hamlett, *Material Relations: Domestic Interiors and Middle-Class Families in England 1850–1910* (Manchester: Manchester University Press, 2011).

[25] Mother, *At Home*, 7.

[26] Mrs Praga, *How to Keep House on £200 a Year* (London: Pearson, 1904), 19.

herself: 'If you wish to be well served, you must look into every room in the house once a day... not timidly as if you were taking a liberty, but with the air of an officer going round his ship and well aware of the dignity of his position; open all the doors... and see if everything is in the state in which you would like your own mother to see it.'[27] Within this spatially segregated framework, authority was also emphasized through the tones of voice, bodily deportment, and posture of the servant-keeping class. As Leonore Davidoff pointed out,

> Middle-class children not only learned that certain social spaces belonged to certain social groups, they also learned to use their bodies to express class and gender boundaries. Little ladies and gentlemen did not sit on steps; they stood absolutely straight; they did not whistle, scuff or slouch. By imitating middle-class adults they learned habits of command through silent body language, through the way they looked at people, through tone of voice as well as accent.[28]

How servants were addressed not only established authority, but also the class status of the employer. The use of strong language or losing of one's temper was not compatible with 'good breeding'. Social conventions required that genteel women did not raise their voices to talk to their servants. Again and again, Victorian advice manuals advised women who wished to show their social superiority that they should display effortless command of their inferiors. Attempts to create social distance by aloof or cold tones of voice were unacceptable. As Eliza Lynn Linton wrote in 1894,

> a duchess will ask a service of her maid with grace and courtesy, and thank her for it when it is performed, while a miserable little snob, aping the gentility she neither feels nor knows, will command hers with rude impertinence, and hold even the coldest acknowledgement beneath her dignity to make. The lower section of the middle-classes for the most part treat their servants with humiliating rudeness.[29]

This highly judgemental advice discourse left many women extremely uncertain about how to talk to their servants; the tone of voice was hard to get right. Robert Graves (1895–1985) recalled in his memoir of his upper-middle-class Edwardian childhood: 'I can well recall the tone of my mother's voice when she informed the maids that they could have what was left of the pudding, or scolded the cook for some carelessness. It had a forced hardness, made almost harsh by embarrassment.'[30]

Linton's comment about the 'miserable little snob' indicates the increasing vitriol directed towards the lower-middle-class mistress—those who managed their (single-handed) servants directly rather than through the intermediary of a housekeeper or butler. Servant-keeping became increasingly affordable lower down

---

[27] Mrs Johnson, *The Bride Elect* (London: Hand and Heart, 1878), 94.
[28] Leonore Davidoff, *Worlds between: Historical Perspectives on Class and Gender* (New York: Routledge, 1995), 112.
[29] Eliza Lynn Linton, 'Mistresses and Maids', in *Ourselves: A Series of Essays on Women* (London: Chatto and Windus, 1884), 92.
[30] Robert Graves, *Goodbye to All That* (London: Penguin, 1976 [1929]), 19.

the social level towards the end of the nineteenth century, as food prices fell and affluence rose amongst the middle classes. As Rose Gibbs encountered in her first job in Edwardian London, when she was 13: 'the first place was with a young couple who were only recently married and wanted to "be big" and able to say "We've got a servant." It wasn't really that they could afford a proper servant, only me as a new "maid of all work." They had a flat, two storeys over a shop in Fulham Road.'[31] In the twentieth century, this kind of smaller-scale servant-keeping became the norm in middle-class homes, and distinguishes twentieth-century domestic service from earlier decades.

The attempts of such lower-middle-class employers to manage their servants were regarded critically and comically by the more secure middle classes, and by their own servants. The polemical journalist Charles Masterman wrote derisively of suburban 'women, with their single domestic servants, now so hard to get, and so exacting when found, [who] find time hang rather heavy on their hands.' Suburban femininity was regarded as mundane, characterized by trivial feuds with neighbours and an intense collective scrutiny of 'manners and fashion, dress and deportment'. It was the ultimate site of competitive consumption and conventionality.[32] Suburban masculinity fared no better, and was also damned through its relationship to domestic work. Geoffrey Mortimer wrote scathingly of the preference for domestic servants in villadom: 'Is there one man in ten in this great sheep-pen who would like to be seen blacking his own boots or sweeping the snow from the front of his house? No, they prefer to ill-pay some man's daughter to do all their irksome and dirty work.'[33] The very same tasks that seemed to unmake a man when undertaken by male domestic servants or securely middle-class individuals were seen as tasks compatible with lower-middle-class manhood by its critics.

It was already apparent to late-nineteenth-century commentators that domestic authority was becoming less secure. In 1895 an article in *The Queen* deplored the tendency of fearful mistresses to make their servants into 'a sort of court of appeal instead of making herself the supreme and ultimate authority.'[34] Many blamed the new spirit of democracy for servant problems; one turn-of-the-century writer fumed against the 'odious and untruthful form of pretence that everyone is as good as everyone else.'[35] Others blamed mass education; nonetheless, the mistress's authority could still be understood as based upon a brute assertion of social and intellectual superiority. In 1912, it was a straightforward assumption of *Cassell's Household Guide* that 'the mistress is of higher mental culture than her servant,' and this gave her the right and ability to command her servants.[36] The servant question

---

[31] Rose Gibbs, *In Service: Rose Gibbs Remembers* (Bassingbourn: Archives for Bassingbourn and Comberton Village Colleges, 1981), 5.
[32] Masterman, *The Condition of England*, 69, 80.
[33] Geoffrey Mortimer, *The Blight of Respectability: An Anatomy of the Disease and a Theory of Curative Treatment* (London: University Press, 1897), 90.
[34] 'On the Management of Servants', *The Queen*, June 1, 1895, 988.
[35] 'A Grandmother', *Macmillan's Magazine*, Oct 1900, 452.
[36] Mrs Stuart Macrae, *Cassell's Household Guide: A Complete Cyclopaedia of Domestic Economy* (London: Waverly Book, 1912), 842.

enabled some Edwardian writers to assert social hierarchy and authority in a way that was becoming unacceptable in other forums. However, in homes around Britain, authority based on social rank was becoming much less tenable in the twentieth century. With increasing pressure for a more inclusive and directly representative polity in the twentieth century, absolutist domestic authority became harder to sustain. The traditional markers of social superiority—educated status, professional standing—were no longer adequate, in an age of mass education and social democracy. Thus the servant problem might be situated as a product of modernity. As one Edwardian feminist argued: 'this [servant] problem is peculiarly a product of the age... We are suffering at the hands of a modern "type"—the slatternly maid-of-all-work.'[37]

In the face of this imagined 'type', metaphors of queenly authority or loving foster-care became less common, and the positive metaphors of mistresshood gave way in the twentieth century to less positive ones. The American feminist and household commentator Charlotte Perkins Gilman noted in her 1903 book, *The Home, Its Work and Influence*, that 'The lady of the house is by no means a captain of industry. She is not a trainer and governor of able subordinates, like the mate of a ship or the manager of a hotel. Her position is not one of power, but of helplessness. She has to be done for and waited on.'[38] As servants began to be more vocal participants in 'the servant question', mistresses became termed prison-keepers and slave-drivers.[39] The metaphors of power and authority were explicitly rejected, and replaced with critical narratives of domestic helplessness and dependency. The British feminist Olive Schreiner, influenced by Gilman, took up the same theme in her 1911 feminist polemic, *Woman and Labour*. She stressed the 'topsy-turvy' idea of men undertaking domestic tasks, to give an added rhetorical edge to her portrayal of women as indolent:

among the wealthier classes, so far has domestic change gone that men are not unfrequently found labouring in our houses and kitchens, and even standing behind our chairs ready to do all but actually place the morsels of food between our feminine lips.... In our modern cities our carpets are beaten, our windows cleaned, our floors polished, by machinery, or extra domestic, often male, labour.[40]

Middle-class mistresses were increasingly being figured as shirkers or parasites, and judging themselves in these terms. Mrs Peel wrote furiously in 1921:

Today we pay dearly for the reign of stupidity, for it is not the war of 1914 which has brought about the servant problem; it is the result of the long slow fight of the working people to gain such conditions as appeal to them, and of the obstinate effort of *stupid women* to stand in the way of progress.[41]

---

[37] Alice Melvin, 'Co-operative Housekeeping and the Domestic Worker', *The Freewoman*, Apr 4, 1912, 386–7.
[38] Charlotte Perkins Gilman, *The Home: It's Work and Influence* (New York, 1903), 112.
[39] A Servant, 'How to Improve the Conditions of Domestic Service' (1894), cited in Judy Giles, *Women, Identity and Private Life in Britain* (London: MacMillan, 1995), 135.
[40] Olive Schreiner, *Woman and Labour* (London: Virago, 1978 [1911]), 50.
[41] Peel, *The Queen*, Apr 30, 1921, 486, emphasis added.

Yet despite powerful discourses of social change and upheaval, in practice there was much continuity between the late nineteenth and twentieth centuries in the management of servants. Many twentieth-century mistresses attempted to surveil their servants during both their work and leisure hours, and authority practices were very varied. One servant in Edwardian Dumfries recalled that

> The first morning I was busy doing the grate—in the dining room when I heard a squeak, I could—I could hear better then, here she's standing at the door to see if... I was doing anything she hadnae told me. And—she just seemed to go about all the time from the time you were up watching... they watched you like hawks,... they sat and watched everything you did.[42]

Some mistresses quizzed their female servants about what they did during their time off, or asked for a summary of the sermon to check on church attendance. Others still found time to investigate the cleanliness of their servants' fingernails. Towards the end of the century, when many cleaners had little interaction with their employers, some still felt motivated to take a close interest in the work of their cleaners. Annette Dobson recalled a mid-1990s employer who 'wanted to boss us about, she insisted on being in, and used to waft about with her baby behind us, interfering with our work'. An overzealous pursuit of surveillance might become perceived as absurd by twentieth-century servants. Dobson and her co-worker christened this employer 'target woman', after her habitual phrase, 'let's target this area then'.[43] Jean Rennie told of the servants' laughter at one employer:

> Part of Mrs Clark's routine was a systematic walk, every morning, armed with sheets of fresh tissue-paper, round the front hall, staircase, and public rooms which the housemaids had left spotless and polished and dustless at five minutes to nine. As soon as she'd finished breakfast, she would get her box of tissue paper out and, with a fresh sheet, she would "dust" every surface she could find. She made not the slightest scrap of difference to the banisters, or the tables, unless it was to make scratches on them. She must have been a godsend to the paper manufacturers.[44]

Other mistresses, however, gave their servants new freedoms, and retreated from the surveillance and moral guidance that characterized Victorian mistresshood. Mrs Hawkins recalled that her Edwardian mother in a wealthy middle-class Manchester household kept her maids

> wonderfully, because... she did not force them to get up early. She said she couldn't see why so long as her breakfast was on time and on the table it mattered whether they be up at five or—six but some people had that feeling in Manchester at that time that their maids must be up by six and moving.'[45]

---

[42] Mrs Martha Shearer (b. 1894), Interview 437, in P. Thompson and T. Lummis, *Family Life and Work Experience before 1918, 1870–1973* [computer file], 7th edn, Colchester, Essex: UK Data Archive (distributor), May 2009, SN: 2000; henceforth cited as *Edwardians*.

[43] Annette Dobson, interview with the author, Sept 3, 2010.

[44] Jean Rennie, *Every Other Sunday: The Autobiography of a Kitchenmaid* (London: Barker, [1955] 1978), 176.

[45] Mrs Hawkins (b. 1899), Interview 4, in P. Thompson, *Family Life and Work Experience before 1918, Middle and Upper Class Families in the Early 20th Century, 1870–1977* [computer file], 2nd edn,

It became common for twentieth-century mistresses to feel that Victorian social norms and scripts of gracious authority no longer helped them in interacting with their servants. One mistress wrote in 1923 of her 'torturing sense of sin when I have given Jane a "good talking to"? Why that feeling of failure and defeat...?'[46] Scolding became increasingly uncomfortable for mistresses at all social levels. One servant, Dora Holtom, who worked as a nanny in London in the 1930s, told of how the previous Finnish nanny had forced the two-year-old child to have a daily cold bath, against both the child and the mother's wishes: 'Why did Mrs Hughes not tell her to stop? I don't know, she hadn't got the guts to I suppose. But she wasn't used to telling people you know.' For suburban mistresses, it was the uncertainty about how to preserve deference and authority in a new landscape that made suburban service so uncomfortable. Mrs Aulton, in service as a single-handed day servant in the 1940s in a bungalow just outside Birmingham found that despite there being no possibility of 'upstairs downstairs' spatial arrangements, her use of the side gate was insisted on, as well as the ceremony of changing into different uniforms at different points in the day. She felt intense resentment at the imposition of social norms and conventions that aimed to establish the differential 'places' of servants and employers in what had been imagined to be more democratic urban spaces.[47]

The spatial segregation of servants from employers declined in the twentieth century, as more servants worked in houses or flats without basements, servants' sitting rooms, and attic bedrooms. Some recalled being able to share rooms like the sitting room and the study with their employers, if they chose to. Servants also recalled eating with their employers, in various rooms in the house (kitchen, dining room, study).[48] By the 1930s, many mistresses had less confidence in simply asserting their preferences and orders. They were increasingly reluctant to invade the rooms or surveil the bodies of their servants, and unwilling to commit to onerous levels of inspection. Domestic informality was thus possible, though there was little uniformity of practice in the twentieth century. This was reflected in the naming of servants. Alice Stroud noted that when she was employed as a servant in Guildford between 1907 and World War I, she had a number of ways of addressing her mistress, and little importance was attached to naming: 'things were getting more general then—she was—she wasn't fussy in that way.' In this job, she was free to undertake the work as she liked: 'I did more as I liked there—I was sort

---

Colchester, Essex: UK Data Archive [distributor], May 2008, SN: 5404; henceforth cited as *Middle and Upper Class Families*.

[46] Fay Inchfawn, *Homely Talks of a Homely Woman* (London: Ward, Lock, 1923), 68.

[47] Dora Holtom (b. 1914), City of Westminster Archives Centre, Upstairs Downstairs Collection; henceforth cited as Westminster, *Upstairs Downstairs*; Mrs Aulton, Birmingham Libraries and Archive Services, Library Services at Home, Upstairs, Downstairs Oral History Project, http://www.birmingham.gov.uk/libraryservicesathome; henceforth Birmingham, *Upstairs, Downstairs*.

[48] This often changed, however, when visitors were present, and it seems that there were frequently two sets of spatial arrangements existing side by side in twentieth-century servant-keeping homes; the presence of visitors made the free circulation of servants and employers who ate and socialized together impossible, and led to a reassertion of spatial segregation. The home was not a static physical space; its boundaries were mobile and evolving according to the physical presence of individuals.

of... your own boss.'[49] A decade later, Dora Holtom, who was a similar age to her mistress, would call her mistress 'dear', though she herself was called 'nanny'. She recalled the intimacy of 'messing about in the kitchen sometimes together'. The mistress in this situation clearly had few strategies that could set her up as an authority figure; when Dora gave in her notice, she recalled, her mistress 'was so upset she didn't speak to me for a couple of days. So I said, "look, it's no good going on like this, my dear."'[50] The servant usurped the role of the mistress in adopting the kind, condescending tone towards the sulky employer. However, naming issues continued to dog domestic service. One servant, Miss Field, declared in frustration to the Domestic Workers' Union in 1947: 'Why should anyone these days be called *Mary Jane, Elizabeth* and so forth. [Mistresses] expect to be called madam every other word, and boys and girls expect one to Miss them every other word also.'[51]

The twentieth century is often thought of as experiencing an 'affective revolution', with the increasing expectation of more informal, emotionally 'authentic' relationships.[52] The last chapter discussed moments of friendship and intimacy between employers and servants, but in the didactic literature aimed at middle- and upper-class women, there was little change between the Victorian and Edwardian periods. Overkindness and sympathy were still seen as likely causes of relationship breakdown. 'Patience', a correspondent to *The Queen* in 1915, explained her own failings as a mistress: 'I was injudiciously kind and over-sympathetic, very impulsive, and when imposed upon, much too seriously disgusted and contemptuous.' She had been forced to acknowledge the social distance between herself and her servants, having foolishly 'expected an equal sense of honour and gratitude to ours, forgetting the very different bringing up.'[53] Advice texts dealing with servants frequently characterized the distinct spheres of class in Britain as so unlike as to be like separate countries. There were clearly disparities between the advice given and the very varied practices, particularly in rural and working-class servant-keeping homes. However, at the level of educated readerships, 'the servant problem' continued to be the most cited example of the social chasm between the classes. One popular interwar writer, Fay Inchfawn, wrote in typical terms of the domestic servant as a foreign and inhospitable country, governed by customs as different from those of employers as savagery differed from civilization.[54] Employers were advised to limit emotional intimacy to paternalistic kindness, rather than any deeper emotions of friendship and empathy.

The reduction in formality in the twentieth century in practices of naming, surveillance, and social interaction did not fundamentally recast the balance of power between employer and servant. The domestic service labour market

---

[49] Alice Elizabeth Stroud (b. 1887), Interview 66, *Edwardians*.
[50] Holtom, Westminster, *Upstairs Downstairs*.
[51] Miss E. A. Field, Feb 21, 1947, at the Modern Records Centre at the University of Warwick (henceforth MRC), MSS. 292/54.76/8, emphasis in the original.
[52] Anthony Giddens, *The Transformation of Intimacy: Love, Sexuality and Eroticism in Modern Societies* (Cambridge: Polity Press, 1993).
[53] 'Patience', *The Queen*, Sept 18, 1915, 523.
[54] Inchfawn, *Homely Talks of a Homely Woman*.

remained set up in such a way that the 'character' giving system gave mistresses considerable authority to determine the career prospects of their servants. While the high demand for servants gave them some ability to resist exploitation, in reality the ability of mistresses to withhold references or give a bad 'character' left servants well aware that they could not 'answer back' or leave any job on a whim. The desperation of employers to find servants led to some erosion of the character system after World War I, but it still pervaded servants' experiences. Jean Rennie, a cook in service in the 1930s, told of being sacked in London without a reference.[55] Her subsequent destitution, despite the high demand for cooks, makes clear the persistent structured power of employers that underlay their domestic authority. Other servants complained that the spread of the telephone now allowed mistresses to 'hint at all sorts of faults—things they wouldn't dare write down in case they had to prove them.'[56] Altering the character system, so that mistresses were compelled to give a written reference, and so might be left open to legal prosecution for slander or libel, was a reform continually requested by individual servants and their advocates.

The payment of wages was also a device that might shore up the authority of employers, perhaps especially for rural households where servants were not expected to need access to cash. Sybil Hayhoe, a housemaid in service in the Fens in the early twentieth century, recalls being paid only four times a year, and this money was immediately spent on necessities, so that she was left permanently without any money reserves. This made for a sense of being beholden to her employer for small loans—a sense that advice manuals explicitly recommended mistresses should develop. A 1912 housekeeping manual recommended paying servants lower wages, in order that the servant learn thrifty ways, and the mistress might have money to spare, 'for bestowing upon her maid little presents and rewards that would encourage her in her well-doing.'[57] The idea of fair wages paid for work done was rejected in favour of the paternalistic relationship in which the mistress could impose her decisions and values.

Gift-giving formed an important part of how an emotional relationship could be established. Jane Hegstrom has identified the one-way giving of gifts by mistresses to servants as a means of imposing authority and control.[58] Amy Clifford, a servant in London to a family who she termed 'just ordinary people like ourselves', described how her mistress 'was quite kind, she gave me a little compact when I was twenty one... just a cheap thing really I think, I don't know what happened to it, but she did give me that, it wasn't wrapped up or anything.'[59] There is a sense of ambivalence here, at the cheapness and lack of preparation of the present, but

---

[55] Rennie, *Every Other Sunday*.
[56] 'I'm Sorry I Entered Service', *Challenge*, Mar 24, 1938, 9.
[57] Mary Chamberlain, *Fenwomen: A Portrait of Women in an English Village* (London: Virago, 1975), 96–8; Macrae, *Cassell's Household Guide*, 843.
[58] Jane Hegstrom, 'Reminiscences of below Stairs: English Female Domestic Servants between the Two World Wars', *Women's Studies*, 36 1 (2007), 15–33.
[59] Amy Clifford, Westminster, *Upstairs Downstairs*.

also an acknowledgement of kindness; on both sides of the relationship, many gifts were kept and treasured after the employment relationship had ended. Yet servants were acutely aware of the paternalism of the gift; one reported that her employers had given her a lace tablecloth at her wedding in 1969, though 'it was not real lace'. Embodied within this shoddy gift was a clear sense of her relative lack of worth, and an acute ability to judge the value of the gift and its intentions: 'They thought they were giving you the world.'[60] Servants sometimes had the opportunity to give gifts themselves, particularly in relation to children. They reversed the gift-giving traditions of domestic service, and gave birthday or wedding gifts, which aimed to make the relationship more reciprocal, as well as to express genuine emotional attachment.[61]

While gifts in each direction were sometimes welcomed, they might also be mocked. Failures of 'taste' in gifting on the part of servants was found amusing. The *Daily Express* published a comic vignette in 1928, for example, recounting the vulgarity of a char, Mrs Briggs, who had broken her employer's antique cup, and to make amends, breezily bestowed an 'English seaside cup', grossly gilded, which her son had won on a Sunday School outing.[62] The gift of a servant to an employer was a comic event in itself, but was found particularly funny when it indicated a misreading of value. In turn, the most traditional 'gift' of the upper-class mistress, of material to be made into servants' uniforms, was often laughed at, or strongly resented. Such a gift clearly violated the norms of gift giving, though it was a common belief amongst employers that servants could not care for 'nice' possessions. Mrs J. E. Panton (1848–1923), a Victorian domestic writer, advised her readers not to bother giving her servants pretty things or well-decorated rooms, because they would feel more comfortable in a room that resembled the austere rooms of their upbringing, sparsely furnished and 'merely places where they lie down to sleep as heavily as they can.' Mistresses were advised to throw out all their own conceptions of the good life or reciprocity and try to imagine a less civilized and child-like mind. The uncertainty around gifting continued throughout the century, and debates around gifts to cleaners are still found in twenty-first-century online chatrooms.[63]

---

[60] Claire Smith (b. 1946), interview with the author, Apr 19, 2007.
[61] See, for example, Mrs Dora Bucknell (b. 1894, Hull), Interview 191, *Edwardians*, and Mrs Hawkins (b. 1899), Interview 4, *Middle and Upper Class Families*. The gifts of children to servants were less common, but where they occurred, parents sometimes disapproved, perhaps reading them as symbolic of the threat to the parent–child intimacy that relationships with servants implied. Joan Evans (b. 1893), for example, as scolded severely by her mother for buying her nanny a gold chain out of her own meagre savings. She considered herself and her nanny 'tacitly banded together against the powers that be', in particular, against a mother who had not wanted her to be born. Joan Evans, *Prelude and Fugue* (New York: Museum Press, 1964), 24.
[62] *Daily Express*, Apr 17, 1928, 10.
[63] J. E. Panton, *From Kitchen to Garret Hints for Yong Householders* (London: Ward and Downey, 1888), 152; http://www.mumsnet.com/Talk/good_housekeeping/882026-Xmas-present-for-cleaner, accessed Aug 8, 2010.

VARIATIONS IN PATTERNS OF AUTHORITY

In such a diverse sector, it is clear that very different regimes and practices of authority were to be found amongst different regions and localities. Lynn Jamieson has suggested that amongst domestic workers in Scotland, distinct authority regimes were experienced by servants in farm households, where older practices of eating together and being treated as one of the family survived.[64] The same seems to be true of those domestic servants working on farms in the West Country or Wales, as described in the Thompson and Vigne interviews. This may partly have been because farming households could rarely afford the higher wages that older servants expected, and so paid smaller sums to younger servants who were local and easily integrated into the household as if they were another child. Amy Clifford, for example, worked for a farmer near Malvern in 1932 when she was 14, doing both domestic and dairy work for 5 shillings a week. She enjoyed the joking relationship she had with the farmer, but had to leave after two years when they couldn't afford to put her wages up. In a similar fashion to domestic servants working on farms, those working in households of shopkeepers, bakers, or publicans, where retailing was closely integrated with domestic work, may have experienced informality.[65] Olive Vigars, for example, worked while at school at her aunt's hotel in Simonsbath, Exmoor, and went there full time when she left at 14 in 1934. She later worked at a pub in nearby Warminster, and after marriage, as a cook and cleaner at a nearby estate house. The work was hard, and in her jobs before World War II, she was dressed as a domestic servant in black dress, white cap and apron. However, the social relationships in each setting were informal, and she recalled the atmosphere as 'down to earth'. The tasks were shared, and she was able to court freely and attend village dances until 1am.[66]

In broad terms, there was no straightforward North/South division in servant-keeping practices, but rather a different set of experiences associated with service in the towns and cities that tended to employ migrant labour as servants, such as Bath, London, Edinburgh, and Brighton, and those towns or rural areas where local workers might be used. The servants of rural origins, who migrated from Wales, Ireland, or Yorkshire to places like London and Brighton were perceived as easier to manage, since they had fewer resources and social networks to fall back on. As one migrating servant wrote of the 1930s, 'you daren't be out of work.'[67] This vulnerability perhaps explains the recommendation by a reader of *The Queen* of

---

[64] Lynn Jamieson, 'Rural and Urban Women in Domestic Service', in E. Breitenbach (ed.), *The World Is Ill-Divided: Women's Work in Scotland in the Nineteenth and Early Twentieth Centuries* (Edinburgh: Edinburgh University Press, 1990), 139.

[65] Clifford, Westminster, *Upstairs Downstairs*. See also Mary Harrison's interviews in the Yorkshire East Riding on service in rural shop and farm households in Yorkshire: Mary Harrison, 'Domestic Service between the Wars: The Experiences of Two Rural Women', *Oral History*, 16 1 (1988), 48–54.

[66] Olive Vigars, The Exmoor Oral History Archive, available at http://www.somerset.gov.uk/archives/exmoor/vigarssummary2.htm, accessed Sept 25, 2008.

[67] Mrs Winifred Cooper née Brown (b. 1919). Westminster, *Upstairs Downstairs*. See also Harrison, 'Domestic Service between the Wars', 53.

Irish maids as friendly and flexible workers, more willing to take on each other's tasks than the status-conscious English servant.[68] One employee of a servants' employment agency reported that 'the country girl was more docile, quieter and ready to do what she was told even if she didn't like it very much.' Londoners, on the other hand, were perceived as more 'uppity'.[69] These myths had persistence across the century, with Annette Dobson noting that when she worked as a cleaner in private homes during the early to mid-1990s, though she was educated to degree level and shared many life-attributes with her employers, her Yorkshire origins were helpful as a means of establishing distance between her and her employers; indeed she was asked on one occasion whether she had 'a proper Yorkshire sense of cleanliness'.[70]

Another solution to problems of authority was to employ foreign servants, reputed to be 'more tractable than English servants', as one late Victorian household manual put it.[71] This, however, raised the anxious prospect of employing men as servants, since it was widely assumed that African and Asian women were unsuitable or unwilling. Few British employers opted for this before the economic and political disruptions of the 1930s.[72] As migration patterns changed, increasing numbers of foreigners did come to work as servants in Britain, but tended to stay in service only while they learnt English, or if refugees, until the initial turmoil of exile had subsided. The refugees of the 1930s briefly formed a new source of servants of both sexes, as many Jewish and other refugees could only enter Britain through a domestic service permit. *Housewife* magazine brutally described the European dislocation as 'Your Opportunity' to its readers in a 1939 article making 'The Case for the Foreign Maid'.[73] The experience of domestic service employment was often excruciating for the disoriented and vulnerable refugees.[74] The professional or 'gentle' status of many such refugees caused particular social discomfort. As one commentator put it, 'the refugees were often well educated, and it must be admitted although it is deplorable, that we were not then accustomed to treating domestic helps as social equals and many awkwardnesses arose as a result of this.'[75] Lore Segal's professional parents worked as a housekeeper and handyman in Kent after fleeing Nazi Austria in 1939, an experience that made evident the continuing discomfort felt by and about male domestic servants. Her mother attempted to dispel the shame that accompanied the habitual address of male domestic servants by their unadorned surname, and asked that her husband be called 'Mr Groszmann'. Her mistress, Mrs Willoughby, responded that 'the cook

---

[68] 'Erin-go-bragh', *The Queen*, Oct 16, 1915, 727.
[69] Dorothy [Jessie] Gould (b. 1909), Westminster, *Upstairs Downstairs*.
[70] Dobson, interview with the author.
[71] Florence Caddy, *Household Organization* (London: Chapman and Hall, 1877).
[72] Martha Major, *Macmillans Magazine*, Aug 1900, 281.
[73] 'Your Opportunity—The Case for the Foreign Maid', *Housewife*, Feb 1939.
[74] Pamela Horn, *Life below Stairs in the Twentieth Century* (Stroud: Sutton, 2001); Tony Kushner, 'An Alien Occupation—Jewish Refugees and Domestic Service in Britain, 1933–1948', in Werner E. Mosse (ed.), *Second Chance: Two Generations of German-Speaking Jews in the United Kingdom* (Tubingen: JCB Mohr, 1991), 553–78.
[75] Doreen Watson, *The Problem of Domestic Work*, MA Thesis, University of Leicester, 1944, 22.

was always "Mrs" and that the manservant was called by just his last name, and she didn't see how they could very well change.'[76] Mrs Willoughby invited the Vicar's cook, an Irishwoman, to have tea with the relentlessly literary Mrs Groszmann, in an awkward attempt to elucidate her 'place'. The indignities of wearing a gardener's pinafore, sleeping on stained sheets, or being refused permission to play the piano went with a deep unwillingness to acknowledge the conditions that had led European Jews to become servants in Britain, and were exceptionally painful for these refugees.

Most of those fleeing economic uncertainty and persecution in the 1930s were of European origins. Over a much longer time span, those of non-European ethnicity found extreme levels of racial prejudice in gaining employment even if they had been raised in Britain.[77] A black footman employed by a late Victorian family, for example, was described as being 'very cheap because so few people would take him'.[78] Forty years later, an orphan, Lilian Bader, found it impossible to leave the Welsh convent in which she was raised through the usual route of domestic service in the late 1930s because of her father's origins: 'My casting out from the convent walls was delayed. I was half West Indian, and nobody, not even the priests, dare risk ridicule by employing me.' Though there had been an earlier aristocratic tradition of employing black servants, this mostly comprised male, liveried servants, and certainly did not extend to twentieth-century middle-class servant keeping.[79] Bader did not leave the convent until she was 20 years old, because of the obstacles to finding work in private service. During a series of institutional service jobs during World War II, she found herself called a 'nazzy', because it was widely assumed that Germans were black.[80] The increasing numbers of migrants from the 'new Commonwealth' countries of the late 1940s onwards were not welcomed as domestic workers in private homes, and if they took cleaning jobs, these tended to be in hospitals and schools. In any case, by the 1950s, many immigrants joined British women in their unwillingness to serve in private homes, though older Irish women continued to be widely employed as live-out chars, child-carers, and cleaners.[81] As Wendy Webster has noted, some migrant women had themselves been brought up

---

[76] Lore Segal, *Other People's Houses* (London: Bodley Head, 1974 [1965]), 82.

[77] Empire and its dissolution influenced the dynamics of domestic service in Britain. Those who had become accustomed to domestic service in the British Empire found it hard to adjust on returning to Britain, and were scathing about British servants, though they also frequently accused native servants of being lazy and dishonest. But empire, with the exception of Ireland, rarely provided domestic workers for British homes. See Maj. C. S. Jarvis, 'East is East', *Cornhill*, Feb 1936; Lt.-Col. Sir K. Fraster-Tyler 'Farewell to Bearers', *Blackwood's Magazine*, 1948; Capt. J. A. Byron, 99/84/1, Imperial War Museum. Ireland itself was located ambiguously, resembling a colonial nation in some respects, yet also regarded as an integral part of the 'mother country', until the conflicts that led to independence in 1921. Its citizens continued to migrate freely to Britain, enabling the flow of domestic servants to continue despite the divide between the two countries.

[78] Olive Haweis, *Four to Fourteen* (London: Robert Hale, 1939), 143.

[79] Giles Waterfield, 'Black Servants', in *idem, Below Stairs: 400 Years of Servants' Portraits* (London: National Portrait Gallery, 2004), 139–51.

[80] The papers of Lilian Bader, 1102 88/2/1, Dept of Documents, Imperial War Museum, London.

[81] Marghanita Laski, 'This Servant Problem', *Spectator*, Mar 24, 1950, 371; Louise Ryan, 'Family Matters: (E)Migration, Familial Networks and Irish Women in Britain', *The Sociological Review*, 52 3 (2004), 351–70.

with servants, and could not envisage themselves in this role. One Jamaican woman recalled: 'I wouldn't be a maid for anyone... The thing is I'd never done it in my own country.' Her family had employed a maid, and she was forced to learn to cook on coming to Britain in 1956.[82]

The small numbers of Filipina, Malaysian, or Sri Lankan maids who mostly came to work for wealthy London-based families from the 1970s often had little time off, and few options for other work, often through the exploitative conditions of their visas. One affluent Asian woman living in London noted in 1978:

for the house (cleaning) I have somebody else. Formerly I had an English couple who used to come every day, that lasted seven or eight years then they got too old. Now I have a girl who comes from—Indonesia? No, Philippines, that's it! She has two days off from her family where she's working, so she comes those two days.[83]

A seven-day working week was not unusual for such migrants, nor regarded as problematic by this employer. More recent waves of migrant workers have undertaken domestic employment as a means of obtaining visas or facilitating the shift into a new labour market. Cleaning and domestic jobs, obtained through personal, informal networks and often on trust, have been common as jobs for Spanish and Portuguese women after their countries joined the EEC in 1986, and later for impoverished Eastern Europeans. Many female Polish workers came illegally as domestic workers in the 1990s, but even legal workers found it an attractive 'toehold' occupation. The relatively highly educated Polish migrants who came to Britain legally in large numbers after the European labour market opening in 2004 have commonly worked as cleaners in private homes, for agencies or in hotels. This work has been undertaken by both men and women. For many Poles, these were temporary jobs, but some have continued to work in this relatively insecure sector, often through their vulnerability caused by lack of language skills and accommodation problems.[84]

The underpinning theme of exploitation in historical narratives of domestic service have made the servant-keeping practices of black and Asian families in colonial societies relatively invisible, and similarly tended to obscure servant-keeping in Britain by working-class or immigrant households. Charles Booth's turn-of-the-century survey of London found servants (many of whom would have been Irish women) employed by prosperous working-class printers and gas workers; there were 29 domestic servants per 100 households amongst the clerks and commercial travellers who hovered between the middle and working classes in his sample.[85] About a sixth of servant-keeping households in nineteenth-century

---

[82] Wendy Webster, *Imagining Home* (London: UCL Press, 1998), 159.

[83] Amrit Wilson, *Finding a Voice: Asian Women in Britain* (London: Virago, 1978), 49. See also Janet Henshall Momsen, *Gender, Migration and Domestic Service* (London: Routledge, 1999).

[84] Kathy Burrell, *Polish Migration to the UK in the 'New' European Union: After 2004* (Farnham: Ashgate, 2009), 44, 155.

[85] Charles Booth, *Life and Labour of the People in London* (London: Macmillan, 1902), 3: 272–3, 449.

Rochdale were identified by Edward Higgs as working class.[86] Jerry White's history of the Rothschild Buildings in early-twentieth-century East London notes that many Jewish immigrant families living in precarious financial circumstances did nonetheless employ daily chars and washerwomen.[87]

Class privilege was not always paramount in determining servant-keeping patterns for some communities, and ethnicity might complicate its operations. A Jewish refugee family based in Rochdale during World War II were sensitive to transgressing their 'place' by taking on a domestic worker. As the son of the family, George Aberdou, recalled, 'my mother took on a char, and even though the people in that area were all what I'd call working class turned middle class, I think there were quite a lot of raised eyebrows when my mother took on a char. I mean not only were they refugee people and therefore suspect, but when my mother actually took on a char, that was something else.'[88] The imagined ethnicity of servant-keepers was mostly indigenous, and despite their self-perception as middle class, the Aberdou family were perceived as unsuitable servant-keepers.

Working-class employers of servants were in many cases less concerned about deference. Mrs Dora Bucknell, born in 1894 into the family of a working-class printer in Hull, recalled that a servant was always kept, who was treated as 'one of the family'. Though her memories may be influenced by nostalgia and the need for composure, she recalled servants as 'always happy and comfortable with us. We were democrats. . . . we would have been in trouble if [my father] had seen the girl wasn't being treated just the same as the family.'[89] Her mother was laissez-faire in her approach to her servants, and didn't ever ask them what they'd done on their evenings off. Even in the dramatic circumstances of the discovery of a dead newborn in the trunk of one maid, Mrs Bucknell insisted that her mother did not attempt to judge or give guidance to this servant, since she saw this as a role only for the servant's own mother. In this household, the servants always ate the same food as the family, though separately in the kitchen. This, however, was remembered as a means of giving them some respite from the family, rather than to create social distance.

The hard lives many working-class women lived, however, often meant poor conditions for their domestic help. One young servant described her mistress, a blacksmith's wife in Scotland, as 'a big overbearing kind of woman', and who expected extremely hard work from her day servant, though the two worked together, and she was treated as one of the family.[90] Her mother's intervention meant that she was removed from the job fairly swiftly. Working in a household where social or lifestyle differences were minimized could easily exacerbate rather

---

[86] Edward Higgs, 'Victorian Domestic Service', *Social History*, 8 (1983), 201–10.

[87] Jerry White, *Rothschild Buildings: Life in an East End Tenement Block, 1887–1920* (London: Routledge and Kegan Paul, 1980).

[88] Mr George Aberdou, Interview 165, in P. Thompson and H. Newby, *Families, Social Mobility and Ageing, an Intergenerational Approach, 1900–1988* [computer file], Colchester, Essex: UK Data Archive [distributor], July 2005, SN: 4938.

[89] Mrs Dora Bucknell (b. 1894, Hull), Interview 191, *Edwardians*.

[90] Jamieson, 'Rural and Urban Women in Domestic Service', 139.

than reduce antagonism between servant and employers. Mrs Macafferty worked as a general servant in rural Wales from 1917 to 1924, for farmers and later for a family running a post office. She felt that they were identical socially, despite her own background of poverty and illegitimacy: 'they had just a little more than we did. They had, you know, just a bit more money to be able to do things with. But there was very little difference really.' Service had been her only job option, and she was motivated by her desire to help her mother financially. However, she hated the work, particularly where working-class employers were socially aspirant. The post office family 'wanted to get their children ahead'; she found them snobbish, refusing to trust her, and making her eat alone after they had finished. They claimed to give her the same food, 'but sometimes I knew they were having something better.' It may have been the economic depression that caused her to stay in the relative security of service: 'I cannot really say I liked anything about it. I just felt I had to stay there because it was a job.'[91] Similar backgrounds sometimes led to friendly coexistence, but for the socially aspiring, it could also lead to petty devices to create social distance between employer and servant.

In addition to these wider patterns of region, ethnicity, social class, and so on, it is also clear that individual preferences and circumstances altered the ways in which authority might be exercised. Single or widowed women, for example, often developed distinctive relationships with their servants. One young servant who worked for a spinster shopkeeper noted: 'Well—she was a maiden lady and she treated me like a—a child, in fact, I got a bit fed up with it. . . . She used to put me in a chair and wrap me up you know and make a fuss of me. I—I didn't have a lot to do there.'[92] Mrs Green, an Edwardian servant in Keighley, Yorkshire, felt that her unmarried mistress was a genuine friend, and they used to have breakfast together when she took it up to her bedroom, as well as taking picnics and daytrips together: 'She was just like, myself, you know.'[93]

Not only marital status but also age was extremely significant in determining authority practices. Those mistresses who were young themselves found it impossible to follow the advice of household manuals in regulating their servants. One Edwardian mistress described how she didn't try to give her servants guidance on their lives, 'because they were both older than me. They could have given me moral guidance, perhaps.' Her servants 'had the freedom of the house', they were addressed as 'Mrs', and she helped them with certain tasks ('if they would allow me').[94] Vivian Hughes, a professional widowed woman who preferred to live without servants between the wars, also found generational divides to be at the heart of her failed experiments with servant-keeping: 'my experience has been either that they are young and you have to look after their health and their morals; or that they are old, faithful, and blameless and at last boss you entirely. And it's so hard to

---

[91] Mrs Laura Macafferty (b.1904), Interview 210, *Edwardians*.
[92] Mrs Edith Annie Lockwood (b. 1887), Interview 129, *Edwardians*.
[93] Mrs Green, Interview 268, ibid.
[94] Mrs Stewart (b. 1889), Interview 177, ibid.

get rid of a saint.'[95] Generation divides and marital status were as important as social class in determining treatment and styles of domestic authority, though they have rarely gained historiographical attention.[96]

MEN, MASCULINITY, AND SERVICE

Gender, of course, also needs to be added to the analysis, and it was not only mistresses who encountered dilemmas in the exercise of domestic authority. Male authority in the home had its own problems, though much less is known about how male employers interacted with their servants, since it stimulated less social commentary. One commentator noted the 'peculiar thraldom [to servants]' felt by men normally used to public command; official authority did not easily translate into domestic authority, and clearly, men used to public roles of authority might feel daunted by their own housemaids and cooks.[97] Men who involved themselves in the management of servants, however, were often mocked as lacking authority and virility. *The Daily Express* mocked a husband's efforts to improve the cooking of their char, Mrs Yoxall, 'a hard-breathing and defiant woman,' in a 1928 sketch. The husband makes a complaint-joke about an inedible pie to Mrs Yoxall, but her failure to see the joke leads to her resignation. Lacking the authority to give clear directions, failed jokes epitomized the frequently edgy relationship between master and servant.[98] R. C. Sherriff's *Greengates*, excerpted in *Good Housekeeping* in 1935, focused on a main character, Mr Baldwin. As a newly retired insurance clerk, Baldwin attempted but failed to exert his authority over Ada, his residential general servant. After provoking an angry outburst from Ada by trying to borrow her broom,

He saw clearly now that he should have gone to the dining-room, spoken first to Edith (wife) and ordered the broom to be sent up to him. By coming into the kitchen he had placed himself on a level with a tradesman's boy: Ada was playing on her own ground: even his costume was too shabby and ridiculous for a show of dignity. But he knew that he could not draw back now... 'I ought to give you notice for this Ada.'

However, his attempt to remind Ada of his status as an employer fails, as she responds, 'I take my notice from the mistress.'[99] The clumsy authority of a master epitomized the decline associated with retirement, though it is possible that the editors of *Good Housekeeping* thought its mostly female readership might simply find Baldwin comic.

---

[95] M. Vivian Hughes, *A London Family between the Wars* (Oxford: Oxford University Press, 1940), 58–9.
[96] For an exception to this, see Katherine Holden, *The Shadow of Marriage: Singleness in England, 1914–60* (Manchester: Manchester University Press, 2007).
[97] Mother, *At Home*.
[98] 'I Speak to Mrs Yoxall', *Daily Express*, Apr 3, 1928, 10.
[99] R. C. Sherriff, 'Greengates', *Good Housekeeping*, Nov 1935, 20, 164.

Though they were more likely to hire and pay the predominantly male outdoor servants, few masters were actively involved in the hiring and management of indoor servants. As one male Edwardian journalist commented, 'Being a man, I am supposed to rule all this [the household], but, fortunately, not to govern it.'[100] Others assumed that men would have few difficulties with servants because they could straightforwardly express their displeasure and then move on from it, in a way unavailable to women. Men might 'give a volley of abuse [to servants], seasoned with a full-flavoured oath or two, and then have done. But some women are at it all day long, with a persistency of ill-temper and an activity of perception simply amazing!'[101] Servants were felt to respond differently to men: 'The master may speak sharply, give unreasonable orders, unnecessary trouble,—on the whole, as from him, it is not resented; but let the mistress do the same, or less, and at once there will be trouble.'[102] It was a cultural stereotype that servants found female authority more rankling than the male equivalent. One interwar maid commented: 'I can't say I wasn't happy there, because though she was a bit school teacher, you know, she would just tick me off sometimes, but the farmer was very nice, you know, he used to make jokes with me.'[103] Edith Baxter enjoyed her relationship with a male employer: 'oh he was a lovely person. Golly, I think if he'd have said "scrub my feet" we'd have done them for him. He was so gentlemanly.'[104]

The easy authority that servants attributed to male employers may have been largely a result of male lack of involvement with the running of the household. However, as John Tosh's work has suggested, Victorian men were in fact intimately committed to their domestic roles, and this sometimes extended to active involvement in managing servants. Tosh suggests that this was less true of middle-class men in the early twentieth century, as they began to find Victorian styles of domesticity increasingly stifling, and preferred the real or fantasy realm of hyper-masculinity.[105] Nonetheless, men did continue to get involved sporadically in some domestic affairs. Edith Baxter, who had worked as a housemaid at the Foreign Office between 1918 and 1923, recalled that 'Lord Curzon used to run his hands over the banisters to check whether they were dusty.'[106] However, this was a rare and faintly comic mention of the domestic role of a male employer, and perhaps was only made possible by the absence of a mistress figure within this institutional setting. Another housemaid, Edith Hanran, found that her employer during World War I, a Scottish Major, simply adopted the same mode of interaction with her that he used with his troops:

I didn't get on well with him because he thought I was one of the troops. He used to shout along the passage 'Dowd.' I said 'did you call me?' . . . he'd just yell at me as if I was one

---

[100] W. L. George, 'The Downfall of the Home', *Harper's Magazine*, June 1916, 49–58, esp. 50.
[101] Linton, 'Mistresses and Maids', 102.
[102] E. Reid-Matheson, 'The Domestic Problem', *The Queen*, Jan 1, 1910.
[103] Clifford, Westminster, *Upstairs Downstairs*.
[104] Edith Maude Baxter, ibid.
[105] John Tosh, *A Man's Place: Masculinity and the Middle-Class Home in Victorian England* (New Haven, CT/London: Yale University Press, 1999).
[106] Baxter, Westminster, *Upstairs Downstairs*.

of the soldiers.... I used to look at him and said—er—'course I couldn't be too rude you see because—er—I had learnt me manners—and I—I used to look at him and I said 'are you speaking to me Sir?'... I weren't scared of his ways so it did no good to shout at me.[107]

Hanran's sense of her own civility and manners provided a means to resist and quietly mock the aggressive and ineffectual authority of her employer.

The relationships between military officers and their servants were one of the few realms in which masters adopted more direct responsibility for managing their servants, and in which male servants took on the tasks female servants normally undertook, of emptying slops, cooking, making beds, and so on. Michael Roper characterizes the relationship between officers and batmen as familial. He stresses the grumbling and teasing accompanied by loyalty, which created intimacies that came to resemble the relationship between sons and mothers. He stresses the dangers of front-line service that shaped the relationship as much as the norms of domestic service. However, the batmen were not entirely insulated from the fears of civilian male servants that their gender identities were compromised by their work. One World War I batman commented that 'somehow I felt less than a complete soldier'; another noted the laughter of officers at their servants: 'a batman himself is a subject for joking, when you come to think of it, although he may not always see the point of the jest.'[108]

The gendered tensions of the servant problem were even more visible when mistresses attempted to exert authority over male servants. Male servants unsettled their late-Victorian and Edwardian employers of both sexes; Max Beerbohm captured their sinister sense of threat in his comic portrayal of male servants:

I have seen a butler in a well-established household strolling around the diners without the slightest droop, and pouring out wine in an off-hand and quite obviously hostile manner. I have seen him, towards the end of the meal, yawning. I remember another whom, positively, I heard humming—a faint sound indeed, but menacing as the roll of tumbrils.[109]

The problem was particularly acute for single mistresses. One household manual delicately advised, 'Widows and maiden ladies find, as a rule, that men servants do not maintain that character for steadiness of conduct and sobriety when there is not a master to be appealed to.'[110] Mrs J. E. Panton advised householders in 1896 to obtain their menservants from old soldiers' associations. A mistress could then make a complaint to their headquarters, with the sanction of loss of pension rights, if they turned out to drink. This was argued to be a much more effective method of dealing with them than the 'talking to' that a mistress might give to the 'ordinary

---

[107] Mrs Edith Hanran (b. 1894), Interview 53, *Edwardians*.
[108] Sources quoted in Michael Roper, *The Secret Battle: Emotional Survival in the Great War* (Manchester: Manchester University Press, 2009), 140, 42. Roper concludes that domestic service as experienced by the children of employers provided the emotional template for the subsequent relationship between officers and their men during World War I (178).
[109] Max Beerbohm, *Servants* (1918).
[110] A Member of the Aristocracy, *The Management of Servants: A Practical Guide to the Routine of Domestic Service* (London: Frederick Warne, 1880), 8.

man-servant'.[111] Alternatively, hiring boys, the disabled, or those of non-English ethnicity might make paternalistic authority over men more sustainable. One upper-middle-class Edwardian household employed a one-armed man who 'cleaned the knives, stoked the boiler, washed the long, flagged passage, cleaned the boots, pumped up the bicycle tyres and caddied for golfers on weekends.' Two decades later, Vivian Hughes recalled her neighbours in Middlesex similarly using a male servant in an ad hoc way:

The Harts had a very efficient servant. During the [First World] war they had befriended a Russian refugee, and now he was acting as a kind of batman, doing any odd job—gardening, woodcutting, whitewashing—and was a perfectly reliable nurse for a few hours. He had few English words, and we loved to hear him addressing the Newfoundland dog thus: 'Kom, kom, mine little hund,' with no effect on the dog. We never knew his name, and called him 'Pardon,' because he always prefaced any remark with this word.[112]

Again there was little compassion shown to the discomfort such refugees had suffered. Internal migrants to England might similarly be regarded as easy to 'manage'. When the government opened a series of domestic service training centres in the 1920s and 1930s, it was only in Wales that they aimed this training at young men, in the belief that Welsh boys had a 'natural aptitude' for work as houseboys and kitchen assistants. Despite the problem of sustaining authority over indoor male servants, their numbers rose temporarily during the Depression.[113]

Male outdoor servants such as chauffeurs and coachman had sources of authority through their mechanical knowledge, and the power to disrupt schedules by 'finding a horse must be shod or a battery charged'.[114] The protagonist of the satirical novel *Diary of a Provincial Lady* noted, 'I don't know if I could bear to launch out into men-servants. For all the time we've had a gardener I've never so much as given him an order, and I'm not a bit at home with the chauffeur.'[115] *The Queen* magazine warned interwar readers that male servants could not be asked to do too much work, as they were more likely than their female equivalents to quit.[116] The decline of employment of men in service outside of the great houses was frequently accounted for by these problems of the exercise of authority by women, and few came up with any workable solutions. Men in service in the interwar years remained figures of fun, or occasionally, as Chapter 5 argues, erotically charged. Employers wavered between responses of laughter, fascination, and anxiety to the disconcerting presence of a 'domestic man'.

---

[111] J. E. Panton, *A Gentlewoman's Home* (London: Gentlewoman Offices, 1896), 410, 11.
[112] Peggy Hamilton, *Three Years or the Duration: The Memoirs of a Munition Worker, 1914–1918* (Wellington: Reed, 1978), 19; Hughes, *A London Family between the Wars*, 14.
[113] Pamela Horn, *The Rise and Fall of the Victorian Servant* (Gloucs: Alan Sutton, 1990), 193. Horn, *Life below Stairs*, 112–13; Ray Strachey, *The Cause: A Short History of the Women's Movement in Great Britain* (London: Virago, 1928), 170.
[114] Winifred Peck, *Home for the Holidays* (London: Faber and Faber, 1955), 201.
[115] E. M. Delafield, *Diary of a Provincial Lady* (London: Folio Society, 1979).
[116] 'Employing a Man Servant', *The Queen*, Apr 5, 1933, 47.

LEGAL CONSTRAINTS, PHILANTHROPY, AND SERVANTS IN COMBINATION

Where scripts and devices within the home failed, it was sometimes necessary to exert or resist authority by resorting to the law. This did not always mean going to the courts; simply knowing the terms of the law was a resource in itself and allowed for the construction of authority. One employer writing in *The Queen* admitted that she had suffered from 'fear of one's servants'. However, 'an old friend initiated me into the laws regulating the terms between master and servant. Since then the most fiery of insolent cooks terrifies me no longer. On the contrary, I find a few calm words soon reduce the bully—and then I can afford to be magnanimous.'[117]

This employer understood the law as operating mainly in her favour. Legally, mistresses could dismiss servants without wages or notice for 'reasonable causes' including drunkenness, immorality, insubordination, and theft. Mistresses also had the right to search the room or personal box of their servants if they suspected theft. In situations of conflict, servants could not defend themselves to their mistresses without grave consequences, since insubordination and 'defiance to proper orders' were legitimate legal grounds for instant dismissal. This left servants with few legal powers to match their employers. Servants could only leave employment without notice if they had 'reasonable cause to fear violence to the person or disease', and this was hard to prove.[118] One female servant sued her mistress for her wages at Shoreditch County Court in 1913, after she was fired for 'answering saucily' and 'slapping things all over the place'.[119] She lost her case, however; the evidence was simply her word against her mistress, and servants could rarely prove unfair dismissal.

Furthermore, since servants could not compel mistresses to give a written character, they could not gain a public hearing for their disputes through accusing their employer of libel. Mrs Gray from Middlesborough wrote vividly of the frustration felt by servants and their families at their marginalization from the legal system in a letter to E. P. Harries, the secretary of the Trades Union Congress's Organization Department, and a force behind the 1938 Domestic Worker's Union (DWU). Mrs Gray had been trying to defend her daughter's right to get a month's pay after being given notice abruptly.

I don't think its right that she [her daughter's employer] can go to her solicitor and say unjust or untrue things and knowing she is at fault and I because I'm poor must submit to her lying accusations about me I have not talked about her to no one except my husband do you think I should write and advise her to take proceedings against me so I can get my side

---

[117] California, *The Queen*, Aug 21, 1915, 370.
[118] *Mistress and Maid: The Legal Position of Domestic Refugees and Their Employers*, issued by the Domestic Bureau, Central Office For Refugees, April 1940, MRC 292/54.76/8.
[119] '"Saucy" Servant', *The Domestic Servants' Advertiser*, May 20, 1913, 12.

of the story told as I resent the accusations strongly as I cannot afford to take a summons out and pay for a solicitor as my husband is unemployed [sic].[120]

What is at issue here is clearly not simply a problem of money, but also the importance of social reputation. Servants felt that they had very few legal resources to defend their good names, on which future employment and personal dignity depended. Harries himself had announced in a 1938 Caxton Hall meeting during the founding campaign of the DWU: 'the need for legal assistance and protection is the most outstanding one so far as this industry is concerned.'[121] However, he was not able to offer Mrs Gray any assistance, simply advising her to consult a lawyer. Servants regarded the law as a tool mainly operating against them, or found it very opaque. One wrote to another trades union organizer in 1947 describing her mistress's rule of excluding her from the house on the servant's day off: 'one of these days, at your leisure, I would really like to know if this is a law—as after all, we go into service to make it our home.'[122]

Some employers also strayed into illegal behaviour in asserting their authority, using physical force against their servants. Much of the evidence for this was anecdotal, but occasional cases of ill-treatment of servants or forcible detention in a home were brought to court. Servants told of being beaten with sticks, kicked and knocked around, and denied the right to leave even when they had handed in their notice. While employers were sometimes convicted for such behaviour, it seems likely that servants had few resources to contest it.

The law did offer servants some resistance to the transgression of their own spaces in the house of their employer. If their box or trunk was opened against their wishes and no theft was proved, they had the right to sue their employer for trespass. Social convention also gave them some protection from instant dismissal; household manuals advised mistresses to pay wages in lieu of notice, rather than dismiss an unsatisfactory servant. Resorting to outright dismissal was regarded as legally risky, since if a servant mounted a challenge, it could be hard to prove the servant's offence at a later date in court. The law was clearly, however, an important shaping factor in the relationship and a resource for the authority of employers, judging by the detailed instructions given in texts advising mistresses as to what legally governed the relationship.

Most servants were well aware that the solution to the servant problem required a recasting of the balance of authority within the home and as interpreted in the courts. The more articulate amongst them frequently argued for combination in trades unions in order to impose standards of pay and hours. Many employers preferred more paternalistic models of cross-class federation and friendship, such as the societies run by privileged servant-keeping women with the aim of aiding servants—the Wayfarer's Guild, the Metropolitan Association for Befriending

---

[120] Mrs Gray, Feb 5, 1938, to Harries, MRC 292/54.76/5.
[121] MRC MSS eph/ew/1621.
[122] Alice M. Pannell, to Beatrice Bezzant, 1947, MRC 292/54.76/8.

Young Servants, the Girls Friendly Society, and so on.[123] While such organizations might provide Sunday leisure facilities, training programmes, and social events, they rarely addressed the real complaints of servants in matters of freedom, pay, and conditions. One commentator noted in 1903 that 'The very societies which aim at the improvement of the conditions of service follow methods unacceptable to nine-tenths of those whom they desire to serve.'[124]

Nonetheless, such bodies proliferated throughout the early to mid-twentieth century. The League of Skilled Housework, for example, was founded by the Girls Friendly Society in 1922. Other organizations were locally based, such as the Domestic Alliance in Surrey, or the Association of Employers of Domestic Workers in interwar Birmingham. This latter aimed to dignify 'housework by putting it on the same level as other skilled labour' and 'to provide an organised body of housewives whose opinion will bear weight with public bodies on domestic matters.'[125] Most such organizations proposed voluntary charters, setting out ideal conditions and duties. They envisaged cooperation across traditional divides of employer–employee, and saw the interwar home as a realm of intimacy and affection between mistress and maid. This intimacy, they argued, was intensified by a shared gender identity and class-crossing domestic skills, and was a realm into which labour politics could not intrude. Servants, however, recognized the impractical nature of the adoption of charters, and the tendency to offer window-dressing solutions of badge-wearing, rather than higher pay or shorter hours.

Domestic servants' unions that were autonomous of employers were founded in various localities in the nineteenth and twentieth centuries, including the Domestic Workers Union of Great Britain founded in 1910, and the Irish Domestic Worker's Union founded in 1918 as a subsection of the Irish Women's Worker's Union.[126] Such unions were rarely successful for very long. Their failure led to a continuing unease within the labour movement at the exclusion of servants from the protections that combination could offer. The circulation of a 1929 Labour Party document, 'What's Wrong with Domestic Service?', led to increased visibility for the problems of domestic workers, and more pressure for some kind of trades union action on their behalf. This document led to a Charter for Domestic Workers, endorsed by the 1931 Labour Women's Party Conference, but no further action in the short term. The major unions found private indoor female servants

---

[123] Brian Harrison, 'For Church, Queen and Family: The Girls' Friendly Society, 1874–1920', *Past and Present*, 61 (1973), 107–38; Horn, *Life below Stairs*, 102–3. On the Wayfarer's Guild, see MRC 292/54.76/1. A summary of the MABYS position was made by M. H. L. Bunting, 'Mistress and Maid', *Contemporary Review*, May 1910.
[124] D. C. Pedder, 'Service and Farm-Service', *Contemporary Review*, Feb 1903, 270.
[125] Unlike many of the other employers committees and schemes, the Birmingham experiment gave specific directions on hours, pay, holidays, naming ('maids to be allowed to choose by what name they shall be called'), and uniforms, and both mistresses and maids were allowed to join a branch of the Workers' Union. MRC 292/54.76/4.
[126] Unions of domestic workers were formed in Dundee and Leamington in 1872, in London in 1891, and Glasgow in 1910. Also in 1910, a general union called the Domestic Workers Union of Great Britain was formed with Grace Neal as its secretary, and while this was fairly short lived, it was revived again under Jessie Stephen in 1926. On the Irish Domestic Worker's Union, see Dora Mellone, *Common Cause*, July 25, 1919.

unappealing as members. Ernest Bevin of the Transport and General Union declared in 1931 that he was not interested in domestic servants in private employment, and would only seek the mostly male gardeners, chauffeurs, and domestic servants employed in public institutions as members; the General and Municipal Workers Union concurred. Local union organizers were able to be more creative in attempting to reach female indoor servants, but there was little support for this at higher levels.[127] In 1932, Dorothy Elliott, National Woman Officer of the General and Municipal Workers Union, set up the Hampstead Domestic Workers' Guild, offering dancing, theatre, table tennis, and a space to bring their young men. She reported in 1933, 'at the present stage they seem very little interested in politics and much more in practical industrial matters which affect their everyday interests.'[128]

The servant problem took on new interest for the labour movement through the influx of foreign maids into Britain in the 1930s, estimated to be around 13,500 in 1938, of whom around 60 per cent were German and Austrian.[129] These foreign maids not only caused anxiety for British workers who feared their competition, but also brought with them experience of union organization amongst domestic servants. One settlement worker in 1936 wrote to the Trades Union Congress (TUC), noting that the Austrian maids she worked with were 'very anxious to re-erect an organisation of their own in this country', having been members of an Austrian domestic workers union.[130] An attempt was indeed made to initiate and sponsor a DWU in 1938, but foreign servants were excluded from membership. There was deep anti-Semitic and anti-alien feeling in Britain at this historical moment, and a widespread perception of the domestic service labour market as being flooded by foreign workers. Members of Parliament testified to the 'considerable feeling about this matter', and in the mid-1930s, some proposed that the tax on male servants of British citizenship might be lifted, while foreign servants of both sexes might be taxed instead.[131] Controls on the numbers of foreign servants had been imposed by the Ministry of Labour in 1931, but were relaxed in 1935 to allow increasing numbers of Austrians and some Germans to enter Britain on domestic service permits. The DWU capitalized on the foreign maids controversy, seeing it as a means of uniting the private domestic workers who had always been seen as fragmented, non-political, and transient. Despite the intensifying European refugee crisis, the union immediately spoke out against the practice of offering domestic service permits to foreign refugees. Its origins were therefore as much a result of fear

---

[127] Bevin to Harries, Dec 2, 1931; Thorne from the Women's Dept of GMW to Citrine, Dec 22, 1931.
[128] Elliott, Dec 13, 1933, MRC MSS. 292/54.76/4.
[129] Diane Aiken, *The Central Committee on Women's Training and Employment: Tackling the Servant Problem, 1914–1945* (Oxford: Oxford Brookes University, 2002); *Hansard*, HC Deb, May 9, 1938, vol 335, cc 1250-1.
[130] R. Gessner of the Toynbee Hall Universities' settlement to Walter Citrine, General Secretary of the TUC, Feb 14, 1936, MRC 292/54.76/4.
[131] Sir Arthur Samuel and Major Mills, *Hansard*, HC Deb, Feb 1, 1934, vol. 285, c. 540.

of foreign competition as of the activist traditions that foreign workers brought to Britain.

The DWU was a unique experiment in the TUC's history, the first time that a union had been actively created in a top-down fashion. The DWU was also unique in seeing itself as 'the first union of workers in a completely non-competitive occupation'. Any suggestion of antagonism between mistress and maid was avoided; one union canvasser noted reassuringly: 'the Union by no means represent a line-up against the mistress as a class.'[132] The TUC organizer E. P. Harries saw the union as aiming not for higher pay, but 'to raise the status of the industry by securing increased leisure, freedom for social contracts, formation of social clubs, legal assistance, and probably the development of a Friendly Benefit side.' The DWU also requested a public system of character giving whereby servants could give their employers a reference, to match that written about the servant.[133]

Initially, membership was strong enough to merit sixteen branches in the greater London area, and three in the provinces. The membership, however, peaked at 1,057 in 1938, and was already dropping by 1939, as the war gave other employment opportunities and curtailed the supply of foreign maids. There was still only a weak commitment from the labour movement to organizing domestic workers, who did not match the image of the predominantly male unionized worker. E. P. Harries commented to the TUC General Secretary in 1939, 'frankly I am disappointed with the new union.' He blamed a set of stereotypically feminine traits: 'the development of cliques, personal quarrels and the very poor standard of intelligence generally with domestic workers.'[134] Without much support from the TUC, and with an annual deficit of nearly £300, the union merged with the TUC Women's Department in 1941, and became little more than a monthly newsletter with a few hundred members. Though correspondence from servants to the TUC continued to demand a union into the late 1940s, there was never again such an ambitious attempt to organize servants. The union continued to exist and sporadic local branches were formed into the 1950s. However, the piecemeal and half-hearted attempts to organize domestic workers over the twentieth century were stymied by the unwillingness to listen to the concerns of servants. Despite the many older women working in service, and the presence of European workers with strong traditions of labour organization, labour leaders still saw the servant as a hedonistic young British girl, transiently employed, and unsuitable for organization. It was not until the grassroots and feminist campaigns around night cleaners of offices in the 1960s and 1970s that more sustained efforts were made, though as in earlier disputes, the larger unions were faulted for their lack of interest in these predominantly female, unskilled workers. The non-domestic setting for these campaigns

---

[132] Celia Fremlin, *The Seven Chars of Chelsea* (London: Methuen, 1940), 163, 73.
[133] Notes on organizations of mistresses, from E. P. Harries to Walter Citrine, June 28, 1938, MRC, 292/54.76/1; *Daily Herald*, Dec 13, 1938.
[134] Harries to Citrine, 1939, MRC MSS. 292/54.76/6.

against contractors, however, made them quite different from the earlier efforts to organize workers in individual houses.[135]

Trade unionism held little promise for domestic workers, and servants tended to resist the depredations of their employers and the unbounded nature of the tasks of service by informal means. Leonore Davidoff has written of the practices of resistance and mockery adopted by servants—spoiling food, serving meals late, feigning not to understand orders, working slowly or sulkily. Peter Bailey noted the uses servants made of noise—'offstage laughter and slammed doors'—to impinge on the privacy of the social spaces of employers.[136] An Edwardian journalist described how a servant might rule her mistress 'with a combination of obstinate humility and rampant remonstrances,' though Alison Light's account of Virginia Woolf's servant Nellie Bloxall's repeated threats to resign reminds us of the relatively few options that servants had to exert agency with respect to their mistresses.[137] Though servants were structurally vulnerable, mistresses believed that maids had formidable experience in such battles, through their knowledge of the practices of different households. It was a commonplace that 'many mistresses are daunted by their maids.' For Ursula Bloom, as for many twentieth-century mistresses her servants 'scared me stiff; and I had no idea how to manage them; in fact, they managed me.'[138]

Servants commonly exercised authority tacitly, often through their intimate knowledge of the household. Employers were acutely aware of the risks the intimate knowledge servants had of their domestic affairs posed to their authority and social standing. One Edwardian servant who worked for an unhappily married couple commented that the servants were 'supposed to go about with our eyes and ears shut, we weren't supposed to see anything, that's it. . . . I think that's why they wouldn't allow you to have friends you see. Because it would be talked about in the village.'[139] Another commentator wrote of how the squabbling married couple might be 'restrained in their outbursts by the maid, who stands in front of the sideboard and who watches her employers as a cat watches mice.'[140]

Those servants who worked in houses with more than one or two servants became authority figures over other servants. Jean Rennie wrote of her promotion to a cook: 'in fourteen years I had come to full authority.' Yet she did not find this easy to exercise: 'I had not yet learned to command. At least, I had never had to command anybody who didn't know their job. I tried to treat [the kitchenmaid] Katie kindly and show her the right way, but I didn't learn for many years

---

[135] May Hobbs, *Born to Struggle* (London: Quartet Books, 1973); Shelia Rowbotham, 'Cleaners' Organizing in Britain from the 1970s: A Personal Account', *Antipode*, 38 3 (2002), 608–25.
[136] Peter Bailey, *Popular Culture and Performance in the Victorian City* (Cambridge: Cambridge University Press, 1998), 211; Davidoff, *Worlds between*.
[137] N. Murrell Marris, 'Servant London', in George Sims, *Living London* (London: Cassell, 1901), 351, part 23, 55–6.
[138] Pedder, 'Service and Farm-Service', 270; Ursula Bloom, *Mrs Bunthorpe's Respects: A Chronicle of Cooks* (London: Hutchinson, 1963), 78.
[139] Mrs Edith Annie Lockwood (b. 1887), Interview 129, *Edwardians*.
[140] Mrs J. G. Frazer, *First Aid to the Servantless* (Cambridge: Heffers, 1913), 2.

afterwards that that was a mistake. And Katie didn't want to learn anyway.'[141] Another cook, Margaret Powell, argued that the reason why cooks were always referred to as 'Mrs' was to give them a modicum of authority over other servants. 'A Butler' wrote in 1892 of the trouble 'higher' servants had in establishing their authority. Many butlers and housekeepers

> possess neither the strength of character nor the tact required to rule others, for they have never learned to rule themselves. They manage by such extraneous aids as assuming the title of 'Mr' and 'Mrs' and retiring to the sacred precincts of the 'room' to procure a little show of respect, which most often veils the heartfelt contempt of their subordinates.

Rosina Harrison perceived this as a gendered phenomenon in 'great house' service, and found it easier to accept the routines and hierarchies of service 'when there were menservants and the butler was in charge.'[142]

For servants as well as employers, the organization of physical space was key to the establishment of authority. Some higher servants had access to domestic spaces where they could resist the intrusion of employers—the cook's authority in the kitchen was such that mistresses would knock and ask permission to enter. The kitchen or servants' rooms might become impenetrable for employers. One mistress commented, 'It requires a very strong sense of duty to make one go where one is so palpably unwelcome, where one's most innocent looks are construed into a mean peeping and prying and the least remonstrance is met by insolence.'[143] As Chapter 4 shows, kitchens were often the location of send-ups and impersonations, made possible by servants' ability to establish spaces of privacy within the homes of their employers.

CHILDREN

Children were often unusually mobile across the spatial boundaries of the household, and might be found in the attics, kitchens, or basements that servants inhabited. Their presence added substantially to the physical hard work undertaken by servants; it was not just nursemaids and nannies who might be expected to wash their clothes and nappies and clean up after them, but also general servants and chars, and this inevitably shaped the relationships established between them. Children problematized authority relationships within servant-keeping households, since it was not clear whether the authority of age could be exerted over the authority of employer status. This was particularly acute for children on the cusp of adulthood. Servants had some level of authority over young children, but their status vis-à-vis older children was often uncertain and difficult to manage. Dora

---

[141] Rennie, *Every Other Sunday*, 219, 160.
[142] 'A Butler's View of Men-Service', *The Nineteenth Century* June 1892, 931; Rosina Harrison, *Rose: My Life in Service* (London: Cassell, 1975), 22.
[143] Caddy, *Household Organization*.

Holtom described an encounter with an aristocratic 11-year-old, while she was his nanny in the 1930s. The child demanded:

'Who said I've got to go and wash now? Why should I?' I said, 'because you don't go to the table in that condition, you know that.' So he said, 'Who do you think you're talking to?' He'd just begun to realise who he was. Must have been listening to conversation. 'One day I'm going to be Lord Allendale, and then nobody will tell me whether to wash or not.' I said, 'all the same, right now, I'm telling you or asking you to go and wash yourself and be back here as soon as you can, please?'

Her equivocation between 'telling' and 'asking' is revealing of her inability to exert her authority in such a situation.[144]

The emotional and social norms governing parent–child relationships had long supplied the script for the interactions of employers and servants, though in practice, styles of parenting were locally and individually specific.[145] However, if employers treated their servants as their 'foster-children', the presence of their actual children necessarily disrupted such models and left the status of the servant uncertain. Most advisers on the home agreed that children must show servants respect, but also that servants must still respect the higher social station of the children of their employers. This made it extremely difficult to impose servants' decisions on their charges. They were warned by mistresses and household manuals not to frighten children into obedience using stories of the supernatural—this was clearly one means by which children might be manipulated in the absence of other forms of authority.[146] Household manuals were concerned to establish the social superiority of children of employers, partly through requiring servants to use formal titles when addressing children. Parents often displayed tolerance or amusement over children's misbehaviour, which made it impossible for servants to sustain their authority over children; the rudeness of children towards servants was a repeated complaint.[147]

Love and intimacy did exist between servants and children, but it was inevitably shot through with awareness of social chasm, and the ephemerality of the relationship. Some child-carers did feel a lasting attachment, and continued to stay in touch with their charges after they had moved on. However, servants had to set boundaries on the love they felt for the children they cared for, though their employers were often insensitive to this. Dora Holtom, who'd deeply loved the child she'd raised for five years, remembered that:

---

[144] Holtom, Westminster, *Upstairs Downstairs*.
[145] C. Fairchilds, *Domestic Enemies: Servants and Their Masters in Old Regime France* (Baltimore: Johns Hopkins University Press, 1984). Eleanor Gordon and Gwyneth Nair's study of the nineteenth-century Glasgow middle classes also stresses a spectrum of motherly behaviour: 'what it meant to be a mother differed according to material circumstances and culture of the middle-class woman as well as the stage of the family cycle' (*Public Lives: Women, Family and Society in Victorian Britain* (New Haven, CT/London: Yale University Press, 2003), 63).
[146] Praga, *How to Keep House on £200 a Year*, 139.
[147] Beatrice Bezzant, 'What's Wrong with Domestic Service?', *The Labour Woman*, July 1938, 105.

Once in the garden the child said 'Nanny will be with us forever and ever and ever, won't she Mummy?' So her mother said, 'yes of course.' I said, 'now wait a minute.... forever and ever and ever only happens in fairy stories darling, it doesn't always happen in real life.' So I had to say something.[148]

Dora struggled to name and set boundaries on her emotional commitment to her employers and their children, and found it corrosive of her own life choices. Despite the love she felt, Dora never returned to visit the family after quitting their employment, preferring to sever her links and return home to care for her own mother.

The children of servant-keeping households fantasized about the unconditional love servants might supply. Violet Markham (1872–1959) nostalgically recalled that 'As we grew older and many dreams had faded in the light of common day, what warmth it was to be gathered to the heart of one of those faithful souls whose eyes were olden to all our faults and who dowered us with virtues and merits which existed alone in their imagination.'[149] Beatrice Webb (1858–1943) similarly recalled feeling gratitude and warmth towards the servants of her childhood, though unlike many others, she was aware of the cost to servants of their emotional commitment to their employing family. She noted of her beloved nurse Martha, 'In middle life, weary perhaps of continuously giving and never receiving solicitous affection, she got married.'[150] The marriage, however, was unhappy, and Martha's apparent desire for autonomy from the emotional burdens of the employing household was not achieved, since her husband became the family's butler.

Many upper- and upper-middle-class children recalled feeling stronger emotional attachments to their nannies or nurses than their mothers. Robert Graves, for example, commented that his nanny 'meant more to us than our mother'. However, such love was often ephemeral and quickly abandoned when the norms of social hierarchy became clearer to older children. Graves went on: 'I did not despise her [Nanny] until about the age of twelve... when I found that my education now exceeded hers, and that if I struggled with her I could trip her up and bruise her quite easily. Besides, she went to a Baptist chapel.'[151] As Michael Roper has noted, middle-class children might suffer split subjectivities as a result of their dual attachment to the domains of servants and employers. The love of servants was rarely unconditional, and children needed to make themselves lovable in their desire to sustain the care and attention of servants. Yet children also recognized their privileged place within the hierarchies of subservience and superiority that inflected domestic service.[152] Webb commented that being brought up in a late-Victorian servant-keeping household gave her 'consicousness of superior power. As life unfolded I became aware that I belonged to a class of persons who habitually

---

[148] Holtom, Westminster, *Upstairs Downstairs*.
[149] Violet Markham, *Return Passage* (Oxford: Oxford University Press, 1953), 36.
[150] Beatrice Webb, *My Life* (1926), 17, quoted in K. Muggeridge, *Beatrice Webb: A Life* (London: Secker and Warburg, 1967), 37.
[151] Graves, *Goodbye to All That*, 20.
[152] Roper, *The Secret Battle*, 170–3.

gave orders, but who seldom, if ever, executed the orders of other people. My mother sat in her boudoir and gave orders—orders that brooked neither delay nor evasion.' This sense of 'place' established in relation to servant-keeping was highly formative, and became recognized as potentially traumatic for children. Increasingly in the twentieth century, the easy authority of Webb's mother was compromised, and the relationships between children and servants were often judged to be morally and socially damaging. Mothers were warned not to delegate the care of their children to servants, nor to employ servants who had children themselves.[153] Strong fears of the influence of servants upon children continued to circulate, often constructed in terms of sexual and social 'contagion'. Children and servants had to negotiate the dangerous erotic charge of service, as the young teenager Sonia Keppel recorded in her account of her relationship with Mr Rolfe, her family's butler. While evacuated to the countryside during World War I, the upper-class Sonia wrote letters 'invariably beginning: "Darling Mr Rolfe" and ending "Your loving Sonia"'. Aware of the unsuitability of this, Rolfe answered her: 'You are getting a big girl now, and you must call me Rolfe. And you must stop signing yourself "Your loving Sonia". It does not do. Yours respectfully, W. Rolfe.' 'He put me in my place,' she concluded.[154]

CONCLUSIONS

Within this very broad sector, there was little consensus on how servants should be treated and how mistresshood was to be understood in the first half of the twentieth century. Divides of region, occupational group, age, ethnicity, and marital status continued to make servant-keeping extraordinarily diverse. The law, philanthropic projects, and the labour movement proved incapable or unwilling to impose uniform conditions. Many servants continued to be treated paternalistically, or were subject to high levels of surveillance, though there were households in which more informal relationships were sustained. Diverse authority strategies were adopted by mistresses in response to criticisms, and in attempts to make sustainable the increasingly strained relationships of domestic service.

This diversity of practices led to a sense of chaotic flux in servant-keeping. The mapping of 'servant-keeping' or 'servantless' homes onto the domains of 'middle class' and 'working class' became precarious in interwar Britain, and there is little evidence of a consolidation of middle-class identity amongst servant-keeping women in this period. A contributor to *Good Housekeeping*, Constance Eaton, argued in 1930 that middle-class women were 'living in a period of transition... To-day the firmly constructed civilisation of the nineteenth century has fallen to

---

[153] Muggeridge, *Beatrice Webb* 37; 'Womanhood', *Good Housekeeping*, Oct 26, 1926; Ann Blyth, 'The Domestic Servant with a child', *The Queen*, Oct 7, 1931, 20.

[154] Sonia Keppel, *Edwardian Daughter* (London: Hamilton, 1958), 110. For a sensitive account of the interactions between children and the often single, mostly female individuals who cared for them, see Leonore Davidoff et al., *The Family Story: Blood, Contract and Intimacy, 1830–1960* (London: Longman, 1999), 221–43.

pieces, and the next era has not yet taken shape. Everything is in a state of flux and instability. There is no counting on anything as fixed and permanent. We are living in a kind of chaos.' Domestic service problems were, for Eaton, the 'most urgent' manifestation of this sense of chaos. Yet what is remarkable in her article and indeed throughout the early to mid-twentieth century is the deep sense of the lack of alternatives for servant-keeping women. Other forms of domestic organization were rarely taken seriously because to do so was to abandon core features of a self-identity of privilege, made up of demarcations of class, ethnicity, and spatial location. Though being a mistress attracted increasing social opprobrium, the authority to command and surveil remained integral to the social imaginary of servant-keeping. Middle-class women remained deeply committed to those public and professional roles that only servant-keeping could sustain, and this was not simply due to its practical contribution in freeing them from domestic responsibilities. It was also the symbolic capital and social authority gained through the establishment of a successfully benign yet distant relationship with servants.

For all the unpleasantness of employing servants, Constance Eaton concluded that 'there will always be human servants as long as the race survives.' Her faith in social hierarchy and class authority was unshaken: 'the human being whose nature it is to obey receives just as much pleasure from obeying and serving as the person born to command receives from giving orders. There is no getting away from the fact that those who serve will always be with us.'[155] This confidence extended into the late 1940s, and as the next chapter notes, into the wistful hopes and fantasies of women in later decades. 'Doing for oneself' was only very tentatively experimented with; fantasies of domestic assistance persisted far beyond its availability in the flesh.

---

[155] Eaton, 'The Gordian Knot of Domestic Service', 48, 49.

3

'Doing for Oneself'

The Servantless Home

Domestic service was a crucial reference point in the formation of twentieth-century social boundaries and identities in Britain. It transcended its domestic significance to affect public, psychic, and emotional life in many ways. The decline in numbers employed in domestic service over the period ironically brought this broad significance into sharper focus, as many who might have been accustomed to having servants during their childhood or early adulthood had to adjust to the condition of 'servantlessness'. This process generated a great deal of reflection and conflict over the significance of domestic service. Many men and women were extremely unwilling to relinquish the lifestyle and identity of being servant-keepers, though this was a dilemma that impacted upon women far more directly than upon men. Other employers, however, could see advantages to relinquishing servants and gaining a more private, intimate domestic setting.

This chapter investigates what one reformer termed 'the holes left by the departed Mary Ann'.[1] I explore how the absence of servants shaped discourses of home and social identity, both during periods when servants were readily available to middle-class householders and in periods when very few would employ a 'servant' as traditionally defined. It offers a study of transition, and suggests that the cultural and emotional work of domestic service, as well as its practical effects on the organization of domestic space, remained important even where servants themselves were not present. Many British homes continued to be organized around the haunting absence of servants well into the second half of the twentieth century. The process of investing new meanings into domestic spaces such as kitchens, sculleries, basements, and attic bedrooms was slow and emotionally laden. Ideas about 'modernity' and 'modern living' continued to be shaped by a discourse of transition towards a servantless state that was rarely understood as completed. Being a middle-class, privileged, educated, modern, or professional woman *and* servantless was not a state that was secure or taken for granted. Instead, it was repetitively assessed, and found to be problematic, across the twentieth century.

---

[1] Mrs M. A. Cloudesley Brereton, 'Domestic Service as a Career for Educated Women: How the Substitution of Gas for Coal Affects the Domestic Service Problem', *A Conference on the Economics of the Home* (London: National Gas Congress and Exhibition, 1913), 17.

'Doing for Oneself'

This suggests a revision of historical narratives concerning the housewife identity, often presented as a popular, class-crossing feminine identity of the mid-twentieth century. From the Edwardian period onwards, housework might be seen as a craft or profession, rather than dreary and dirty. It therefore became a potential component of middle-class femininity. The socialist feminist Clementina Black (1854–1922) declared after World War I that 'a great revival of interest in domestic principles and practices has arisen among educated women' especially the 'intelligent and active minded'.[2] The establishment of the housewife as an available and attractive identity, appealing to large numbers of British women from the 1920s to the 1950s, has been seen as contributing to new forms of domesticity and ideas of citizenship. It is also seen as reviving conservative gender norms that would anchor women in the home and eventually lead to feminism in the later twentieth century.[3] This has formed a dominant narrative of women's history. Judy Giles talks of the 'upgrading and revaluing of domestic work that took place particularly after the First World War.' She argues that between 1920 and 1950, the housewife role offered dignity and purpose to working-class women, who relished the material circumstances of greater affluence that went with it.[4] Historians of the post-war years have also described housework and the 'housewife' identity as gaining cross-class appeal in the 1940s and 1950s: 'working-class and middle-class women seem to have been equally exposed to post-war ideologies of domesticity and homemaking.'[5] In the mid-twentieth century housewifery and ideas of hygiene were powerfully linked to ideas of modernity and science, giving domestic work greater significance. It became an emotional expression of care, a contribution to individual *and* national physical welfare. These trends culminated in World War II, as housewifery became depicted as a crucial contribution to the war effort, and inspired fantasies of secure and comforting British homes.[6]

The success of the 'housewife' identity has been widely linked to the decline of domestic service. This chapter questions the extent to which middle-class women termed themselves 'housewives', and points to the continuing attraction that servant-keeping had, despite the diminishing appeal of the 'mistress' identity charted in the previous chapter. The focus here is on feminine identities, because to 'do for oneself' was a far more complex thing to imagine for a woman than

---

[2] Clementina Black, *A New Way of Housekeeping* (London: Collins, 1918), 5–6.
[3] See, for example, Elizabeth Darling, '"A Citizen as Well as a Housewife": New Spaces of Domesticity in 1930s London', in Hilde Heynen and Gulsum Baydar (eds), *Negotiating Domesticity: Spatial Productions of Gender in Modern Architecture* (London: Routledge, 2005), and Alison Light, *Forever England: Femininity, Literature and Conservatism between the Wars* (London: Routledge, 1991).
[4] Judy Giles, 'Good Housekeeping: Professionalising the Housewife, 1920–50', in Krista Cowman and Louise Jackson (eds), *Women and Work Culture: Britain c.1850–1950* (Aldershot: Ashgate, 2005), 70–86, esp. 73; Matthew Hilton, *Consumerism in Twentieth-Century Britain: The Search for a Historical Movement* (Cambridge: Cambridge University Press, 2003), 109; Claire Langhamer, 'The Meanings of Home in Postwar Britain', *Journal of Contemporary History*, 40 (2005), 341–62.
[5] N. Gregson and M. Lowe, *Servicing the Middle Classes: Class, Gender and Waged Domestic Labour in Contemporary Britain* (London: Routledge, 1994), 234.
[6] Evidence of the power of this identity during World War II is found in Ruby Grierson's 1940 propaganda film *They Also Serve* (Realist Film Unit).

a man. As Clementina Black acidly noted in 1918, men might lightly propose doing without servants, because they 'know nothing of the processes by which their households are kept going'.[7]

VARIETIES OF SERVANTLESS HOMES

To be servantless was a condition that might be attached to a variety of different circumstances across the twentieth century. In the early decades, it was often seen as an affliction of the lower social orders. The homes of the lower middle classes and working classes had been evocatively described in the 1901 serial *Living London*, imaginatively located in

a desolate region lying below high-water mark, not very far from the Victoria Docks—a region where still the pools on the waste land are salt when the tide is high, and where thousands of grey-faced houses, built squat upon the reeking earth, lean towards each other for mutual support.

This is the servantless land.

These endless rows of expressionless grey houses, with their specious air of comfort and gentility, their bay window and anti-maccassar-covered table, are tenanted by two, it may even be by three, families housed in the four rooms. These are the people who 'do for themselves.'[8]

This dramatic prose conveys something of the horror felt at the condition of being servantless, drawing on clichéd descriptions of slum dwelling, combined uneasily with the antipathy directed towards the lower middle classes, summed up in the fussy anti-maccassar. Having aspirations to gentility, yet not having the servants needed to realize them, was for Edwardians comic, yet also degrading and comfortless.

When referring to more securely middle-class households, being 'servantless' was taken by Victorians and Edwardians to refer to a temporary state of being 'between' servants. Its irritations and trials provided comic stories for middle-class Edwardian householders to recount at dinner parties, or weave into amusing memoirs. Servantlessnes was also a vehicle for improving moral exhortations. One American author, Adeline Whitney, described to a British audience strategies for reducing 'the terror of servantless interregnums'. She recommended that middle-class girls should learn all domestic tasks, in order to be able to stand in temporarily for servants. This had moral as well as practical value; in wiping, polishing, and dusting, she argued, 'you will be setting up your own character at the same time.'[9] Servantlessness represented an irritating disruption to domestic routines, but might nonetheless be usefully character-building. There was a hint in her exhortation to wipe and dust of the diminishing popularity of the mistress identity,

---

[7] Black, *A New Way of Housekeeping*, 11.
[8] N. Murrell Marris, 'Servant London', in *Living London*, 351–2, part 23.
[9] Mrs Adeline D. T. Whitney, 'Spinning and Weaving', *St Nicholas*, Aug 1, 1876, 634.

which as the previous chapter discussed, was increasingly associated with parasitism and laziness.

Becoming servantless might also be an abrupt transition caused by loss of economic means or bereavement, and many novels relied on it as a staple of melodramatic or romantic fiction. It might also result from transitions of location, as those living with the domestic staff of colonial or military environments relocated back to Britain.[10] It might be expected during exceptional periods such as war, or at specific points in the life-cycle, such as during the early days of setting up one's own home. Nonetheless, it was clear that around the turn of the century, middle-class women could take on only limited tasks without loss of gentility. Mrs Panton, for example, advised late Victorian readers of the periodical *Woman at Home* that certain 'dainty' tasks were acceptable—washing china and glassware, laying the table, mending socks, and retrimming hats.[11] However, there was no mention of the work characterized as 'the rough'—scrubbing floors, heavy cleaning of boots, knives, and pans, removing ashes, and blackleading stoves. This work was still widely expected to be done by servants or chars. Laundry was seen as particularly physically onerous and degrading. Those without regular household help mostly sent out their washing to be done in laundries; if it was done at home, one writer warned, 'the unmistakeable odour asserts itself and the lady of the house feels that her prestige in the neighbourhood is considerably lessened.'[12] If fewer live-in servants were available to undertake such tasks in the first half of the twentieth century, day workers were largely brought in to replace them. The numbers of chars recorded in the census, which almost certainly underestimated the total numbers working in this mostly informal sector, suggests a large expansion between 1901 and 1911. As day servants increasingly began to be employed, servantlessness might become a transition made nightly, as those used to residential domestic service adjusted to having domestic assistance at only certain times of the day, and their houses became sites of shifting geographies of access and domain.

In public debates, fiction, and memoirs, becoming servantless was most commonly understood in apocalyptic terms, as a profound change. It was a transition that inspired intense fascination and anxiety. For established middle-class families, servantlessness represented the progressive unmaking of 'home'.

---

[10] One daughter described the deep disorientation of her mother, who had transferred from having a house of servants in India, to working in a factory in England; Mrs Ruth Tilley (b. 1933), Interview 142, in P. Thompson and H. Newby, *Families, Social Mobility and Ageing, an Intergenerational Approach, 1900–1988* [computer file], Colchester, Essex: UK Data Archive [distributor], July 2005, SN: 4938. For further exploration of the colonial transitions associated with servant-keeping, see Elizabeth Buettner, *Empire Families: Britons and Late Imperial India* (Oxford: Oxford University Press, 2004).

[11] Mrs Panton, 'Simple Homes and How to Make them', *The Woman at Home* (London), 1899, 488. See Helen Long, *The Edwardian House* (Manchester: Manchester University Press, 1993), 89–96, for a useful overview of Victorian household advice manuals, including those of Mrs Panton.

[12] Mrs Agatha Willoughby Wallace, *Woman's Kingdom: Containing Suggestions as to Furnishing, Decorating, and Economically Managing the Home for People of Limited Means* (London: Archibald Constable, 1905).

They mourned a loss of a lifestyle of 'cultured living' and comfort, which had formed distinctive features of middle-class self-identity alongside notions of public service and respectability, and which had only been made possible by employing domestic servants. During World War I, the Scottish novelists Mary and Jane Findlater expressed these feelings in their memoir of a summer spent without servants, published in 1916. They blamed wartime middle-class poverty for the profound changes in lifestyle they expected. As servants became scarce, 'the whole standard of outward refinement will suffer. Perhaps the flower of civilised living may fade in the meanwhile amongst people of moderate income, and a way of life much less elegant take its place.'[13] The Findlaters experienced intense anxiety at the prospect of two months without help in a Scottish holiday cottage: 'we were like unaccustomed swimmers suddenly thrown into deep water. All must now depend upon our own energy; there was no one to be appealed to for any help.' However, the experiment was made possible by hiring a largely unacknowledged daily domestic help, to deal with the fires, washing up, and cleaning boots. They did find cooking to be rewarding and relatively straightforward, and this was one area where doing for oneself might be managed without loss of status, though they found the damage to their hands troubling. Not being able to afford rubber gloves, they frequently rubbed their hands in glycerine and lemon juice.[14] Eventually, they came to enjoy the 'simple routine' of domestic work, which was monotonous but not taxing, although they did not expect it to last beyond their rural holiday.

ETIQUETTE

The fear of damage to one's hands runs through the advice and memoir literature on doing for oneself, and it captures the continuing social unacceptability of housework. One of the reasons being servantless rarely featured prominently in early- to mid-twentieth-century labour-saving advice literature was precisely the continuing concern for social prestige and norms of etiquette. It had been the etiquette functions of servants that, Theresa McBride argues, made them a necessity to middle-class status from the mid-nineteenth century, as the increasing formality of upper-class 'Society' influenced social norms of other social levels.[15] For much of the first half of the twentieth century, there is evidence of a deep resistance to the removal of servants as mediators of the boundary areas of middle-class houses. Mrs J. G. (Lily) Frazer, a translator and academic wife in Cambridge, published *First Aid to the Servantless* in 1912. She called on middle-class householders without servants to give up entertaining (except for two weeks in the year when, in order to keep up with social obligations, hired help could be brought in), to use paper napkins, and to eat breakfast in the kitchen.[16] She

---

[13] Mary Findlater and Jane Helen Findlater, *Content with Flies* (London: Smith, Elder, 1916), 3.
[14] Ibid. 24, 38.
[15] Theresa McBride, *The Domestic Revolution* (London: Croom Helm, 1976), 18.
[16] Mrs J. G. Frazer, *First Aid to the Servantless* (Cambridge: Heffers, 1913).

also advocated the use of labour-saving devices, such as a 'parcel receiving device'. Devices such as 'receivadors' ('the silent servant of the household, giving orders and receiving parcels'[17]) continued to be included in much later visions of the labour-saving home, aiming to reduce the contact between middle-class women and tradesmen. The concerns of social etiquette were to be modified, or confined to an annual fortnight, but by no means abandoned; Mrs Frazer still stressed that it was vulgar to receive packages in person, or to answer the door to callers.

The atmosphere of World War I, however, led to numerous proposals for servantless homes or simpler living, and less social affirmation for 'mistresshood'. A contributor to *The Queen* in 1915 directly challenged the standards of society that she perceived to be dominated by goals of 'parasites', whose customs 'makes life so difficult for less moneyed folk who have not the strength of mind to remain unimpressed by the fashion'.[18] She noted: 'the only way to solve the problem seems to me to set up a different social standard. Why should we not carry our own parcels? Why should we not cook, do housework and open our own front doors? Why when Lady Jones or Mrs Smith comes to tea can I not fetch the tray and make the tea?' This was not yet, however, an entirely self-sufficient vision of the home—the author still felt that one servant was needed, even with the self-sufficiency of opening one's own front door. She rejected the ceremonial and display aspects of service, but not the 'rough' work that should be done within the house. And those who managed with fewer or no servants still actively attempted to disguise this; one mistress wrote in 1917, 'I have people to lunch now and then and intimate friends to dinner, and by means of my hot plate and careful choosing of food, our Jane is dressed for lunch and able to wait at table, and I doubt if it occurred to anyone that there was not a cook in the kitchen.'[19]

Servantless homes did not only evoke responses of panic and loss. Being without servants might be felt to be a release from the crushing conventionality of domestic routine and propriety. Robert Graves recalled the constraints imposed by servants in his Edwardian childhood: 'My mother, being *gemutlich* by nature, would, I believe, have loved to dispense with servants altogether. They seemed a foreign body in the house.'[20] J. B. Priestley commented on becoming servantless: 'ill feeling, nay downright hatred, has now left the house. It is terrible to live under the same roof with people who would appear to resent your very existence, to hate the very sight of you.'[21] Feminists such as Alice Melvin recommended cooperative living to readers of *The Freewoman* journal, with domestic workers inhabiting 'colonies' and enrolled in guilds. Yet Melvin's scheme prompted the

---

[17] *Daily Mail Ideal Labour-Saving Home* (London: Associated Newspapers, 1920).
[18] 'Interested Reader' *The Queen*, Oct 23, 1915, 773. Curiously though, she classed herself as one of these weak-minded women: 'I confess that I for one find it hard to be content to live in a different manner from other people in my own circle of friends and acquaintances. I know I am silly... but there it is!'
[19] Anon., quoted in Mrs C. S. Peel, *The Labour Saving House* (London: John Lane, 1917), 83.
[20] Robert Graves, *Goodbye to All That* (London: Penguin, 1976 [1929]), 20.
[21] J. B. Priestley, 'Servants', *Saturday Review*, Mar 19, 1927, 429.

critical assessment of the domestic servant Kathlyn Oliver, who responded in a letter to the editor:

> When the words 'abolition of domestic drudgery' caught my eye, I eagerly went over Mrs Melvin's scheme, but, alas! I found that the abolition of domestic drudgery was not for me, but was for the middle-class people who could, by combining their resources, achieve a far better home life than they have hitherto known.... Methinks that this common ownership of domestic drudges would not be quite so satisfactory from the domestic drudge's point of view.

Melvin had declared that 'Woman's duty to herself should lead her to come out of the home as quickly as she can, until the old basis of home life has been readjusted'. Oliver, however, was acutely aware that female servants were not included in this address to 'woman'.[22]

Across the political spectrum, middle-class commentators wrote of their longing for new forms of home life without servants that were less emotionally stunted, more private and intimate, and more demonstrative.[23] One domestic manual claimed: 'We need fantasy, imagination, wit in our houses. We want to relax, to enjoy intimacy, to feel, as well as actually to be, comfortable.... We require our homes to be quieter, more informal, more personal.'[24] Another claimed that 'domestic comfort is far greater, that home is far more really "home" in the fullest sense of the term, without servants than with them.'[25] Yet middle-class commitments to dainty, comfortable, or 'cultured' living, to national and civic service, and to professional or philanthropic work were slow to be relinquished. There was an irresolvable ambivalence about domestic service, an institution that middle-class Britons felt they could neither live with or without. The upper-middle-class Gwen Raverat insightfully noted:

> Of course I disapproved of having servants on principle, even when they were treated with affection and respect, as ours were at home. But this was just an abstract theory; for I had never considered in the least how we should get on without them; in fact it seemed to me quite inevitable that they should be there, a necessary and very tolerable arrangement, both for them and for us.[26]

For all the fascination with domestic transitions and change in the twentieth century, it should not be forgotten that there had long been well-off households

---

[22] Alice Melvin, 'Co-operative Housekeeping and the Domestic Worker', *The Freewoman*, Apr 4, 1912, 386–7; Kathlyn Oliver, *The Freewoman*, June 20, 1912, 98. Marilyn Boxer, however, notes the more successful incorporation of the needs of domestic servants into some versions of European feminism, in 'Rethinking the Socialist Construction and International Career of the Concept "Bourgeois Feminism"', in Karen Offen (ed.), *Globalizing Feminisms 1789–1945* (London: Routledge, 2010), 286–301, esp. 296.

[23] Arthur M. Edwards, *The Design of Suburbia* (London: Pembridge Press, 1981), 28; Jane Hamlett, *Material Relations: Domestic Interiors and Middle-Class Families in England 1850–1910* (Manchester: Manchester University Press, 2010).

[24] Dorothy Todd and Raymond Mortimer, *The New Interior Decoration: An Introduction to Its Principles, and International Survey of Its Methods* (London: Batsford, 1929), 28.

[25] An Engineer and His Wife, *The Ideal Servant-Saving House* (London: Chambers, 1918), v.

[26] Gwen Raverat, *Period Piece: A Cambridge Childhood* (London: Faber and Faber, 1952), 49.

that did not employ residential workers, even when the supply was relatively plentiful and wages were low. A substantial minority of middle-class homes preferred to deploy the labour of wives and daughters, though normally with the employment of daily chars or causal help for the dirtier 'rough' tasks. Leonard Schwarz has estimated that a fifth of class I households in York did not keep residential servants in the 1890s, while this was true of more than half of class I families in Lincoln, Bolton, and Coventry.[27] Lynn Jamieson's research suggests that doing for oneself was also a widespread practice in many parts of Scotland.[28] It is clear that being servantless was regionally uneven. It was particularly high in areas where working-class women had access to industrial work. Doing for oneself might embrace a very wide variety of domestic arrangements, but it had long been possible even in relatively well-off families. As early as 1883, an anonymous Liverpool woman published an account of 'how she managed without a servant', and the 1880s saw a focus upon cooking and domestic skills for those of 'middling' incomes in manuals and magazines.[29] However, this is emphatically not the point at which servantless living began to become socially acceptable. Indeed, the subsequent decades were to witness an increase in the employment of one or two servants in modest villa homes. One Edwardian newspaper noticed the numbers of 'people who twenty years ago would have done all the housework themselves now wishing to keep a maid to help them in the work.' The editor concluded: 'more people keep maids than was formerly the case.'[30] However, the scarcity and difficulties of managing maids did encourage experimentation with new categories of domestic workers.

LADY HELPS AND NANNIES

One solution to the discomfort with domestic service was to employ a domestic worker of a class status equal to that of the employer. This was the basis of the experiments with 'lady helps', widely discussed from the 1870s and sometimes described as a form of servantless living. The 'lady help' idea was intended to employ the 'gentlewomen' who were unlikely to marry and had few marketable skills. It was proposed that these so-called 'superfluous' genteel women might be taken into households in a role somewhere between servant and kin. Training

---

[27] Leonard Schwarz, 'English Servants and Their Employers during the Eighteenth and Nineteenth Centuries', *Economic History Review*, 52 2 (1999), 236–56, esp. 253. Schwarz suggests that there was a long-term decline in numbers employed in service from the eighteenth century onwards, and he discounts the nineteenth-century census figures that suggest otherwise as misleading. The frequent changes in categorization of domestic work have led to an overestimate of the numbers in nineteenth-century domestic service, though it remains a very large sector of employment. Schwarz notes regional variations, and the buoyant labour market for servants that persisted in London.

[28] See Lynn Jamieson, 'Limited Resources and Limiting Conventions: Working-Class Mothers and Daughters in Urban Scotland, c. 1890–1925', in Jane Lewis (ed.), *Labour and Love: Women's Experience of Home and Family, 1850–1940* (Oxford: Blackwell, 1986).

[29] A. E. L. L., *How She Managed without a Servant* (Liverpool: J. Burniston, 1883).

[30] 'The Servant Problem', *Domestic Servants' Advertiser*, June 24, 1913.

organizations, such as the Guild of Aid in Bath and the Guild of Dames in Cheltenham, were founded to facilitate the entry of 'ladies', under the euphemism of 'helps', into service. Mrs Caddy, in an 1877 household manual, for example, recommended that 'a lady help could be found more useful as well as more ornamental than the "dolly-mop"'. She noted, however, that such a domestic worker could be expected to do nothing menial, and later prescriptive literature advised that they were best suited to the homes of elderly couples or ladies living alone. The lady-help could be regarded as 'an adopted "daughter of the house"', and was only to take on the standard duties of a house-parlourmaid.[31]

As might be expected, experiments with lady helps were dogged by ambiguities of social standing. These 'daughters' or 'guests' must be given a separate bedroom and sitting room, to preserve their social status, yet could not be fully integrated into the household: the most fatal mistake, one Edwardian manual noted, would be to treat them as members of the family: 'it is no pleasure to them and a great tie to the lady of the house, not to mention her visitors.'[32] In a fictional account of the employment of a lady help published in the Victorian household magazine *The Ladies' Treasury*, the mistress agonized over whether the lady help should sit to dinner with the family, and if so, whether her husband would have to serve her. And how, practically, could she join them at meals in a presentable state, having just cooked them herself? The *Ladies Treasury* asserted unconvincingly that any real lady 'will not be dirty or unpresentable in any work she may undertake', but this fantasy of effortless service was only to be achieved by appointing other servants to work under the lady help.[33]

The class status of a lady help could not remain unchallenged by her association with dirt and personal service. A 1905 commentator concluded: 'her position was undefined and she was miserable and unhappy. If she came as a cook or housemaid she was condemned to mingle in daily intercourse with the servants and just because she was a lady they hated her and rendered her life unbearable.'[34] Domestic commentators conceded that it was only possible to retain a domestic worker from higher social classes if the whole household was staffed by the middle or upper classes. Yet even under those conditions, the lady help was advised that she should not 'rush to the piano when her mistress is out'. As ever, the piano symbolized class distinctions and the boundaries of domestic hierarchies.[35] There was comic potential in these ambiguities of status and dilemmas of etiquette, and the press ruthlessly satirized the whole idea. *The Daily Mirror* pictured a supercilious 'Lady Domestic' in 1922, who when asked what duties she would undertake, answered 'I'll be happy to arrange the flowers and help you in receiving guests' (Figure 3).

The limitations on the tasks that might be undertaken, and the need for symbolic spaces of gentility such as sitting rooms, largely doomed lady helps to

---

[31] Florence Caddy, *Household Organization* (London: Chapman and Hall, 1877), 33.
[32] Wallace, *Woman's Kingdom*, 148.
[33] 'My Lady-Help, and What She Taught Me,' *The Ladies' Treasury: A Household Magazine*, Mar 1, 1876, 156.
[34] 'The Domestic Tyrant', *Chambers Journal*, July 29, 1905, 546.
[35] Ibid.

'Doing for Oneself'

Figure 3. W. K. Haselden, 'Lady Domestic', *Daily Mirror*, February 24, 1921 (Mirrorpix).

be an abstract rather than actual solution to 'the servant problem'. *The Englishwoman's Review* had concluded in 1907, 'The experiment [with Lady Servants] is as a rule too expensive for the ordinary household, where two or three servants are kept, and in which the income cannot be stretched to cover large wages, nor the houses to give the accommodation expected.'[36] Nonetheless, lady helps continued to be proposed well into the twentieth century. Where economic conditions were depressed, it seems that arrangements of this sort did provide a lifeline for some single women. 'Miss P.' wrote from Worcestershire to the DWU describing her domestic circumstances as a companion to an elderly woman in the mid-1930s, 'I have a small private income and I read to Miss A, take her out etc. I am giving my services for a home and food.'[37] She hoped to recruit a servant to 'cook our simple food and do the work of the house', also for no salary.

The lady help role proved unsuccessful in attempting to raise or blur the social standing of domestic service through the intangible cultural assets of class; middle-class origins were easily obscured by associations with dirt and domestic labour. However, in one role, middle- and even upper-class women were recruited and regarded as skilled workers—as nannies. The 'nanny' had been an upper-class institution, but became more widely employed in twentieth-century middle-class households, while retaining a social distance from 'servantdom'. Nannies hovered on the cusp of being servants, or being social equals with a professional status. Their professionalization was enabled by the growth of training institutions and qualifications. The Norland School was founded in 1892, with the explicit aim of attracting 'genteel' and 'refined' young women to the career, and provided certified training that could command premium wages. The domestic writer Mrs Peel recorded paying her Norland Nanny the generous salary of £48 per year in the early 1900s, compared to the £28 her cook earned. Only her manservant, a former head footman in a stately home, was paid more, receiving £70.[38] Like lady helps, Norland Nannies would mostly expect to be waited on, and to be addressed using their surnames and honorifics of 'Miss', 'Nanny', or even 'Sister'. The clothes of a nanny diverged from the standard print dress and apron of a domestic servant, and resembled the more professional garb of a nurse. The more prestigious training colleges offered their own distinctive capes and dresses.[39] Most nannies would not undertake the 'dirty' aspects of raising children, and delegated the washing of nappies and scrubbing of nursery floors.

The success of the Norland training college inspired others, and by the 1920s, nannying was a well-established career for middle-class young women. Nannies might be given relative freedom in arranging their own time off and work schedule,

---

[36] Review of 'Lady Servants for and against', reprinted from *Women's Employment*, *Englishwoman's Review*, Apr 1907, 138.

[37] Quoted in the Report of Our First Year's Work, Household Service League and National Union of Domestic Workers, 1938, MRC 292/54.76/8 [53.3].

[38] Mrs C. S. Peel, *Life's Enchanted Cup: An Autobiography (1872–1933)* (London: Lane, 1933), 125.

[39] Jonathan Gathorne-Hardy, *The Rise and Fall of the British Nanny* (London: Hodder and Stoughton, 1972), 174.

though they often did not have their own bedrooms and shared their rooms with the children they looked after. In practice, working-class women still predominated in this role, and continued to become nannies through promotion from nursery maid, or without any training. Nonetheless, they took occupational prestige from the Norland-inspired rebranding of their role.[40] In the second half of the twentieth century, and somewhat unevenly in earlier decades, nannies and the parents who relied on them successfully constructed a social identity that was divorced from the discourses of social inequality that pervaded domestic service. The nanny occupied a distinct space that did not relate to the 'servant' category, but is better described as fictive or false kinship.[41] This was made possible in part through the powerful emotions that existed in the relationship between children and their carers, discussed in the previous chapter, which established a very different emotional register from that of other kinds of domestic work.

The concept of employing a nanny or 'mother's help' (rather than a general servant who would undertake some childcare) spread down the social scale as postwar affluence increased. *The Times* commented in 1963 that individuals of a lower annual salary range (£2,000–5,000) were now looking to employ nannies and mother's helps, where before they would have had less specialized domestic help, or none.[42] Studies of domestic workers in the 1980s suggest that the late-twentieth-century nanny or mother's help was an increasingly dominant category amongst other domestic workers.[43] These workers did not escape the conflicts around surveillance, emotional dependency, and hierarchy. An account of the early 1980s recorded the experiences of 'Mandy', a Cambridgeshire domestic worker. Her mother was a 'washer-up' at a study centre and cleaner at a school. On leaving school Mandy

> went with my mum to an agency and signed up as a mother's help. I like children. I got a job straight away. My mum wanted me to be a mother's help. She liked the idea of me being under supervision and I suppose it did mean that I'd leave home—we'd had our ups and downs. I was very happy in my first job and stayed for over a year...I still keep in touch. The next job never really worked out well. The boy was very difficult to handle. His parents...wouldn't tell him off if he was really rude to me. The little girl, who was three, was no bother, but I just couldn't take to her. I had held back from the offer of another job which I would have loved, because I didn't want to leave them in the lurch—it was just before their holiday—when they sacked me, giving me a week's notice. They said it wasn't my fault, but I just couldn't handle the boy. The trouble with being a mother's help is that the pay isn't very good, so it's difficult to save, and if you lose your job you lose your place to live...I'd had enough of looking after other people's children and other people's homes.[44]

---

[40] Ibid. 171.
[41] Gregson and Lowe, *Servicing the Middle Classes*, 190–206.
[42] 'Rising Popularity of the Hired Footman', *The Times*, Mar 19, 1963, 5.
[43] Gregson and Lowe, *Servicing the Middle Classes*, 13–17.
[44] Deidre Sanders and Jane Reed, *Kitchen Sink, or Swim? Women in the Eighties—The Choices* (Harmondsworth: Penguin, 1982), 106.

There are strong parallels here with the emotional and material concerns of earlier decades. The *Good Nanny Guide* of the late 1980s also described many of the same tensions that had fuelled 'the servant problem' of earlier decades; employers complained of high turnover, of finding themselves obsessively discussing the nanny, and of struggles to assert their authority. Late–twentieth-century nannies complained of humiliations, mockery, and snooping employers.[45] With the decline of the servant problem as a means of framing such problems for both employees and employers, there were fewer ways of conveying the tensions in the relationship, though Internet discussion forums such as 'Mumsnet' contain familiar discussions of conditions and expectations for those workers looking after children. A thread from 2010, for example, discussed why au pairs use such large amounts of toilet paper, and whether it is acceptable to buy them cheaper brands.[46] The fascination with these intimate, awkward relationships conducted within sites that are both home and workplace has continued; what seems different is that mothers and child-carers both contribute on relatively equal terms. Relationships with other forms of domestic workers, however, lack any particular cultural or social framework for expression, and have become relatively unexamined.

LABOUR-SAVING HOMES AND HOUSEHOLDS

Technological, infrastructural, and demographic changes first became evident in the late Victorian period, and significantly changed the nature of middle-class homes. Middle-class couples began to limit their fertility from the 1870s through delaying marriage and practicing sexual abstinence within marriage.[47] This was a shift achieved slowly and unevenly, but as households got smaller, the heavy physical tasks associated with childraising were reduced. New forms of work associated with the emotional and educational needs of children expanded and began to be seen as tasks that should not be delegated to servants. Motherhood became a more exacting role, but not in ways that precluded other social and professional commitments for married wealthy women, who continued to employ nurses and nannies, or at least general servants and chars who would undertake the washing and scrubbing of childraising.

The beginnings of the demographic shift coincided with the late-nineteenth-century economic depression that affected the incomes of some middle-class families, and their ability to afford servants. It prompted manuals such as Mrs Caddy's 1877 *Household Organisation*, which instructed mistresses in doing

---

[45] Charlotte Breese and Hilaire Gomer, *The Good Nanny Guide: The Complete Handbook on Nannies, Au-Pairs, Mother's Helps and Childminders* (London: Century, 1991).
[46] Available at http://www.mumsnet.com/Talk/childminders_nannies_au_pairs_etc/1013822-au-pairs-and-toilet-paper, accessed August 8, 2010.
[47] Simon Szreter, *Fertility, Class, and Gender in Britain, 1860–1940* (Cambridge: Cambridge University Press, 1996).

their housework 'in the cheapest and pleasantest way', though the author stressed the need to use the labour of servants more efficiently rather than living without them.[48] Talk of doing without servants was still rare, and even with smaller families, few commentators took seriously the idea that one might manage without servants for long. An advice columnist in the sixpenny women's fashion magazine *Myra's Journal* complacently advised a correspondent who had complained in 1890 of her 'servantless condition' to advertise in the national dailies, 'and you will be certain to receive a great number of answers.'[49] Another manual offered tips on 'How to Keep House on £200 a Year'. This was an income that barely reached the level normally understood as a middle-class income at this period. Nonetheless, readers were advised that 'there are plenty of strong strapping girls from fourteen to fifteen years of age who are glad to come for a mere trifle of wages, 1s 6d or 2s a week at the outset, and a good home and food.'[50]

Demographic change was accompanied by a changed built environment. Suburban villas, often owner-occupied, became more common for middle-class householders, and generated new concepts of 'the home' and its management. Victorian domestic prescriptive literature had stressed forms of 'saving', and obsessively documented the need to avoid waste. Indeed, wastefulness had been a chief ingredient of early versions of the servant problem. Weighing purchases made, and obsessive using up of scraps featured prominently in Victorian domestic literature, and was a means of reconciling the expanding luxury of employing servants with older discourses of austerity and thrift that had been central in establishing middle-class identities.[51] Wastefulness of materials and food continued to be a major complaint made about servants, but the discourse on housekeeping shifted in the late nineteenth century, to give greater prominence to making economies of *effort* rather than economies of consumption in the new suburban villas. 'Labour-saving' was coined first in the United States and popularized in Britain through Mrs Christine Frederick's popular manual, *Household Engineering: Scientific Management in the Home*.[52] This Edwardian text ran to many editions, and was promoted in Britain by Frederick, who lectured at British universities and associations, accompanied by toy kitchens peopled by dolls. The 'labour-saving movement' linked attention to science and engineering with concepts of hygiene and health. Labour saving worked well with new ideas of a simpler 'ideal home'. Edwardian domestic interiors had reacted against the fussy, overfurnished aesthetic of Victorian middle-class homes, and became modelled on cottage-style interior design and architecture, with plain furniture and comfortable surroundings. Experiments such as Hampstead Garden Suburb, Letchworth Garden City,

---

[48] Caddy, *Household Organization*.
[49] Myra's Answers on Household Management, *Myra's Journal*, Mar 1, 1890, 24.
[50] Mrs Praga, *How to Keep House on £200 a Year* (London: Pearson, 1904), 136.
[51] Leonore Davidoff and Catherine Hall, *Family Fortunes: Men and Women of the English Middle Class, 1780–1850* (London: Hutchinson, 1987), 36–42.
[52] Janice Williams Rutherford, *Selling Mrs Consumer: Christine Frederick and the Rise of Household Efficiency* (Athens: University of Georgia Press, 2003), 60–1.

Knebworth in Hertfordshire, and Harborne in Birmingham aimed to extend the cottage home ideal of 'simple living' to the more affluent.[53]

Christine Frederick's message was simple; housework was needlessly time-consuming and wasteful, though she believed that 'far from being dull drudgery, home-making in all its details is fascinating and stimulating if a woman applies to it her best intelligence and culture.'[54] Her work, however, led others to voice a rather different idea—it might also be dull and unsatisfying. In 1916, a manual titled *The Home of Today: By a Woman who Keeps One* offered an account of how to perform the 'cruelly dull and repetitive' housework using all the labour-saving devices available—there was no defence of traditional, time-consuming methods as somehow morally superior or satisfying to feminine instincts, and the drudgery of housework was openly acknowledged. Manuals that stressed elaborate preparation of polishes and time-consuming tasks such as blackleading began to sound out of date, though servants testified that these practices extended well into the twentieth century. *The Home of Today* showed a new willingness to think flexibly about the tasks traditionally allocated to servants, motivated by the belief that servants themselves were reluctant to use new methods or devices. If they would not use a vacuum cleaner, the author advised the mistress herself to use it, leaving the scrubbing and polishing to the maid.[55] It was typical of the early-twentieth-century labour-saving literature that it did not envisage a servantless home, but a redistribution of tasks and perhaps a reduction in hours of labour.

The household efficiency approach was widely feted in the British press as solving the conundrums of the servant problem, yet Frederick herself was ambivalent about domestic service. Though her book included a chapter on 'servantless living', this was postponed to a late part of the book, and does not seem to be a major motivating factor for her work.[56] Frederick had argued in the American *Ladies Home Journal* that scientific management would allow for 'team work' between mistress and servant, and the improvement of the latter's working conditions—though her approach also implied a reduction of freedom for the servant, who was expected to follow detailed 'scientific' routines. There was little stress on the practicalities of a servantless home, and Frederick's radicalism at this stage was limited to suggesting that servants lived in their own flats.[57]

Labour-saving was premised on the new domestic technologies that slowly percolated into British homes. Bathrooms had not been widely present in middle-class houses of the 1870s, with most households relying on cumbersome hip baths and washstands. The growing availability of running water made bathrooms

---

[53] Adrian Forty, *Objects of Desire: Design and Society, 1750–1980* (London: Thames and Hudson, 1986), 111–12; David Jeremiah, *Architecture and Design for the Family in Britain, 1900–70* (Manchester: Manchester University Press, 2000), 22–3.
[54] Christine Frederick, *The New Housekeeping: Efficiency Studies in Home Management* (Garden City, NY: Doubleday, 1913), 186.
[55] Paul Oliver, Ian Bentley, and Ian Davis, *Dunroamin': The Suburban Semi and Its Enemies* (London: Barrie and Jenkins, 1994), 181.
[56] June Freeman, *The Making of the Modern Kitchen: A Cultural History* (Oxford: Berg, 2003), 36.
[57] Christine Frederick, 'The New Housekeeping', *Ladies Home Journal*, Dec 1912, 16; 'Suppose our Servants Didn't Live with Us?', *Ladies Home Journal*, Oct 1914, 102.

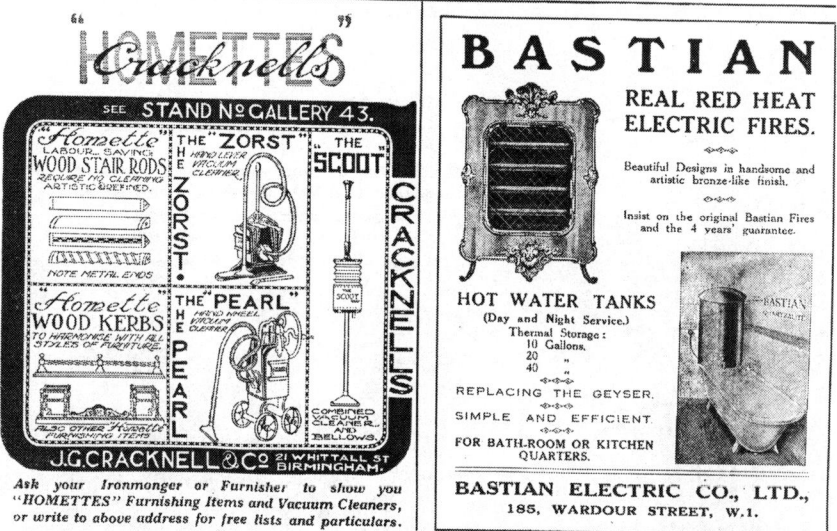

Figure 4. Advertisements, *Daily Mail Ideal Labour-Saving Home*, 1920.

viable over the next 20 years, and cast-iron enamelled fitted baths became widely marketed from 1910, though servants were usually forbidden from using them.[58] Carpet sweepers and floor polishers were available, often personified as servants, such as the 'Our Susan' mop (Figure 4). A highly cumbersome form of the vacuum

---

[58] Ibid. 97.

Figure 5. 'The Hard Hit Middle Classes', British Commercial Gas Association advertisement, *The Times*, March 19, 1924, 18.

cleaner was invented in 1901 and would have been a major financial investment; one 1908 domestic manual advised women to ask for one as a wedding present.[59]

It had become fairly common during the nineteenth century for townhouses to have gas for lighting; by 1885, there were 2 million gas-lit houses in Britain.[60] Gas was still a relatively dirty form of illumination, and by 1914, electric light was starting to prove a more efficient alternative, removing some of the need for the annual spring clean. The Edwardian electricity industry was deeply oriented to solving the servant problem, branding their product 'the new servant in the home'. Gas and electric fires were heralded as 'lend[ing] themselves most readily to the absence of servants', and began to gain ground as alternatives to open coal fires, though they remained more expensive forms of heating until after World War I.[61] Electricity, in particular, was hampered until the 1930s by the lack of wiring in British homes, and the high cost; in 1918, only 6 per cent of British homes were wired, and the majority of these were only wired for lighting.[62] Some early washing machines and gas ranges were available, but they did not reach many homes until the 1920s. The pre-World War I changes were slight. Most Edwardian homes saw a change in small appliances rather than major transformations of layout and infrastructure. Mrs Peel noted that when she modernized a house in the early 1900s, 'neither architect nor builder suggested central heating, a second bathroom, or indeed, any labour-saving arrangements.'[63] Moreover, most manufacturers preferred to hedge their bets on who was to undertake housework, and spoke of their products lightening the 'daily routine cheerfully undertaken by mistress or maid' (Figure 5). The housewife identity was not yet seen as appealing to middle-class women and did not have wide cultural circulation. Where 'gentlewomen' were addressed in a domestic setting, as in the three-penny illustrated *Hearth and Home* magazine, there was very little discussion of housework, other than through controversies such as that presented in a 1913 issue, 'Are servants a pampered class?'[64]

INTERWAR DOMESTICITY

New domestic products became more visible in British homes after World War I. Hire purchase made appliances more affordable, and shops such as Woolworths began to provide cheap household goods. Most middle-class householders between the wars inhabited or aspired to a suburban bungalow or semi-detached house. The newly built houses of this kind rarely possessed attic bedrooms and basement kitchens designed for servants, and with their bathrooms and modern heating,

---

[59] Edith Waldemar Leverton, *Housekeeping Made Easy: A Handbook of Household Management Appealing Chiefly to the Middle-Class Housekeeper* (London: George Newnes 1910).
[60] Long, *The Edwardian House*, 89.
[61] Quoted ibid. 100.
[62] Forty, *Objects of Desire*, 188.
[63] Peel, *Life's Enchanted Cup*, 159.
[64] Mrs Alfred Sidgwick, 'Are Servants a Pampered Class?', *Hearth and Home*, Nov 13, 1913, 133.

seemed compatible with ideals of servantlessness.[65] Kitchens began to sport white enamel surfaces, and living rooms might use imitation leather. The reduction in clutter and in the ornamentation of furniture made rooms and objects easier to clean. There was some decline of ceremony in middle-class homes; less formal dining meant that meals might be served without tablecloths.[66] Servants became less necessary as symbolic mediators of food, dirt, and visitors, and the more formal roles of parlourmaid and footmen declined. Their work became more practical, associated with cleanliness rather than with deference and gentility. Symbolic tasks that provided an appearance, but not the substance, of cleanliness—such as whitening the front steps, or blackleading the range and grates—slowly declined. The cookery writer Elizabeth Craig wrote of 'Doing away with the servant problem' in a 1932 article in *The Queen*. She recommended that *The Queen*'s upper- and upper-middle-class readers withdraw their household silver from circulation, and use the bottled and tinned food that had formerly been regarded as vulgar. Craig also called for the limitation of the heaviest household tasks—the outdoor steps, in her view, only needed to be sluiced down once a day—though it seems unlikely that many of *The Queen*'s readers would envisage themselves doing the sluicing. Craig, indeed, concluded ambivalently about the benefits of living without servants—with all the expense needed to obtain labour-saving devices, 'you may in the end wonder if it pays to run a house without a maid.'[67]

Good Housekeeping, launched in Britain in 1922, has been seen as the periodical most unequivocally committed to new forms of domesticity directed towards middle-class women. Its pages projected an ideal, educated housewife whose work was scientifically informed:

A complete revolution appears to have occurred in modern housekeeping. The young wife is up-to-date in her knowledge of food values and bases her selection of food on their vitamin properties. She makes her own calorie chart. The day's shopping (done by car) provides an amusing theme for conversation during the evening—she shops around for the best buy. As a mother she must be up-do-date and know a great deal of hygiene... This will entail a great deal of reading and perusing of suitable literature and attending a course of lectures and demonstrations.[68]

Good Housekeeping concluded emphatically in its first UK issue that labour-saving would enable 'the educated classes to be independent of domestic help.'[69]

World War I and its immediate aftermath has thus been taken as a historical turning point in domestic discourses and material organization, but this overstates its influence. It was still possible for *The Queen* to conclude unequivocally in 1919: 'The middle-class woman with a family cannot solve the question by becoming her

---

[65] On the interwar semi, see Alison Ravetz, with Richard Turkington, *The Place of Home: English Domestic Environments, 1914–2000* (London: SPON, 1995), 153–4.

[66] Robert Graves and Alan Hodge, *The Long Weekend: A Social History of Great Britain 1918–1939* (Manchester: Carcanet, 2006), 137–9.

[67] Elizabeth Craig, 'Doing Away with the Servant Problem', *The Queen*, Nov 2, 1932, 36.

[68] Lady N. Spencer Churchill, 'Woman, Yesterday, Today and Tomorrow', *Good Housekeeping*, 1930, 280.

[69] 'The Reason for Good Housekeeping', *Good Housekeeping*, Mar 1922, 11.

own servant. The care of her children, the cooking and serving of meals, and the cleaning of the house are more than she can undertake without detriment to health.'[70] In practice, affluent households still varied dramatically in their purchase of appliances, and the impact of new technologies on the home was very uneven in its penetration. Even where a bathroom might be present, many middle-class families preferred to use jugs of hot water delivered by servants to their bedrooms. Mrs Kemp, in service in the mid-1920s, recalled her irritation at having to carry such jugs upstairs each morning, only to have the daughter of the house opt for the bathroom.[71] Despite the new cleaning products and tools, Mrs Kemp was also still sweeping carpets with tea leaves to lay the dust. Major appliances were out of the reach of many, or seen as not worth the investment. However, small ones spread rapidly, to middle-class and more affluent working-class homes. By 1923, *The Lady* magazine advised its upper-middle-class readers facing 'servant problems': 'I presume you have a carpet sweeper, vacuum cleaner, knife machine, komo mop, longhandled dustpan and brush.' By 1939, there were 6.5 million electric irons in British homes.[72] There was no abrupt transformation of housework in the early to mid-twentieth century, but rather an easing of some of its physical drudgery.

In characterizing the twentieth century, historians have often posited a simplistic narrative of a social transition towards servantless living brought about by the technological changes that proliferated after World War I. Jonathan Gershuny has argued that 'needs that are satisfied by domestic servants, train tickets and theatre seats are met later by domestic machinery, motor cars and video recorders'.[73] Such an explanation does not acknowledge the role of domestic service in postponing the deployment and mass marketing of available technologies. Historians of the domestic realm have largely retreated from the belief that technological changes—appliances such as the vacuum cleaner or gas cooker, or new manufactured commodities such as tinned food and cleaning products—were causal factors in the declining reliance on servants. Instead, it is widely accepted that the development of domestic appliances and the shift to electricity and gas in heating and cooking were *delayed* by the continuing reliance on servants, which prevented the development of middle-class consumer demand until after World War II. Domestic technologies only proliferated when the absence of servants required a rethinking of the market for household appliances.[74] Even in the post-war era of mass availability of heavy appliances such as refrigerators and washing machines, technological developments did not drive the social world. There is no simple association between technological advances and a lightening of domestic labour; as

---

[70] Mrs Peel, 'Le Menage', *The Queen*, Mar 29, 1919, 368.
[71] Mrs Kemp, T/Z 25/265, AC 'My First Job' (1961), Essex Record Office.
[72] *The Lady*, May 10, 1923; Forty, *Objects of Desire*, 200.
[73] Jonathan Gershuny, 'Economic Development and Change in the Mode of Provision', in Nanneke Redclift and Enzo Mingione (eds), *Beyond Employment: Household, Gender and Subsistence* (Oxford: Blackwell, 1985), cited in Gregson and Lowe, *Servicing the Middle Classes*, 80.
[74] Forty, Objects of Desire; Freeman, *Making of the Modern Kitchen*, 35; Frank E. Huggett, *Life below Stairs: Domestic Servants in England from Victorian Times* (London: Book Club Associates, 1977), 157–8; Jeremiah, *Architecture and Design*, 146.

Avner Offer has argued, 'technology did not save women's time because it was not associated with any rearrangement of the gender division of labour at home.'[75] Nor did new technologies necessarily reorganize domestic labour. Demographic and technological changes *did* make servantless living more practically viable, but 'labour-saving' did not translate into a simple retreat from practices of employing domestic labour.

Indeed, for servants the interwar period often meant more intense domestic labour. Faced with higher labour costs, more households were employing one servant where they might have employed two before the war, while nonetheless expected a similar lifestyle. And some practices of the upper classes, such as late dinners, were spreading to smaller households, creating more work for the servants. There was no real 'death of Society' in these decades, and the new rich still absorbed themselves in the 'cult of gentility'.[76] Formal rituals retained their power even in quite modest households. One interwar day servant described her mistress's horror of answering the door herself, and the solution—placing a hat on her head, the mistress would pretend to callers that she was going out, and had only opened the front door by chance. Siegfried Sassoon, on the other hand, simply refused to answer to callers if he would have to open the door himself. Hatches and ways of receiving goods, and of dealing with answering the door to all kinds of callers, continued to be the subject of considerable public debate and commercial interest well into the twentieth century.[77]

Most commentators remained uncertain or uncommitted about the social implications of changing domestic practices and equipment. Many early-twentieth-century advocates of the 'simple lifestyle' for more affluent households continued to prefer servants to modern gadgetry, or combined both, as W. K. Haselden imagined in his 1905 cartoon (Figure 6). When John Gloag and Leslie Mansfield produced their utopian vision of 'the house we ought to live in' in 1923, it was to be 'a house where work is simplified, cleaning reduced, and convenience increased. It will not contain an unmanageable museum of labour-saving mechanism, nor will it be a costly and spacious palace.'[78] Simplicity and practicality were the keynotes for their ambiguously named 'houseworker', but the authors conceded that their ideal household would still employ a cook and a maid. Even those homes explicitly named as servantless might paradoxically include domestic workers. *The Times* classified columns began to advertise 'ideal detached, labour saving, electrically fitted servantless houses' in the 1920s, but in this context, servantless was

---

[75] Avner Offer, *The Challenge of Affluence: Self-Control and Well-Being in the United States and Britain since 1950* (Oxford: Oxford University Press, 2006), 179. See also Ruth Schwartz Cowan, *More Work for Mother: The Ironies of Household Technology from the Open Hearth to the Microwave* (New York: Basic Books, 1983); Christine Hardyment, *From Mangle to Microwave: The Mechanisation of Household Work* (Cambridge: Polity Press, 1988).

[76] Ann Pope, 'The Domestic Service Report', *The Spectator*, Nov 3, 1923, 630.

[77] 'The Quiet Revolution', narrated by Veronika Hyks, *Timewatch* (1995), V3588 British Library; Alison Light, *Mrs Woolf and the Servants: The Hidden Heart of Domestic Service* (London: Penguin, 2007); 'Tradesmen's Calls', *The Times*, June 23, 1928, 10.

[78] John Gloag and Leslie Mansfield, *The House We Ought to Live In* (London: Duckworth, 1923), 15.

'Doing for Oneself' 119

THE ELECTRIC KITCHEN.

At the Electrical Exhibition will be shown a kitchen in which almost everything may be done by electricity. Woman's sphere in the future will be pressing buttons, instead of sewing them on.

Figure 6. W. K. Haselden, 'The Electric Kitchen', September 26, 1905, *Daily Mirror* (Mirrorpix).

intended to convey a sense of modern living—many such advertisements also noted the housekeepers or daily maids supplied with the house.[79] When *The Times* hosted a correspondence on domestic service in 1929, the many letters received mostly recommended a better training regime and the possibility of living-out as a solution to servant problems. Only one mistress, Dorothea Da Fano, proposed, 'In all seriousness... it is time we faced the changed situation, time we refused to be dependent upon unwilling and inefficient labour, time, in fact, we raised the standard of domestic work by doing it ourselves and bringing up our children to do it.'[80] Yet there was little resonance for her utopianism, and for her middle-class contemporaries, 'housewife' might still be a euphemism for 'mistress'. Similarly, labour-saving was still associated with retaining servants rather than doing without them. Mrs Noble, the author of *Labour Saving in the Home* (1930), declared that 'the well-trained servant is more ready to accept and to remain in a situation where

---

[79] *The Times*, Aug 4, 1922, 20; Mar 18, 1925, 26.
[80] Da Fano, 'Domestic Serivce', *The Times*, Febr 23, 1929, 11.

she finds suitable arrangements are made for running the house on labour-saving lines.'[81]

Even *Good Housekeeping* offered a deliberately ambiguous visual iconography of the 'domestic worker'. The figures depicted operating labour-saving devices or new appliances were always feminine; occasionally, they were obviously servants, in black and white uniforms. More often, however, dainty, 'modern' figures were depicted, always aproned, but open to interpretation as mistress, maid, or housewife. This went with persistent uncertainties about nomenclature. Around the turn of the century, the domestic adviser Mrs Panton preferred to talk of 'servantless mistresses' rather than housewives, in identifying those of small means who could not afford servants.[82] In 1922, *The Spectator* also tried to avoid 'housewife', and termed the middle-class woman who did not employ servants a 'housemistress'.[83] The *New Survey of London Life and Labour* noted that 'housekeeper' had newly emerged in the 1920s to characterize *both* a new class of servant, mostly employed by professional women, *and* the domestic role that these employing women might undertake themselves.[84]

Good Housekeeping often presented dissenting voices to its domestic prescriptions of pleasurable, modern housekeeping. Its editors published the views of Violet Bonham Carter, daughter of former Prime Minister Henry Asquith, in 1923, in which she argued that middle-class women 'grudge spending time and energy on anything so dull [as housework]. Servants liberate us. By standing like buffers between us and the leaden routine of daily drudgery they endow our lives with freedom, spaciousness and scope.'[85] The women's pages and magazines found it hard to reflect the contradictory and changing expectations that middle-class women had of their lives, particularly as interwar feminists offered critical evaluations of domesticity. Though women were widely presented with positive narratives of housework, feminist Pippa Strachey had defiantly declared 'to be born a woman is not to be born a domestic worker'. It is not clear, however, that she extended this to working-class women. Feminist writer Naomi Mitchison (1897–1999) heralded the 1930s modern domestic interior as a feminist innovation, rather than a celebration of a domestic modernity: 'these bare walls, plain curtains, clean-lined, simple furniture and labour-saving devices which are typical of the very modern home, *are a sign that women have other things to do*.'[86] The 'professionalization of housework' through discourses of hygiene and engineering had not made it more attractive to middle-class women, who largely continued to expect domestic workers of some sort, even if they were to be non-residential. Moreover, many

---

[81] Mrs Robert Noble, *Labour-Saving in the Home: A Complete Guide for the Modern Housewife* (London: Macmillan, 1930), 81.
[82] Mrs Panton, 'Simple Homes and How to Make Them', *The Woman at Home* (London, England), 1899, 488.
[83] Caia, 'Household Prestige—I', *Spectator*, Jan 21, 1922, 72.
[84] H. Llewellyn Smith, *New Survey of London Life and Labour* (London: King, 1929), 2: 435.
[85] Violet Bonham Carter, 'The Servant Question', *Good Housekeeping*, June 1923, 11.
[86] Strachey, quoted in *Daily Telegraph*, June 2, 1923; Naomi Mitchison, *The Home and a Changing Civilisation* (London: John Lane, 1934), 88–9, emphasis added.

middle-class women found the domestically oriented women's periodical press too conservative, failing to reflect their interests.[87] The periodical advice literature is thus an unreliable guide to the actual subjectivities constructed around domesticity, many of which were critical of its constraints.

KITCHENS AND COOKING

One domestic pleasure that seemed more convincing to many middle-class women was that of cooking. Though there were strong continuities in other areas of domestic organization across the apparent divide of World War I, the resignification of the kitchen in the early to mid-twentieth century did reflect real change. While 'rough' tasks continued to be of questionable respectability, cooking was a task that increasingly could be taken on by middle-class women with greater equanimity as to its genteel status. Nonetheless, many twentieth-century middle-class women still found cooking highly daunting. Victorian urban middle-class kitchens had been associated with the darkness of their basement locations, with domestic smells, and with infestations of black beetles and other creatures. The kitchen was unequivocally the domain of servants, who might both work and sleep in it, and was the one room in the house to which mistresses were uncertain of their access and might be expected to knock on entry. One proposal for servantless living thus argued in 1918 that 'where there are no servants there need be no kitchen in the ordinary sense of the term.' The authors preferred a 'workroom', supported by public kitchens from which food could be delivered.[88] Yet more typically in 1935, *The News Chronicle* headlined its discovery that 'Women want kitchen to be best room in house.'[89] When Monica Dickens worked as a servant in the late 1930s, she commented on the attractiveness of this domain to which her upper-class upbringing had denied her access: 'it would be marvellous to have the run of a kitchen to mess in to my heart's content.'[90] The kitchen replaced the drawing room as the imagined 'heart' of the middle-class home. It became a room in which all might feel at home, or even a room of public display, and this represents a profound change in the emotional and functional organization of British homes.[91]

Christine Frederick had pictured the labour-saving, scientific kitchen to British readers as a compact space, decorated with white, enamelled surfaces. British writers such as Mrs Peel called for a kitchen that 'should not be used as a sitting-room; it is the place in which food is prepared, and should be a place which can be kept exquisitely clean.'[92] Her labour-saving manual depicted institutional-looking

---

[87] Mrs H. A. L. (Lettice) Fisher, for example, was highly critical of the trivial content of journalism aimed at women, in 'The Woman's Page', *Cornhill Magazine*, Feb 1923.
[88] An Engineer and His Wife, *The Ideal Servant-Saving House*, 16.
[89] 'Women Want Kitchen to be Best Room in House', *News Chronicle*, July 17, 1935.
[90] Monica Dickens, *One Pair of Hands* (London: Joseph, 1939), 25.
[91] Forty, *Objects of Desire*, 114.
[92] Peel, *The Labour Saving House*, 41.

Figure 7. Mrs Peel, *The Labour-Saving House*, 1917, plate xiii.

kitchens, still peopled by servants, with large-scale catering equipment (Figure 7). *Good Housekeeping* similarly presented the kitchen as central to modern middle-class domesticity but still in institutional terms, noting in 1922: 'the kitchen is the working centre of the house, the laboratory in which the family meals are prepared and the health of the household depends to a large extent on this department.'[93] These ideas were further developed in the European-led 'modern movement', whose proponents declared that the kitchen should be a functional room, dedicated to cooking rather than a living space. Le Corbusier argued that it should be placed at the top of the house, to avoid cooking smells. Other modernist texts proposed the small galley kitchen or open-plan kitchen-diner, furnished with kitchen cabinets, continuous work surfaces, and built-in appliances.[94]

Where the kitchen was simply an upgraded institutionalized space, the presence of servants did not seem intrusive. Where it was imagined as a compact recessed

[93] Anon., 'The Bride's Kitchen', *Good Housekeeping*, Apr 1922, 58.
[94] Freeman, *Making of the Modern Kitchen*, 37–49. Lynn Abrams and Linda Fleming, 'From Scullery to Conservatory: Everyday Life in the Scottish Home', in Lynn Abrams and Callum G. Brown (eds), *A History of Everyday Life in Twentieth Century Scotland* (Edinburgh: Edinburgh University Press, 2010), 48–75.

space, intimately connected to the dining and living areas of the house or flat, servants might seem out of place. Yet interwar advice texts that advocated such spaces seemed persistently untroubled by their presence. The author and cookery writer Geoffrey Boumphrey broadcast a series of BBC radio talks, collected under the title *Your Home and Mine*, in 1938, in which he argued that 'the modern idea is to reduce household work to a minimum—partly because of the difficulty of getting a staff to do it, and partly because of the growth of consideration for our domestics.' He clearly only had middle-class listeners in mind, despite the inclusive, populist title of his broadcast, and rhetorically asked, 'where are the servants to be found who will devote to [furniture's] upkeep the conscientious labour our parents demanded of their staffs?' Influenced by time-and-motion techniques, Boumphrey stated that 'the modern kitchen is kept as compact as possible, to avoid unnecessary movement.' It seems extraordinary, however, that he still recommended that the space saved by reducing the kitchen to a minimalist, functionalist cooking area 'should be used for a servants' hall or maids' sitting room'.[95] Although it was often imagined as being collectivized and professionalized, domestic service continued to intrude upon celebrations of modern living.

In practice, there were a number of different visions of the kitchen at play, and the transformation of the kitchen in interwar Britain was slower and more uneven than in continental Europe and the United States.[96] Though they were inundated with advice and speculation as to what modern kitchens should look like, few British households used the fitted cabinets and continuous work surfaces that began to be used in European innovative designs such as the Frankfurt Kitchen. Modernist buildings like Kensal House in West London, built in the 1930s, still offered small and fairly conventional, though brightly lit, kitchens. Householders preferred to make small changes, such as the incorporation of new free-standing storage options, described by June Freeman as 'commodious cupboards'. These were marketed through the ubiquitous reference point of the servant; one company described their kitchen cabinets as 'the best servant in your house', able to 'make kitchen work a pleasure'.[97] Yet in the interwar period, as Adrian Forty notes, the actual appliances available did not match the seductive discourses available of the fulfilment and modern status of housework. The fantasy of the 'staff of silent, efficient, electrical servants ready at a touch to minister to our wants' proved hard to realize.[98]

In middle-class townhouses, basement kitchens were still widespread. The journalist Mary Wylde commented in 1936 that she had 'envisaged a bright kitchen, well-equipped pantry, and floods of light in the house that should be mine.' However, the basement kitchen of her house in Kensington bore little

---

[95] Geoffrey Maxwell Boumphrey, *Your House and Mine* (London: Allen and Unwin, 1938), 160–3.
[96] Deborah Cohen, *Household Gods: The British and Their Possessions* (New Haven: Yale University Press, 2006), 184–7.
[97] Freeman, *Making of the Modern Kitchen*, 41–2; 'Sellers Kitchen Cabinets', *Daily Mail Ideal Labour-Saving Home*, viii–ix.
[98] Forty, *Objects of Desire*, 195; Dora J. Moore, 'The Servantless House: Solving the Problem of Costly Living', *Good Housekeeping*, June 1923, 28.

resemblance: 'the kitchen, sandwiched in between a scullery and the maids' bedroom, had no window of its own, but received what light there was from the scullery beyond. The paint was dark green, and the kitchen range was enormous.' She found the kitchen inconvenient and unsettling: 'at times, my hatred of that basement and the problems it gave rise to, shattered my mind and made it quite impossible to settle down to anything.'[99] The old taboos on the sounds and smells of cooking were slow to shift, and even where middle-class kitchens were lifted from the basement, they continued to be organized so that visitors to the house could not observe the process of cooking. The use of hatches and lobbies between kitchens and dining rooms remained more common than the kitchen-diners that many architects preferred. The Ideal Home Exhibition in 1927, for example, displayed a 'soundproof service hatch between the kitchen and the dining-room', which was designed to 'avoid conversations in the dining-room being overhead in the kitchen.'[100] The presence of servants was still very tangible.

If the design and location of kitchens was slow to correspond to fantasies of servantless living, foodstuffs and cooking practices were more fluid. Robert Graves and Alan Hodge noted the changes in foods after World War I; ingredients became more standardized, and easier to prepare, and a wider range of tinned food became available and socially acceptable. Where the Edwardian domestic reformer Alice Melvin had bemoaned the use of 'tabloid soups and coffee essences', these cooking shortcuts had become permissible only a decade later.[101] Bloomsbury innovators such as Virginia Woolf and Vanessa Bell attempted to lighten their dependence on servants by using the shop-bought cakes that they had been brought up to consider vulgar. However, perhaps still motivated by taboos on an open-plan kitchen, Bell's used appliquéd curtains to screen off the cooking and cleaning activities of the servants in her kitchen.[102]

In some circumstances cooking was becoming an acceptable, or even elevated pursuit. Virginia Woolf declared that she would cook, though she still felt that cleaning and washing-up went too far. Advice manuals began to recommend that mistresses should cook, if only to better manage their servants. Mrs Peel argued in *The Queen* in 1921 that she had lacked authority to put her point of view to servants until she had been abandoned by a cook, and was forced to learn to cook herself.[103] This was perhaps a startling revelation for the relatively well-off readers of *The Queen*—but also an indication that the opposition between gentility and some aspects of housework was crumbling. Indeed, discussions of being servantless were often a means of establishing the capability of middle-class women to carry out domestic tasks, and in doing so, to *revalidate* forms of mistresshood. Winifred

---

[99] Mary Wylde, *A Housewife in Kensington* (London: Longmans, Green, 1937), 51, 55, 73.
[100] *Daily Mail Ideal Labour-Saving Home* (London: Associated Newspapers, 1927), 113.
[101] Graves and Hodge, *The Long Weekend*; Melvin, 'Co-operative Housekeeping and the Domestic Worker', *Freewoman*, Apr 4, 1912, 386–7. See also Joanne Hollows, *Science and Spells: Cooking, Lifestyle, and Domestic Femininities in British Good Housekeeping in the Inter-war Period* (Aldershot, Ashgate, 2006).
[102] Light, *Mrs Woolf and the Servants*, 230.
[103] Mrs Peel, 'The Memoirs of a Housewife', *The Queen*, May 21, 1921, 578.

Peck's 1942 novel *House-bound* illustrates this; the main character, Rose Fairlaw, an upper-class Scottish mother whose children are grown, undertakes her own cleaning as a contribution to the war effort. She had come to believe that servant-keeping women were 'useless and helpless and—unproductive'. As a housewife, Rose was portrayed as capable, but physically unsuited to the tasks, and is eventually rewarded by a self-elected live-in servant, the comical Mrs Childe. With semi-irony, Peck concluded 'the Fairlaws will live a feudal life in their fortress again.' The novel reads as a vindication of the view that, as Rose's husband puts it, 'Women like you uphold the standards of civilisation . . . leisured people keep culture and beauty alive in the world.' To employ servants was a means to this still valid end.[104]

Curiously though, cooking is one task that Rose Fairlaw could not 'do for herself'. Mrs Peel observed in her autobiography that 'the way in which educated women have become skilled cooks or house-parlourmaids with very little teaching other than that obtained from books is rather surprising.' She claimed that 'none of them makes any to-do about it'.[105] Yet the cookery advice supplied to upper- and middle-class women belies this claim, and described the transition to cooking for yourself in dramatic terms. Advice focused on new dishes and methods of cooking that might be substituted for more complex food. One journalist declared in 1939: 'the once despised tinned food is now so well prepared that it can take its place in any cookery,' and provided recipes for casseroles and other slow-cooking meals that might be prepared in a single dish by those without servants. It was a remarkable signal of the 'felt absence' of servants in affluent British homes that these dishes continued to be referred to as 'servantless dishes' for at least the subsequent three decades.[106]

When her cook walked out abruptly in 1936, Mary Wylde chronicled the resulting year of domestic chaos in her regular *Evening Standard* column, later published as a book entitled *A Housewife in Kensington*. Left alone in the kitchen, she reflected, 'I hardly knew where to begin or how long to allow for roasting the meat.' She also felt emotionally bereft: 'strangely quiet was the house. Clocks ticked all round me, and ashes dropped from the kitchen range.' Nonetheless, she produced a meal and 'with hands spoiled by peeling potatoes and contact with the greasy meat-tin, and an unusually red countenance, I sat down to dinner.' In common with most twentieth-century domestic experimenters, she continually worried about the state of her hands: 'In spite of the rubber gloves, my hands are rough on the palms . . . what a blessing it is that one's face does not betray menial work.'[107] The experiment with cooking for herself was practically feasible, though portrayed as unpleasant. When she finally employed a cook, after a year of very intermittent or incompetent help in the kitchen, Mary Wylde commented in melodramatic terms: 'I feel born again. This last month has seemed ten years of years, and I must try to pick up the threads of life that have been lost in that

---

[104] Winifred Peck, *House-Bound* (London: Persephone Books, 2007 [1942]), 14, 289, 53.
[105] Peel, *Life's Enchanted Cup*, 262.
[106] A Correspondent, 'Housekeeping without Tears', *The Times*, July 31, 1939, 17.
[107] Wylde, *A Housewife in Kensington*, 188.

time.'[108] The housewife identity claimed in the title of her book was surely an ironic gesture and should not be read at face value.

While kitchens and cookery showed signs of resignification in the years before World War II, other tasks remained unrespectable. Mary Wylde had concluded that 'I can do lady-like jobs such as dusting and polishing furniture without perishing of fatigue, but these other tasks [scrubbing, heavy cleaning] are exhausting to a degree.' Daintiness persisted as a component of middle-class femininity. Claims that the housewife identity allowed interwar middle-class women to imagine their homes without servants need to be critically revisited. The debates about being servantless strongly suggest that the 'housewife' identity was not class neutral before World War II, and was not particularly attractive for many middle-class women. Its insecure status made it still acceptably comic for a mistress to recount how she managed her servants in 1923 in *The Queen*: 'As for doing things myself— no. I tell everyone I don't know how and just sit there and then everyone does them for me.'[109] Even households of 'only moderate needs', described in 1934 by Helen de Guerry Simpson's *The Happy Housewife*, were still assumed to employ a cook, general servant, and a char; she also advised that in a medium-sized house, a male gardener–chauffeur should be employed. Domestic manuals had become wary of referring to mistresshood, preferring ambiguous euphemisms like 'housekeeper' or even 'housewife', but often with little significant change in the role envisaged. Middle-class women still had a deep sense of entitlement, and neither labour-saving, hygiene or the 'professional' housewife identity was sufficient to dislodge their feeling that they deserved domestic servants.

Many interwar descriptions of managing without servants still envisaged this as a temporary, and sometimes entertaining state of affairs, rather than a sign of a new democratic social order playing out in the home. *Good Housekeeping* ran an article in 1923 entitled 'The Servantless Home' depicting 'doing for oneself' as a holiday experience. The article described the need for a 'simpler' life given the rising cost of living, which led to servantless experiments on a caravanning holiday. The author smugly declared: 'one begins to realise how unnecessarily encumbered is domestic life for the average housewife,' and enthusiastically described using central heating and a 'kitchen-cum-diner'.[110] In 1930, *Good Housekeeping* presented a description of the housewife as flexibly taking on all roles in her household, but still only servantless in the older sense of being 'between' servants:

The woman of today is compelled to assert her personality and conserve her energies as she has to depend upon herself so much, owing to the instability of labour. From week to week, the modern woman is never quite sure of her domestic staff, whether she will have to turn cook, housemaid, nurse, chauffeuse, or act as her husband's secretary.[111]

---

[108] Wylde, *A Housewife in Kensington*, 18–19, 207.
[109] 'Diary of a 20th Century Woman', *The Queen*, Jan 1923.
[110] Dora J. Moore, 'The Servantless House: Solving the Problem of Costly Living', *Good Housekeeping*, June 1923, 28.
[111] Churchill, 'Woman, Yesterday, Today and Tomorrow', 280.

'Doing for Oneself' 127

The uncertainties of the supply of domestic help meant that she might be regularly between servants, but doing without them entirely was not envisaged. The 'self' being presented here is a competent managerial one—still a form of mistresshood rather than an autonomous housewife.

By 1939, the rhetoric had barely changed. *The Times* ran a story describing the joys of a 'servantless bungalow' that combined a holiday retreat with a place in which daughters might be trained to cook and clean.[112] This weekend retreat was not expected to set the tone for everyday living, and was a diverting curiosity, akin to camping out, rather than a realistic proposal for how to manage a household. Nonetheless, as more working-class women were absorbed into industrial work and re-armourment, the tone of domestic advice tended to become more sanguine. *Housewife* magazine declared: 'If you have a maid, do not expect her to cook, dish up and wait at table as well. No human can do all three well. Be frank as most of us are and help—and invest in a service trolley.'[113] World War II intensified the need to consider managing without servants. On a single day in 1942, *The Times* 'situations wanted' column advertised the availability of a motley group of domestic workers: a 'youth with nervous complaint' sought 'au pair work'; a butler offered his services but noted that he was 'over 50, [and] a little deaf'; a cook described herself as 'elderly' and 'lame', but would oblige for £1 a week; and a 'gentlewoman' was willing to 'help' between 10am and 3pm, as long as there was no shopping and she could bring her dog. In the same column, a solution to the transition to servantless living was offered: 'Gentlewoman who has been staying in ladies' houses, showing them how to manage and cook for themselves when maids have been called up, is now willing to do the same thing from her London home by the half day or hour.'[114] The transition to a servantless home still required coaching and encouragement, but had become more immediately imperative.

POST-WAR 'SERVANTLESS HOMES'

After the war, manuals such as the 1949 *How to Run Your Home without Help* had finally began to give details of the tasks that had been termed 'rough'—how to wash nappies and do laundry.[115] However, feminine identities of privilege still resisted an easy internalization of a class-crossing, ethnically neutral housewife identity. Journalist Roy Lewis and Conservative politician Angus Maude commented in their 1949 survey of the English middle classes:

if their music and drama are to be purveyed to them only through the radio; if good furniture, good silver and good pictures (all of which need careful maintenance) are to be

---

[112] 'Housekeeping without Tears', *The Times*, July 31, 1939, 17.
[113] *Housewife Magazine*, Feb 1939.
[114] *The Times*, Aug 10, 1942, 8.
[115] Kay Smallshaw, *How to Run Your Home without Help* (London: Persephone Books, 2005 [1949]).

banished for ever to museums; and if entertaining is to be permanently restricted for all but Cabinet Ministers, then emigration to Eire or South Africa seems the only hope.[116]

They insisted that domestic service be perpetuated for the sake of this lifestyle of high culture, which they felt had deep national and cultural significance. Others, perhaps more in touch with their times, argued that the value of domestic service lay in freeing married servant-keeping women up for public service rather than leisured living. Violet Markham, and Florence Hancock of the Trades Union Congress, argued in their 1944 report to the Minister of Labour: 'An educated woman fitted by training and experience to make a real contribution to the national life must, if married, provide primarily for the needs of her household, her husband and her children. If no help is forthcoming in carrying out these duties, inevitably she must discharge them herself. Waste of energy and capacity ensues.'[117]

Markham and Hancock also had more apocalyptic concerns. They concluded: 'A woman who cannot be a companion to her husband and share his leisure and amusements will not undertake the burden of childbearing. Behind domestic problems stands the greater issue of the birth rate and our menaced existence as a great nation.'[118] 'Servantless homes' connoted a decline not only in middle-class lifestyles and public service opportunities, but also in the reproductive work of middle-class women. The concerns over middle-class fertility had become commonplace in the early to mid-twentieth century. The prominent Anglican author Dean Inge stressed the demographic implications of being servantless in a 1920 public lecture: 'I have no doubt that in the professional classes especially we shall have thousands of childless and servantless households in which the tradition of culture and refined living shall be maintained at the heavy price of family suicide.'[119] This concern with fertility was not confined to conservatives such as Inge and Markham. Clementina Black had prophesied that if middle-class women with their 'intensified passion for cleanliness' had to manage without servants, they would limit their fertility, to the detriment of the nation.[120] Being servantless was thus linked to some cues for moral panic, and resonated with the long-standing degeneration and decline narratives that proved so persistent in twentieth-century Britain.

There was, however, a surprising mood of optimism amongst middle-class women in the immediate post-war years that domestic service could and should be perpetuated. Markham and Hancock concluded that dignity and skill might still be its hallmarks. They recommended the establishment of a national training body that would regularize conditions and make of domestic service a skilled profession. The resulting National Institute of Houseworkers (NIH) was set up in 1949;

[116] Roy Lewis and Angus Maude, *The English Middle Classes* (Bath: Cedric Chivers, 1973 [1949]).
[117] Violet Markham and Florence Hancock, *Report on the Organisation of Private Domestic Employment* (London: HMSO, 1944).
[118] Ibid. 18.
[119] Dean Inge, 'Eugenics and Religion', public lecture at the Wigmore Hall, reported in 'Family Suicide', *The Times*, Nov 17, 1920.
[120] Black, *A New Way of Housekeeping*, 14.

Hancock believed: 'The setting-up of the Institute has opened up a new era for the domestic worker.'[121] She expected it to work with the National Union of Domestic Workers, to secure skilled status. However, the union was never an active force, and the NIH found that its graduates (around 500 annually) preferred to go into institutional jobs rather than private domestic service. NIH training centres received diminishing levels of state financial support. Their network was reduced, until the entire organization was wound up in the early 1970s, never having achieved its aim of creating a skilled profession. Nonetheless, there was still considerable support in government for delivering domestic workers, usually blandly termed 'home helps', to what Angus Maude termed in 1951 'the hard-pressed, harassed, overworked, professional or middle-class family.'[122]

Discussions of the servant problem pervaded post-war domestic advice literature. The architect Morrison Hendy's 1950 *Planning Your Home for Tomorrow* still included a chapter devoted to 'The Maid Problem'. Hendy advised readers that a maid was simply too expensive for post-war budgets; houses therefore 'should be planned, both in size and in convenience, so that it may be run without whole-time domestic help.' He was convinced that labour-saving techniques could make servantless living feasible, though it was clear that providing for servants was still a contentious issue for architects, prompting serious debate and meriting lengthy discussion in Hendy's book.[123] Manifestos of 'modern living' from the post-World War II years continued to be ambivalent about domestic service. A vision of 'houses for the atomic age, rather than of the early steam age', for example, outlined in Henry Dalton Clifford's 1963 *Houses for Today*, was still tentatively proposing a role for servants. Clifford was a regular writer for *Country Life* and well known for supporting radical and novel modes of living such as prefabricated houses. He stated unequivocally:

This is an age of social revolution and scientific progress. Our standards of comfort and sanitation are far higher than those of a hundred and fifty years ago. The housemaid has been superseded by mechanical and electrical devices. Instead of a cook the lady of the house presides in the kitchen. We have almost done away with coal fires and all the dust, soot, smoke, ash, draughts, labour and fire-hazard that went with them. We no longer need a separate room for every domestic activity—a dining-room, sitting-room, drawing-room, library, breakfast room, study and boudoir. With no servants to spy on us, and with clean automatic heating systems to keep every corner of the house at a comfortable temperature, we can, if we want to, have one large all-purpose living-room.[124]

The absence of servants profoundly informed Clifford's vision of modern living (which continued to be gendered in traditional ways). Yet whatever his intentions, the possibility of service continued to shape the houses he described. Devices such as the fold-down table were proposed for 'a family house', designed to offer two folding flaps on either side of a serving hatch. This offered the family a curiously

---

[121] Florence Hancock, 'On Domestic Employment', *Labour Woman*, Oct 15, 1946, 210.
[122] Maude, *Hansard* HC Deb, Apr 27, 1951, vol 487, cc 802–12.
[123] Morrison Hendy, *Planning Your Home for Tomorrow* (London: Faber, 1950), 178–9.
[124] Henry Dalton Clifford, *Country Life Book of Houses for Today* (London: Country Life, 1963).

semi-shared dining space, with 'children and their nurse on the kitchen side and the parents in the dining-room'. 'Staff quarters' and 'maid's bedrooms' pervaded the well-heeled homes reviewed in Clifford's *Houses for Today*. A pattern in post-war texts emerged, where a polemical statement of 'modern living' foregrounded the departure of domestic servants as a primary shift of modernity, only to have this contradicted by the detail of the designs and descriptions of actual living arrangements. Features of modern life, such as the advent of the take-away meal, were still interpreted in the light of the absence of servants. In 1961, *The Spectator* described a 'fetch-your-own-curry service in Camden Town' as being designed to 'fill the gap left by the vanished race of servants'.[125] Elizabeth David's cooking column in the same paper was aimed at those learning to cook for themselves, but was still illustrated by a black and white uniformed figure who was unmistakably a cook. Servants were a haunting presence; whether absent or present, they were a continued reference point for those thinking about and depicting British homes.

How did this influence quotidian domestic practices? A survey of au pair employment concluded in 1961, 'women who grew up in a home where help was taken for granted find themselves married and without household assistance. Despite modern flats and houses and labour-saving devices, those who have always been used to "servants" do not wish to do without them.'[126] For young women during and after World War II, the transition to doing for oneself was still a traumatic and disorienting one. Elizabeth Arthur left a middle-class home to work as a nurse, and had to be instructed how to clean a toilet.

I had to put my hand in the lavatory and scrub all round it by hand. Another thing I hadn't done was to cut bread, and I remember that was difficult. We'd had a cook, a housemaid, a tweeny—whatever that was—and a charwoman . . . I always wondered why I found it hard to do housework in my own house later. But as a child home meant to me sitting down and being waited on.[127]

One member of a small national correspondence club, using the pen name 'Accidia', described her domestic role with considerable honesty and insight:

People gasp on learning that I have five children and wonder how on earth I manage. Clearly they envisage either an efficient squad of family retainers or complete squalor. Actually we have neither. Two mornings a week a 22-year-old girl comes up from the village and lays about her with relative efficiency whilst I, an exile from the kitchen which cannot contain two (for purely physical, not temperamental, reasons), do as many of the numerous postponed small jobs as possible; for the rest of the week I 'do' for myself.[128]

She had no washing machine, no vacuum, and very few technological aids. Though Accidia claimed that this hard work was rewarding and acceptable, she did resent

---

[125] 'Leslie Adrian' [Jean Robertson], 'Dining Out at Home', *Spectator*, Dec 29, 1961, 962.
[126] Sheila Williams and F. D. Flower, *Foreign Girls in Hendon: A Survey* (London: Hendon Overseas Friendship Association, 1961), 38.
[127] Wendy Webster, *Imagining Home* (London: UCL Press, 1998), 157.
[128] Accidia, 'Ergs of Work', Dec 1951, in Jenna Bailey, *Can Any Mother Help Me?* (London: Faber and Faber, 2007), 44–5.

the gendered inequity of her household: 'Lucky lucky Daddy who dresses placidly and half-asleep, unconscious of the turmoil around him and unmolested by the throng!' And some years later in 1955, she acknowledged that:

there are times... when a black accidie descends; I wake to a feeling of 'what the hell?' seeing the years' relentless passage, so little time, so little accomplished, and my life endlessly spent in tidying the muddles of others, cleaning the horrid little house, trying to fit a gallon-size family into a pint-pot establishment.... My own life at the moment seems a dull waste, a vale of (unshed) tears, an empty vessel, a froth of frustration... I am bored, bored, BORED.[129]

This was the frustration of the 'housebound mother' identified by Hannah Gavron in *The Captive Wife* (1966), and which eventually led to a radicalization of attitudes to the domestic division of labour and new forms of feminist activism. Gavron directly linked this to the experiences of 'the now servantless middle-class wives with young children [who] are leading a life not dissimilar to that of many workers' wives.' Post-war feminists proved inadequately attentive to the disadvantages of class and ethnicity experienced by those women to whom domestic work was still delegated. Germaine Greer notoriously advocated a utopian solution to the emancipation of women in the 1971 *Female Eunuch*, which envisaged a form of 'collective living' in an Italian farmhouse: 'the house and garden would be worked by a local family who lived in the house.'[130]

The frustration of women like 'Accidia' in the 1950s was exacerbated by the cultural presentation of middle-class domestic life as leisured. The middle-class families presented by the media, such as the Dales of the hugely popular BBC radio series *Mrs Dale's Diary* (1948–69), and the Conover family on BBC television (1949–50), employed domestic workers—a char and a cook, respectively. The relationship between Mrs Dale and her char, Mrs Morgan (later Mrs Maggs), was still transacted in simpler, more limited language than other conversations of the programme. One Polish refugee to Britain, Danuta Gradosielska, commented: 'I had a radio and listened to "Mrs Dale's Diary." In this program she used to give her maid detailed instructions, and that's how I learnt English.'[131] Servant-keeping was still being presented, and interpreted, as central to middle-class femininity, a subject position defined by ethnicity alongside class and gender.

Print culture was equally haunted by servant-keeping and its new permutations. *Housewife*, a glossy women's magazine of the 1950s and 1960s, still referred commonly to domestic 'helps' and featured chars in its cartoons. Despite its title, the editors addressed 'the business girl or wife with a job' or to complex, clumsy identities such as the 'single-handed cook hostess'. When one reader wrote of her hatred of housework in 1957, another reader glibly advised her to get a job and employ 'domestic help' for a couple of hours each day. *Householder Magazine*,

---

[129] Feb 1, 1955, ibid. 51–2.
[130] Hannah Gavron, *The Captive Wife: Conflicts of Housebound Mothers* (London: Routledge & Keagan Paul, 1966); Germaine Greer, *The Female Eunuch* (London: Flamingo, 1993), 264.
[131] A436870, http://polishdiaspora.net/_wsn/page13.html, accessed June 30, 2009.

founded in 1939, become *Modern Housewife and Householder* in 1950. 'Modern Housewife' must have proved unappealing, however, because the magazine quickly changed its title again, to the more directly individualistic *You*. Its editors were perhaps seeking a readership of self-consciously modern young women, those at whom the popular journalist Katharine Whitehorn aimed her highly successful book in 1961, titled *Cooking in a Bedsitter, or Kitchen in the Corner*. Whitehorn termed herself and her envisaged readers 'the domestically incompetent' or 'sluts'. She actively presented herself as epitomizing the post-war democratic blurring of 'above and below stairs' social distinctions, commenting in 1960: 'When I am in luck I have a char; when out of luck I have occasionally *been* a char.'[132] Yet her autobiography reveals the extent of her own reliance upon domestic help; she had a daily cleaner, working from 10am to 3pm, when still childless. After the arrival of her two sons, she variously obtained the help of an Austrian refugee, a daily 'help', and some residential 'mother's helps'. These habits continued for educated women; a 1964 survey of members of the British Federation of University Women found that over 90 per cent of respondents employed domestic help, ranging from residential servant to mother's help or au pair.[133]

'These servantless days' was a repeated cliché of the 1950s and 1960s, used to usher in a discussion of any domestic or family item in the media. Advertisers still exploited the middle-class sense of entitlement and loss associated with being servantless. An advertisement for oil-fired domestic appliances in *The Times* in 1959 addressed a harassed housewife, 'Mrs 1970': 'You—Maid of all work. Cooking. Cleaning. Laying the fires. Encouraging them with sheets of The Times. Rushing back to see to the boiler. Servantless. And bored!' To drive home their point, they also included a 'then and now' comic strip, illustrating 'Fanny', an imagined maid of the past, who 'wrapped Grandma round in a devoted cocoon of cosy comfort' (Figure 8). The housewife did not appear as a settled identity willingly embraced by post-war women, but rather as a problematic subject position into which middle-class women from formerly servant-keeping families had been forced.

Figure 8. 'How to Live Your Life without Servants—and Enjoy It!' *The Times*, September 18, 1959, 9.

---

[132] Katharine Whitehorn, 'Nought for Homework', *Spectator*, Nov 25, 1960, 874.
[133] Katharine Whitehorn, *Selective Memory* (London: Virago, 2007), 152; British Federation of University Women, *The Occupational Outlook for Graduate Women* (London, 1964), 25–6, quoted in Webster, *Imagining Home*, 157.

Professional women were still fantasizing about domestic help, though they may have realized it to be unrealistic. *Good Housekeeping* reported a professional working woman in 1969 as claiming: 'I'd trade in my vote if I thought I could get a good, old-fashioned nanny who would also cook and wash-up', though the editor commented that such a desire was 'pie-in-the-sky'.[134] *The Spectator's* consumer column, in contrast, was less pessimistic. In 1960, its main contributor, Jean Robertson, noted that 'everyone has—or is looking for—a "little man" or a "little woman" round the corner to do odd jobs at reasonable prices.'[135] Though *The Spectator* referred gloomily to 'these servantless, family-divided days', domestic help agencies such as Domestics Unlimited or Universal Aunts were continually reviewed in its pages in the early to mid-1960s.[136]

New categories of domestic workers did indeed fill the gap to some extent. In 1967, Katharine Whitehorn wryly commented on her 'Hampstead friends', 'Lately we have all been edging round to some sort of help—not a *nanny* of course, but an *au pair*, a mother's help, a part-time student, or a Girl.'[137] Au pairs seemed the most promising and widely used of these options. The idea of light household tasks undertaken by a young 'visitor' in exchange for language learning, plus room and board had been available in Europe since the 1890s, but it was not portrayed as a solution to the class tensions of the servant problem until considerably later. The *Manchester Guardian* articulated with honesty the post-war hope that the au pair would solve 'a delicate social problem for the professional and middle classes who cannot quite afford a full time domestic and whose accommodation is limited so that it is easier for the housewife to have someone around of her own standing. One does not apologise to social equals.' *The Times* estimated that around 17,000 such workers were coming to Britain each year in the 1950s. The numbers of those migrating to improve their language skills as au pairs across Europe was in the tens of thousands in the late 1960s.[138]

Commentators attempted to position the au pair within the social landscape of domestic service, as 'not quite a guest and not quite a servant'. There were few established norms governing how such 'guests' should be treated, and as a result, *The Spectator* commented in 1950, the 'home help from abroad' created even more difficulties than the maid.[139] Au pairs drew on the eroticized overtones of domestic

---

[134] Kenneth Passingham, 'The Troubled Double Life of a Working Wife', *Good Housekeeping*, Aug 1969, 38–9.
[135] 'Leslie Adrian' [Jean Robertson], 'Odd Jobs', *Spectator*, Oct 21, 1960, 626.
[136] 'Leslie Adrian' [Jean Robertson], 'Mrs Mopp', *Spectator* Sept 28, 1962, 45; Spectator's Notebook, Apr 16, 1965, 502; Dec 9, 1966, 767; 'Leslie Adrian', 'Help Wanted', Feb 25, 1966, 235.
[137] Katharine Whitehorn, 'Good Old Nanny, by Any Other Name', *Observer Review*, Nov 12, 1967.
[138] *Manchester Guardian*, Nov 3, 1958; *The Times*, Jan 9, 1956; *Observer*, Apr 30, 1961; European Agreement on 'au pair' Placement (ETS 68). Online at http://conventions.coe.int/treaty/en/Reports/Html/068.htm; *The Times*, Oct 21, 1960. On the contemporary representations of au pairs, see Rosie Cox, 'The Au Pair Body: Sex Object, Sister or Student?', *European Journal of Women's Studies*, 14 3 (2007), 281–96.
[139] 'Home Help from Abroad', *Spectator*, Dec 15, 1950, 700.

service, discussed in Chapter 5, and were frequently portrayed as a disruptive sexual presence.[140] A survey undertaken in 1957 in Hendon noted considerable ambiguity of status for both the part-time au pairs and the full-time foreign workers whose Ministry of Labour permits termed them domestics or 'mothers helps'. Both these groups were included by surveyors under the capacious category of 'foreign girls'. More than 80 per cent of the workers in the affluent London 'dormitory' suburb of Hendon were classed as middle class by the authors, and a large majority came from Germany. The work conditions of the full-time workers closely resembled that of a general servant, with two half-days off a week and around £3 a week in wages. Only two-thirds of them ate with the family and the majority reported that despite their intentions of learning English, they had no conversations that went beyond childcare and family matters. Both groups found the class ambiguities of their position hard to negotiate. The report's authors noted that

Most girls are aware that they are taking the place of the pre-war 'servant' and they often resent it. There is little difference in attitude between au pair girls and full-time girls. They think of themselves as students, as typists, as glamour girls, but not as domestic workers... [Yet] if their employers wish to regard them as servants they have no protection. They are, legally and actually, in the same position as old-fashioned 'servants' were.

They listed the resulting tensions:

one girl felt very humiliated because she had to hand round biscuits to guests but was not allowed to take one. Another complained that she had to eat her tea in the kitchen when her employer's sister made a weekly visit. These employers took the girl with them to a fortnight's holiday at a seaside hotel, where they stopped using her name and dressed her up in a white uniform and called her 'Nannie'.[141]

A comedy of nomenclature emerged from these accounts of post-war domestic employment. Both sides recognized that 'maid', 'master', and 'mistress' were unacceptable terms, while employee was too formal. Uncomfortable innovations such as 'mister' were used to address the 'hosts' of au pairs. 'All this is decidedly comic to the English ear, but there really are no words to describe the odd relationship. "Girl," "lady" and "mister" are all indications of the anomalous social situation.' The survey's authors instead proposed the bland identity 'part-time workers', preferring to leave the work and worker unspecified. British households enthusiastically imported au pair labour, and numbers rose in the late 1960s and early 1970s. However, the status problems persisted; Joan Vickers, MP for Plymouth, noted in 1971 that 'the girls are semi-servants for people who cannot afford servants, who do not like doing the work themselves, and who in most cases do not pay National Insurance or selective employment tax'.[142]

---

[140] See for example, Margaret Belsky, '"I'm Terribly Worried about Charles and the Au Pair Girl"', *The Sun*, May 5, 1965; Williams and Flower, *Foreign Girls in Hendon*, 42–4.
[141] Williams and Flower, *Foreign Girls in Hendon*, 33–5.
[142] Ibid. 75; *Hansard*, HC Deb, Feb 15, 1971, vol 811, cc 1499-510.

The euphemism of 'help' did become more widely adopted in the middle years of the century as a means of differentiating new kinds of domestic workers from servants, alongside other terms such as 'treasure', and 'gem'. 'Help' was still the preferred term in the 1980s, by which time 'daily' or 'char' had come to seem demeaning or used ironically. One Hampshire employer noted in 1983, 'I dislike "housework" as such, and am fortunate enough to have help once a week for 3 hrs (twice when mother is home). I do all the laundry, all the cooking and shopping. I like the copper, brass and silver to be well polished and I enjoy doing this.'[143] To term these workers 'helps' acknowledged that domestic tasks might be shared, but also denied them the status of employed worker, and made their informal employment seem acceptable.

Most post-war domestic workers sought the distance from 'servantdom' that au pairs had attempted to achieve through renaming. When the government founded the National Institute of Houseworkers (NIH), the aim had been to distance this institution from any hint of domestic service through the 'home worker' identity that spanned paid and unpaid domestic work. It was clear, however, that this rebranding was met with considerable resistance, as cultural frames of 'Mrs Mopp' persisted. 'Houseworker' was never widely adopted, and in 1963 the *Daily Telegraph* reported a competition to find a new name; 'home carer' was a strong contender, but in the end, the NIH was renamed, in 1968, the National Institute for Housecraft.[144] This was chosen despite the majority of NIH graduates going into non-residential posts in institutions such as hotels and schools rather than private homes.

At the specific historical and spatial location of the Hendon survey, the large numbers of Jewish families in the area also produced tensions of ethnicity for the au pairs. The 1961 report noted the hostility that Jewish or non-European employers faced from the casual anti-Semitism of the 'girls': 'many girls seem to think nearly all employers are Jewish... In the complex interplay of emotions which often, though not always, exists when a Jewish family employs a German girl, both sides are made unhappy.'[145] The inappropriateness of servant-keeping for those othered by their ethnicity or religion was still implied, though the domestic workers here were also portrayed as intrusive of domestic privacy and equilibrium. *The Observer* was sympathetic to employers in its discussion of the 'au pair problem' in 1961, and concluded that 'one may prefer to see one's friends without an extra presence, and to be able to be alone with oneself or one's marriage partner is the essence of home.'[146] Versions of the home defined by privacy were clearly available, and gained in significance during the post-war years, forming a component of white British ethnicity in contrast to the imagined chaos of immigrant domestic life, as Wendy Webster has argued. The 'private' home was also linked to more domestically oriented versions of masculinity, smaller working-class families, and the

---

[143] S531, Mass Observation reply to Autumn 1983 Directive 'Household Tasks'.
[144] *Daily Telegraph*, July 18, 1963; *Hansard*, HC Deb, Jan 19, 1968, vol 756, cc 2163-76.
[145] Williams and Flower, *Foreign Girls in Hendon*, 50–1, and unnumbered appendix.
[146] *Observer*, Apr 30, 1961.

transformation of the built environment during the municipal and private building programmes of the 1950s and 1960s.[147]

By the later 1960s, there seemed a distinct shift in the cultural presentation of the domestic realm. Being servantless was no longer a central discursive element of being a housewife. Household manuals rarely mentioned domestic workers in the home, or acknowledged that they were now employed by very few, and would expect 'consideration and courteous treatment'.[148] In the experiences of the less affluent, beyond the pages of the colour supplements and design books, servantless middle-class homes were becoming a reality. The census in 1971 showed a large drop in the already small numbers working as residential domestic servants in England and Wales, from around 100,000 in 1961, to only 32,000 in 1971.[149] These remaining servants were concentrated in London and the South East, and served only a tiny proportion of households. Clumsy efforts to name domestic roles continued, with *The Times* in 1970 terming the professional woman who cooked at home 'the working cook housewife', who might devote herself to what were still called 'servantless dishes'.[150] Patrick Hutber's 1976 polemical text, *The Decline and Fall of the Middle Class, and How It Can Fight Back*, suggested that domestic service continued to shape 'middle-classness'. Hutber's correspondents were all drawn from the *Sunday Telegraph* readership; one commented that defining features of being middle class included: 'To be able to provide the family with a holiday, be it only a week at a local coastal resort and to ease the burden of household chores through domestic help.' Another, an architect, commented on the sense of anxiety of the mid-1970s; he felt 'up against the wall. I haven't seen a play in London in two years. I only eat in restaurants on business. Can't afford the gardener once a week any more.'[151] However, in the main, the 'felt absence' of domestic servants in contemporary British homes evoked in the discourse of being servantless had faded; the servant problem was no longer an effective channel for the tensions generated by social and economic change.

Mary Ingham's survey of her 30-something peers, undertaken in 1977, revealed strong conflicts over housework between heterosexual couples. Men's failure to help with housework continued to motivate the employment of domestic workers. Most of the women Ingham interviewed acknowledged their sense of low status if they stayed at home to raise children, and found they had conflicting feelings over housework. Some enjoyed it, or found it a source of power, though one housewife

---

[147] Webster, *Imagining Home*, 67, 73. See also Stephen Brooke, 'Gender and Working Class Identity in Britain during the 1950s', *Journal of Social History*, 34 4 (2001), 773–96; Mark Clapson, 'Working-Class Women's Experiences of Moving to New Housing Estates in England since 1919', *Twentieth Century British History*, 10 3 (1999), 345–65.

[148] Norman Hartnell, *The Complete Housewife* (London: Evans, 1960). See also Aileen King, *Better Home Management* (London: Mills and Boon, 1961); Joan Storey, *Running a Home: A Guide to Efficient Household Management*. (London: Faber and Faber, 1968).

[149] Penny Radford, 'Keeping an Open House', *The Times*, Aug 10, 1972, 10; Judy Hillmann, 'Census and the Serving Classes', *Guardian*, Aug 21, 1975.

[150] 'Food in Britain' *The Times*, Feb 16, 1970, p. I of supplement.

[151] Patrick Hutber, *The Decline and Fall of the Middle Class, and How It Can Fight Back* (Harmondsworth: Penguin, 1977), 29, 37.

feared 'simply acting like my mother, wanting kitchen omnipotence.' Some employed cleaners consciously to resolve the tensions with their partners, while others worked as cleaners themselves during the economic downturns of the 1970s.[152] There was far less sense of social chasm attached to this employment, and in some local labour markets, women had a degree of power. One Mass Observation correspondent (who had worked as a cleaner herself) noted that when she advertised in 1979 for a cleaner, it took six months to find anyone, and women she encountered were choosy about hours and wages. The more intense economic downturn of the 1980s, however, pushed larger numbers of vulnerable women into insecure, casual cleaning jobs, and the same correspondent noted that in 1983, she had only to advertise by putting a notice up in a local newsagents for less than a day, and managed to find a cleaner to come daily for two hours. She hired a young married woman with two children who also worked at as an office cleaner in the evenings. This employer was well aware that the arrangement was within the 'black economy', but noted that women were pleased to get any work.[153] Such work became economically and culturally invisible, and many such 'helps' rarely encountered their employers, who were mostly out at work. Except in relation to childcare, the powerful emotional links and conflicts that marked earlier forms of domestic service had faded, though Annette Dobson's experiences of private cleaning in the 1990s suggest that it still had a low status and connotations of compulsion. She herself stopped this work when it became clear that her wages were unlikely to go up, since there was no formal means to discuss pay: 'you're hitting your head on the glass ceiling before you've even straightened up.'[154] As Chapter 6 will discuss, in the 1980s domestic service became a powerful and evocative component of public memory and British 'heritage', effacing the actual presence of domestic workers in large numbers of British homes.

CONCLUSIONS

This chapter has suggested that there was deep ambiguity over what 'a servant' was, and when one might be considered servantless in twentieth-century British society. Talk of being servantless was loaded with moral judgements; some households might be seen as deservedly or appropriately servantless. It was a condition that the established, indigenous middle-classes wished to see imposed upon those of limited means or minority ethnicity, who if they did hire servants, were widely felt to be living 'above their station'. The cliché of 'these servantless days' was not always used to indicate the shortages of servants, but rather to distinguish between competing definitions of privilege and belonging. The upper-middle-class magazine *The Lady*,

---

[152] Mary Ingham, *Now We Are Thirty: Women of the Breakthrough Generation* (London: Eyre Methuen, 1981).
[153] A015, Mass Observation Archive (University of Sussex), reply to summer 1983 directive on Work, Leisure and Unemployment.
[154] Annette Dobson, interview with the author, Sept 3, 2010.

for example, acknowledged in 1938: 'It looks as though a good deal of suburban elegance will have to be abandoned and simpler household ways adopted. The luxury of an attendant almost constantly on duty will have to go the way of candlelight, open fires and other amenities now only possible to the rich.'[155] This was less a mourning for the passing of a way of life than an attempt to distinguish the 'suburbans' from their social superiors.

The absence of servants became a more pressing concern for more affluent households in the later 1930s, and a range of new identities and monikers attempted to convey new styles of living and social statuses. Housekeeper, house-mistress, hostess, home worker, home carer, housewife, girl, and help competed, and made the divide between servant and employer increasingly permeable and anxious. 'Housewife' was an identity that many mid-twentieth-century working-class and ethnic minority women found to offer satisfaction and agency, in comparison to their marginalization in paid employment, or their mothers' experiences of poverty. With the affluence and greater consumption of the 1950s and 1960s, more working-class women began to aspire to and achieve standards of comfort and cleanliness that had previously been part of the cultural capital of being middle class. Historians have constructed sensitive accounts of the relationship working-class women sustained to domesticity, but this seems unconvincing for more privileged women. The identities and worldview of servant-keeping were persistently at play in the construction of 'domesticity' for such women during the interwar period and for two decades after World War II. Servant-keeping was widely presented and understood as capable of being modernized and imagined as progressive, rather than obsolete. The shift to a housewife identity was partial and half-hearted, and while it is clear that to speak as a housewife had its political uses, particularly in the 'austerity years' after World War II, it was far from being deeply internalized in middle-class female subjectivities.

Post-war consumer culture continued to evoke the 'holes left by the departure of Mary Ann', often for commercial motives. Adverts such as Shell's 'Mrs 1970' sought to summon up a feeling of the oppression of servantless housework, a sensation of injustice at being 'the maid of all work'. Yet a sense also emerges from the sources of this period that many middle-class, indigenous women genuinely felt uninspired by domesticity, and frustrated at being forced to do more of it than they had expected. Yet mid-twentieth-century middle-class women aspired to careers, and opportunities for self-development in other realms. Katharine Whitehorn asserted in 1960, 'we have heard the words "labour-saving" and "career" too often for us to feel that we are being finally judged as women by the way we run our houses.'[156]

In the discussion of 'servantlessness' there was a discussion of the domestic contributions that men might make. It was not until 1943 that *Housewife* magazine brightly announced that 'the new mother's help is—father'.[157] Most advice texts

---

[155] *The Lady*, Jan 1938.
[156] Katharine Whitehorn, 'Nought for Homework', *Spectator*, Nov 25, 1960, 875.
[157] Ann Blythe, *Housewife*, 'The New Mother's Help Is—Father', Mar 1943.

continued to be highly tentative about masculine forms of domesticity until the 1970s, presenting men only as helpers to their female counterparts. The continuing employment of domestic workers enabled the gendered domestic division of labour to be sustained for the rest of the century, and for the men of servant-keeping households to neglect childcare and housework.

When one professional woman wrote to *The Times* in 1962 describing her pleasure and mental release in mopping, vacuuming, and washing-up, she acknowledged that these were 'heretical views' that she had been very cautious of airing in public.[158] The apparent celebration of domesticity associated with her era was not publically voiced amongst her peers. Instead, middle-class women pursued more individualistic versions of selfhood; they increasingly attended higher education, and put off having children. Young middle-class women in the 1950s were offered literature encouraging them to choose a career, in the form of magazines, annuals, and 'career girl' novels in which working and professional women were presented as glamorous and capable.[159] The twentieth-century association of middle-class, indigenous female identities with a cosmopolitan, path-breaking, trend-setting mode of being—in other words, with a version of 'modernity'—rendered the long-standing association between middle classness and servant-keeping problematic, but did not sever it. The identity options for privileged women proliferated, and modified, hard-to-name, yet still recognizable versions of servant-keeping continued to be the practical and symbolic means of realizing their aspirations.

---

[158] 'Relaxation', *The Times*, June 18, 1962, 15.
[159] Deborah Philips and Ian Haywood, *Brave New Causes: Women in British Postwar Fictions* (London: Leicester University Press, 1998).

4

Kitchen-Sink Laughter

Domestic Service Humour

As we have seen in previous chapters, the instability of the performances associated with domestic service could easily shade into farce, and laughter might intrude. The idea of domestic service as a realm suitable for jokes and laughter has had a long cultural heritage. Carolyn Steedman and Jane Thaddeus have written of eighteenth-century domestic servant jokes and 'Mollspeak', the pretentious and colloquial language put into their mouths that made servants so funny to their employers.[1] Jokes and laughter at the expense of employers and servants were equally prominent and persistent in late-nineteenth- and twentieth-century British society. Humour was an ingredient in the highly emotionally charged nature of domestic service—the invocations of loyalty, love, betrayal, and loss that went with the emotional and spatial proximity of employers and servants.

Victorians had for the most part regarded their jokes about servants as harmless, or even as a healthy way of ensuring that servants knew their place. However, from around the turn of the century, reformers habitually talked of the comedy value of servants as a major problem, indicative of the lack of respect and dignity of the profession. The widely debated 'servant problem' was often recast as a 'humour problem', a damaging tendency to laugh at all involved with domestic service. A 1919 government enquiry into domestic service described how the press represented servants as 'comic or flippant characters...held up to ridicule', while the domestic difficulties of employers were also commonly portrayed as 'ignoble and laughable'.[2] Opportunities to laugh were important means of gaining authority, of resisting indignities, or even for abandoning the social scripts that governed interactions between employers and servants.

Looking at the jokes told about domestic service provides an alternative means of understanding the servant problem, which as Chapter 1 argued, has mostly been

---

[1] Carolyn Steedman, 'Servants and Their Relationship to the Unconscious', *Journal of British Studies*, 42 (2003), 316–50; Jane Thaddeus, 'Swift's Directions to Servants', *Studies in Eighteenth-Century Culture*, 16 (1986), 107–23. Earlier traditions can also be identified; see Sarah Gordon, 'Humour and Household Relationships: Servants in Late Medieval and Sixteenth-Century French Farce', in Susan Broomhall (Ed.), *Emotions in the Household, 1200–1900* (Basingstoke: Palgrave, 2008), 85–102.

[2] Gertrude Emmott, *Report of the Women's Advisory Committee of the Ministry of Reconstruction on the Domestic Service Problem* (London: HMSO Cmd. 67, 1919), 22–3.

investigated by historians as a social and economic issue, shaped by a powerful tendency to find victims. Accounts of service as an institution within British society have frequently assumed that the servant problem is best analysed through the conditions of work—the wages, the hours, and so on. Attention to humour and laughter enriches such accounts of domestic service with an additional cultural and emotional dimension. It both joins and extends a well-established historiography in reading class as a complex phenomenon, influenced as much by language, culture, and emotional experiences, as by socio-economic circumstances.[3] Investigating the humour problem captures the deep socio-cultural significance of domestic service in Britain, and reveals the ways in which laughter and comedy could sustain or undermine statuses and identities. It is clear that the alignment of an individual with forms of social identity is, as Michael Roper reminds us, a selective and partial process, and humour is one unpredictable vehicle for this kind of identification.[4] The study of humour sheds light on how representations of otherness work. So the history of humour, the traditions and 'knowingnesses' on which jokes and cartoons rely, can tell us something of how the representations and exclusions that shape our social world were and are received, transformed, and passed on. Humour is an important component of how culture and language intervene between social experiences or 'social being' and subjectivity. Like many emotions, laughter is a subjective and even uncontainable physical human response, but is also culturally codified. Laughter operates as a site of the exercise of power, in providing a means of naming, belittling, imitating, and making ridiculous. As Andy Medhurst has argued, 'Being laughed at is a surefire way of feeling put in your place—your place being absolutely not the place of those doing the laughing.'[5] It also, on occasion, promotes social inclusion, informality, and friendship. As Gatrell has recently argued, 'studying laughter can take us to the heart of a generation's shifting attitudes, sensibilities and anxieties'.[6]

Laughter at domestic service was evident amongst readers of cartoons, audiences at cinemas and music halls, and radio listeners. Some characters were long lasting and named, such as Mrs Sudds the charlady (1912–18) and Pansy Pancake the cook (1912–29), found in the penny comics. In addition, there were innumerable comic sketches of anonymous servants littering British journals and newspapers, novels, and memoirs. Laughter was also a frequent response to serious attempts to reform domestic service; when anxious ministers sponsored three public enquiries into domestic service, in 1919, 1923, and 1945, the response from the mass media

---

[3] Patrick Joyce, *Visions of the People: Industrial England and the Question of Class, 1848–1914* (Cambridge: Cambridge University Press, 1991); Gareth Stedman Jones, *Languages of Class: Studies in English Working Class History 1832–1982* (Cambridge: Cambridge University Press, 1982); Gareth Stedman Jones, *Outcast London: A Study in the Relationship between Classes in Victorian Society* (Oxford: Clarendon Press, 1991).

[4] Michael Roper, 'Slipping out of View: Subjectivity and Emotion in Gender History', *History Workshop Journal*, 59 (2005), 57–72, esp. 67.

[5] Andy Medhurst, *A National Joke: Popular Comedy and English Cultural Identities* (Abingdon: Routledge, 2007), 20.

[6] Vic Gatrell, *City of Laughter: Sex and Satire in Eighteenth-Century London* (London: Atlantic Books, 2006), 5, 159–76.

was invariably levity. A typical *Evening Standard* 'investigation' into service in 1939 set the tone; it opened: 'When I read about the servant question, I just laff and laff and laff.'[7] However, laughter was also evident in the myriad interactions that took place in kitchens and drawing rooms, and were related and recalled at middle-class dinners, 'below stairs', and in working-class homes. Domestic service humour can thus be understood to span two intersecting realms—the cultural representations of domestic work, and the everyday interactions in homes that employed servants or chars. Laughter at domestic service was both a response looked for by comic productions and an unpredictable, unstable element of the individual encounters of domestic service. This chapter will explore both successful and unsuccessful attempts to make domestic service laughable, dividing the laughter found at all levels of British cultural life from that found within homes, while acknowledging the interdependence of these realms. These are brought together with a concluding exploration of shared jokes and failed jokes of the second half of the twentieth century, and an assessment of the changes over time that can be traced in relation to domestic service humor.

Attention to humour in these kinds of sources allows for an expansion of the range of any historical inquiry into domestic service and class relations, since the texts and performances that carried domestic service humour frequently had a far wider circulation than the 'serious' treatment of the servant problem in the public enquiries, pamphlets, and articles that historians have largely drawn on. Yet there has been little attention to the laughter that accompanied domestic service—as if, lacking 'seriousness', the jokes about servants and employers did not have weight. Or perhaps it simply has not been evident that some texts were comic, since the jokes are often no longer funny to a modern reader. Why, for example, did the children of a late Victorian servant-keeping household in which a servant had been caught stealing money record that 'we were all astonished at Mother's cleverness' when she posed the joke, 'why is a thief like a dirty carpet? Because the sooner it is taken up and beaten, the better.' Yet as Robert Darnton's work suggests, it can be the 'unfunny' jokes of the past that are the most revealing.[8]

Humorous acts and texts, funny or unfunny to later interpreters, differ from other historical sources. Jokes have a performative dimension, and rely on gestures, pantomime, timbre, and rhythm. Historical work on humour is hampered by the difficulty of recovering this performative dimension, as well as the distances of a historical perspective—the passage of time and space, the translation in some cases from oral to written form, or the ambiguity of the visual form when read from a different context—all these factors make humour hard to pin down. Humour is

---

[7] 'Maids Say, "We Are Treated Like Machines" But This Mistress Just Laughs', *Evening Standard*, May 20, 1939, 17.

[8] Olive Haweis, *Four to Fourteen* (London: Robert Hale, 1939), 65. Robert Darnton's analysis of an eighteenth-century cat massacre by Parisian printing apprentices connects the older symbolic economies of charivari and rough music to what now seems an 'unfunny joke' of cat-torture, in order to uncover and explain the 'Rabelaisian laughter' and resistances of this episode: 'Workers Revolt: The Great Cat Massacre of the Rue Saint-Severin', in *The Great Cat Massacre and Other Episodes in French Cultural History* (London: Penguin, 2001), 75–106.

often timely, and not easily carried outside its historical context.[9] What was intended as satirical may now read as neutral, as social realism, or as grotesque.

Reading humour also requires a close attention to reception, and as an ambiguous and unstable medium, to the possibility of very different receptions by different audiences or individuals. What one finds funny is highly context-dependent, and this makes it hard for a historian to judge the success of comic performances and texts. Comic discourse is richly unstable, and sometimes escapes the intentions of the author or performer. Finally, it is important to be sensitive to the conditions of production of humour; much nineteenth- and twentieth-century humour was produced in commercial contexts, and needs to be read as a 'humour industry' rather than a direct vox populi or expression of mentalities. The production of, for example, nineteenth-century music hall songs as a commercial medium was in some senses 'just entertainment'—songs were intended to amuse and not to provoke. The material context of their production therefore can limit the meanings that can be read into them.[10]

The historiography of humour is dominated by two competing interpretations of the significance of humour. First, there is a literature (primarily located in sociology and anthropology) on the subversive power of humour, typified in political humour as the 'underground culture of dissent'.[11] Mary Douglas, drawing on Henri Bergson and Freud, offered a classic reading of jokes as essentially subversive, 'levelling of hierarchy, [a] triumph of intimacy over formality, of unofficial values over official ones'.[12] Such dissident humour can operate through symbolisms, can be overtly political, or can be simply socially irreverent.[13] In this guise, humour tends to be seen, following James Scott, as a 'weapon of the weak'. It is also identified with the grotesque inversions and licence of carnival, explored by Mikhail Bakhtin.[14]

The apparent 'dissidence' and subversive power of jokes, however, can be ambiguous to interpret; they can also shade into a second interpretation of the role of humour—to act as a kind of social vent that dissipates unrest. Umberto Eco has argued that carnival is an '*authorised* transgression', and thus reinforces established forms of identity.[15] Anthropologist Susan Seizer notes that jokes

---

[9] Darnton, 'Workers Revolt', xii; Walter Nash, *The Language of Humour: Style and Technique in Comic Discourse* (London: Longman, 1985).

[10] Dave Russell, *Popular Music in England, 1840–1914: A Social History* (London: St Martin's Press, 1997).

[11] Mary Lee Townsend, 'Humour and the Public Sphere in Nineteenth Century Germany', in J. Bremmer (ed.), *A Cultural History of Humour: From Antiquity to the Present Day* (Cambridge: Polity Press, 1997), 200–21.

[12] Mary Douglas, *Purity and Danger: An Analysis of the Concept of Pollution and Taboo* (London: Routledge, 2002), 152.

[13] For examples, see Gatrell, *City of Laughter*, and Peter Bailey, 'Ally Sloper's Half Holiday: Comic Art in the 1880s', *History Workshop*, 16 (1983), 4–31.

[14] James C. Scott, *Weapons of the Weak: Everyday Forms of Peasant Resistance* (New Haven, CT: Yale University Press, 1985). Mikhail Bakhtin, *Rabelais and His World*, trans. Helene Iswolsky (Bloomington: Indiana University Press, 2008 [1968]).

[15] Umberto Eco, 'The Frames of Comic Freedom', in Thomas A. Sebeok (ed.), *Carnival!* (Berlin: Mouton, 1984), 6.

paradoxically 'often serve to reinscribe the very conventions they blatantly taunt'.[16] Humour can depict abuse or exploitation as reassuringly funny, or can, through humiliation of outsider groups, create emotional affinities and satisfactions within social groups. Humour formed an important ingredient of what Gareth Stedman Jones labelled the 'culture of consolation' of late Victorian working-class leisure, and can serve as a substitute for political action, releasing social tensions and making the status quo seem more sustainable.[17]

Peter Bailey has extended the historiography beyond these two options with his influential account of Victorian music hall comedy as based on 'knowingness', a 'culture of competence' that was both subversive *and* complicit. The commercial genesis of late Victorian and Edwardian music hall and its attempts to appeal to broad audiences limited the potential for subversive or challenging content. Yet Peter Bailey has argued that there was a level on which music hall humour worked to 'destabilise the various official knowledges that sought to order common life through their languages of improvement and respectability and the intensifying grid of regulative social disciplines that marked the period.' This made for a 'counter-discourse' potential, but one that 'was limited to the infraction rather than the negation of the dominant power relationships.'[18] In other words, Victorian and Edwardian music hall—and possibly other contemporaneous forms of popular humour such as postcards, comics, and cinema—might mock and satirize official, elite, or establishment concerns, but rarely challenged or changed the terms of the status quo in any profound sense. Andy Medhurst similarly argues that popular comedy represents a temporary 'invitation to belong', built on the 'survival laughter' prompted by recognition of the grimness of daily life. He refuses to identify this with any ideological bent, concluding that popular humour 'is primarily a politics of defense not attack, of refusal not uprising, of embracing your own, of consolidation against condescension.'[19]

Servants were the ideal candidates for the kind of humour that relied upon social transgression and juxtaposition. The illustrator John Leech of *Punch* continually drew attention to the snobberies of servants in two series, *Flunkeiana* and *Servantgalism*. The language of servants was a persistent cause of laughter, centring on their attempts to imitate middle-class speech and accent. Other cartoons based their humour not on the snobbery of servants but on their desire for a social life, for contact with other workers, or for social activities such as reading literature or playing music. Such 'foibles' of servants were a stock topic for illustrated and comic magazines throughout the nineteenth century, as well as for collections of jokes, or jestbooks. Servants' undainty and odorous bodies, their dirty faces, the unseemly

---

[16] Susan Seizer, 'Jokes, Gender, and Discursive Distance on the Tamil Popular Stage', *American Ethnologist*, 24 1 (1997), 62–90.
[17] Stedman Jones, *Outcast London*. See also Gordon, 'Humour and Household Relationships', 90; Marjolein 't Hart and Bos Dennis, *Humour and Social Protest* (Cambridge: Cambridge University Press, 2007), 6–7.
[18] Peter Bailey, 'Conspiracies of Meaning: Music-Hall and the Knowingness of Popular Culture', *Past and Present* (1994), 138–70, esp. 139, 149.
[19] Medhurst, *A National Joke*, 19, 69.

physical positions their work required (scrubbing front door steps, for example), their names, and their misapprehension of middle-class social norms, all were long-established components of humour. Ethnicity was a component of such humour, and though Irish servants were not as ubiquitously funny in British cultural life as they were in US jokes, the voluble but illiterate 'Bridget' featured, usually speaking in dialect. As one interwar mistress recounted in the *Daily News*: 'in the intervals of her volubility [Bridget] did small domestic tasks in my kitchen' and aspired to visit 'Ameriky'.[20]

Jokes at the expense of servants can be read as a form of disciplining mockery—to perceive someone as ridiculous challenged their freedoms, habits, and lifestyle. The Edwardian humorist Max Beerbohm cheerfully recalled the incongruous servant character in *Punch* of the 1860s as maintaining appropriate social distinctions:

Absurd that Jemima Jane should imitate the bonnets of her mistress and secretly aspire to play the piano! 'Punch' and his artists, as you will find in his old volumes, were very merry about her, and no doubt his readers believed that his exquisite ridicule would kill, or his sound good sense cure, the malady in her soul.[21]

For mid-Victorians, laughing at domestic servants had been part of the solution to the servant problem. It was a useful means of establishing social distance and 'place', and nineteenth-century print culture returned again and again to the social faux pas of the pretentious, provincial, or foolish servant. Leonore Davidoff has commented on the use of 'a form of humour which reinforces social difference' in Victorian servant-keeping families, though she argues that 'fear can be sensed behind the stories which belittle the servant's grasp of middle class language and customs.'[22] Employers were aware that servant-keeping made themselves vulnerable to being seen as figures of fun. Incongruity was a device that could be reversed, and employers were also laughed at for their vulgarity and pompous aspirations. Servants used laughter and humour to form what James Scott has termed 'a "hidden transcript" . . . spoken behind the back of the dominant.'[23]

---

[20] Ronald Pearsall, *Collapse of Stout Party: Victorian Wit and Humour* (London: Weidenfeld and Nicolson, 1975), 17, 33–6, 72–4; Nina Condron, *Daily News*, Nov 1, 1923, 4. See also Andrew Urban's account of the jokes associated with Irish servants in the United States: 'Irish Domestic Servants, "Biddy" and Rebellion in the American Home, 1850–1900', *Gender and History*, 21 2 (2009), 263–86.

[21] Max Beerbohm, *Servants* (1918).

[22] Leonore Davidoff, *New Society*, Apr 26, 1973, 183. On the humour of role incongruity that aims to discipline the behaviour of social subordinates, see Angus McLaren's account of the courtroom and popular press laughter aroused by working-class men who had hoped to marry above their social station through the use of a matrimonial agency: *The Trials of Masculinity: Policing Sexual Boundaries 1870–1930* (Chicago: University of Chicago Press, 1997), 47–51. It was mostly female domestic servants who were on the books of the matrimonial agency, and who were understood as the appropriate marriage partners for such men—and the men's rejection of matrimony with these comic figures, who were also laughed at for having aspirations above their station, must have added to the humour of the situation.

[23] J. C. Scott, *Domination and the Arts of Resistance: Hidden Transcripts* (New Haven, CT: Yale University Press, 1990), xii.

Jokes and sketches about servants could also be seen as a defensive reaction by non-domestic workers, a tendency to mock those workers who had a lower status or worse conditions than themselves—a consolation of sorts. They partially satisfied the 'deep-seated need that people have to tell jokes about a group of stupid outsiders.'[24] Both workers who were not servants and insecure servant-keepers of the lower middle classes might use domestic service humour to shore up and distinguish their own social position. This leaves uninvestigated, however, the process by which domestic servants, rather than the workers of other despised occupations, came to be the 'outsider group'. Nor does it tell us when domestic service no longer fulfilled this function, and why. Domestic service humour does not easily fit into any simple category of the 'function' of humour, and indicates the limited usefulness of looking for an overarching, transcultural, or transhistorical explanation for how humour operates.[25] While there do seem to be repeated features in jokes about service (such as the idea of role incongruity), what is held to be incongruous must inevitably be historically and culturally specific. As Andy Medhurst has argued, 'Every comedy belongs simultaneously to both its own moment and its wider cultural antecedents.' What is funny is highly historically contextual, though there may be certain persistent cues that work across many cultural and historical contexts, termed 'deep comedic structures' by Medhurst.[26] The fine-grained exploration of why it was domestic servants who so often functioned for eighteenth- to twentieth-century audiences as 'stupid outsiders' cannot be solved by sociological, literary, or psychological generalizations. I turn now to a historical narrative of domestic service humour in late-nineteenth- and twentieth-century Britain to shed more light on when, why, and for whom domestic service was funny.

Laughter had long been prompted by the vulgar, the gross, and the lewd, often seen as qualities intrinsic to working-class status. George Orwell noted in 1937: 'Look at any number of *Punch* during the past thirty years. You will find it everywhere taken for granted that a working-class person, as such, is a figure of fun.'[27] Nonetheless, according to Alfred L'Estrange, a cleric and commentator on British life, the closing decades of the nineteenth century had seen vulgarity, rather than poverty and low station, become the target of humour and satire. This was best represented by 'those slightly below [middle-class people]', and L'Estrange specified 'the artifice and cunning of the waiter of the Hotel in Yarmouth' as a typical example of the comically vulgar.[28] It was both the lower-middle-class employers of servants *and* the servants themselves who epitomized the incongruous

---

[24] Christie Davies, *Jokes and Their Relation to Society* (New York: Mouton de Gruyter, 1988), 3.

[25] Jan Rüger discusses this point in a recent article, and calls for recognition of the 'inherent ambiguity' of humour: 'Laughter and War in Berlin', *History Workshop Journal*, 67 1 (2009), 23–43, esp. 26.

[26] Medhurst, *A National Joke*, 12, 11.

[27] George Orwell, in Peter Davison (ed.), *Orwell's England: The Road to Wigan Pier* (London: Penguin, 2001), 141.

[28] A. G. L'Estrange, *A History of English Humour* (New York: Burt Franklin, 1970), 2: 233.

and vulgar pretensions to gentility that for L'Estrange remained a legitimate object of humour, while other working-class targets had become exempt.

When the American journalist Elizabeth Banks caused a sensation by her impersonation and two-week employment as a housemaid in London of the early 1890s, she intended her write-up in the *Weekly Sun* to be read as funny. Banks recalled in her autobiography that:

> whatever was sad, whatever was tragic, and, to a certain extent, whatever was serious, I determined to leave out of my 'In Cap and Apron' series. I knew there were plenty to write fiction, plenty to write tragedy, so I chose what afterwards proved to be the better and more popular part of trying to write brightly and entertainingly of my brief experience as a servant.[29]

Banks had correctly assessed the market in recognizing that many were willing to be entertained by a narrative of domestic service, and she became an overnight celebrity through her incongruous portrayal of a young middle-class woman, still possessed of her own long-serving personal servant, impersonating a housemaid. Domestic service humour circulated in different forms within 'popular' and 'educated' cultural performances, though there were overlapping audiences for each of these genres and no very firm distinction can be made—Banks reported that servants, employers, and reformers wrote to her copiously after the series had been published—all were consumers of her 'bright' articles in a mass newspaper.

Not everyone, however, found the series amusing. After the publication of 'In Cap and Apron', Banks was called to account for her 'serious' aims in going into service at a meeting of a late Victorian reformist women's club. Her reply, that gaining entertaining copy had been her motive, caused outrage amongst her audience: 'I shall never forget the shocked expression on that woman's face, nor fail to remember her exclamation of surprise and disgust, as she replied:—"Copy! You mean to confess you had no philanthropic aim?"' The reaction exemplifies the new sense of unease at the entertainment to be derived from domestic service. 'The humour problem' was widely identified as diminishing the supply of servants. The domestic reformer Ellen Darwin wrote in 1902:

> The class of jokes which depends entirely on the inherent ridiculousness of the demands of servants for air, exercise and society, indicate the current state of mind of the subject. I call them jokes; because they appear in the pages on comic journals, so I suppose they are intended to raise a smile. But to those who don't smile, they appear as curious and significant instances of class stupidity—of that want of imagination in employers, who have done all they can to isolate servants as a class, and to lower the type of person who enters domestic service.[30]

The twentieth-century concerns over who was laughing and in what fashion were intensified by the new ability of servants to consume humour in sources such as the

---

[29] Elizabeth Banks, *Autobiography of a Newspaper Girl* (London: Methuen, 1902), 89. See also Lucy Delap, 'Campaigns of Curiosity: Class Crossing and Role Reversal in British Domestic Service, c.1890–1950', *Left History*, 12 2 (2007).

[30] Ellen Darwin, 'Lady Servants', *National Review,* June 1902, 609.

Weekly Sun. Where Victorian servants had sometimes been socially and culturally isolated, those of the twentieth century could read newspapers and novels, and were more likely to also access realms of culture and leisure such as the music hall, radio, and cinema. This aroused extensive controversy over the 'problem' of servants' consumption of culture and leisure.[31] While the reading habits of servants had long been seen as problematic (distracting them from their work and inflating their romantic ambitions), it was the specific content of what they read and what they saw at the cinema and music hall that became troubling. Servants could now access the cultural representations of domestic service, leading to disaffection, or worse, to service appearing comic in their own eyes. A writer in *The Spectator* wrote in 1914 of the shift in the direction of domestic service laughter, from employer to servant:

> Thackeray dealt a blow at domestic service which it has never quite recovered. He made it ridiculous.... The literature of his day reflected his point of view. Servants did not like reading novels—they were 31s 6d each—neither did they belong to lending libraries. The derisive smiles of their employers were hardly understood by them.... Meanwhile, education has made rapid progress. A class which never read before is reading now... the result is that the class from which servants are drawn is beginning to laugh at domestic service.[32]

Though domestic service comedy was beginning to be thought to be inappropriate and damaging, comic plays, essays, and serials, such as J. M. Barrie's 1902 *The Admirable Crichton*, Jerome K. Jerome's 1909 *Fanny and the Servant Problem*, Max Beerbohm's 1918 *Servants*, or the interwar *Diary of a Provincial Lady* by E. M. Delafield, continued to use domestic service as a key vehicle for humour, and a means of making semi-serious comments on recent social trends.[33] Some standard comic tropes emerged, such as the self-important or snobbish servant, the savvy or workshy servant, the deadpan, witty manservant, and the frivolous or fashion-loving maid. Overall though, it is hard to say exactly what is meant to be funny about many such sources. The humour is very implicit; to some degree, servants were simply funny in essence, much as bicycles had been in the 1890s, without needing to engage in much overtly comic activity.[34]

Domestic service was sometimes a vehicle for the domestic concerns that dominated both the comic/illustrated papers aimed at educated readers and the popular media of the music hall and halfpenny comic. One Victorian songwriter wrote of the 'pathos, homely humour—something to do with the wife and mother-in-law and so on' of the 'catchy' songs he produced.[35] Servants were easy to add to

---

[31] See Margaret Beetham, 'Domestic Servants as Poachers of Print: Reading, Authority and Resistance in late Victorian Britain', in Lucy Delap, Abigail Wills, and Ben Griffin (eds), *The Politics of Domestic Authority in Britain since 1800* (Basingstoke: Palgrave Macmillan, 2009).

[32] *The Spectator*, November 14, 1914, 663–4.

[33] E. M. Delafield published her very popular tales of 'servant trouble' from a mistress's perspective in 'Diary of a Provincial Lady', in the weekly *Time and Tide*, and they were collected in Delafield, *Diary of a Provincial Lady* (London: Folio Society, 1979).

[34] Thanks to the work of Michael Epp for this insight.

[35] Felix McGlennon, *Era*, Mar 10, 1894, quoted in Russell, *Popular Music in England*, 109. See also Pearsall, *Collapse of Stout Party*, Chapter 2.

this list—they served to add a romantic or sexual element to a plot, they conveyed sartorial anxieties and oddities, and domestic service was a feature of everyday life in which large sectors of the population were invested, as current or former servants or as employers. Servants were a convenient vehicle for slapstick, and for introducing sexual horseplay into plots, without necessarily serving as characters in their own right. This was particularly evident in early cinema productions where female servants are kissed or seduced by their masters.[36] Other standard tropes in early cinema were the stupid servant (*Mary Jane's Mishap; or, Don't Fool With The Paraffin*, G. A. Smith, 1903), or (just as commonly) the servant who turns the tables and humiliates or exploits the employer (*Accidents Will Happen*, 1907, Charles Urban Trading Co.; *Milkmaid*, 1905, Gaumont). This was a persistent feature of servants in all forms of popular culture—though they inhabited degraded circumstances, they were rarely just derided characters, but more often wily and cunning.

While there is a great deal of evidence that employers found their servants funny, it was not the laughter of employers that inspired early twentieth-century commentaries on the 'problem' of domestic service humour. Instead, it was the laughter of the working classes or servants themselves that seemed most problematic and threatening. Dramatic reviews such as the 'comic absurdity', *The Silly Servant*, which played at the Hulme Hippodrome in August 1906, were feared likely to convince working-class audiences that domestic service was an undignified profession.[37] In music hall songs, domestic service humour mocked the pretensions of those who employed servants but were themselves barely middle class.[38] Many songs had semi-serious content, drawing attention to the hard life and low pay of domestic servants, and seemed sympathetic to the servant's perspective.[39] Some portrayed the smart servant who managed to confuse employers and so evade work, resonating with a long-standing British popular comic tradition of sending up those in authority.[40] Where stupid servants were mocked, it was also the employer who emerged as comic. Adroitly picking up on anxieties over the reading skills of servants, a 1912 Edgar Bateman song, *Our Martha Jane Can't Read*, mocked the employers' preference for an illiterate 'treasure' and their concern over the reading habits of servants:

> We used to have a servant Constance Leonora May,
> She'd sit up reading half the night, and sit down all the day.
> So after Ma had sack'd her, and her penny novellette,
> A girl who couldn't read at all we thought we'd like to get.
> At last we came across one quite a proper Martha Jane!

---

[36] See for example, *Hanging Out The Clothes; Or, Master, Mistress And Maid*, G. A. Smith, 1897; *The Magic Glass*, Hay Plumb, 1914.
[37] 'Provincial Theatricals: Manchester', *Era*, Aug 11, 1906, 9.
[38] See for example, *Mary Ann, Mary Ann Come in*, Fred Murray and Charles Collins, c.1912; *The Bell Goes a-Ringing for Sai-rah*, G. W. Hunt, c.1873.
[39] See *The Servant Question (by one who knows)*, Harry Ivimey, c.1901.
[40] *I never does nothing at all*, composed by T. German Reed, written by William Brough, c.1862. See Medhurst, *A National Joke*, 76.

> Her face is like her cooking, well, it's homely and it's plain.
> A thorough maid of all work, and she suits us very well,
> Tho' she's rather hard of hearing and she cannot taste or smell,
> Chorus: And the poor dear girl can't read. We've found a perfect treasure indeed!
> But lately when the landlord came to get his quarter's brass,
> We found the rent had vanish'd that we'd saved for him, alas!
> Said Martha, 'Were they banknotes that I used to light the gas?
> Because our Martha Jane can't read. Etc.

Interpreting the implications, ironies, and tacit meanings of music hall and popular performances requires 'knowingness', often hard to reconstruct at a historical distance. Servants were represented ambiguously. In reviews of music hall acts, female servants (almost always portraying those at the bottom of the hierarchy of service, the maid-of-all-work, or 'slavey') were persistently described as 'quaint'. An actress playing at the Dover Theatre Royal in 1906 was described as 'the quaintest of quaint little slaveys'; a music hall maid-of-all-work in 1924 was declared 'the essence of quaint comicality'.[41] Most reviews gave little detail on what this meant, though a write-up of a play at the Hackney Empire in 1906 gives a fuller picture of a 'quaint' comic role:

> Jemima is a London slavey, in service of a widow . . . [There is] a good deal of funny comedy business, in which Jemima takes a prominent part . . . Miss Louie Freear quite revels in the part of Jemima, the lovelorn 'domestic', and her embodiment of the quaint looking little slavey is marked throughout by a genuine humour which delights the audience. Her by-play is excellent. Everyone laughs when Jemima washes the seats of the chairs with a flannel cloth dipped in water and then, proceeds to dry them by a highly original method.[42]

Clearly there was an element of slapstick in this performance. However, 'quaintness' had quite different connotations from its contemporary meanings—to be quaint for Edwardians was to show a combination of ingenuity, wilyness, and affectation.[43] This last value was perhaps the most insulting to servants, since it was often believed to be a comic 'affectation' on their part to seek some very natural human goals—to have a love life, a social life, or any pursuits outside of their work. The tennis- or piano-playing servant was a very common comic figure in cartoons aimed at educated readers, though the same targeting of pretentiousness also surfaced in popular humour. There was certainly no clear divide to be found between 'elite' and 'popular' humour, which often depicted the same comic figures—though mostly to quite different effect. The 'lovelorn Jemima' was a typical figure within the music halls, where the desire amongst servants to have a love life was, I suspect, regarded with irony rather than being straightforwardly incongruous or comic. Most working-class members of the audience would have

---

[41] 'Provincial Theatricals: Dover', *Era*, Aug 11, 1906, 7; 'Love and Laughter at Shoreditch Olympia', *Era*, Sept 16, 1924, 14.
[42] *Era*, July 14, 1906, 21. The play was *Snooks*, by Mr B. Soane Ruby.
[43] N. Porter, *Webster's Revised Unabridged Dictionary* (Springfield, MA: Merriam, 1913).

Figure 9. Pansy Pancake, *Comic Cuts*, February 22, 1913, 4–5.

been aware that to marry was the only way to get out of a labour market sector that was not kind to older single women.

Edwardian and interwar comic papers reveal an amalgamation of these comic tropes; the servants they portray are gross and ineffective, but by chance or design, with they always end up with the whip hand over the master or mistress. Perhaps lampooning in their turn employers' jokes about musical servants, comic papers repeatedly portrayed musically active servants who used this to 'get one over' their employers. Pansy Pancake, the long-running 'comic cook' character in the halfpenny paper *Comic Cuts*, was portrayed in 1913 using her awful singing voice to irritate her mistress into getting her a singing teacher, by whom she then smuggled food out of the kitchen for her family (Figure 9).

Another character from 1913, Mrs Sudds the Charlady, featured in another cheap comic, *Picture Fun*. This character was much less wily (or quaint) than Pansy Pancake, and almost every week she was physically abused by her employers. Her strip is hard to interpret; it reads as an unfunny joke to a modern reader, in relying simply on the slapstick value of physical mishap. However, a note of irony does creep in—the commentary to one strip ends with a typical humorous attempt to

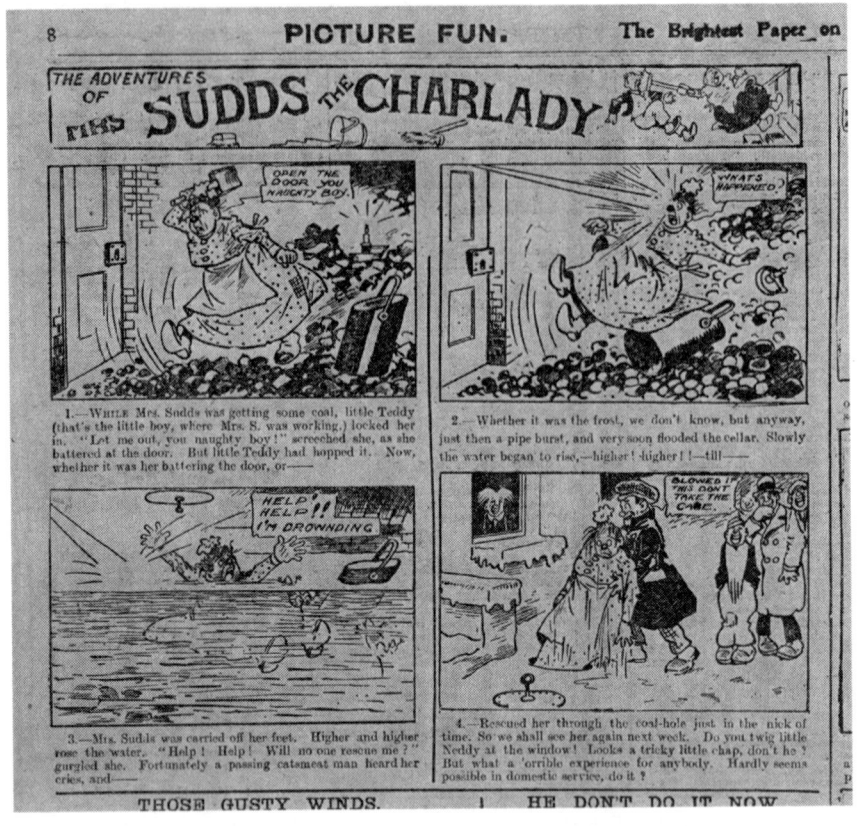

Figure 10. Mrs Sudds the Charlady, *Picture Fun*, February 11, 1913, 8.

imitate the missing aspirate that servants were associated with: 'But what a 'orrible experience for anybody. Hardly seems possible in domestic service, do it?' (Figure 10).

While this strip still mocks the language of servants, there's a sense that the audience being addressed is one that knows that ill-treatment is not only possible in domestic service, but common. Mrs Sudds addressed a 'knowing' audience, who were well aware of the hypocrisy of the very common claims made by employers and public officials that service was the highest honour and privilege. As Nicholas Wolf notes, 'popular culture does not straightforwardly assimilate the goals and tactics of elite culture.'[44] In relation to servants, the laughter elicited by British popular culture vehicles was equivocal and ironic. Despite the grossness and affectation of its comic servants, popular culture seemed relatively supportive of the dignity and aspirations of servants, and its satire was aimed more at employers.

[44] Nicholas Wolf, 'Scéal Grinn? Jokes, Puns, and the Shaping of Bilingualism in Nineteenth-Century Ireland', *Journal of British Studies*, 48 1 (2009), 51–75, esp. 56.

> SPREAD OF THE SERVANT-GIRL GRADUATE IDEA.
> (*Interior of a super-kitchen.*)
> *Mistress.* "WOULD YOU MIND LEAVING YOUR SOPHOCLES FOR A MOMENT, MARY, AND RUNNING TO THE POST?"

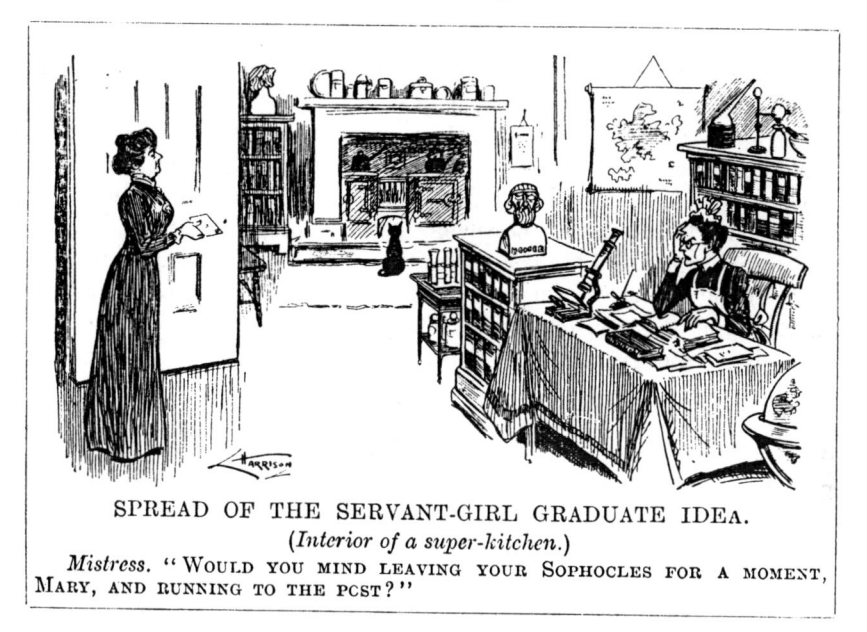

Figure 11. 'Spread of the Servant-Girl Graduate Idea', *Punch*, 146, January 14, 1914, 36.

During and after World War I, a tendency emerged to find humour in the reversal of social esteem and circumstances that seemed to favour the domestic servant over the employer in interwar Britain. *Punch*, for example, depicted a 'servant-girl graduate' studying in plush academic surroundings while a mistress requested: 'Would you mind leaving your Sophocles for a moment, Mary, and running to the post?' (Figure 11). *Punch* readers were offered some incongruous announcements in 1919, motivated by the fear that the war had created more independent-minded young women who would refuse to serve:

'A Servant Girls' Trade Union has been formed. So far there is no suggestion of interfering with the mistresses' evening out.

We understand that a West-End lady has just been appointed mistress to a young parlourmaid.[45]

The popularity of P. G. Wodehouse's *Jeeves* novels from the 1920s was partly based on the social reversal of the incompetent employer and masterly valet. However, the extent of the reversal was always limited, and usually both parties were mocked for their foibles. Despite the apparent reversal of *Punch*'s 'Servant-Girl Graduate' with a strong labour market position and aspirations to educated status, she is depicted as pretentious and shrewish, and her aspirations seem

---

[45] 'Charivaria', *Punch*, Mar 5, 1919, 173. See also Evoe, 'The Domestic Problem', *Punch*, Jan 14, 1920, 22.

laughable and spinsterish. The ageing profile of twentieth-century domestic service perhaps contributed to the comic value of the unmarried female servant, as 'servant humour' tended towards 'spinster humour'.

Nonetheless, as the social divide between employers and servants decreased after World War I, there was a narrowing of the characteristics of servants that could be laughed at. The cartoons of George Belcher, published in *Punch* and *The Tatler* in the 1920s and 1930s, dwelled heavily on servants, and particularly on the comic figure of the char. In a 1933 collection titled *Potted Char*, Belcher continued to ridicule the 'mollspeak' of domestic workers ('shall I serve the rabbit up in the camisole, mum?'), but his employers and servants had come to look physically similar—both tended to be large, aproned women, depicted in shared domestic spaces, rather than in domains that could be identified as belonging to 'upstairs' or 'downstairs'.[46]

Social reversals and blurring of distinctions did not only prompt laughter, of course, but also intense anger. In the early 1920s, there was outrage amongst middle-class public opinion over the possibility that working-class women might be drawing unemployment doles rather than going into available domestic service jobs. The *Daily Mail* ran a scaremongering campaign on 'Scandals of the Dole' in 1923, which prompted an enquiry by the Ministry of Labour into the supply of domestic servants.[47] The authors of the resulting report attempted to defuse the *Daily Mail* readers' outrage by blaming humour rather than the dole for keeping women out of service. Indeed, the humour problem had an extraordinarily high profile in the domestic service reform literature. The 1923 report claimed that 'the constant caricaturing of maidservants as dirty, harassed, impertinent and somewhat grotesque creatures, and the use of contemptuous terms such as "skivvy" and "slavey," are significant.' Although it was mainly the educated classes who had the power to shape the representations of the media, the authors denied that this issue could be laid at the door of employers themselves. Rather, it was claimed that it was the working-class 'friends and relatives' of servants who found their occupation ridiculous and thus damaged the profession. Curiously though, of the servants quoted in the final Report on this issue, only one parlourmaid blamed the 'snobbery of our own class' for the problem of servants being laughed at. Others named the daily papers, the stage portrayals of servants, and most importantly, the attitude of employers. Clearly, employers were still making servants feel inferior through their ridicule. The only suggestion that the Report's authors could make was to appeal to 'the Press, the dramatist, and the humorist' to realize that their 'cheap jokes at the expense of the "general"' were actually inflicting genuine pain.[48] They were unwilling to acknowledge that the laughter of employers might be to blame.

[46] George Belcher, *Potted Char and Other Delicacies* (London: Methuen, 1933). I am grateful to Stella Moss for pointing me to Belcher's work.
[47] Adrian Bingham, *Gender, Modernity, and the Popular Press in Inter-war Britain* (Oxford: Clarendon Press, 2004), 68–9.
[48] E. M. Wood, *Report to the Committee Appointed to Enquire into the Present Conditions as to the Supply of Female Domestic Servants by the Ministry of Labour* (London: HMSO, 1923), 15–16.

The educated classes, at whom books such as Monica Dickens' 1939 *One Pair of Hands* were aimed, were, however, reluctant to stop laughing. Dickens' experiences as a servant were read by critics as portraying 'unforced enjoyment in the spectacle of life below stairs', despite the reform intentions of the author.[49] Alison Light records the laughter amongst 1930s Bloomsbury literati, aimed at their casual domestic workers and chars, alongside their deep personal dependency.[50] In 1939, *The Evening Standard* published a comic story about a servant sitting down in an armchair to listen to her employers' music-making; another employer wrote to the paper with a 'funny' story of how her maid had asked for time off to see her children, and to play tennis.[51] The jokes rested on the familiar incongruity of transgressing one's place without being aware of it, though the humour of the situation is barely evident to a twenty-first-century reader.[52] The 1944 report to the Ministry of Labour, attempting to rationalize and perpetuate domestic service within plans for the post-war reconstruction of Britain, concluded that little had changed in 'the humour problem' since 1923, despite the challenges to domestic service that wartime full employment offered. The authors, Violet Markham and Florence Hancock, gave a detailed account of the problem as they saw it:

Ugly adjectives such as menial and servile were increasingly in use, and the domestic worker found herself often subject to contempt and ridicule from acquaintances who taunted her with being 'a mere servant.' A social stigma intensely humiliating to a sensitive girl began to take shape... In our opinion the music hall and the popular song have no little responsibility to bear in this matter. Infinite damage has been done to the status of the domestic worker by jests at her expense on the stage and in the Press. An intelligent and competent maid going to the theatre with friends is often humiliated by seeing her own skilled trade held up to ridicule. Work in which she takes a pride is 'guyed' by some minor character who almost invariably is represented as a drunken, dishonest and incompetent. The house may be relied on to rock with laughter at any turn which caricatures a servant girl in a shapeless dress, with her cap askew and a smut on her nose. Illustrations in comic papers often elaborate the same theme. It is superfluous to stress the reaction of such ridicule on a girl hesitating as to whether or not she shall take up domestic work.... Improved status cannot be achieved if the domestic worker is made to feel there is something ludicrous, if not contemptible, about her trade.[53]

To what extent did domestic service humour became culturally marginal or 'poor taste' as servant-keeping declined after World War II? The portrayal of servants in

---

[49] *Booklist*, Dec 1, 1939, 132. Also in the review, K. John, 'Cook General', *New Statesman*, July 1, 1939, 21.

[50] Alison Light, *Mrs Woolf and the Servants: The Hidden Heart of Domestic Service* (London: Penguin, 2007), 234–5.

[51] 'Tennis "Her Game"', *Evening Standard*, May 17, 1939, 10, and 'Maids Say, "We are treated like machines"', May 20, 1939, 17.

[52] *Evening Standard*, May 20, 1939. It was also challenged by contemporaries. Celia Fremlin noted that it was 'an extraordinary comment on present-day society', that such anecdotes were still seen as funny in 1930s Britain (*The Seven Chars of Chelsea* (London: Methuen, 1940), 160).

[53] Violet Markham and Florence Hancock, *Report on the Organisation of Private Domestic Employment* (London: HMSO, 1944), 6–7.

'popular' mediums stayed in a burlesque mode right into the 1940s, with characters such as Mrs Tickle and Mrs Mopp the charwomen in the wartime radio comedy *It's That Man Again*.[54] The association of female servants and 'dirty jokes' also persisted; the British Broadcasting Corporation had produced a list of subjects on which jokes were banned which included chambermaids, alongside jokes about lavatories, effeminacy in men, and ladies' underwear.[55] Comic papers such as *Blighty* and *Razzle* continued to portray domestic service as a site for laughter, though the char came to predominate over the maid. Domestic service humour was still viable in 1960s and 1970s Britain, decades more usually imagined as ones in which servants and the serio-comic anxieties they induced had disappeared. Reformers such as Mrs Wales, president of the Institute of Home Help Organisers, were still concerned about the impact of comic domestic workers in the 1960s. She assertively and somewhat defensively insisted on the difference between a Home Help and the comic charlady Mrs Mopp.[56]

However, much laughter at servants had transferred to the new domestic workers—au pairs, cleaners, and home helps. The extensive social and economic transformation of post-war Britain had been marked by an underlying continuity in the cultural realm of what was funny—the comic does not map closely onto direct social experience, but often has its own trajectory. However, the laughter directed at cleaners and chars was milder, denoting fewer social anxieties. These workers, as Nicky Gregson and Michelle Lowe have argued, were more autonomous than the domestic workers of the early to mid-twentieth century, and had less potential as sites of social incongruity. They still sometimes sustained relationships of emotional debt and complex intimacy with their employers, but often worked with a much higher degree of control over their working conditions than their counterparts in earlier decades.[57] There was therefore less need to establish social boundaries through laughter. The comic productions that did emerge, such as Pam Brown's 1984 cartoon collection *Mutterings of a Char*, were wry rather than biting, published alongside her comic accounts of life with teenagers and hapless men.[58]

THE LAUGHTER OF EMPLOYERS

Laughter at domestic service was not only elicited through reading illustrated papers or at the theatre. Throughout the twentieth century, employers and servants

---

[54] Mrs Mopp became such a popular character that she merited her own radio series in 1946, entitled *The Private Life of Mrs Mopp*. On the humour associated with chars, see Light, *Mrs Woolf and the Servants*, 252–3.
[55] *The Variety Programme and Policy Guide for Writers and Producers*, produced in 1949, cited in Adrian Bingham, *Family Newspapers?: Sex, Private Life, and the British Popular Press 1918–1978* (Oxford: Oxford University Press, 2009), 39.
[56] *Daily Telegraph*, Sept 21, 1961, quoted in E. S. Turner, *What the Butler Saw* (London: Penguin, 2001), 294.
[57] N. Gregson and M. Lowe, *Servicing the Middle Classes: Class, Gender and Waged Domestic Labour in Contemporary Britain* (London: Routledge, 1994), 215–28.
[58] Pam Brown, *Mutterings of a Char* (Watford: Exley, 1984).

could experience their relationships in the domestic setting as funny, on a daily basis. The laughter in the home was responsive to or even scripted by the available cultural representations. However, it was also on occasion a realm of resistance and reinterpretation, and was not determined by the cultural repertoire of jokes associated with service. This is a more problematic realm for historical investigation—fewer textual accounts survive to describe it. Such humour 'in the home' is captured in some memoirs, journalism, autobiographies, and oral histories, and consisted of both sides of the relationship mocking each other's pretensions and idiosyncrasies. Capturing something of the laughter within servant-keeping homes provides a counterpoint to the continuities and shifts of the cultural history discussed in the preceding section. It reminds us of the diverse and unpredictable reception and uses of the forms of comedy offered through cultural life and the media.

While it is hard to recover the conversation of middle- and upper-class 'at homes' and tea parties, many commented on the dominance of the servant problem in polite society talk. It is likely that much of such talk consisted of complaints disguised in humorous anecdotes that served to release the frustration of employers and to share strategies for coping—that which Carolyn Steedman and Tim Meldrum have characterized as 'a routine and ritualized moaning about their household servants.'[59] An enquiry sponsored by *The British Weekly* in 1889 recorded the anecdotes of a group of mistresses who had been asked to talk about their servant troubles; almost all used humour as their mode of addressing the problem.[60] Despite *The Spectator*'s claim that in 1914, 'the employer has forgotten that he ever laughed', in reality, employers continued to find their interactions with servants funny well into the twentieth century.

The basis for the humorous value of servants varied—they were judged to be odd, pretentious, innocent, or wily; employer laughter was motivated by a range of emotions, from condescension, to ignorance of working-class lifestyles, to a desire to tease and bait. A revealing comic story was told by one woman who recalled her Edwardian childhood in a middle-class London household that employed three servants. The humour of her anecdote rested on the long-standing comic trope of servants seeking cultural expression: her mother, the mistress, heard

the strains of a violin [coming] downstairs. She said 'Where on earth is that coming from?'—waiting for afternoon tea you see. Goes upstairs, there's one of them—it's an easel up in the bedroom with music on it and there she was playing away and the other one sitting back in her chair with her feet on an ottoman cushion. Oh, they went faster than they came in.[61]

---

[59] Steedman, 'Servants and Their Relationship to the Unconscious', 329; Tim Meldrum, *Domestic Service and Gender, 1660–1750: Life and Work in the London Household* (Harlow: Longman, 2000), 7.
[60] The 'British Weekly' Commissioners (ed.), *Toilers in London, or, Inquiries Concerning Female Labour in the Metropolis* (London: Hodder and Stoughton, 1889).
[61] Mrs A. Grace Hargrave (b. 1889), Interview 178, in P. Thompson and T. Lummis, *Family Life and Work Experience before 1918, 1870–1973* [computer file], 7th edn, Colchester, Essex: UK Data Archive (distributor), May 2009, SN: 2000, henceforth cited as *Edwardians*; also quoted in Paul Thompson, *The Edwardians: The Remaking of British Society* (London: Routledge, 1992), 82.

Laughter at servants with musical or artistic ambitions was not limited to the press and theatre, but was incorporated into family histories and personal biographies. This story was clearly narrated in a formula that suggested that it had been told on numerous occasions, the sort of anecdote one might 'dine out' on in well-to-do circles.

Employers laughed at their servants, to ease the social discomfort and ambiguities of the relationship, and to create or perpetuate social distance. Laughter at servants might also serve to create intimacy within servant-keeping families and to close up other forms of social distance; Graham Cross, a child of a servant-keeping household in Eastbourne, recalled moments of closeness to his mother through their shared laughter at the servants in the interwar years.[62] 'Denise', the name of the daughter of the long-serving housemaid, for example, was a family joke because it suggested pretensions to middle-class status, though Cross noted that the laughter was not malicious, but gentle. Yet the boundaries of whom one might laugh with or at were strictly policed. His own sharing of a mild joke at a family member's expense with his mother's housemaid was forbidden in strong terms. Laughter in this household both established and transgressed social hierarchies and intimacies.

As Cross's forbidden laughter with servants suggests, employers also used mockery to disrupt the intimacies that unsettled the hierarchies of servant-keeping, particularly those that flourished in the ambiguous emotional space between servants and the children of employers. In her memoir of a late Victorian childhood, Olive Haweis recalled that when a long-serving servant, Ann, had been jilted by her fiancé, the response from her mistress was a hurtful joke: 'What did she expect with a face like that?' This might be read as heartless mockery, but the aftermath to this joke suggests that it was also motivated by this mistress's disquiet at the relationship sustained between Ann and her daughter, Olive, as well as the threat to domestic composure that Ann's courtship offered. Ann gave notice when the daughter reported the joke to her. The mother responded with an acknowledgement of the underlying problem of excessive intimacy between servant and child, commenting to her husband: 'there you see she's got such a hold over her, it is just as you said, it's time she went.' In response, her daughter declared: 'I hate her and I love Ann.'[63]

The children of employers of servants sustained ambivalent, often emotionally intense relationships with the servants who helped raise them, and also used laughter to mediate and manage their relationships. One child of a Victorian clergyman recalled the attraction of the 'vulgar kitchen jokes' they overheard. She and her sister sought to elicit more laughter by dressing up and impersonating their own relatives to the servants.[64] Children were also sensitive to the permitted laughter *at* servants, and sometimes made the mockery of servants more overt

---

[62] Graham Cross, interview with the author, May 8, 2007.
[63] Haweis, *Four to Fourteen*, 78–9.
[64] Agnes Maud Davies, *A Book with Seven Seals: A Victorian Childhood* (London: Chatto and Windus, 1974), 82–3.

than their elders would have thought seemly. Ursula Holden, educated at a girls' boarding school the 1930s, recalled discussing with her friends who they would least like to kiss: 'One maid in particular got the vote. She was hideous, cretinous, and she smelled. Would anyone dare? Wanting to be thought brave and outrageous and so increase my popularity, I volunteered. We trapped her in a passage and I kissed her greasy face amid cheers. I was the female Judas and I think she understood the mockery.'[65] The joke lay in combining disgust, transgression and erotic charge—and reminds us that these elements might be at play and manipulated between females, and between different generations, rather than as conventionally imagined between male employers and female servants. Humour, indeed, allows for an ironic, parodic adoption of discourse and rituals of power by groups such as children whose access to them is uncertain.

While employers were forced to acknowledge the labour market power of servants, they continued to find servants ridiculous. Monica Dickens commented on the constant exposure of servants to employers' ideas of what was humorous in the late 1930s:

It is a curious game that people like to play sometimes, drawing out the maid (baiting the butler in some houses), in order to get amusement out of the screechingly funny idea that she may have some sort of a human life of her own.... Once you get used to the idea of being suddenly hauled out from the oblivion of servitude into the spotlight of attention, and expected to provide entertainment until they just as suddenly tire of you, and intimate that you have said your piece, it's quite an easy game to play. You have to humour them by saying amusing and slightly outrageous things so that they can retail them to their friends, or 'dine out' on quotations from your conversation.[66]

It is hard to know how much this kind of laughter on the part of employers persisted into later decades, but an anecdote from the mid-1960s suggests that it was still in play; the novelist Ivy Compton-Burnett and her private secretary laughed together at the pretentious language of Mary, a housekeeper. As the secretary explained, 'Old servants, having heard the talk of their superiors for most of their lives—and this was true of Mary—set an example to those beneath them by talking "above their station," lifting their vocabulary too high, the result being a kind of burlesque of "refined" speech.'[67] Mention of domestic service still caused laughter in the House of Commons, though those who laughed were vulnerable to criticism. One Scottish Labour member who sought a wages council for domestic servants in 1961 was incensed by the response to his intervention: 'this is not a matter which should cause hilarity on the part of some hon. Members opposite who are themselves possibly guilty of such abuses.'[68] Twenty years later, the employment of domestic workers had risen dramatically across the 1980s, and

---

[65] Ursula Holden, 'More about Maids', 4, unpublished mss., undated, in possession of the author.
[66] Monica Dickens, *One Pair of Hands* (London: Joseph, 1939), 260–1.
[67] Cicely Greig, *Ivy Compton-Burnett, a Memoir* (London: Garnstone Press, 1972), 116, cited in Alison Light, *Forever England: Femininity, Literature and Conservatism between the Wars* (London: Routledge, 1991).
[68] Archie Manuel, *Hansard*, HC Deb, May 3, 1961, vol 639, cc 1390–1.

in a direct revisiting of the concerns of the interwar 'humour problem', the 1988 *Good Nanny Guide* advised employers not to humiliate their nannies by requiring comic performances from them at dinner parties, and reminded nannies that comic impersonations of their employers were likely to land them in trouble.[69] The power of laughter to belittle and discipline was undiminished in this late-twentieth-century phase of increased reliance on paid domestic workers.

THE LAUGHTER OF SERVANTS

Historians of humour have suggested that the 'knowingness' of comedy works to set up a sense of group membership, to which only those who 'get' the conventions of humour belong. If domestic service humour was 'knowing', could servants themselves be included in this 'knowingness', or did the humour inevitably exclude and humiliate them? Though there are few sources showing how servants felt about the issue, it is clear that some servants resented their status as objects of humour. The Edwardian servant Kathlyn Oliver was enraged in 1911 by the cultural depictions of servants: 'In literature and on the stage it is common to depict the domestic servant as *non compos mentis*, indeed as scarcely human.'[70]

John James, a house steward in service in the first half of the twentieth century, regarded himself as well read and educated. He complained of the comic presentation of servants as 'misusing the aspirate', commenting, 'surely this sort of ridicule is unsporting since the objects are not free to retaliate?'[71] James's comment reveals awareness of his relative inability to intervene in public opinion or print culture, or even to respond in everyday interactions. This, however, was a rare complaint from a male servant. Male servants had a comic value distinctive from that of female servants, and were characterized as funny because of the feminization of twentieth-century domestic service. There was a pervasive sense that the domestic male was faintly ridiculous, as James Hammerton has argued for lower-middle-class 'domestic husbands'.[72] In the early twentieth century, it was felt that, as *The Spectator* put it in 1914, 'some very faint aroma of ridicule still clings to... the thought of domestic service, at any rate for men.'[73] Judy Giles has argued that 'the humour problem' was mainly to the detriment of female servants: 'whilst the fictional conventions and cultural discourses for representing male servants emphasise an equality of intelligence, wit and resourcefulness between man and master', female servants were depicted 'as comic and often unattractive figures'.[74]

---

[69] Charlotte Breese and Hilaire Gomer, *The Good Nanny Guide* (Century: London, 1988), 218.
[70] Kathlyn Oliver, *Domestic Servants and Citizenship* (London: People's Suffrage Federation, 1911), 13–14.
[71] John James, *The Memoirs of a House Steward* (London: Bury, Holt, 1949), 96–7.
[72] A. James Hammerton, 'Pooterism or Partnership? Marriage and Masculine Identity in the Lower Middle Class, 1870–1920', *Journal of British Studies*, 38 3 (1991), 291–321.
[73] 'Dignity and Domestic Service', *The Spectator*, Nov 14, 1914, 663–4.
[74] Judy Giles, *Women, Identity and Private Life in Britain* (London: MacMillan, 1995), 138.

Certainly, comic traits such as 'quaintness' were associated with femininity, and laughter at female domestic servants sometimes shaded into a gendered sense of disgust at their physical presence. Their bodies combined connotations of contamination and erotic charge, and this created a distinctive comic-erotic gendered role, which is further explored in the following chapter. The bodies of male servants were not portrayed as comically gross in the same way. Nonetheless, male servants were not simply witty and resourceful. Their masculinity was compromised by what one Victorian etiquette manual derided as 'this heaping of gold lace, gaudy colours, blooming plushes on honest John Trot'. Interwar depictions of 'the house-parlourman' were clearly intended to be belittling.[75] Men in service were effeminized and thus laughable, though they might also access the intimacies of shared laughter with female servants. Margaret Powell described a valet in one of the households she served: 'nobody treated him as though he was a man. They all spoke and made jokes with him as if he was a woman. His hands were so soft, and he was so soft spoken, he didn't seem masculine. More like a jelly somehow, to me.... We used to look on him as one of us.'

In contrast, some forms of masculinity were compatible with domestic work, and maritime masculinities had long been admired for their domestic handiness. *The Mirror* in 1914 offered an admiring comic strip detailing the tasks of a sailor-domestic servant, prompted by its press report of a mistress who had sought a male servant from an agency, and was advised to try a sailor (Figure 12).[76] However, most men in service found the humour problem to demean them in gender-specific ways. Men, however, had more opportunities to change their employment, and it was women who felt that domestic service was their only employment option who were most vocal in contesting their comic status.

The report on domestic service to the Minister of Labour in 1923 gives us a valuable set of opinions from female servants on the humour problem. The report dwelled at length on this issue, and it was only in relation to jokes that any direct speech of servants was given. When asked whether the ridicule servants suffered was so problematic, one 'ex-maid' responded with dignity: 'Not only servants but parsons, etc., are held up to ridicule by the stage. Why should servants object more than the others? For the very good reason that parsons, having an assured standing as the first gentleman in the district, could well afford to ignore it. Servants cannot.'[77] Servants continued to feel excluded from shaping public representations of themselves and vulnerable to the belittlement of laughter, despite their increased access to education and achievement of citizenship rights in the interwar decades. They pleaded for social and cultural dignity: when asked to describe a good mistress, one cook-general was cited, 'Her hand is not continually on the bell-punch. Her sense of humour is kindly.'[78] Interwar servants still complained of

---

[75] *******, *Mixing in Society*; Delafield, *Diary of a Provincial Lady*; W. K. Haselden, 'When Jack Tar Takes Mary Ann's Place', *Daily Mirror*, July 22, 1914.
[76] Margaret Powell, *Below Stairs* (London: Pan Books, 1968), 67–8.
[77] 'An Ex-Maid', quoted in Wood, *Ministry of Labour Report*, 15.
[78] E. P. Harries, *Plight of the Domestic Workers*, Publicity Dept of TUC (1937 or 8), Modern Records Centre at the University of Warwick, 292/54.76/3.

WHEN JACK TAR TAKES MARY ANN'S PLACE.

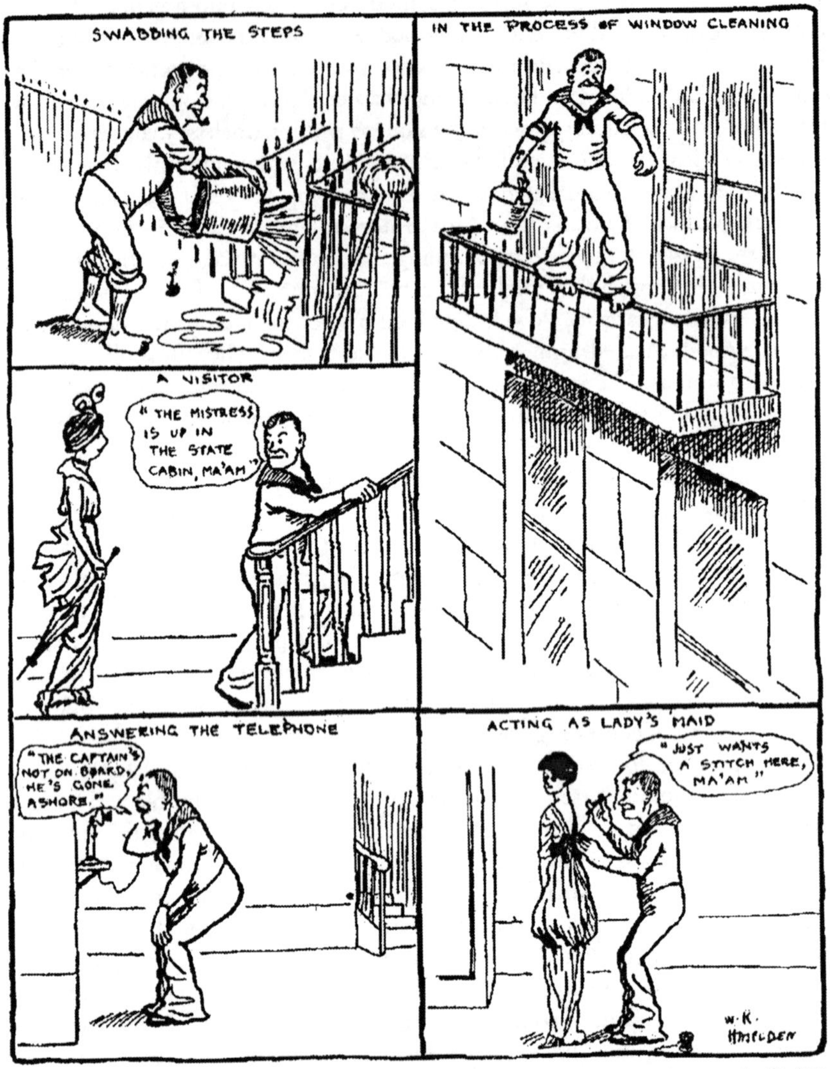

Retired bluejackets are, it appears, becoming more and more popular as domestic servants, in view of the extreme difficulty of procuring competent specimens of that class. A further advantage of employing these men would be, no doubt, that they would throw a refreshingly nautical atmosphere over the humdrum duties of the house.—(By Mr. W. K. Haselden.)

Figure 12. W. K. Haselden, 'When Jack Tar takes Mary Ann's place', *Daily Mirror*, July 22, 1914 (Mirrorpix).

their cultural isolation and the clichéd representations they encountered in British culture. Many attempted to parry the laughter of their employers by cultivating dignity in their public voices.[79]

[79] See, for example, Jean Rennie, *Every Other Sunday: The Autobiography of a Kitchenmaid* (London: Barker, [1955] 1978), 157.

Servants also deployed their own laughter, to the infuriation of their employers. One servant, caught laughing at the ugliness of her employer's relations during family prayers around 1907, recalled being 'hauled up on the carpet';[80] middle-class employers clearly found such laughter an invasion of their privacy and subversive of their authority. It punctured attempts to establish serious or sacred spaces or rituals, such as family prayers, and prompted strenuous efforts to police it throughout the first half of the twentieth century. Nonetheless, servants continued to purvey what one TUC publication in the 1930s called a 'bitter humour'.[81] Kitchenmaid Margaret Powell was well aware of the comic and degraded status of being a 'skivvy'. Powell and many of her contemporaries pretended to boyfriends that they had other occupations. However, she also resisted the stresses of her social status with mockery and impersonations of her own, staged in kitchens and attic rooms in the 1920s and 1930s: 'Even if you've got a mistress who's disagreeable, if the other servants are young and lively you can extract some humour from the place even if it's only making a combined attack on her upstairs. We used to give them a sort of kitchen psycho-analysis.'[82] The upper-middle-class Monica Dickens wrote of her discomfort at the constant jokes and satires of employers made by servants while she worked as a servant in the late 1930s, and employers also found it troubling. One house parlourmaid wrote in 1939 of how her mistress was peculiarly troubled by the laughter of her servants: 'When she catches us passing a joke she shouts at us instantly and gives us an unnecessary job to do to keep us apart.'[83]

Servants especially found the pretensions of suburban and middle-class employers amusing. The affluence and changing economic structure of the late nineteenth and early twentieth centuries had extended servant-keeping to the 'insecure bourgeoisie'. These employers were deeply sensitive to questions of social status, and felt themselves to be walking 'a social tight-rope' that left them vulnerable to ridicule.[84] There was considerable resentment and mockery of attempts to keep servants and chars within lower-middle-class or suburban households, regarded by the upper middle classes and many working-class observers as a snobbish affectation. Comic depictions of suburban lower-middle-class employers of servants foregrounded their anxious domesticity, a central component of which was their inability to manage their servants. Charles Pooter, satirized in *Punch* and in the comic novel *Diary of a Nobody*, suffered from the indignity of too-familiar servants. One caller reported to him that 'Your maid opened the door, and asked me to excuse her showing me in, as she was wringing out some socks.' Satirists also drew attention to

---

[80] Interview with Miss Spence (b.1891), George Ewart Evans collection, British Library Sound Archive ref. T1442R.
[81] Harries, *Plight of the Domestic Workers*.
[82] Powell, *Below Stairs*, 135.
[83] *Evening Standard*, May 20, 1939, 17.
[84] Harold Perkin, *The Rise of Professional Society: England since 1880* (London: Routledge, 1989), 81.

the uneasy relationship to jokes and physical expressions of laughter more generally amongst the lower middle classes; Pooter confided to his diary: 'I don't often make jokes,' though the comedy of the diary rests on his assiduous recording of all the occasions on which he did. When he offered a clumsy quip to a friend, his laughter and that of his wife was inappropriately excessive: 'I could not help roaring at this, and Carrie said her sides quite ached with laughter. I never was so immensely tickled by anything I have ever said before. I actually woke up twice during the night, and laughed till the bed shook.'[85] Suburban servant-keepers were laughable, both for their pretensions and for their vulgar, convulsing laughter. Comically, they shared these traits with their servants.

Like the embarrassingly excessive laughter of the Pooters, it was not only *what* servants laughed at but *how* they laughed that was troubling and subversive. The bodily expression of servants' laughter was felt by critical employers to be physically overwhelming and yet coyly expressed; how one laughed was a distinctive marker of alterity. Victorian magazines had commented on the 'sniggering slavey' who would 'grin in a gurgling manner at the most commonplace remarks' or 'conceal[ing] her giggles in a shame-faced manner behind her hand, or the coal shovel or any other domestic implement, without regard to its dirtyness.'[86] Hinting at the fascination bordering on disgust employers might feel for the laughter of servants, Ursula Holden recalled the physical presence of her nursery maid and nanny of the early 1920s: 'Didi was red faced and cheerful. I remember her and Nanny laughing so hard at some joke that Nanny's teeth fell into the basin in the bathroom. Those red gums and the clatter they made frightened me.'[87] Servants laughed in unacceptable ways, drawing attention to their mouths and bodies and transgressing norms of genteel physicality.[88] Servants also used laughter to navigate the tensions of the relationships that they maintained with children—often relationships of intimacy, yet shot through with awareness of social disparities. Servants could not maintain

---

[85] George Grossmith and Weedon Grossmith, *The Diary of a Nobody* (London: Collector's Library, 2008), 71, 56, 61. On the gendered comic value of lower-middle-class men and women, see Hammerton, 'Pooterism or Partnership?'; James Hammerton, 'The Perils of Mrs Pooter: Satire, Modernity and Motherhood in the Lower Middle-Class, England, 1870–1920', *Women's History Review*, 8 2 (1999), 261–76.

[86] Quoted in Pearsall, *Collapse of Stout Party*, 17.

[87] Holden, 'More About Maids'. A similar anecdote was told by George Abedou: 'I remember another early childhood memory, when [Mrs Ogden, the char] showed me that her teeth were not real and she dropped her upper set and I ran out the room utterly horrified. A total nightmare.' Mr George Aberdou, Interview 165, in P. Thompson and H. Newby, *Families, Social Mobility and Ageing, an Intergenerational Approach, 1900–1988* [computer file], Colchester, Essex: UK Data Archive [distributor], July 2005, SN: 4938.

[88] A feminist writer, Margaret Macnamara, was concerned about the expressions of laughter that might be prompted by her comic sketch that featured a servant who attempted to set up a labour-saving home, and her resistant mistress, published in the feminist periodical *Time and Tide* in 1920. She warned her readers: 'this little play is comedy, not farce. The audience should be moved to smiles and laughter, but not to guffaws and giggles.' Margaret Macnamara, 'A New Idea', *Time and Tide*, May 14, 1920, 17–21.

the authority normally given to adults, and so used less confrontational strategies. Ursula Holden recalls her exclusion from the laughter of the servants who helped to raise her. Though the servants often laughed amongst themselves, 'Nanny never smiled for me.'[89]

As servant-keeping spread down the social scale in the early twentieth century, indicators of status such as names, educational level, dress, food, hobbies, and ambitions were less resonant of a comic social gulf between employer and employee. Interwar servants such as Margaret Powell came to be able to claim without humour: 'The trouble with me and Mrs Hardacre was that I knew she was my inferior: . . . I was better educated, I read more and understood more, and as a result of my time in service I had better taste and better manners. She was a dried up, embittered, ignorant thing.'[90] While some larger and aristocratic households may have genuinely felt alone and uninhibited while in the company of servants, smaller, middling families complained of having to curtail their behaviour and speech for fear of looking ridiculous. They suspected (rightly) that their servants were often laughing at them, and indulged in harsher forms of humour, in attempts to shore up dissolving social boundaries. Many servants noted the discomfort of serving such employers, and felt anxiety intermingled with laughter over their social proximity to their employers. Celia Fremlin, a socialist writer who investigated domestic service in the late 1930s by taking jobs as a servant or cleaner, described in comic terms her interview with a 'lower-middle-class housewife' looking for a general servant. The mistress, on answering the door, apparently suffered intense uncertainty:

Was I a visitor still, so that she should show me in? Or was I already a servant, so that she should go in first herself? A few seconds' agony on both our parts, and then she solved the problem by going in first herself, making an agonized but sufficiently indeterminate noise in her throat, which could have been interpreted as 'excuse me' if I wished, and not if I didn't.[91]

Fremlin's description of this encounter as comic attempts to convey the new sense of egalitarianism and self-worth of young women in the 1930s, resulting from greater access to education, leisure opportunities, and civic rights, alongside the influence of feminism, and their relatively strong labour market position.[92] While young women workers continued to be paid less and to have significant curtailments on their freedom relative to their male peers, even those employed as domestic servants were aware that they had alternatives and might negotiate better conditions.

---

[89] Holden, 'More about Maids', 1.
[90] Margaret Powell, *My Mother and I* (London: Joseph, 1972), 92–3.
[91] Fremlin, *Seven Chars of Chelsea*, 23–4.
[92] Selina Todd, *Young Women, Work and Family in England, 1918–1950* (Oxford: Oxford University Press, 2005).

SHARED JOKES

The new cultural and economic confidence of younger domestic servants did not easily lend itself to emotional intimacy with employers. Shared laughter had been occasionally part of the texture of domestic service, but was impermissible in most of cultural scripts, and was mostly recorded in the less strictly policed interactions between children and servants.[93] The impossibility of a shared joke between adult employers and servants had been satirized by H. M. Bateman in *Punch* in 1922 (Figure 13).

The servant's laughter in Bateman's cartoon was depicted as physically overwhelming; her mouth wide open, she lets drop the dish she holds. In contrast, the dinner party guests retain their genteel posture while laughing at the same joke. Nonetheless, both servants and employers were pictured as diminished and disempowered by their inability to laugh together. Bateman's cartoon makes clear that the things that one might find funny and the physical style in which one laughed were still part of the repertoire of cultural, emotional, and physical scripts that made up divides of gender and social class in 1920s Britain. The shared joke was potentially subversive of these norms and hierarchies of laughter, and moments of shared laughter function as indicators of the changing relationship between servant and employer in 1930s Britain.

Mrs Sturgeon's description of her work as a housemaid in the 1930s dwelled on laughter as symbolic of changing social relationships. Having recounted her experiences of intense exploitation in service in Suffolk, she contrasted this with working in London for Charles Laughton, a Bloomsbury actor. At the centre of the contrast was a tale of the cook, Nellie Boxall, being able to share a joke with Bertrand Russell, a houseguest; both laughed at the bald head of another guest at the house. The genuine shared laughter in the Laughton household was remarkable and noteworthy for Mrs Sturgeon, as representing the new possibility of dignity and respect in domestic service. Service was not a static institution, and this anecdote reminds us that it could be constructed along more egalitarian lines in interwar Britain.[94] Nonetheless, the slapstick content of the bald head joke still suggests a confined emotional and cultural range for such encounters. Monica Dickens also found humour a significant marker of social relations, but did not see the shared joke as indicative of change. She concluded gloomily in 1939: 'Nice people like the Vaughans laugh with you, others laugh at you; but it comes to the same thing in the end.'[95]

---

[93] See, for example, the shared laughter described in Davies, *A Book with Seven Seals*, 82–5, and Haweis, *Four to Fourteen*, 99–101.

[94] Interview with Mrs Sturgeon (née Powley, b.1917), George Ewart Evans collection, British Library Sound Archive ref. T1434WR. See Light, *Mrs Woolf and the Servants*, for a sensitive account of the life in service of Nellie Boxall.

[95] Dickens, *One Pair of Hands*, 214.

Figure 13. H. M. Bateman, 'The Maid who was but Human', *Punch*, December 13, 1922, Fitzwilliam Museum.

During and after World War II, it seems that the willingness of bohemian London to laugh *with* rather than *at* their servants spread beyond their relatively unusual households. Mrs Mathias, a married daily servant to a Jewish family in Belsize Park, London, between 1939 and the 1960s, recalled that her employers, Mrs and Mrs Meres, used to do the cooking. I used to prepare—the stuff and they used to—we all used—three be in the kitchen. We had a lovely time there. And—it's a long kitchen, with a table—and a—table there and the sink here. And Mrs Meres used to be down there, the stove was down there, and—he used to say—we're boompsy-daisying again darling. 'Cos he used to bump—bump into me and we used to have a laugh. That was the happy days there.[96]

It is possible that Jewish servant-keeping households were untypical in having less investment in the rigid boundaries of social class; nonetheless, such interactions were still in a clowning mode. More sophisticated forms of humour were less acceptable within the servant-keeping relationship. Mrs Groszmann, an educated Jewish refugee working for a British couple in the Home Counties, found that her love of wordplay and puns was lost on her mistress, who was unable or unwilling to follow the jokes. Mrs Groszmann's laughter had been a gesture towards a potential friendship, but came to serve another function, perceived by her daughter as a weapon in Mrs Groszmann's continuing battle for dignity and status.[97] Laughter continued to be subtly or overtly defined by the complex othernesses of class, ethnicity, and gender, and few moments of shared laughter emerge from the historical sources describing domestic service.

CONCLUSIONS

How should historians read and contextualize the phenomenon of domestic service humour? Laughter and humour signal the interplay of the domestic and cultural realms—servant-keeping was a private employment relationship, but its relationships were mediated by cultural scripts and expectations, which predominantly worked in a comic mode that has been neglected by historians of domestic service. Laughter was frequently elicited by cues and performances that have little contemporary resonance, as the discussion of the 'quaint' servant reminds us, and some of its allusions and looked-for responses are likely to remain opaque.

Where we can recover their meanings, the frequently 'unfunny jokes' of domestic service reveal the complex textures of domestic service relationships, as sites of negotiation of power. In particular, examining laughter reveals the persistent intolerance of employers for their servants' social and cultural aspirations, their strategies for asserting authority, and the ambiguous intimacies and emotional dependencies of the relationship with the 'distant companions' they employed in their homes. Acute anxieties can be discerned about whether servants themselves were laughing at their work and their employers, and about whether the whole institution of service was sustainable in the face of such laughter. Indeed, it was not simply the alternative jobs available to working-class women that (temporarily) made domestic service residual by the 1950s, but also the harsh laughter and bitter

---

[96] Mrs Mary Ann Mathias (b. 1899), Interview 409, *Edwardians*.
[97] Lore Segal, *Other People's Houses* (London: Bodley Head, 1974 [1965]), 83.

humour of both servants and employers that was corrosive of ideas of intimacy, homeliness, and the dignity of housework, and began to make the 'servantless home' more and more attractive.

Understanding the humour problem is also central to understanding attempts made to reform domestic service, because it was the perceived problem of domestic service humour that shaped the solutions offered to the servant problem. Rather than better wages and conditions, reformers sought more symbolic and cultural resources for servants—a uniform that conveyed trained status, badges for long service, and calls for an end to music hall jokes. These solutions of course were not only relatively cheap, but also were often ones strongly resisted by servants, who regarded uniforms as yet another area of intrusion by employers. While many servants complained of hours, social isolation, and rates of pay, reformers returned compulsively to the comic status of the profession.

There certainly was a subversive element to laughter about domestic service, due to both the emotionally charged nature of the servant-keeping relationship and the disproportionately large amounts of cultural and political resources devoted to anxieties around service. The many public and private enquiries and press discussions about the servant problem created opportunities for a script that satirized these concerns, for a chance to mock the earnest and intrusive reformers who sought to ensure their own continuing lifestyle reliance on domestic service. The heavy weight such reformers gave to the humour problem suggests that finding servants, service, and employers of servants ridiculous was a powerful weapon of resistance to the indignities of service. It may have been the persistent portrayal of servants in popular culture as smarter than their employers and 'on the fiddle' that really rankled. Nonetheless, the extent to which servant jokes challenged the status quo was limited, and servants themselves did not often deploy them. It is notable that when the *Evening Standard* invited its readers to submit funny anecdotes about service in the late 1930s, the jokes published were almost entirely recounted by employers, while servants whose voices were included gave detailed, humourless statements about why they disliked domestic service. The comic voice was not easily adaptable to their perspective and 'the quaint slavey' was not an identity they could easily manipulate. Domestic service humour was not straightforwardly a 'weapon *of* the weak'. The depictions of domestic service in the comic papers, music hall reviews, and *Punch* cartoons offered few resources for servants to reinterpret their experiences. It is clear that humour offered as much consolation as subversion—consoling to employers who could laugh at the servants who caused them so much trouble, and consoling for other workers who could see their own factory job or unemployment as better than this low-status trade.

Overall, the laughter prompted by domestic service cannot effectively be read as either consoling or subversive, but instead, offers a richer set of insights than these two historiographical options allow. A historical reading of laughter requires going beyond the identification of power and resistance, and talk of the dominant and the weak, to chart the essential ambiguity of laughter. It promoted and connoted authority, mockery, and social distance, but might simultaneously be an ingredient of intimacy and friendship in servant-keeping households.

The sources explored here also demonstrate that laughter is not simply a cultural response, but somatically expressed. Its norms of physical expression are as significant as the *content* of what was laughed at, and in this role it forms a part of the performances of class, ethnicity, and gender in British homes. Laughter in this somatic sense can tentatively be equated to the influence of smell, which George Orwell identified in *The Road to Wigan Pier* as functioning at a deep level at which class is enacted in bodily, sensory terms.[98] The somatic expression of laughter tends to be neglected in historical and cultural studies of the comic, but suggests the ways in which social distinctions may be 'written on the body'.

It may have been the changes in the media in twentieth-century Britain that in the end made service jokes redundant, or transmuted them into the gentler humour of Mrs Mopp or *Upstairs, Downstairs*. From Edwardian times, music halls attempted to reach a socially mixed audience, a process that ended with the more bland and commercial 'variety show' of the interwar and post-war years. Cinema and, to some degree, radio were not aimed specifically at working-class audiences, but became mass entertainment, relatively untethered to particular class cultures.[99] And print media were also transformed in the interwar decades: general women's magazines such as *Good Housekeeping* were founded, supplanting the pre-war divide into a dual magazine market specializing on the one hand in sensational fiction aimed at working-class women and, on the other, in domestic material aimed at middle- and upper-class women running homes with servants.[100] Editors built their interwar reading public around images of the housewife or business girl, and this attempt to amalgamate audiences disrupted the 'knowing economy' of domestic service humour.[101] The addressee of 'domestic service humour' was becoming ambiguous and fluid. In 1939, *Housewife* magazine ran a story entitled 'My Maid and Me'. 'If you have a maid,' the byline promised, 'you'll enjoy this article, if you haven't, you'll enjoy it still more.'[102] It is clear that those who might employ servants, the servantless, and even servants themselves might all be anticipated as amused readers of such a text.

More generally, servants no longer undertook a key bridging function between social groups or audiences, and thus their power to convey humour through juxtaposition and incongruence slowly faded. This was a change, however, that developed in an uneven fashion; comic discourse has the power to interweave older meanings and symbolisms with newer ones, and it has a certain degree of autonomy from its immediate circumstances. British culture may have partially reorganized itself around less divisive domestic figures such as the housewife, but *Housewife* magazine remained wedded to the comic servant in the 1950s. Although the magazine's practical advice on running a home assumed the absence of residential

---

[98] Orwell in Davison (ed.), *Orwell's England*, 141.
[99] Ross McKibbin, *Classes and Cultures: England 1918–1951* (Oxford: Oxford University Press, 1998).
[100] Billie Melman, *Women and the Popular Imagination in the Twenties* (London: Macmillan, 1988).
[101] Judy Giles, *The Parlour and the Suburb: Domestic Identities, Class, Femininity and Modernity* (Oxford: Berg, 2004), 5–6. See also Bingham, *Gender, Modernity, and the Popular Press*, 85–6.
[102] Gil Chard, 'My Maid and Me', *Housewife*, Jan 1939.

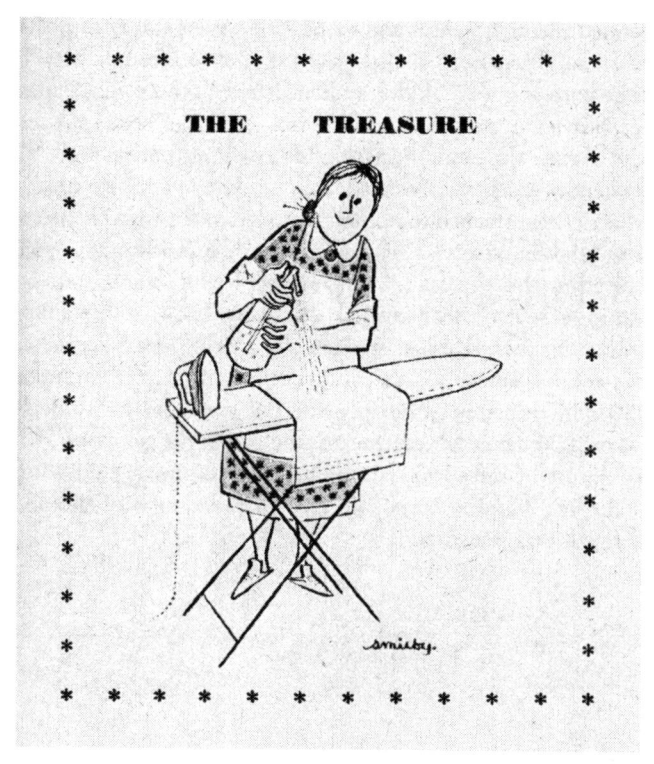

Figure 14. 'The Treasure', *Housewife*, November 1956, 185.

servants, a long-running comic feature, entitled 'The Treasure', still used many of the same jokes as prewar print culture (Figure 14). Depicting an overweight, overall- and slipper-clad older domestic worker, the jokes revolved around her determination to subvert the normal or efficient uses of household objects, or laughed at her sexual interest in men.

A moment of resistance to the invitation to laugh at 'The Treasure' by a *Housewife* reader in 1957 suggests, however, that the knowingness needed to find her an amusing character was no longer reliably felt by readers. Mrs D. K. Tolley wrote to the editors from Cirencester: 'While I saw the funny side of "The Treasure" smilingly "sprinkling" her ironing board with a soda water siphon in the November issue, well, if it's full of scrupulously clean water, *why not?*'[103] Housewives, like domestic workers, might also prefer to take shortcuts and use objects 'against the grain', and no role incongruity could be established in this unsuccessful joke.

Finally, laughter suggests a revised periodization for the 'servant problem', with jokes about service persisting well into the later twentieth century. Domestic service

---

[103] Mrs D. K. Tolley, 'Treasure's Tip', *Housewife*, Jan 1957, 101.

humour operated through genres and tropes still found funny in post-war Britain despite their uncoupling from mass social experience, though Mrs Tolley made clear that the 'knowingness' of the audience had become unreliable. Domestic service jokes proved a persistent vehicle for anxieties around the encounters between social classes, the establishment of domestic authority, and the willingness of young women to undertake domestic labour. They were also implicated in the complex sexual desires attached to domestic service, as the next chapter will explore. The persistent laughter at service reminds us that the serio-comic servant question was not resolved at the apparent watershed of World War II but continued to function within a society that turned decisively back to the employment of domestic workers in private households in the 1980s. Much had changed in the late-twentieth-century labour market, and commentators have emphatically denied that pre-1939 domestic service can provide the paradigm for understanding the resurgence of paid domestic labour towards the end of the century.[104] Nonetheless, the enduring nature of the comic cultural cues surrounding paid domestic labour suggest that the two periods cannot be seen in isolation, and should be situated within a single cultural imaginary.

[104] Gregson and Lowe, *Servicing the Middle Classes*.

5

'The Good, the Bad, and the Spicy'

Servants in Pornography and Erotica

A girl (though she wore long skirts her figure was unformed and her waist had a stiff youthful curve) ran quickly into the room. Her eager bright-coloured young face—that also not yet fully formed—was overshadowed by a flapping decorated hat obviously constructed less for a woman's head—less still for a maiden's—than for a cash draper's window. Her chest was plastered with a motley collection of cheap jewellery and lace. Her boots had not been cleaned.

This description of a servant returning home for a visit was offered in 1909 by Stephen Reynolds, a middle-class 'social explorer' who lived with Devon fishermen from 1907 to 1918.

Reynolds' description seems a sympathetic portrayal of a child worker. However, his gaze lingered disconcertingly on her sexual attributes and in what followed, he conveyed the flavour of that strange mixture of sexual attraction and disgust that might attach itself to Edwardian servants:

Poor brave small servant girls, earning your living while you are yet but children! I see your faces at the doors, rosy from the country or yellowish-white from anaemia and strong tea; see how your young breasts hardly fill your clinging bodices, all askew, and how your hips are not yet grown to support your skirts properly—draggle-tails! . . . I see your floppety hat which you cannot pin down tightly to your hair, because there isn't enough of it;—your courageous attempts to be prettier than you are, or else your carelessness from overmuch drudgery; your coquettish and ugly gestures mixed.

Having speculated on the romantic fantasies that might preoccupy such a servant, Reynolds went on to offer his own fantasy:

In mind, I follow you also into your little bedroom under the roof, . . . What will you try on to-night? A hat, or a dress, or the two-and-eleven-three-farthing blouse? Shift the candle. Show yourself to the looking-glass. A poke here and pull there—and now put everything away carefully in the box under the bed, and go to sleep.

His final description was of disavowal of his voyeuristic gaze at the servant girl's body, mirrored, undressing, or asleep:

Though I say that I follow you up to your attic, and watch you and see you go to sleep, you need not blush or giggle or snap. I would not do you any harm; your eyes would plague me. And besides, I do not entirely fancy you. You are not fresh. You are boxed up too much. But I trust that some lusty careless fellow, regardless of consequences, looking not too far ahead and following the will of his race—I trust that he will get hold of you and whirl you heavenwards, and will fill your being full to the brim; and will kiss you and surround you with himself, and will make you forget yourself and your mistress and all the world.[1]

The reader is left with an impression of Reynolds' curious voyeurism, and attraction to this coquettish but stale child. The servant has no privacy, and may be observed at her most intimate moments, even in her fantasy life. Reynolds' intriguing portrayal of an Edwardian servant signals the close relationship established between domestic servants and sex. This is of course a long-standing relationship—the sexual insult 'slut' was seventeenth-century shorthand for slattern or kitchen maid, and the links between domestic service and sex have been intense for many centuries. Two names widely recognized as 'servants names', John Thomas and Mary Ann, were also nineteenth-century sexual slang. Servants were strongly associated with illicit sex, and were over-represented amongst the mothers of illegitimate children in the nineteenth century. The jokes made about domestic service and the obsessive watching of servants by employers and reformers had a sexual element central to the cultural elaboration of 'the servant problem'. I have suggested that domestic service was influential in shaping and conveying British emotional life; and this is borne out when we examine the importance of sexual fantasy in defining the service relationship. Servants and employers of both sexes encountered, constructed, and circulated images, fantasies, and narratives of themselves as erotic or sexually innocent beings, and these continued to flourish in British society long after live-in domestic service employment had become residual. Domestic service played out in the fantasy realm as powerfully as it did in the everyday domestic encounters between employers and servants, and erotic fantasies profoundly shaped and nuanced domestic encounters.

Thinking about the sexual fantasies domestic service inspired offers the chance to set some unusual texts alongside the oral histories and reformist reports that have typically formed the substance of historical work on domestic service—to look, for example, at pulp, comic, and pornographic periodicals, 'saucy' postcards, striptease, and cinema. The existing literature on domestic service has sometimes acknowledged the prominence of sex in the servant problem,[2] but has largely failed to broaden its evidence base to reflect this. Moreover, this work has tended to depict only the sexual objectification or exploitation of the servant. Servants were, as Ronald Hyam puts it, 'subordinate and sexually accessible women'.[3] My

---

[1] Stephen Reynolds, *A Poor Man's House* (Oxford: Oxford University Press, 1982), 133–4.
[2] See, for example, Karen Tranberg Hansen, *Distant Companions: Servants and Employers in Zambia, 1900–1985* (Ithaca, NY: Cornell University Press, 1989); Phyllis Palmer, *Domesticity and Dirt: Housewives and Domestic Servants in the United States, 1920–1945* (Philadelphia: Temple University Press, 1989).
[3] Ronald Hyam, *Empire and Sexuality: The British Experience* (Manchester: Manchester University Press, 1990), 59. See also Standish Meacham, *A Life Apart: The English Working Class 1890–1914* (London: Thames and Hudson, 1977), 187–8, on the sexual vulnerabilities of servants.

account, in contrast, dwells on the powers of both employers *and* servants to narrate the servant problem in terms of sex. The sexual charge of domestic service is documented not only in social reform and entertainment, but also in the everyday interactions of servants and employers. I focus on the changing power of domestic service to direct and give meaning to sexual desire, and to allow for voyeurism and sexual interactions. The association between sex and domestic service was not a static one; in the twentieth century, new kinds of intimacies within the home, new styles of courtship, expanded sources of sexual knowledge, and changes in sexual aspirations, all mediated and shaped the eroticization of service.

As well as challenging existing accounts of domestic service, the eroticization of service raises some historiographical and political questions about reading pornography and erotica. In the historiography of pornography, there has been a welcome expansion beyond issues of censorship, to its wider cultural role.[4] There is, nonetheless, still a tendency to focus on the medium rather than the content, which is assumed to be repetitive and predictable in the modern era.[5] It has also been tempting for historians interested in discourses of sex and the erotic to turn to more extreme and graphic sources in order to determine patterns and representations of sexual desire. The sentimental, the comic, and the mildly titillating have been neglected as bearers of erotic charge. Sources in this mode often had a much higher circulation than the more explicit forms of pornography, though they have been less well preserved in library collections. 'Knowing' servants was portrayed in music hall, in cheap Edwardian periodicals such as *Pick-me-up, Judy,* and *Fun,* and in early cinema. Their depictions do not lend themselves to a straightforward account of sexual exploitation and subjugation. Sexual desire and 'sexual charge' do not work only in the mode of dominance and subjugation, and are not only organized through clandestine texts. While it may be harder to give historical readings of ambiguous sources such as the fantasy of Stephen Reynolds quoted above, it is important to expand our sense of the channels through which meanings of the erotic have been established and contested. The line setting pornography apart from other kinds of erotically charged texts has long been extremely blurred.

The framing category of the 'erotic imaginary' is adopted in this chapter to juxtapose pornography to less explicit but nonetheless titillating texts and indicate this wider throw. It draws on the idea of the 'social imaginary', a term that, as Lisa

---

[4] See Carolyn Dean, *The Frail Social Body: Pornography, Homosexuality, and Other Fantasies in Interwar France* (Los Angeles: University of California Press, 2000); Lisa Sigel, *Governing Pleasures: Pornography and Social Change in England, 1815–1914* (New Brunswick: Rutgers University Press, 2002); eadem, *International Exposure: Perspectives on Modern European Pornography, 1800–2000* (London: Rutgers University Press, 2005); Sarah Toulalan, *Imagining Sex: Pornography and Bodies in Seventeenth-Century England* (Oxford: Oxford University Press, 2007). This chapter largely avoids discussing the thriving pornographic subcultures associated with sadomasochism, transvestism, and other sexual preferences, and also largely focuses on print culture, only touching on cinema and erotic performance, though these might form fruitful areas for further research. The discussion concludes in the 1980s, at a time when increasing use of pornographic home videos allowed for a proliferation of the niches of pornography, to such an extent that it becomes hard to make any generalizations about 'erotic imaginaries'.

[5] Isabel Tang, *Pornography: The Secret History of Civilisation* (London: Channel 4 Books, 1999).

Sigel summarizes it, describes 'the mental structures, which allow[s] people to organize their culture, to understand the actions, behaviours, artefacts, symbols and signs among which they live. It is mobile, and acts not only on people but also through people as they continually cast, recast, and reconstitute their milieu in meaningful ways.'[6] 'Erotic imaginary' designates the changing social and cultural organization of desire, and transcends the contested distinctions among porn, erotica, smut, and so on. There are historical moments when the erotic imaginary can be linked to a single and relatively dominant 'worldview', but more often we can describe competing 'imaginaries' operating in those textual and cultural spaces in which sexual desire and practices are given symbolic meanings through human agency.[7] Erotic imaginaries offer a range of coexistent and sometimes contradictory image clusters. We can discern persistent patterns—for example, the gendered pattern by which mainly female servants are desired or surveilled by mainly male employers. However, mistresses and male servants are also represented, and it is clear that the eroticization of servants was not simply heterosexual or 'patriarchal'; relationships between mistresses and their female servants were eroticized in a complex or 'queer' fashion. Moreover, the pornographic sources examined below offer no simple gender pattern of male dominance and female sexual objectification, and were not only constructed for men. Women were also sometimes expected as readers and viewers, or formed an unexpected audience.[8]

Pornography and erotica provided some 'scripts', highly ambiguous and variable, that allowed servants and employers to imagine, name, condemn, and practice their desires, and through this to establish authority and identity. Power imbalances

---

[6] Sigel, *Governing Pleasures*, 2. As developed by Cornelius Castoriadis, the social imaginary 'builds upon but always exceeds the material conditions of human life', and elaborates itself through the symbols and myths by which society self-identifies in an ongoing and mutable fashion (Cornelius Castoriadis, *The Imaginary Institution of Society* (Cambridge: Polity Press, 1987)).

[7] An account that centres on erotic imaginaries seems to hover at the level of 'discourse history' and may struggle to incorporate individual experiences, agency, and physical bodies into its narrative. Some feminists have insisted that pornographic discourse and sexual experience must coincide, since 'the definition of women articulated systematically and consistently in pornography is objective and real in that real women exist within and must live with constant reference to the boundaries of this definition.' For Andrea Dworkin, for example, pornography offers systematic and consistent definitions of women, and she neglects the possibility of variation over time or the conflicting uses to which pornography may be put (Andrea Dworkin, 'Pornography: Men Possessing Women', in Hilaire Barnett (ed.), *Sourcebook on Feminist Jurisprudence* (London: Cavendish, 1998), 443–5, 444). This, however, seems reductive and negligent of issues of reception and agency. More usefully, historians such as Lyndal Roper have noted that somatic experiences may occur at a level that is sometimes independent of discourse, This is a level, however, to which we do not have unmediated epistemic access. Sex, bodies, and desire exist 'outside' of discourse and can sometimes intrude in unexpected ways, but they are usually experienced in historically contingent and culturally mediated ways. The erotic imaginary is a conceptual framework that acknowledges this mediation, while remaining attentive to the ways in which discourse is established through human agency and the material, unpredictable, presence of bodies (Lyndal Roper, *Oedipus and the Devil: Witchcraft, Sexuality, and Religion in Early Modern Europe* (London: Taylor and Francis, 1994), 17).

[8] I build on Ellen Rosenman's account of Victorian women's relationship to sensual and erotic texts, and their own bodies. Rosenman argues that though there is often an implied male spectator of erotic material, women nonetheless might identify with fantasies on offer (Ellen B. Rosenman, *Unauthorized Pleasures: Accounts of Victorian Sexual Experience* (Ithaca, NY: Cornell University Press, 2003), 9–12).

certainly governed their relationship, and different scripts achieved greater cultural prominence at different moments. Pornography, as Sarah Toulalan has argued, tells us about how the sexual was interpreted within the social in complex ways that cannot be reduced to a simple description of being oppressive or liberating for women.[9] It is therefore unhelpful to see the eroticization of servants as organized around simple binaries of good and bad, licit and illicit. Instead, I argue that pornography should be seen as a site of ongoing negotiation between competing sexual narratives—and it is this set of negotiations, which takes place in culture and through fantasies, that can be characterized as an erotic imaginary.

TRANSFORMATIONS OF THE EROTIC IMAGINARY

Explicit erotic texts entered into a mass circulation heyday more or less at the same time as domestic service was at its height, towards the close of the nineteenth century. The invention of the stereoview, cinema, and new forms of image reproduction enabled what has been termed an intensification or 'frenzy' of the visual in British society.[10] There was a swift expansion of the audiences and channels of circulation of erotica in the late nineteenth century, and these channels extended transnationally. What had been an elite item of consumption, published in small print runs in graphic and explicit expensive editions, became a mass commodity traded across national boundaries, recast as the 'saucy' or 'fast' publication. 'Naughty' penny postcards, often produced and distributed in Paris, became cheaply available in late-Victorian Britain. There was also a huge increase in periodical publishing, much of it mixing titillating content with new tabloid techniques. The nature of the pornographic became uncertain and fragmented in legal terms and in publishing genres. Historians have seen this as a moment of opportunity for more scrutiny of the erotic, beyond the limited distribution of elite pornography, deploying more 'democratic' media, better suited to the 'more democratised, heterosocial world of sex and sociability' characterizing the early twentieth century.[11] Pornography became more threatening to cultural elites, as it became cheap and visual. With the shift to greater sexual openness went a loss of richness in the kind of language used to describe sex, with sexual cursing beginning to predominate in descriptions of sex and women's bodies reduced to 'the sum of their polluted parts'.[12] Representations of sex became democratized, but also commodified to a greater degree in the late nineteenth century.

---

[9] Toulalan, *Imagining Sex*.
[10] Linda Williams, *Hard Core: Power, Pleasure and the 'Frenzy of the Visible'* (Berkeley: University of California Press, 1989); Lynda Nead, 'Strip: Moving Bodies in the 1890s', *Early Popular Visual Culture*, 3 2 (2005), 135–50, esp. 139.
[11] Peter Bailey, *Popular Culture and Performance in the Victorian City* (Cambridge: Cambridge University Press, 1998), 173; Sigel, *Governing Pleasures*, 123.
[12] Sigel, *Governing Pleasures*, 418.

The erotic imaginary was peopled by a shifting set of sexual actors. The governess had served as a focus for nineteenth-century erotic fantasies, fuelled by her lack of clear social status. She was sexually vulnerable, though sometimes also cherished her own sexual and social aspirations to marry into the employing household or social circle. For the mid-Victorians, governesses were deeply saturated with sexual charge because unlike lower servants, their sexual or courting interests might be directed at any social level. However, the governess held a fading erotic appeal in the early twentieth century, as fewer were employed in this role. Governesses came to act as a pornographic focus for flagellation fantasies but otherwise became rarely represented.[13] She gave way to the housemaid, 'slavey' or maid-of-all-work, presented in saucy postcards, stereoviews, or the newly invented mutoscopes that became a feature of mass leisure in the 1890s. Often depicting female nudes, these hand-cranked 'penny in the slot machines' were also known as 'What The Butler Saw' machines.[14] Domestic service was thus immediately foregrounded as a realm of male voyeurism and female sexual availability; male servants were very rarely figured in these texts, except as voyeurs. Sex became something increasingly to be watched, and female servants were figured as a class of 'public women' without privacy. Cultural representations of servants were omnipresent in 'fast' or 'naughty' periodicals, in the 'smoking concert' films of early cinema, and in the 'knowing', eroticized comedy of music hall. Kissing and seducing servants featured very prominently in Edwardian cinema. An early pornographic or explicit film, *A L'Ecu d'Or, ou la bonne auberge* (1908), for example, centres on the sexual liaison between a servant and a soldier, and servants continued to be slapstick figures of desire and sexual horseplay in cinema productions of the 1920s such as *Le Telegraphiste*.[15] Their erotic role was intensified through the shift identified by Lisa Sigel, who argues that around 1880, 'eroticism in some fundamental way became equivalent with dirtiness. The eroticised body had been stripped of its potential as a repository of complex and contradictory metaphors and instead had become a site of pollution beliefs.'[16] The lack of privacy and associations of dirt with female domestic servants lent themselves well to increasing eroticization.

Servants' proximity to dirt made them polluted in ways that added to the sexual charge of service. Early twentieth-century servants were still intimately connected to disposing of human waste, in slop buckets, nappies, and chamber pots. And many had an enforced intimacy with their own waste, through being forbidden the use of bathrooms. Mrs Barton was in service at her local vicarage between the wars: 'The house did have a bathroom but I was not allowed to use it. I had to go to a little house in the garden. The first time I saw it I was horrified, it had four seats in

---

[13] Trev Broughton and Symes Ruth, *The Governess: An Anthology* (Stroud: Sutton, 1997), 180.
[14] Simon Brown, 'Early Cinema in Britain and the Smoking Concert Film', *Early Popular Visual Culture*, 3 2 (2005), 165–78, esp. 168. On stereoviews, see Serge Nazarieff, *The Stereoscopic Nude 1850–1930* (Cologne: Benedikt Taschen, 1993).
[15] Williams, *Hard Core*, 74.
[16] Lisa Sigel, 'Name Your Pleasure: The Transformation of Sexual Language in Nineteenth-Century British Pornography', *Journal of the history of sexuality*, 9 4 (2000), 395–419, esp. 410.

a row—was I expecting company?'[17] Mary Douglas's influential analysis of dirt as 'matter out of place' has helped to relativize and contextualize the pollution threat that 'dirty work' and 'dirty workers' seem to offer. Douglas stressed that 'there is no such thing as dirt; no single item is dirty apart from a particular system of classification in which it does not fit.' 'Clean', she argued, should be reread as 'proper to its class'. The powerful taboos around pollution are often spelt out in the 'exaggerated avoidances' of sexual cultures.[18] Influenced by Douglas, Phyllis Palmer has argued, 'in the Western unconscious of the past two centuries, dirt and sex live in close association, and women who clean up things associated with bodies find themselves mysteriously deemed sexual and powerful'.[19] This, she argues, has enabled both men and women to split women into 'good' and 'bad' women.

Through their association with pollution, domestic servants have been the prime candidates for an association with illicit sex as 'bad women'. Leonore Davidoff describes the relationship between Hannah Cullwick and Arthur Munby, which so dominates the historical landscape of eroticized domestic service, as a means of capturing a mid-Victorian worldview or social imaginary in which certain social categories are paired, setting up hierarchical and erotically charged divisions—purity/dirt, white/black, human/animal, Madonna/Magdalene, and so on.[20] These accounts are important, though as we shall see, they do not fully capture the erotic charge of domestic service.

Servants were also symbolically equated with animals, and their sexuality was understood as, in its rankness, closer to nature. 'Nature', in its turn, was eroticized and associated with 'animal functions'. Servants were often characterized as 'feeble-minded' or below average intelligence, and this also symbolically linked them to 'nature'. The distribution of space in servant-keeping homes and the material objects associated with servants conveyed powerful messages of revulsion and otherness. Robert Graves wrote:

I remember the servants' bedrooms. They were on the top landing, at the dullest side of the house, and by a convention of the times, the only rooms without carpets or linoleum. Those gaunt, unfriendly-looking beds and the hanging-cupboards with faded cotton curtains,

---

[17] Mrs Barton (b. 1913), AC 'My First Job' (1991), ERO T/Z 25/2495. On the relationship between privies and eighteenth-century servants, see Carolyn Steedman, *Labours Lost: Domestic Service and the Making of Modern England* (Cambridge: Cambridge University Press, 2009).
[18] Mary Douglas, *Purity and Danger: An Analysis of the Concept of Pollution and Taboo* (London: Routledge, 2002), xvii, 180.
[19] Palmer, *Domesticity and Dirt*, 138.
[20] Leonore Davidoff, *Worlds between: Historical Perspectives on Class and Gender* (New York: Routledge, 1995), 105. This polarized social imaginary is evoked in the 1956 study of a socially conservative mining area of Britain, *Coal is Our Life*, an environment in which the authors believed 'women can only be objects of lust, mothers and domestic servants' (Norman Dennis, Fernando Henriques, and Clifford Slaughter, *Coal is Our Life* (London, 1956, 1969), 231). Within such a social imaginary, it is the transgression of the boundaries that is most haunted by erotic associations, and this helps to explain why dressing up as a servant was so persistently popular amongst employers. See Lucy Delap, 'Campaigns of Curiosity: Class Crossing and Role Reversal in British Domestic Service, c.1890–1950', *Left History*, 12 2 (2007).

instead of wardrobes with glass doors as in the other rooms. All this uncouthness made me think of servants as somehow not quite human.[21]

The different grade of soaps and toilet paper often given to servants inevitably associated them with inferior standards of cleanliness in the minds of their employers.[22] One child of a servant-keeping Edwardian household, interviewed in the 1970s, returned again and again to her unresolved question of how the servants in her childhood home had kept themselves clean, since they were forbidden to use the household bathroom.[23] Disgust has an important role to play in determining wider power relations, as Sara Ahmed suggests: 'Disgust at "that which is below" functions to maintain the power relations between above and below, *through which "aboveness" and "belowness" become properties of particular bodies, objects and spaces.*'[24]

The sexual connotations of service, linking servants to nature, animals, and dirt, went beyond the interest in the visual that has dominated the historical literature on pornography, and was linked to other senses, in particular, the smell of servants. As Leonore Davidoff writes of the Victorian period, 'Children soon learned that servants talked differently, walked differently, even smelled differently. Memories, for example, are evoked of a maid's hands which smelled of dishwater when dressing a child, or of the fusty smell of servants' bedrooms.'[25] Body odour and cheap perfume were commonly recalled in early-twentieth-century descriptions of servants, capturing this polluted erotic charge. As Stephen Reynolds put it in his address to a servant girl: 'I follow you into your kitchen, with its faint odour of burnt grease (your carelessness) and of cockroaches, and its whiffs from the scullery sink, and a love-story that scents your life, hidden away in a drawer.'[26] Servants' distinctive smell seems linked not only to pollution, but also to their comfort value. One employer recalled her childhood servants as 'an amiable crowd who smelt of stale hair-oil, patchouli on occasions, and always of B.O., but I loved them all.'[27] Dirt and its smells, then, did not only convey social distance, but also had the power of reassurance and comfort that could be figured in sexual terms. *The Times* talked in 1914 of servants 'assaulting us in the very nostrils with culinary flavours and soapy scents'.[28] Servants' role as comforting nannies and mother substitutes gave them an erotic appeal established during childhood that perhaps prompted the pervasive depiction of them as a consoling sexual presence, as, for example, in

---

[21] Robert Graves, *Goodbye to All That* (London: Penguin, 1976 [1929]), 20.
[22] Graham Cross, interview with the author, May 8, 2007.
[23] Mrs Philpot (b. 1888), Interview 1, in P. Thompson, *Family Life and Work Experience before 1918, Middle and Upper Class Families in the Early 20th Century, 1870–1977* [computer file], 2nd edn, Colchester, Essex: UK Data Archive [distributor], May 2008, SN: 5404.
[24] Sara Ahmed, *The Cultural Politics of Emotion* (Edinburgh: Edinburgh University Press, 2004), 89, emphasis in the original.
[25] Davidoff, *Worlds between*, 110.
[26] Reynolds, *A Poor Man's House*, 133.
[27] Ursula Bloom, *Mrs Bunthorpe's Respects: A Chronicle of Cooks* (London: Hutchinson, 1963), 35.
[28] 'The Servant Question', *The Times*, Apr 21, 1914, 11.

Walter's adventures with numerous servants in *My Secret Life*.[29] This was a sexualization of women figured as 'ordinary', 'natural', and encountered everyday. It flourished in the nudist and physical culture or 'cult of the body' movements that emerged after World War I. The *Sun Bathing Review* was a semi-titillating journal of the 1930s, which juxtaposed health features with shots of airbrushed coy nudes. Servants, especially those of immigrant origin, were lauded in the journal as in touch with nature, their bodies and sexuality, contrasted to effete mistresses.[30] An 'earthy' sexual charge was thus quite ambiguous, and might simultaneously convey pollution, threat, *and* a liberated, 'natural' sexuality of plenitude and consolation.[31]

The body of the female servant as 'dirty' and 'natural' associated it with other realms of Victorian and Edwardian erotic fantasy—the empire and the orient. Servants' bodies were both a familiar, intimate presence in middle-class homes, but also signified what Gertrude Koch terms 'foreign imperialist eroticism', with its overtones of openness to exploration and annexation.[32] In a self-consciously 'homely' collection of popular domestic advice essays, Fay Inchfawn described a servant, Jane, as best approached as an explorer would tackle a 'foreign soil': 'You have strange and unintelligible landmarks. Here, you will probably meet with opposition. The natural conditions of the country may prevent you from making rapid headway. You may encounter icebergs, landslips, tropical heat, poisonous plants. You are certain to light upon the unexpected.' The process of 'exploration' mistresses were advised to use in their dealings with servants was one of paternalistic colonialism: 'the true explorer . . . attempts his perilous journeyings that he may bring this hitherto unknown territory into a helpful relation with the rest of the world . . . This is the only spirit in which you should begin to explore Jane.'[33] The erotic subtext is clear—the process of imperial exploration had a sexual component, and scantily dressed natives featured prominently in the expanding 'naughty postcards' trade of the early twentieth century. It was no accident that images of servants and 'natives' were mainstays of the erotic postcard trade.

'PUBLIC WOMEN'

Edwardian representations of servants as highly sexually charged link them to some other eroticized groups of working women. Historians have focused on specific groups of Victorian and Edwardian working women whose roles, like those of

---

[29] Walter, *My Secret Life* (Wordsworth editions, 1996), vol 1, Chap 3. See Bruce Robbins, *The Servant's Hand: English Fiction from Below* (New York: Columbia University Press, 1986), 196–8.
[30] In one article, a mistress's Irish servant had given notice because 'the Spring had entered her blood', and this inspired her mistress to adopt nudism: Leila Barford, 'Susanna Greets the Spring', *Sun Bathing Review* (1935), 23.
[31] Robbins, *The Servant's Hand*, 199.
[32] Gertrude Koch, 'On Pornographic Cinema', *Jump Cut: A Review of Contemporary Media*, 35 (1990), 17–29. See also Collette Colligan, *The Traffic in Obscenity from Byron to Beardsley: Sexuality and Exoticism in Nineteenth Century Print Culture* (Basingstoke: Palgrave, 2006).
[33] Fay Inchfawn, *Homely Talks of a Homely Woman* (London: Ward, Lock, 1923), 71–2.

servants, were sexualized—actresses and barmaids.[34] Their accounts have stressed the links barmaids and actresses sustained to the world of glamour to define their sexual appeal; through the distancing effect of the stage or bar counter, these smartly dressed women were both available yet inaccessible to their customers. Peter Bailey has outlined the concept of 'parasexuality', a sexuality that is 'deployed but contained . . . In vulgar terms, it might be described as "everything but".'[35] The appeal of actresses and barmaids was of an 'open yet licit sexuality', on display, open to the male gaze, performing a role. The eroticization of these kinds of working women, then, was through their being objects of display and voyeurism, allied to their links to the glamour of fashionable dress, amusement, and celebrity.

Domestic servants clearly drew on some of these dimensions of attraction—indeed, Bailey acknowledges that barmaids in smaller bars were in effect maids-of-all-work. Like barmaids, servants wore a uniform, and were on display to the male gaze. Service could be figured as a stage, a realm in which the gaze was supremely important. Like the actress and the barmaid, the female domestic servant was visible and a lack of privacy was built into her job. Towards the middle decades of the twentieth century, the well-dressed servant picked up a smattering of glamour, and some girls fantasized about the servant's smart black dress and ribboned cap.[36] Through their association with great houses and aristocrats, service had some glamorous connotations, particularly for those upper servants such as lady's maids, who might travel and had to care for dresses and jewellery.

However, the inaccessibility of 'parasexuality' cannot capture the ways in which most Edwardian servants were sexually depicted. Instead, servants were more closely associated with another group of 'working women' in the early decades of the twentieth century. As the sex psychologist Havelock Ellis wrote, 'by the conditions of their lives servants, more than any other class, resemble prostitutes. Like prostitutes, they are a class of women apart; they are not entitled to the considerations and the little courtesies usually paid to other women; in some countries they are even registered, like prostitutes.' For Ellis, it was the servant's experience of observing a superior social world, and not her poverty and low wages, that tempted her to a life of sexual vice:

the servant is deprived of all human relationships; she must not betray the existence of any simple impulse, or natural need. At the same time she lives on the fringe of luxury; she is surrounded by the tantalizing visions of pleasure and amusement for which her fresh young nature craves. It is not surprising that, repelled by unrelieved drudgery and attracted by idle

---

[34] Bailey, *Popular Culture and Performance*; Tracy C. Davis, 'The Actress in Victorian Pornography', in Kristine Ottesen Garrigan (ed.), *Victorian Scandals: Representations of Gender and Class* (Athens: Ohio University Press, 1992).

[35] Bailey, *Popular Culture and Performance*, 151.

[36] Indeed, Bailey interprets the wider possibilities for twentieth-century women to partake of glamour through their growing access to makeup and fashions as a 'closing up' of the 'parasexual' effect of distance between the everyday and the glamorous (ibid. 163). I argue below that parasexuality was not uniquely associated with the late Victorian period, but also had purchase in the late twentieth century.

luxury, she should take the plunge which will alone enable her to enjoy the glittering aspects of civilisation which seem so desirable to her.[37]

Servants were thus sometimes attributed with overwhelming desires that might lead them to vice or sexual misdemeanour.

Servants did often come into contact with the borderlands of paid sex, as the Christian feminist reformer Maude Royden made clear in her 1916 book on the causes of prostitution, *Downward Paths*.[38] Former domestic servants were held to make up around 40–50 per cent of prostitutes in the late Victorian years, and the memoirs of twentieth-century servants dwelt on their proximity to sex workers. Winifred Foley, when employed as a maid at a boarding house in the late 1920s, quickly noticed that some of the lodgers were nightclub hostesses, while others were luggage-less couples who simply took the room for a night.[39] She was comfortable with this environment, repelling 'the skirmishing attacks on my virtue that were inevitable in a setting like a Paddington terrace boarding-house', but without offering judgement on the casual sex that surrounded her. Jean Rennie, a maid in the 1930s, was briefly a nightclub hostess herself while out of a position. Many women employed as servants in lodging houses, or in the trade parallel to domestic service, the uniformed Lyons waitress (the 'nippy'), spent evenings with customers, and received presents in return, though there may have been no actual sex or money exchanged. Margaret Powell recalled two housemaids who let their employer fondle their hair curlers at night, in return for cosmetics and stockings.[40] The sociocultural and economic links between service and prostitution were reinforced by these proximities. This led to widespread fears that servants were a source of sexual corruption; most disturbingly, that they might undertake sexual experiments with the children of the house, or might bring practices of working-class sex and courtship into middle-class homes.

COURTING AND COMIC EDWARDIAN SERVANTS

Though in popular memory, servants have been widely depicted as victims of cross-class seduction, the desires of servants were normally represented by early-twentieth-century commentators as directed towards men of their own class. It was not, in fact, the cross-class sexual encounters between employers and servants that dominated Edwardian representations of domestic service, though historians have focused on this dimension. Instead, erotic images of servants functioned predominantly as a means of imagining sexual and courting encounters between

---

[37] Havelock Ellis, 'Studies in the Psychology of Sex' (Philadelphia: Davies, 1897), 6: 265, 91. On the longer term associations of servants and prostitution, see Carolyn Steedman, *Master and Servant: Love and Labour in the English Industrial Age* (Cambridge: Cambridge University Press, 2007), 52.
[38] A. Maude Royden, *Downward Paths: An Inquiry into the Causes Which Contribute to the Making of the Prostitute* (London: Bell, 1916).
[39] Winifred Foley, *A Child in the Forest* (London: Futura, 1974), 237.
[40] Margaret Powell, *Below Stairs* (London: Pan Books, 1968), 135–6.

working-class individuals. In early-twentieth-century sources, fantasies about cross-class sexual encounters were far outnumbered by the 'scopophilia' of observing 'working-class' sexual practices. *Punch* magazine, aimed at the employing classes, portrayed the love life of servants as ridiculous and irritating, yet compulsively observed. Indeed, the power to observe, and its pleasures, formed a component of modern middle-class identity, epitomized in the *flâneur/se* identity.[41] Though servants were sexually vulnerable, it was less their sexual availability to their employers that explains their erotic charge, and rather their capacity to be observed.

Female servants, as John Gillis has described, had trouble in fulfilling the norms of working-class courtship, and resented being made to court in hurried snatches, or in unsuitable public places.[42] Their 'walking out' took place outside of the sites of working-class courtship, such as street promenades, homes, and music halls. Margaret Powell, in service in the 1930s, stressed that female servants were particularly vulnerable to being pressured into premarital sex. They felt an especially urgent need to get married because they were, as Powell put it, 'dying to get out of domestic service', and were aware of the harsh life of older unmarried female servants. Furthermore,

the ratio of girls to young men was so high that if you had a young man and you cared about him and he suggested [sex], it seemed to be the only way to keep him. You had a hard job not to do it if you were not going to be stuck without a young man at all.[43]

The problems of meeting men and the stigma of service were much complained of by servants, who became more likely to be older and never-married women in the twentieth century.[44]

Servants were active in courtship and flirtation, though not always on their own terms. Many of their memories dwell on pranks and flirting; Alice Harrison recalled throwing notes to male servants wrapped around coffee beans, as well as the constant sexual innuendo of jokes at work. Margaret Cox, who described herself as 'boy-mad', told of how she enjoyed scrubbing the front steps in the early mornings because she could wave to the footmen cleaning the brass on the doors of the other houses.[45] So when servants offered their own narratives of themselves as desiring subjects, they stressed their strong links to the world of working-class heterosexual courtship, though many also noted the limits set by their lack of sexual

---

[41] Mica Nava, 'Modernity's Disavowal: Women, the City and the Department Store', in Mica Nava and Alan O'Shea (eds), *Modern Times: Reflections on a Century of English Modernity* (London: Routledge, 1996), 38–76; Janet Wolff, 'The Invisible Flaneuse. Women and the Literature of Modernity', *Theory, Culture and Society*, 2 3 (1985), 37–46.

[42] John Gillis, 'Servants, Sexual Relations, and the Risks of Illegitimacy in London, 1801–1900', *Feminist Studies*, 5 (1979), 142–73.

[43] Powell, *Below Stairs*, 168.

[44] See, for example, 'Domestic Service, The Status Difficulty', *The Times*, Dec 17, 1930.

[45] Mrs Alice Harrison (b. 1908), Mrs Margaret Cox (b. 1922), City of Westminster Archives Centre, *Upstairs Downstairs* Collection, henceforth cited as Westminster, *Upstairs Downstairs*.

knowledge: as Powell put it, 'the only thing that kept me and those like me from straying off the straight and narrow was ignorance and fear. Ignorance of how not to have a baby and fear of catching a disease.'[46]

Literary depictions of courting servants, in contrast, often deployed a language of grotesque pollution, stressing the sexual availability implied in their public courtship. The lack of privacy for female servants' courtship and their familiarity as eroticized figures positioned them as epitomizing working-class promiscuous sexuality. The courtship of servants served as the means of representing the sexual practices of the working classes *tout court*. In his Edwardian short story, *Two Gallants*, James Joyce invested a 'slavey' with the marks of prostitution and degradation. Observing and then approaching the 'slavey' and her lover, Joyce's protagonist, Lenehan,

found the air heavily scented and his eyes made a swift anxious scrutiny of the young woman's appearance. She had her Sunday finery on. Her blue serge skirt was held at the waist by a belt of black leather. The great silver buckle of her belt seemed to depress the centre of her body, catching the light stuff of her white blouse like a clip. She wore a short black jacket with mother-of-pearl buttons and a ragged black boa. The ends of her tulle collarette had been carefully disordered and a big bunch of red flowers was pinned in her bosom stems upwards. Lenehan's eyes noted approvingly her stout short muscular body. Rank rude health glowed in her face, on her fat red cheeks and in her unabashed blue eyes. Her features were blunt. She had broad nostrils, a straggling mouth which lay open in a contented leer, and two projecting front teeth.[47]

This description of gaudy, vulgar clothes is linked to the concerns of many mistresses and reformers over the 'cheap' finery and fashions worn by their servants. For some, this was a fear of servants' aping middle-class fashions and becoming sartorially indistinguishable from themselves. However, others were motivated by a sexual disgust at the 'polluted' nature of servants' adornments. Capturing this disgust, one mistress described her lipstick-wearing servant as having a 'mouth [that] looked like a cockerel's behind'.[48]

A less grotesque, but still voyeuristic account was offered to middlebrow readers in the 1901–3 serial, *Living London*, published by the 'slum investigator' George Sims. In the section titled 'London's Sweethearts', female domestic servants were depicted as the chief actors in working-class courtship. The love life of servants was served up to mass consumption in a sentimental mode (an alternative to the more typical comic mode):

The area gate is open, and on the top step a pretty London housemaid is taking the air. She looks anxiously towards the corner, every now and then throwing a furtive glance at the drawn blinds. Presently a young man comes sauntering along. He saunters until he catches sight of the fluttering strings of a little white cap. Then he quickens his pace, and the young

---

[46] Powell, *Below Stairs*, 89.
[47] James Joyce, *Dubliners* (London: Penguin, 1996), 59–60. My thanks to Maria DiCenzo for pointing out this reference.
[48] Elizabeth Young, *Bessie Remembers* (Braunton: Merlin, 1989), 17.

housemaid trips light to meet him. In the shadow of the house next door, out of the line of sight of any eyes that may peer from the house in which she is a handmaid, Mary lingers with her lover for a while. He holds her hand in his and they talk earnestly together. The policeman passes with a nod and a smile. The young man knits his brow a little, but it is only a summer cloud. Presently the clock of a church close by strikes ten. Mary gives a little start. 'I must go!' she exclaims. Then there is a long lingering pressure of hands, and then—we discreetly turn our backs, but a familiar sound strikes our ears, and a minute later Mary softly closes the gate, and disappears down the area steps.[49]

'London's Sweethearts' was not a text aimed particularly at middle-class employers, though its relatively high price (6d), many illustrations, and presentation on glossy paper placed this publication out of reach of most working-class readers. Nor does it seem particularly aimed at men, or establishing a male voyeuristic gaze. It suggests nonetheless a fascination with the courting of domestic servants that went beyond the comic portrayals of courting servants in the illustrated papers. In 'London's Sweethearts', the issue is presented more sympathetically, appealing to the reader's senses. The 'familiar sound' of Mary and her young man moves the text beyond the visual gaze to the aural—but what act causes this sound is left untold; the reader can imagine a kiss, endearments, or something more. The reader is very directly evoked as a voyeur in this description, despite the concern of the couple to avoid prying eyes, and the titillation offered by the fantasy surveillance of the courting servant is clear. As in Stephen Reynolds' vignette, the erotic charge around service frequently centred on the idea of privacy and its violation, and apparently gave both male and female observers vicarious pleasure, despite the distancing effect of depicting such courtship as comic, tragicomic, or pathetic.

Laughter at the 'saucy' nature of domestic service was prominent in mass entertainment. Voyeuristic accounts of the courtship of servants pervaded *Punch*, and other cheaper comic papers, and formed a running gag in popular media such as music hall and stereoscope views. Jokes were organized around servants' courting ruses while also dwelling on their sexual needs. In music hall performances such as the Edwardian 'slavey' depicted by Vesta Victoria (Figure 15), songs were largely about the ups and downs of courting.[50] Early cinema depictions of servants were located ambiguously between the comic and erotic, as servants were sexually assaulted in a slapstick style.[51] Yet servants were also often represented as desiring, smart, and more knowledgeable about sexual affairs than their masters; a French maid in *Judy*, a 2d Edwardian 'serio-comic journal', was pictured asked by her mistress:

---

[49] George Sims, *Living London* (London: Cassell, 1901), part 13, 16–17.
[50] See 'Through the Opera-Glass', *Pick-me-up*, Feb 8, 1902, 311.
[51] See for example *Hanging out the Clothes or Master Mistress and Maid* (1897), *The Baron and the Maid* (Pathe 1902), *Mistress and Maid* (1907), discussed by Brown, 'Early Cinema in Britain and the Smoking Concert Film'.

Figure 15. 'Through the Opera-Glass', *Pick-me-up*, Feb 8, 1902, 311.

MISS JAY: 'Young Trevor has been making love to me the whole summer, but he has not yet proposed, nor spoken to papa in any way. I wonder what he really wants of me!'
FIFINE: But mademoiselle must surely know that by this time!'[52]

The humour here is not always mocking, nor are servants always its target. Sometimes both servant and employer were depicted as sexually complicit, but more often, servants were depicted as sexually knowing and critical, observing and laughing at their employers, who were figured as sexually ignorant or unattractive and lecherous.[53] There was a satirical whiff of 'old corruption' around many of the depictions of the debauched male employer, whether welcomed or rebuffed by the servant, perhaps intended to appeal to a male working-class or artisanal concept of the sexual defence of 'their' women. Humour was a highly ambiguous medium, which cannot be easily pinned to a narrative of class or gender exploitation, but which clearly featured as prominently in early-twentieth-century pornography and erotica as it had done in earlier periods.

This titillation was not only experienced in print culture; many employers, both male and female, were fascinated by working-class courtship, and took a vicarious

---

[52] 'Honi Soit Qui Mal'y Pense', *Judy*, Apr 7, 1906, 157. Nationality was not commonly a component of the sexual charge of domestic service, though occasionally French maids were figured as sexually knowledgeable, while Irish maids were sometimes characterized as more 'earthy' or 'natural'.
[53] See, for example, 'Making It Sure', *Judy*, Feb 24, 1906, 85; *Bits of Fun* frontpiece, Mar 17, 1917.

pleasure in observing it amongst their own servants. As the novelist Ursula Bloom, growing up in Warwickshire at the turn of the century, described it:

> we accepted the love affairs of rectory maids as being part of their lives. They went through the formula of 'keeping company,' which meant that the affair was budding; then they 'walked out,' which was 'going steady.' The engagement came long after they had promised each other, and, immediately after that, full plans for the wedding. The walking-out period was exciting.

In a rare mention of the sexuality of male servants, she observed the kitchen boy, 'Buttons', flirting with maids and imagined him 'teaching the tweeny the facts of life in his spare moments'. Bloom was absorbed in this imagined circulation of sexual knowledge and courting rituals amongst her family's servants. Other middle-class children recall the excessive and very public teasing to which courting servants were subject.[54] The 'no followers' rule had become more relaxed in the twentieth century, but authoritarian discipline and confinement were still common responses both to the courtship of servants, alongside teasing, personal involvement, and laughter.

Female servants also recalled the 'ribald remarks' aimed at those scrubbing on their knees.[55] Mrs Happy Sturgeon, in service in Suffolk in the early 1930s, recalled the humiliating laughter of boys she had been to school with, who witnessed her kneeling and scrubbing the front steps while wearing a dress that was too short.[56] The link to laughter, however, was not always at the expense of the servant, and the comic servant was often associated with an active and knowing sexuality, contrasting to the innocent or ignorant employer. Ursula Holden described the laughter of her parents' servants in the interwar years as 'knowing', 'racy', and 'naughty', a means of deliberately flaunting their greater sexual knowledge: 'When my mother knitted bathing suits for [my brother] and me she made the gussets between the legs too large. They were baggy and had to be remade. The maids sniggered, whispering "Are your gussets alright now?" The word "begat" from the book of Genesis was another source of mirth.'[57] Servants thus might deliberately deploy laughter to indicate an adult status and to manipulate their interactions with their employers' children.

As the previous chapter suggested, reading the comic element of erotic discourses is challenging, as innuendo and jokes become opaque through the passage of historical time, and as laughter thrives on ambiguity. Nonetheless, it is clear that as for so much 'saucy' or 'bawdy' erotic material, a comic element was inseparable from the erotic in depictions of the 'everyday' sensuality of servants. Laughter, sometimes seen as akin to sexual pleasure in its physical abandonment and release,

---

[54] Bloom, *Mrs Bunthorpe's Respects*, 18, 16; Miss Thompson (b. 1891), Interview 2, *Middle and Upper Class Families*.
[55] Powell, *Below Stairs*, 82.
[56] Interview with Mrs Sturgeon (née Powley, b. 1917), George Ewart Evans collection, May 18, 1973, British Library Sound Archive, T1434WR.
[57] Ursula Holden, 'More about Maids', 4, unpublished mss., undated, and interview with the author, Dec 16, 2008.

is strongly associated with erotic power. It accompanies the breaking of sexual taboos, exposure, and the carnal gaze.[58] Some commentators have accused modern pornography as being distinguished from earlier periods by its depiction of a 'grim, grey, spiritless universe', in which humour is absent and only the sexed body is represented.[59] This is premised on a disembodied, abstract sense of the male gaze, and a privileging of the visual as the paramount erotic sense. A broader account of sensation and affect can recognize that modern erotic imaginaries are saturated by humour and laughter.

Overall, there were tensions or complexities in the Edwardian sexualized imagery of domestic service. The characterization of the female servant as vulnerable, young, and sexually available coexisted with her as knowing, savvy, and 'close to nature' in her sexual impulses. Her association with dirt and degradation connoted both pollution *and* comfort. Servants possessed passive bodies that could be gazed at and lacked privacy, but also were pictured as actively pursuing their own sexual desires, as courting, seducing, and knowledgeable. They were not simply observed, but also encountered through smells, sounds, and flavours, in ways that extended and vivified the class and gender privileges of observation. The high profile of domestic service as a realm of laughter, lust, and desire points to its role in establishing eroticized and gendered concepts such as authority, class, and station, but also its role in subverting these concepts.

CONTINUITIES AND CHANGE

The sexual charge of domestic service was far from static, and indeed, sexual norms were in flux in the mid-twentieth century, though the pace of change was uneven. Despite the apparent shift towards more 'democratic' sexual cultures in the early twentieth century, the vastly expanded trade in erotic postcards in the 1910s and 1920s continued to rely on familiar images of servants. Women, identified as servants by their cap and apron, were pictured with duster or water jug in varying states of undress. Mistress and maid might feature on erotic postcards as vehicles of lesbian desire.[60] It is clear that the eroticization of servants continued to affect profoundly the fantasy life and sexual practices of British men and women after World War I. One adolescent of a servant-keeping family in the 1910s and early 1920s, Geoffrey Grigson, recalled obsessively re-reading the seduction of a servant in Tolstoy's *Resurrection*, which had been hidden away by his mother. He also described how a day servant employed by his parents had provided an emotional centre in his childhood, and how this 'pagan' woman who was 'rich and racy in her mind and in her speech' imparted knowledge about working-class sexual habits to

---

[58] Koch, 'On Pornographic Cinema', 2.
[59] Steven Marcus, *The Other Victorians: A Study of Sexuality and Pornography in Mid-Nineteenth Century England* (London: Weidenfeld and Nicolson, 1966), 251.
[60] See, for example, the two sets of postcards reproduced in Paul Hammond, *French Undressing: Naughty Postcards from 1900 to 1920* (London: Jupiter Books, 1976), 64–5, 89–91.

him. Servants, then, were set up as a powerful sexual presence in his narrative. Grigson undertook his first sexual encounters with servants, furtively giving kisses to servants within his own household, and at boarding school. However, his description of such encounters indicates a sense of dismay and unfulfilment; the expected comfort and earthiness of servants is absent in his description of kissing 'the peculiarly cold, and paper-like cheek of an otherwise unattractive housemaid' at his boarding school. Despite his sentiments of disgust, seducing servants continued to dominate his fantasy world.[61]

Servants themselves continued to suffer from forms of sexual harassment. Mrs Kemp, in service in Essex in the 1920s, recalled the atmosphere of flirtation between her employer, 'the Colonel' (a roguish drinker), and the maids. She termed it harmless, but felt nonetheless that it was a situation that could have got out of hand, and she was relieved that her employers had no son. It also created an atmosphere of mistrust and anxiety between the mistress and the maids. Many other servants describe a similar background of flirtation or mild sexual advances, which sometimes became more overt. Edna Forder described a post in one household: 'the woman was harsh and the man too friendly. I couldn't lock my bedroom so I put a chair behind [the door, so that] at least there would be a clatter if he did try to visit me—but I measured my waist with a tape measure each morning in case he had given me a baby in the night in my sleep! I was 22 but we didn't know much in those days.'[62]

Other anecdotes from servants describe experiences that cannot be categorized as sexual harassment, though they have an erotic element. Edna Forder also described how, when serving an invalid mistress in another job, she was asked to clean the room with her sleeves rolled up, so that the mistress could see her 'beautiful arms': 'Miss Christina had noticed my arms when I did her bedroom grate. She had at one time painted water colours and said she would like to paint my arms.'[63] Forder recalled being terrified of touching her mistress's body when putting her into whalebone corsets, or of their knees touching when they went in the brougham together to church. There clearly was a queer sexual dynamic here, which left the servant feeling distinctly ill at ease.

By the 1930s and 1940s, however, the eroticization of service was much less prominent in popular periodicals such as the new mass market 'men's' magazines—*Lilliput*, *London Opinion*, and *Razzle*—which featured air-brushed nudes and titillating stories. The erotic imaginary was in flux, in a shift that was much longer and more uneven than simplistic labels of the 'permissive 1960s' imply. Earlier concerns over the prominence and availability of titillating and pornographic material gave way in the 1930s to a broader acceptance of newly imported American forms. Erotic material began to gain in cultural standing during and

---

[61] Geoffrey Grigson, *The Crest on the Silver* (London: Cresset Press, 1950), 50–2, 83–4.
[62] Edna Forder (b. 1910), 'From Pillar to Post', unpublished autobiography, Westminster, *Upstairs Downstairs*. See Monica Dickens, *One Pair of Hands* (London: Joseph, 1939), 46–7, on sexual harassment during her impersonation of a servant in the 1930s.
[63] Edna Forder, Westminster, *Upstairs Downstairs*.

after World War II, sometimes through its association with the wartime morale boosting.[64] British publishers adopted the more mainstream and socially acceptable device of the pin-up girl, and the cheap pre-war porn pulp magazine morphed into the modern, colour 'glamour magazines' of the 1960s, and more mainstream pornographic movies of the 1970s.[65]

Within this newly sexually confident mid-century erotic imaginary, servants were often introduced in a way that parodied earlier 'saucy' depictions. The weekly humour magazine *Blighty*, for example, opened a 1949 issue with the following:

When I rang the bell, a smart little piece, in a brightly coloured overall and one of those mob caps the maids in Restoration Comedies always wear, answered the door. 'My, my,' I said appreciatively, 'a new maid!' And I gave her a friendly little spank on the place provided by a bounteous Nature for such tokens of appreciation. 'Sir,' said the wench, drawing herself up indignantly. 'Your mistress at home?' I inquired with an air.[66]

However, the comic resolution of this sketch is that the 'maid' turns out to be his wife. The humour centred on the manipulation of the characteristic erotic images of domestic service, parodying them as stale and predictable, but also suggesting that domestic service continued to be a site of erotic role-play.

A similar cheap comic paper, *Razzle*, was published from the early 1930s to the late 1950s with an initial monthly circulation of more than 100,000, under the sometime byline: 'Ensure that for yourself and your friends there is at least one day in the month in which the depression is not depressing.'[67] Servants featured mostly as comic-erotic characters; a series of 'joke classifieds' in 1939, for example, announced: 'Titled Lady requires services of handsome Butler... Exit by back door when necessary. No dogs kept.' and 'Housemaid. Live out. Sleep in. Apply "Three Muskateers" pub.'[68] However, equally, servants sometimes served as a dowdy contrast with a more glamorous version of femininity. Night club dancers or secretaries seemed to be newly favoured as objects of desire. Servants became featured as onlookers in *Razzle* cartoons, rather than as sexualized objects being looked at in their own right.

Leonore Davidoff highlights the fascination with female youth that predominated in mid-Victorian erotic imagery. Wives might be depicted as children, and servants were perhaps so prominent in the erotic imaginary because they could be assumed to be young. In the twentieth century, as servant numbers dropped, the average age of those who continued to work in domestic service rose. As a vehicle

---

[64] Adrian Bingham, *Family Newspapers?: Sex, Private Life, and the British Popular Press 1918–1978* (Oxford: Oxford University Press, 2009); Dean, *The Frail Social Body*.
[65] H. G. Cocks, 'Saucy Stories: Pornography, Sexology and the Marketing of Sexual Knowledge in Britain, c. 1918–70', *Social History*, 29 4 (2004), 465–84; Marcus Collins, *Modern Love: An Intimate History of Men and Women in Twentieth-Century Britain* (London: Atlantic Books, 2003); Sigel, *International Exposure*, 15; Tang, *Pornography*. On the increasing acceptability of the pin-up, see the write-up of the Mass Observation study, 'What Is a Pin-Up?', in *Picture Post*, Sept 23, 1944.
[66] Harris Deans, 'White Tie and Tails', *Blighty*, Nov 26, 1949, 4.
[67] *Razzle*, Mar. 1933, no. 6; Cocks, 'Saucy Stories', 478.
[68] *Razzle* 1939 [undated].

for eroticizing youth, they were no longer suitable, and this perhaps explains the partial substitution of the secretary and temp, and later the predominance of the nurse in the 1950s 'seaside' bawdy postcard. The film and television equivalents produced from 1958—the 'Carry On' films—also centred on these figures as vehicles for erotic slapstick.[69] Nonetheless, those domestic workers who were predominantly young—au pairs, for example—continued to feature large in fantasy and pornography. *Parade*, a mildly sexually explicit weekly that had recently incorporated *Blighty*, ran a salacious feature in 1961 on the exploitation and sexual vulnerability of foreign au pairs.[70] Au pairs were also figured as a sexual threat in middle-class households, likely to attract the attentions of husbands or sons.

Charwomen and cleaners also found themselves sexually objectified, despite their predominant portrayal as comic. Live-in domestic service was no longer experienced by large numbers of working-class women by the middle decades of the twentieth century, but 'day servants' or 'helps' might still be figured as comforting and earthy. The popular magazine *Lilliput* featured a romantic story in 1951, in which a farmer proposed to 'the girl who came up from the village every day to clean the farm-house and cook Mr Ford his meals': 'He watched Lily with new eyes when she brought his supper and laid it steaming hot before him. She was a lovely sort of girl, he thought, more rounded and solid and sweaty than anything out of a dream ... He observed her as she moved about in her pink cotton dress. Lily's arms were always bare and cotton seemed to keep her warm, even in winter.'[71] Even when situated beyond the more formal, deferential relationships of live-in service, the bodies of young domestic workers could still be eroticized as intrusive, hot, odorous, and sweaty.

The older female domestic worker, however, was also portrayed in sexual terms. This was sometimes the sexually repressed elderly maid, about whom Margaret Powell wrote: 'their own lives were so devoid of excitement that they had to find all their life vicariously. Sexual life, social life, every sort of life.'[72] This sexual stereotype was repeated by Celia Fremlin in her 1940 *Seven Chars of Chelsea*, in her description of the residential domestic servant.[73] Fremlin, however, saw chars as vigorous, earthy figures, though also as comic. The humorous dimension of the eroticized servant became concentrated on those older workers, usually titled 'Mrs Maggs', 'Mrs Dangle', or 'Mrs Scrubb', at the mid-twentieth century. Cartoonists emphasized the char's sexual inquisitiveness—an interest in nude male statues while cleaning is a joke repeatedly featured in *Razzle* and in interwar postcards.[74]

---

[69] *Carry On Emmanuelle* (1978) is perhaps the only *Carry On* film which foregrounds domestic service, with a narrative of the erotic pursuits of a household of stock 'upper servant' figures (housekeeper, butler, etc.), in keeping with the later rediscovery of the erotic potential of great house service. See Andy Medhurst, *A National Joke: Popular Comedy and English Cultural Identities* (Abingdon: Routledge, 2007).

[70] 'Au pair can mean Slave Labour in Britain', *Parade*, July 8, 1961, 10–11.

[71] Emma Smith, 'The Farmer Who Wanted Lily'. *Lilliput*, Nov–Dec 1951, 35, 36.

[72] Powell, *Below Stairs*, 86.

[73] Celia Fremlin, *The Seven Chars of Chelsea* (London: Methuen, 1940); Judy Giles, *The Parlour and the Suburb: Domestic Identities, Class, Femininity and Modernity* (Oxford: Berg, 2004), 81–4.

[74] *Razzle*, ud [1950], 31; Feb 1949, 12.

The charlady Mrs Mopp supplied an iconic catchphrase of sexual innuendo with her 'Can I do you now Sir?' in the 1940s radio show, *It's That Man Again*. The persistent voyeurism of the relationship between mistress and char is illustrated in the 1962 memoir *Jam Tomorrow*, in which the author acknowledged her fascination with the 'love life' of 'Mrs Kemp', particularly with her exploits while wearing a 'saucy camisole'. There is almost no mention of Mrs Kemp's domestic work, and the entire memoir revolved around the life of crime, violence, and sex that Mrs Kemp revealed to her shocked and fascinated employer.[75]

The traditional focus on the *female* domestic servant was much less marked in mid-twentieth-century representations. The male butler and chauffeur featured quite prominently, as did the sexually 'innocent' figure of the valet or serving boy. These figures had long had power to unsettle through their erotic overtones. As one letter from a Scottish reader to the *Morning Post* noted 1857, 'To us country people, when we go up to town, there is no class with whom we are so ill at ease as [men servants].' Young male servants were described in reformist literature as 'exposed to even worse influences and more degrading temptations that those which overcome the young girls.'[76] Male servants were also associated with 'oriental', slave-keeping societies, and so were exoticized, and sometimes viewed as sexually queer. Margaret Powell observed of the valet in one household: 'I assume of course he could sire children. But you couldn't imagine him trying.'[77] However, it was more common to see male servants as heterosexual predators. As Gwen Raverat recalled of her turn-of-the-century Cambridge childhood, the 'charming' Swiss manservant employed by her parents, Rittler, who was 'sent away because the women servants *would* fall in love with him.... After that, we only had woman servants.' Edwardian commentators advised against menservants, seeing them as sexually disruptive: 'An excellent servant once said to me she wished there were no men-servants. They did very little work, their habits were bad, and they amused themselves by beguiling the younger servants to their harm.' Their employers were advised in veiled terms to 'recognise the danger to their servants of both sexes and do their best to provide against it.'[78] The dangers menservants were subject to were never openly named, and they hovered between sexual victims and sexual agents. Their sexual charge was too ambiguous to feature strongly in the early-twentieth-century erotic imaginary, which opted instead for the more clear-cut 'naughty' sexuality of the housemaid.

Very small numbers of men worked in twentieth-century private domestic service, but they became newly prominent in titillating material of the mid-twentieth century, as having the power to penetrate the private spaces of women. Depictions of male servants (mostly in great homes) in sources such as *Razzle* had a

---

[75] Margaret Norton, *Jam Tomorrow: Portrait of a Daily Help* (London: Victor Gollancz, 1962).
[76] 'QQ', *Morning Post*, Jan 23, 1857; 'On the Education of Young Servant Girls', *Englishwoman's Review*, Apr 1868, 413.
[77] Charlotte Perkins Gilman, *The Home: It's Work and Influence* (New York, 1903), 107; Powell, *Below Stairs*, 68.
[78] Gwen Raverat, *Period Piece: A Cambridge Childhood* (London: Faber and Faber, 1952), 81–2; M. Bunting, 'Mistress and Maid', *Contemporary Review*, May 1910, 601.

strong nostalgic or fantasy element. Drawing on long-standing traditions of the sexual privileges of male servants, a typical story in *Razzle* is the 1948 'Grande Dame', in which a butler awakens his mistress by kissing her sleeping body.[79] Male servants also connoted the sometimes eroticized homosocial relationship between master and servant, a relationship that Michael Roper has argued might resemble that of mother and son. This was a relationship long explored in literary accounts, and repeatedly presented to the public through figures such as Peter Wimsey and Mervyn Bunter as a form of acceptable intimacy between men.[80]

Later issues of *Razzle* in the 1950s, and a similar 'saucy' magazine, *Men Only*, in the 1960s, show relatively few portrayals of servants of either sex. Butlers occasionally surface, but there is nothing like the systematic representation of servants in earlier pulp magazines and on saucy postcards. Instead, detective stories, tabloid-style news, and cartoons of glamorous women and playboys feature. The post-war erotic imaginary centred on glamour-girls, with a few mother-in-law jokes thrown in. Service had become less central to the everyday experiences of the majority of people, and the influence of American erotic print culture was becoming apparent in pornography, marriage manuals, agony aunt advice, and an overall less inhibited approach to sexual issues.[81] Though permissiveness has proved to be a historically slippery concept, courtship and marital sexual relationships were being (unevenly) transformed in the 1950s and 1960s. Discussions of sex became more explicit and less reliant on vehicles of comedy and melodrama.[82] Servants were therefore less prominent as characters that culturally connoted sexual slapstick or illicit pleasures.

DOMESTIC SERVICE RE-EROTICIZED

While there was a mid-century dip in representations of female domestic servants in 'naughty' magazines, they reappeared from the later 1960s in large numbers in the newly expanded publishing world of more explicit pornographic magazines. The expansion of pornography and its blurring with other genres may have had earlier roots—Harry Cocks argues that we can see pornography becoming more available

---

[79] J. Penn, 'Grande Dame', *Razzle*, spring 1948, 46–50. Kristina Straub has argued that the sexuality of eighteenth-century male servants was less threatening and troubling to the cultural imagination than that associated with female servants, and that male servants might be situated as sexually charismatic and virile (*Domestic Affairs: Intimacy, Eroticism, and Violence between Servants and Masters in Eighteenth-Century Britain* (Baltimore: Johns Hopkins University Press, 2009)). There is, however, little evidence for this in the twentieth-century eroticized male servant, who served mainly as a foil for the aggressive sexuality attributed to upper-class women, or when serving men, as a feminized caring figure.

[80] Wimsey and Bunter were fictional characters in the detective fiction of Dorothy L. Sayers, set and written in Britain between the wars. I'm grateful to Deborah Thom for drawing my attention to these sources.

[81] Hera Cook, *The Long Sexual Revolution: English Women, Sex and Contraception, 1800–1975* (Oxford: Oxford University Press, 2004), 225–6.

[82] On the scope of changes in permissiveness, see Kate Fisher, *Birth Control, Sex and Marriage in Britain 1918–1960* (Oxford: Oxford University Press, 2006); Jeffrey Weeks, *The World We Have Won: The Remaking of Erotic and Intimate Life* (London: Routledge, 2007), 67–70.

in Britain and sharing a cultural space with sexology from the 1920s.[83] However, Marcus Collins emphasizes a new phase in pornographic publishing in the 1960s, when naturist, photographic, and artistic magazines were transformed into a new style of commercial magazine. These were initially American imports such as *Playboy*, but British versions followed. Titles such as *Penthouse*, *King*, and *Club International* began to publish in large, full-colour format, with more upmarket lifestyle articles and portrayals of nudes that tested the limits of legality. As Collins puts it, pornographic magazines had moved from under the counter to the top shelf. This went with a national expansion of the 'porn industry' of sex shops, cinemas, strip shows, and massage parlours.[84] Pornographic films developed from the furtively made and technically limited 'stag films', to the 'porn chic' era of the 1960s, when full-length 'hard core' films began to use storylines and developed porn celebrities. The audiences for pornography became too large to prosecute, and in any case, there was public uncertainty over the boundaries of the obscene. Women were sought as readers and viewers, and the pornographic element in magazines was integrated with readers' interests in fashion and design.[85] Nonetheless, the market was still divided not only by sexual preferences but also by class, as some magazines adopted glamorous nude shots and evoked an imagined reader as affluent, cosmopolitan young men, while others such as *Whitehouse* were more downmarket, specializing in 'strong' poses by 'ordinary' girls, and celebrated the everyday sex lives of 'readers wives'.[86] In comparative terms, British pornography remained much less explicit than its continental counterparts.

Despite its comparative tameness, this mid- to late-twentieth-century flourishing of pornography was often directly linked to an idea of *modern* Britain, specifically, to 'swinging London'. Domestic service might initially have seemed out of place within this apparently forward-looking cultural production, but curiously, female servants began to feature quite prominently. Collins describes the establishment of a Penthouse Club by *Penthouse* magazine in the late 1960s, in which hostesses wore 'abbreviated maid's outfits', and made elaborate curtseys to guests.[87] Revealing maid's costumes became established as standard in erotic fancy dress, and were featured in both pornographic and mainstream cinema, and in their associated magazines (Figure 16). Maids and 'serving wenches' featured prominently in pornographic films and novels.[88] Strip-tease performances in the expanding Soho

---

[83] Cocks, 'Saucy Stories'.
[84] Collins, *Modern Love*, 141; Frank Mort, 'Striptease: The Erotic Female Body and Live Sexual Entertainment in Mid-Twentieth-Century London', *Social History*, 32 1 (2007), 27–53.
[85] Cocks, 'Saucy Stories'.
[86] Clarissa Smith, 'A Perfectly British Business: Stagnation, Continuities, and Changes on the Top Shelf', in Lisa Sigel (ed.), *International Exposure: Perspectives on Modern European Pornography, 1800–2000* (London: Rutgers University Press, 2005), 146–72, esp. 150.
[87] Collins, *Modern Love*, 154.
[88] Pornographic novels used as a standard plot the idea of male sexual initiation undertaken by knowing and lustful female servants in a 'great house' context. See for example *Margery*, a fairly typical anonymous and undated typescript novel from the British Library's Private Case collection (pc.14. i.17), describing a youth's sexual initiation by servants, dated by Patrick Kearney to be from 1967: Patrick J. Kearney, *The Private Case: An Annotated Bibliography of the Private Case Erotica Collection in*

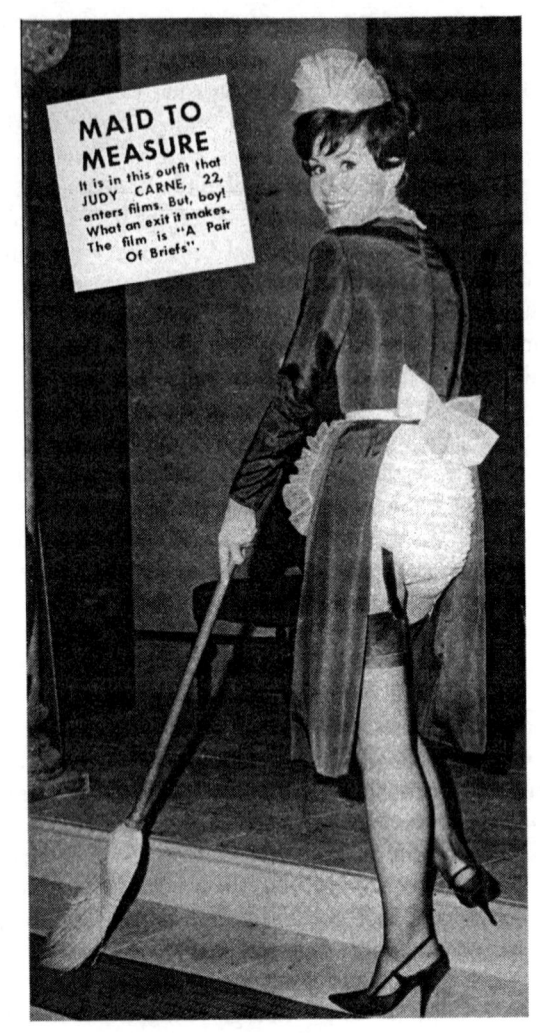

Figure 16. Judy Carne in 'Maid to Measure', *Parade* June 30, 1962, 12.

sex club scene also featured servants, and one performer offered this description of a lesbian act from the early 1970s:

Curtains open on a naked woman in the bath-tub, splashing away with her back to the audience, to the accompaniment of dreamy, 'Milk Tray' advert music. After a minute or so, the maid totters on carrying a jug of water, which she empties into the tub. She washes the Countess then wraps her in a bath towel, dries her, and leads her over to a chair set right at the front of the stage. The Countess kneels on the chair whilst her maid rubs Baby Lotion

the British (Museum) Library (London: Jay Landesman, 1981). See also Richard Wortley, *Skin Deep in Soho* (London: Jarrolds, 1969), 81.

into her back. Then she turns round and rips off the maid's costume, which is held together by a spit and a prayer. Then on to the rug for the lezzie bit.[89]

Domestic service continued to be a popular feature within the pornography of the 1970s. *New Vibrations*, a magazine 'for sexually aware adults', published a string of articles in 1977, featuring 'sexy service from a hotel maid', 'confession from a rich white girl who seduced a black servant', 'erotic au pair girl', and 'lusty hotel maids'. Cumbersome devices were used to suggest why women might still be working in domestic service in the late twentieth century. In a 1977 lesbian maid story in *New Vibrations*, the protagonist stated:

I'd never have dreamt about getting a job as a maid—I always used to think it was just about the lowliest work a girl could do. But not many women would turn down the chance to act as personal maid to one of Hollywood's biggest film stars... and as for it being a menial job... well, I looked on it as a kind of role I'd been playing—acting a part so that I could move on to higher things.[90]

Domestic service then was acknowledged to be menial and residual, but was given glamour through its association with luxurious houses and celebrities, imaginatively located in Hollywood. The performative nature of domestic service was also foregrounded, as placing women onto a stage, subject to the desiring gaze of others.

Women (and occasionally men) in 'traditional' domestic service jobs (mostly presented as maids) were placed alongside those in 'new' service jobs—chambermaids, waitresses, usherettes, and au pairs.[91] The black and white uniforms of these newer service jobs often linked these women visually to domestic service, and they were depicted as sexually knowledgeable and insatiable. The char or cleaner, however, largely disappeared from the erotic imaginary.

What was the continuing appeal of fantasies around domestic service? The maid–mistress relationship was frequently a vehicle for the representation of lesbian desire. A 1970s pornographic magazine titled *Curious: A Magazine of Sex Education for Men and Women* published a typical photograph of a maid in cap and apron adjusting the shoes of a reclining and semi-undressed mistress in highly glamorous surroundings (Figure 17). Service conveyed a world of female intimacy that lent itself easily to depictions of lesbian sex. *New Vibrations* published tales of a 'Lesbian Maid: extra duties become a pleasure when a young girl takes up an exciting new position with a seductive mistress.'[92] Servants had also become closely associated with submission and sadomasochism. One reader of *Curious* wrote to the editor in 1973 to admit his longing to cross-dress as a 'submissive maid':

the thought of being a woman's slave and doing household chores in return for a few punishments and beatings certainly turns me on.... I can't imagine any woman having a

---

[89] Nickie Roberts, *The Front Line* (London: Grafton Books, 1986), 47–8. My thanks to John Davis for pointing out this reference and other material on the London sex clubs scene.
[90] 'Lesbian Maid', *New Vibrations*, 5 9 (1977).
[91] Ibid. 5 4–9 (1977).
[92] Ibid. 5 9 (1977).

198 *Knowing Their Place*

Figure 17. *Curious*, May 1973, no. 39, 50.

man in her home so as to dress him up as a maid and put him to work, and after a few jobs have been done, she would tie him up, gag him and humiliate him; it just cannot be true![93]

However, the idea of subservience and submissiveness did not feature very widely beyond the niche of sadomasochistic pornography. Within less specialized pornography, it was the knowing and lusty servant who was portrayed, rather than the helpless or submissive. Perhaps this shift can best be described as a resurgence of the erotic charge of 'parasexuality'—the effect of distance and fantasy that was able to come into play in relation to domestic service because the institution had become historically distant or the preserve of the super-rich, rather than everyday reality by the 1970s. Placed at a geographic distance—in Hollywood—or at a historical distance—in an imagined Victorian period—the servant could be 'parasexually charged' as glamorous and hypersexualized, as actresses and barmaids had been in earlier eras. Servants were no longer polluting, comforting, sweaty, and earthy, but removed from the everyday and sexually deviant.

The comic mode also persisted, though it had become much less dominant as a means of eroticizing servants. *Curious* published in its edition of May 1973 a reproduction of an interwar American comic strip, 'Ella Cinders', from the 'Tijuana Bible' genre of comic pornography.[94] The strip depicted a 'transgressive' moment

---

[93] *Curious*, Apr 1973, 45.
[94] Iva Snatch, 'Such a Grief', *Curious*, May 1973, 13.

whereby a Jew, stereotyped as lascivious and money-grabbing, bought sex from a willing applicant for a maid's post. The depiction of the Jew was aimed at much earlier American anti-Semitic concerns about the sexual transgression of ethnic boundaries, and seems unlikely to resonate within the late-twentieth-century British erotic imaginary. Yet it was reproduced without comment for a British audience some 40 years after its initial publication. *Whitehouse* magazine reproduced the same strip in 1975, this time with an apology for its 'racialist element', but a claim that the humour outweighed the offence of the strip. The recycling of material within pornography makes it hard to trace definitive shifts in erotic imaginaries, which are clearly eclectic and overlapping.

How did readers and viewers react to these images? Here, I offer only very tentative conclusions, as few accounts of reading or viewing pornography are available to historians. Even where readers do offer their own responses to pornography, in form of the fantasies submitted to the letters pages of pornographic magazines, these tend to be formulaic, and are acknowledged by publishers to be heavily edited, to maintain certain boundaries of 'decency'. We do know, however, that the strip-tease performer Nickie Roberts, who portrayed 'a Lowly Maidservant' in the early 1970s, commented that while her lesbian performance was meant to be 'sexy and dramatic', to her 'it just sounded bloody daft'. What of her audience? Roberts surmised that 'lesbian acts are always popular with the punters. They think, "Those sweet little girls, what they need is a man"'[95]; but this is only her speculation, and most 'punters' have remained anonymous and mute. Perhaps the only sure guide available to reception lies in the commercial nature of pornography. As a responsive commercial genre, publishers or purveyors of pornography were unlikely to continue to produce performances, texts, and images that did not sell. We can therefore assume that viewers and readers found a continuing fascination and appeal in domestic service, though its titillation power varied according to its social and historical proximity.

PERIODIZATION

This narrative of shifting erotic imaginaries across the twentieth century has suggested a number of changes in the erotic charge of domestic service, as servants variously became vehicles for representing earthy knowingness, sexual slapstick, pollution, glamour and luxury, and lesbian desire. But no simple chronology can be offered, in part because domestic service drew on such a diverse set of erotic imaginaries.[96] The historical literature on domestic service has tended to focus on its sexual connotations in the Victorian period, perhaps motivated by the Victorians' reputation for sexual hypocrisy, and by the sense that in this period, 'sexual designations and class segregations were closely interwoven.'[97] This has tended to

---

[95] Roberts, *The Front Line*, 80.
[96] This point is discussed in Harry Cocks, 'Modernity and the Self in the History of Sexuality', *Historical Journal*, 49 4 (2006), 1211–28.
[97] Davidoff, *Worlds Between*, 105.

result in relatively static accounts of pornography that fail to chart its changes over time. Steven Marcus's classic account, for example, argued that 'by the mid-Victorian period the pornographic scene had established itself in very much the same modes, categories, and varieties as exist today.'[98] This does not acknowledge the changeability of twentieth-century erotic imaginaries, which are well illustrated in domestic service.

Nonetheless, any attempt to trace change over time in erotic representations is made problematic by the indiscriminate and opaque publishing habits of 'racy' or 'fast' publications. As we have seen, material was recycled without identifying source or date. There was clearly a transnational borrowing of content, with much British pornographic material originating in France or the United States. Publishers frequently tried to disguise the origins of their material, attributing novelty to old sources or offering a 'new translation' of older texts. An Edwardian pornographic novel, for example, that had been initially published in 1900, *Flossie: A Venus of Fifteen*, was advertised in a 1970s edition of *Curious* as a text 'never before published', without any indication of its long publishing history and origins. It is therefore unhelpful to look for a simple sequential chronology, in which 'erotic discourses' steadily supplant each other. The recycling of material created possibilities for a re-eroticization of old 'sexual stories' and their tropes. Such material defies an easy chronology.[99]

Periodization is further complicated by the self-conscious construction of fantasy epochs within pornography. British pornographic magazines began to publish what were termed 'Victorian classics': *Lady Pokingham*, for example, was initially serialized in *The Pearl* between 1879 and 1880, and was reprinted in *Curious* in 1973. There was an explicit construction in the late twentieth century of a genre termed 'Victorian erotica', in which domestic service and the sexual antics of the aristocracy were centre stage. An advertisement for the 'glamour magazine' *Park Lane* promised that it would 'specialise in the most advanced modern sex photographs—but this will be combined with the very best in Victorian style literature—giving you the very best of the "old" and "new".'[100] As *Whitehouse* magazine put it in 1975, 'there can be no doubt about it whatsoever. The Victorian sex scene is a complete goldmine for those who really are interested in the seamier side of life, or who want to know what life was like in the raw in those far-off days.'[101] Features in *Whitehouse* included 'Confessions of a Victorian White Slaver', 'Memoirs of a Victorian

---

[98] Marcus, *The Other Victorians*, 65–6.
[99] See Smith, 'A Perfectly British Business', 161, for a discussion of recycling in contemporary soft-porn magazines. The periodization offered by Marcus Collins that pornography can be easily divided into pre- and post-1960s phases, the former offering images of dominated and exploited women, and the latter briefly offering a recognition of women's sexual agency and then turning back to misogyny, pays little attention to this recycling and recontextualizing of material such as *Iva Snatch* from different decades. Furthermore, by generalizing about depictions of *all* women, this account conceals the diversity of pornography of both pre- and post-1960s.
[100] *Park Lane* advertisement in 'Summer Sex Guide', *Piccadilly*, 4 (1975).
[101] *Whitehouse*, 5 (1975), 18.

Traveller', and 'Memoirs of a Victorian Jockey'; predictably, servants featured prominently in these stories as sexual figures. Advertisements in 'glamour magazines' circulated for self-consciously 'Victorian' erotic books such as *A Man with a Maid* (first published in 1968), which promised: 'it is Victorian erotica at its best—the sexiest story of all time'.[102] Within this genre, the Victorian maid had become re-imagined, no longer as a figure of pollution or comedy, nor as standing in for the courtship practices of the lower orders. The mid-century prominence of male servants and older servants faded; the servant was not coded (or scented) as sexually consoling. Instead, she became a 'parasexual' figure of sexual availability and transgression, aimed at a masculine consumer, with imagined sexual encounters now always framed as crossing class barriers.

Domestic service has in recent decades become a projected fantasy, set in a historically distant epoch. The comic element became obscured, and instead, servants became loaded with the sexual frisson of transgression of social boundaries. This was not new—social transgression clearly underlay the erotic play of Hannah Cullwick and Arthur Munby. However, in cultural terms, this has become dominant only in the late twentieth century, and was not the predominant mode by which servants were erotically charged across the first half of the twentieth century. Instead, earlier depictions purveyed a voyeurism available to both sexes, and more diverse erotic registers.

COUNTER-NARRATIVES

There is little historical evidence to show how servants felt about their portrayals as erotic figures in British society and culture. They protested at constantly being rendered comic, and this may have been motivated by the sexual subtext of many of these jokes. They also protested against their portrayal as polluted and degraded 'skivvies' or 'the lowest of the low', which also carried sexual connotations. Servants' complaints of lack of privacy and personal freedom frequently related to their freedom and privacy to court or flirt, and can be read as a strategy to counter the sexual voyeurism they encountered. But servants had few resources to counter their relentless depictions as heavily sexualized. One narrative available was to reverse the discourse and render their employers hypersexualized in return. As Mary Douglas has argued, 'pollution beliefs can be used in a dialogue of claims and counter-claims to status.'[103] Many servants displayed a sanctimonious attitude to sexual morality, and wrote of or recalled their sense of outrage at the sexual antics of their employers. One said of the daughter of her mistress: 'she was a tart, or she was no better than a prostitute really,' and complained that another mistress never wore knickers, and openly conducted an adulterous affair.[104] Another recalled the entire staff quitting

---

[102] Advertisement in 'Summer Sex Guide', *Piccadilly*, 4 (1975).
[103] Douglas, *Purity and Danger*, 4.
[104] Mrs Amy Clifford, Westminster, *Upstairs Downstairs*.

in protest at a scandal over a kept woman; the mistress was forced to employ male servants in their place.[105]

This prudishness was in part a consequence of labour market vulnerability; no servant could afford to have her name associated with scandal, or to be furnished with references that lacked moral authority. But it was also an ongoing argument or negotiation about sexual meanings and designations. Erotic imaginaries are not created though a one-way process of objectification or identification of sexual victims and protagonists. Rather, a number of possible erotic narratives are usually co-present, around which power struggles are conducted. Servants had their own powers of observation and narrative resources, which frequently named employers as highly sexed and morally corrupt. Increasingly in the interwar decades, they were able to insert these into print media. The counter-narrative stories about the antics of employers of both sexes had their own titillation value, alongside the hypersexualized depictions of servants. One servant, for example, offered in the pages of the *Daily Chronicle* a 'pollution anecdote' in 1923, about a mistress who made her maid use the mistress's dirty bath water, and sleep in her soiled sheets.[106] The disgust usually associated with the bodies of servants was effectively turned back towards the mistress and her domestic organization. Leonore Gregory, a popular fiction writer, wrote a piece entitled 'Pity the Servant' in 1938, published in the cheap liberal daily, the *News Chronicle*, in which she described the experiences of maids confronted with an alcoholic mistress, a prostitute mistress, and a mistress who held orgies.[107] Mrs Barton's horror at the four-seat outside toilet she was required to use projects a sense of (sexual) decency sullied by the practices of a servant-keeping household. Servants became adept at stigmatizing and sexualizing their employers, while also, in the case of female servants, claiming their own sexual ignorance as a kind of moral high ground. Servants may have been sexually ignorant due to their relative social isolation, but as Kate Fisher and Simon Szreter have argued, sexual ignorance can be a strategic choice or element of self-fashioning, rather than simply a lack of knowledge.[108]

Servants sometimes had limited powers to give their stories wider cultural prominence, and would perhaps have preferred respect rather than pity to be elicited by them. Nonetheless, it is clear that employers were often represented in the jokes, cartoons, and journalism of mass culture as lustful and lascivious, while servants could be coded as innocent and uncorrupted. This, however, was ultimately a weak strategy for those seeking dignity in domestic service, since the trope of the lascivious employer and innocent servant was perfectly compatible with the pornographic emphasis on cross-class seduction that became more prominent as

---

[105] Mary Humberstone, 'The Story of My Life', unpublished manuscript (1972) in possession of the author.
[106] 'A Servant's Point of View', *Daily Chronicle*, June 16, 1923.
[107] Leonore Gregory, 'Pity the Servant', *News Chronicle*, March 5, 1938.
[108] Kate Fisher and Simon Szreter, '"She Was Quite Satisfied with the Arrangements I Made": Gender and Birth Control in Britain 1920–1950', *Past and Present*, 169 (2000), 161–93, esp. 173; Ross McKibbin, *Classes and Cultures: England 1918–1951* (Oxford: Oxford University Press, 1998), 316–17.

the twentieth century went on. As with the jokes associated with domestic service, the erotic imagery was not easy for servants to manipulate for their own ends, and the available counter-narratives could simply add weight to the sexually stigmatized nature of domestic service.

The stories servants told, or threatened to tell, carried echoes of ones that had long circulated—of aristocratic libertines—and which carried a particular political resonance in Britain.[109] Servants in the twentieth century extended the scope of such salacious scandal, so that not simply aristocrats and politicians but any employer of servants might be implicated. Margaret Powell recalled:

[servants] used to tell scandalous stories about the gentry. Anybody upstairs was called gentry in those days. We would hear all about their employers. The good, the bad, the spicy. They used to talk about their affairs. A lot of male gentry had what was known in those days as a love nest, a flat they'd set up for some woman, and the chauffeurs used to drive them to it.

Such stories were sometimes a form of self-aggrandisement for the servants who were party to sexual secrets, often when told by male servants about male employers. Powell went on: 'to listen to them you would have thought that they'd partaken of the love feast. Using the royal "we"... they would take us through the whole ceremony in all its amorous details. They couldn't have known it.'[110] But telling such stories also had a deeper purpose, as a means of countering the eroticization of domestic servants.

Charting these competing narratives is complicated by the fact that servants not only used the narrative resources of libertine accusations against employers, but also at times themselves depicted and described hypersexualized servants. Winifred Foley's account of her naïve desire for a lodger at her boarding house is a good example. She described innocently falling for her 'ideal lover,... as remote and desirable as a Hollywood film star.' However, she was horrified to discover that he was sleeping with another housemaid, Rosie, whom she described with the full power of the pollution and hypersexual narratives long deployed against servants:

one could picture her a thin grey little rodent climbing out of the Paddington Canal and nearly turning into a girl... Narrow is the word that comes to mind to describe Rosie physically. She had a long thin pallid face, well sprinkled with pimples and blackheads; her nose was long and just kept her small grey eyes apart. She looked as sly as a ferret... Sex to her was like fish and chips, enjoyable, but nothing to make a fuss about.[111]

Rosie is the earthy, yet somehow revolting, servant found in saucy postcards, 'naughty' magazines, and the fantasies of employers, here described by a fellow

---

[109] Anna Clark, *Scandal: The Sexual Politics of the British Constitution* (Princeton: Princeton University Press, 2004). Occasional court cases and convictions for blackmail suggest that some servants, the vast majority male, attempted to extort money from their employers through the servant's knowledge of their sexual secrets. See for example *The Times*, Mar 1, 1928, 11; Nov 22, 1929, 5; Dec 7, 1933, 11.
[110] Powell, *Below Stairs*, 85.
[111] Foley, *A Child in the Forest*, 241–2.

servant. We should bear in mind the wide range of moral and sexual codes amongst servants, about whom it is hard to make generalizations, as well as their powers to usurp narratives that historians have tended to read as victimizing.

CONCLUSIONS

Female servants have tended to be seen historically as sexual victims, available to their employers, leered at, and put on display. Historians have stressed their sexual vulnerability, and have focused on their experiences of casual sex, or seduction and abandonment, by middle-class youths and men.[112] This is supported by the numerous upper- and middle-class memoirs that describe stealing kisses or caresses from them, while servants frequently offer memories of sexual harassment. For early- and mid-twentieth-century servants, there were sometimes high personal costs to the erotic imaginary that coded servants variously as earthy, polluted, homoerotic, or knowing, or coded employers as salacious and promiscuous. Servants could clearly be sexually exploited with relative impunity, and in a revealing aside, 'Walter', the narrator of *My Secret Life*, noted that he gave the real names of servants he alleged to have seduced, while all other categories of women were given the anonymity of false names.[113] For Hyam, 'the evidence is overwhelming that for many boys the first experience of the opposite sex was with a female servant living in the family home.'

However, the sexual availability of servants did not necessarily make them only cast as sexual victims. Indeed, the historical narrative needs to move beyond depictions of victimhood, Victorian sexual hypocrisy, and cross-class seduction, to an awareness of how servants occupied a range of sexual subject positions as polluted, degraded, earthy, natural, accessible, and consoling sexual figures, and within these, could be attributed sexual agency and desire. The story is not straightforwardly one of male employers desiring their female servants and projecting qualities of 'bad women' or pollution onto them. Pollution figured, though so did discourses of sexual naturalness. Fantasies of boundary crossing and class transgression were at play, though servants were most commonly the vehicle for a middle-class vicarious fascination with working-class courtship, which was not only limited to male voyeurs of female servants but also proved fascinating to middle-class women. Comedy was often intimately connected with the eroticization of service, and both servants and employers could be the butt of jokes, or seek sexual dignity through humour strategies. Servants were sometimes objectified in mass culture, but had their own resources of parody and eroticization. I have argued that prudishness and ignorance were not just the characteristics of individual servants,

---

[112] Marcus, *The Other Victorians*, 129; Palmer, *Domesticity and Dirt*, 144. The sacking of Samuel Pepys' servant Deb Willetts, after his wife discovered Pepys with his hand up Willets' skirt, epitomizes this vulnerability and is widely cited. Pepys speculated, 'I fear I shall by this means prove the ruin of [her].' Quoted in Toulalan, *Imagining Sex*, 27–8.

[113] Preface, Walter, *My Secret Life*.

but also components of an alternative sexual narrative that servants used to counter their own hypersexualization through accusing their employers of being sexually uncontrolled, dirty, and libertine. The desires and pleasures attached to domestic service were in flux, but this erotic imaginary was clearly a resource that both servants and employers could exploit, despite its asymmetry.

Recent work on the history of sexuality has stressed that there is no single predominant erotic imaginary of an 'age'. It is unlikely that we can tell one singular story about any aspect of sexual desire, and the erotics of domestic service are no exception. In the early to mid-twentieth century, the 'available' domestic servant—young, vulnerable, and figured as sexually compliant and passive—coexisted with the 'knowing' servant, with active sexual desires. Female servants were mostly eclipsed as repositories of sexual desire in the 1940s and 1950s, though male servants and older, married female chars did figure, and the comic element persisted. Servants returned in a different guise in subsequent decades, as a vehicle for a nostalgic identification of sexual desire with social transgression and hierarchy. The experiences of the single-handed 'skivvy' that had been prominent in the early twentieth century were replaced by the increasing attention to the large staffs of 'great house' service. Servants in the late twentieth century stood in for sexual victims, with a stronger 'parasexual' appeal to the male gaze.

As domestic service employment waned in Britain from the mid- to late twentieth century, fantasy became correspondingly more important as a means of remembering and re-narrating domestic service. As British people became more willing to see class as a feature of 'past times', a crude version of its erotic element was foregrounded, as fantasies about domestic service became more about upper-class male seduction and working-class female submissiveness. Class and its transgression was given greater currency and prominence as a vehicle for sexual desire in the post-war decades. The diversity, queerness, and indeterminacy of the earlier erotic imaginary—the mistress viewing with pleasure her maid's arms, the defiant counter-eroticization aimed at employers by servants, the backhanded humour of sexual jokes about service—all became homogenized into a late-twentieth-century erotic imaginary in which gender and class seemed to operate in clear-cut and polarized ways in the nostalgic historical fiction of the pornography industry.

6

Heritage Nostalgia

Domestic Service Remembered and Performed

In 1891, Thomas Hardy depicted a conversation between his fictional farm servant and victim of seduction, Tess Durbeyfield, and her middle-class admirer, Angel Clare, who asked Tess: 'Wouldn't you like to take up any course of study—history, for example?' Tess responded:

What's the use of learning that I am one of a long row only—finding out that there is set down in some old book somebody just like me, and to know that I shall only act her part; making me sad, that's all. The best is not to remember that your nature and past doings have been just like thousands' and thousands', and that your coming life and doings'll be like thousands' and thousands'.[1]

A history of domestic labour was imagined as disempowering, a depiction of monotonous repetition and historical stasis.

However, Tess's 'long row' of those engaged in domestic labour across historical time now engages and enthuses popular imaginations. As the previous chapter suggested, it has also proved titillating. Imaginatively located in great homes, service has been remembered as an institution through which differentials in power, authority, and resources might be sexually enacted. This has proved to be a powerful and marketable mode of remembering domestic service, found also in the playfully eroticized and costumed interactions of Japanese 'maids cafes', and commodified in the maids' outfits available worldwide in 'adult' shops. It still resonates in the erotic banter centring on maids in early-twenty-first-century 'reality TV' depictions of domestic service.[2] This erotic mode of representation is, however, one amongst many, and in British society, domestic service remains compulsively 'over-represented'—in other words, it serves as an overdetermined set of stories about the past retold and re-enacted for their symbolic and personal meanings. In scores of stately homes, television comedies, costume dramas and

---

[1] Thomas Hardy, *Tess of the D'Urbervilles* (London: Vintage Classic, 2008) quoted in Jesse Freedman, '"To Feel Fiercely": Tradition, Heritage, and Nostalgia in English History', *The History Teacher*, 39 1 (2005), 107–15, esp. 109.

[2] See, for example, the sexual banter depicted amongst servants in 'Monument to Folly', a National Trust/Heritage Lottery Fund youth cinema production filmed at Ickworth House (2008, Forest Films), and the sexual speculations about maids in *The Edwardian Country House*, Wall to Wall Media Ltd, screened by Channel 4, 2002.

'docusoaps', art galleries, advertising campaigns, cinema productions, novels, memoirs, the oral history movement, and educational curricula, domestic service has come to take centre stage as an evocative, fantasized means of dramatizing the past in Britain.

The symbolic meanings of these depictions of domestic service are multiple and ambiguous. 'Service' establishes diverse encounters with the past, and its 'memory work' offers no neat form of identity politics or single message. This chapter looks at some of the narrations and performances of domestic service available in late-twentieth- and early-twenty-first-century Britain, and reflects on their meanings and reception. It is concerned with the historicity of domestic service—the way in which the past plays a social role in the present through the staging of memory, or to use Arlie Hochschild's concept, its 'cultural weight'.[3] The first section of this chapter will focus on the recent fascination with representing and re-enacting domestic service in television and cinema, from *Upstairs, Downstairs* in the 1970s, to the reality television show *The 1900 House* and the drama *Downton Abbey* of the twenty-first century. This will be set alongside a second discussion, exploring depictions and re-enactments of domestic service within British stately homes, allied to the rise of what has been termed the 'experience attraction' or 'live interpretation'.

Both these realms can be understood as offering 'heritage performances', foregrounding particular narratives of the past, while eclipsing others. The term 'performance' is understood in the broadest sense of the presentation and enactment of the past in textual, visual, material, and theatrical form, often without posing any deep divisions between 'audiences' and 'performers'. Audiences may be active participants in this process, and can embrace, interpret, or reject these narratives, according to their social and emotional purchase upon memory and life histories.[4]

HERITAGE AND MEMORY

The term 'heritage' defies any neat definition, but is used here to capture the social production of memory, usually linked to material objects, landscapes, and cultural products.[5] Heritage operates at both the macro level of the nation and the micro

---

[3] Arlie Russell Hochschild, *The Commercialization of Intimate Life: Notes from Home and Work* (Berkeley: University of California Press, 2003), 58.

[4] Gaynor Bagnall, 'Performance and Performativity at Heritage Sites', *Museum and Society*, 1 2 (2003), 87–103, esp. 88. Sociologists of museums and their visitors suggest that in contemporary Britain 'the distance between audiences and performers has diminished; people perform and they see others as performers, they perform for an audience yet they are also members of a range of audiences' (ibid. 87). The rise of reality television has further obscured the distinction between audience and performer, as has the use of live interpretation in heritage settings. Visitors are invited to dress up, handle artefacts, and respond to the overtures of actors in historical roles.

[5] Popular Memory Group, 'Popular Memory: Theory, Politics, Method', in G. McLennan, R. Johnson, B. Schwarz, and D. Sutton (eds), *Making Histories: Studies in History-Writing and Politics* (London: Hutchinson, 1982), 205–52.

level of locality and personal remembrance. It has been widely seen as expanding into a major commercial and political phenomenon in the second half of the twentieth century, and in the process, deeply influencing our relationship with the past. Critical definitions would term heritage an 'industry', a 'commodification of history', or 'the *use* of the past for contemporary purposes'.[6] Robert Hewison's *The Heritage Industry* represented a genre of historical polemics of the 1980s and 1990s, which situated this memory work as intrinsically linked to the 'New Right' Thatcherite project, and argued that the past had been 'shaped and moulded to the needs of the present, and in the process, filtered, polished and drained of meaning.'[7] More specifically, Hewison noted that the English 'cult of country houses' represents a conservative vision of 'hierarchy, a sturdy individualism on the part of their owners, privilege tempered by social duty, a deference and respect for the social order on the part of those who service and support them. They reinforce these values in the present.'[8] Patrick Wright similarly pointed to an upper-class social world as the focus of nostalgia in the 1980s. He argued that 'In a world where values are in apparent disorder and where the social hierarchy has lost its settled nature, it is not so surprising that old forms of security become alluring (the upstairs/downstairs style of traditional integration where everybody in the house—servant or "family"—has an unproblematic place at the beginning and end of every day).' This kind of history, he argued, is 'closely connected to the impulses of contemporary conservatism' and offers a frozen, static view of the past.[9]

Other historians have preferred to set heritage within a broader ideological and historical context, and situate its popularity over a longer time period. Peter Mandler's study of English country houses helpfully adopts a broader historical context than earlier polemical histories, and sets the 'turn to heritage' in the context of the broad changes to British society—the post-war slum clearances and transformation of the built environment, the changing nature of consumption, property ownership, and of state powers—alongside the 'peculiarly violent' British reaction to 'the modern' or 'permissive' society experienced in the 1960s, which created an 'intense affinity for "heritage," and a country-house heritage in particular, in British

---

[6] David Lowenthal, *The Past Is a Foreign Country* (Cambridge: Cambridge University Press, 1985), 6; J. Tivers, 'Performing Heritage: The Use of "Live" Actors in Heritage Presentations', *Leisure Studies*, 21 3 (2002), 187–200, esp. 188.

[7] Robert Hewison, *The Heritage Industry: Britain in a Climate of Decline* (London: Methuen, 1987), 99. John Baxendale and Christopher Pawling have argued that a key feature of Thatcherism was its success at colonizing the past as well as dominating the present, and explore how heritage, in various constructions, was a key component of the New Right's appeal: John Baxendale and Christopher Pawling, '"A Feeling for Tradition and Discipline": Conservatism and the Thirties in Remains of the Day', in *eidem* (eds), *Narrating the Thirties: A Decade in the Making, 1930 to the Present* (Basingstoke: Macmillan, 1996). See also Patrick Wright, *On Living in an Old Country: The National Past in Contemporary Britain* (London: Verso, 1985).

[8] Hewison, *The Heritage Industry*, 53.

[9] Patrick Wright and Michael Bommes, '"Charms of Residence": The Public and the Past', in Mclennan et al. (eds), *Making Histories: Studies in History-Writing and Politics*, 253–302, esp. 264; Wright, *On Living in an Old Country*, 22.

culture in the 1980s.'[10] This also led, Mandler argues, to a sharp turn to the political Right from the mid-1970s, expressed both culturally and electorally. These wider social changes, rather than Thatcherism, created a 'post-permissive' sense of a break with the past, and spurred the construction of new 'sites of memory' or collective engagements with the past.

Understood within this broader perspective, 'heritage performances' may be imbued with both conservative and critical elements, and nostalgia is found across the political spectrum, as Raphael Samuel has argued. He offered an influential account of the political indeterminacy of heritage, noting its capacity for sustaining popular participation across the twentieth century, and its fluctuations according to contemporary tastes and contexts. Heritage is viewed as a mobile, fluid discourse, and for Samuel, its expansion into an 'industry' is based as much on the work of progressive historians and Left-wing governmental initiatives as on the values of the entrepreneurial New Right.[11] Howard Malchow, similarly, warns against attempting to establish a simple link between popular culture and political ideology. Instead, he perceives a 'quite complicated dialogue—an often mutual process of transforming and enabling—that exists between "every day life" and political ideology.' He traces a shift from popular interpretations of heritage sparked by the nostalgic and chaotic 1970s, to the versions of heritage purveyed in the consumption-driven 1980s. This latter decade, for Malchow, saw heritage become premised on notions of possessing the past, in private hands, alongside an 'erosion of the distinction between the authentic and the simulated past'.[12] The reshaping of British engagements with the past after the disruptions of World War II, the consumer boom of the 1950s, and its aftermath should not therefore be seen as a singular shift, but a multifaceted and ongoing process of 'memory work'.

These historiographical developments in the study of heritage are also reflected in the literature on memory. Historians initially focused on the role memory plays in creating national communities, through the influential work of Pierre Nora and Benedict Anderson, and drawing on earlier ideas of 'collective memory' developed by Maurice Halbwachs.[13] Nora introduced the influential idea of a *lieu de mémoire*, a site of memory, 'where memory crystallizes and secretes itself', and which is invested by the imagination with a 'symbolic aura'.[14] Jan Assman's account of

---

[10] Peter Mandler, *The Fall and Rise of the Stately Home* (New Haven, CT: Yale University Press, 1997), 411.

[11] Raphael Samuel, *Theatres of Memory: Past and Present in Contemporary Culture* (London: Verso, 1994), 205–42. See also Chris Waters, 'Autobiography, Nostalgia and the Changing Practices of Working-Class Selfhood', in G. K. Behlmer and F. M. Leventhal (eds), *Singular Continuities: Tradition, Nostalgia and Identity in Modern British Culture* (Stanford: Stanford University Press, 2000).

[12] Howard Malchow, 'Nostalgia, "Heritage," and the London Antiques Trade: Selling the Past in Thatcher's Britain', in Behlmer and Leventhal (eds), *Singular Continuities*, 213.

[13] Benedict Anderson, *Imagined Communities: Reflections on the Origins and Rise of Nationalism* (London: Verso, 1982); Maurice Halbwachs, *On Collective Memory* (Chicago: University of Chicago Press, 1992 [1950]); Pierre Nora, *Realms of Memory: Rethinking the French Past* (New York: Columbia University Press, 1996).

[14] Like Halbwachs, Nora argues for a distinction between history and memory, the first a critical process of representation, and the latter a more organic 'affective and magical' realm. However, the distinction between memory and history seems to obscure rather than shed light on the ways in which

'cultural memory' has also been influential, defining it as 'that body of reusable texts, images, and rituals specific to each society in each epoch, whose "cultivation" serves to stabilize and convey that society's self-image.'[15] However, just as heritage has become seen as a mobile and politically flexible discourse, so too has memory become regarded as less consensual, a site of 'counter memory', power play, and manipulation, rather than a force for cohesion and collective identity.[16]

Memory, understood as increasingly plural and personalized in the late twentieth century, is now seen as less directly connected to national identities.[17] This helps elucidate the many ways in which the memory work of domestic service has operated. Though elements of domestic service—the formal 'English butler', for example—can be seen as components of the visual iconography of English national identity, there are no clear 'official' or state-sanctioned 'dominant' narratives being told about domestic service, and no formal sites of commemoration. Service and servants have been depicted broadly across British popular culture, and serve no single political purpose. Instead, the 'memory work' of domestic service is worked into narratives of individuals, families, locations, artefacts, or individual houses. Memories of domestic service tend to be intensely personal, though they have a significance that goes beyond the personal. Domestic service can usefully be seen as a *lieu de mémoire*, yet it does not fit easily into the categories of memory and counter-memory that predominate in the historiography. This chapter demonstrates the ways in which a single 'site of memory' can offer a number of diverse relationships to the past, not only over time, but simultaneously, and can also be reinterpreted and manipulated by different audiences. The dominance of domestic service in heritage performances and as a site of memory in Britain poses a number of questions: what does it mean to think of domestic service as a site of memory? Does domestic service become relegated to a past that is 'resolved' and distant, and thus unrelated to present inequalities, particularly those associated with the rise of paid domestic employment since 1980? Or is domestic service as a site of memory an attempt to work through and clarify the more opaque ways in which class, gender, and other social hierarchies now function in contemporary times? And finally, what forgetting and displacement of memory is bound up with the heritage performances of domestic service?

---

domestic service is remembered, and I prefer to use 'memory work' as a more capacious term, spanning what I see as the deeply interconnected realms of scholarly and popular history. Pierre Nora, 'Between Memory and History: Les Lieux De Memoire', *Representations*, 26 (1989), 7–24, esp. 7, 19, 8.

[15] Jan Assmann, 'Collective Memory and Cultural Identity', *New German Critique*, 65 (1995), 125–33, esp. 132.

[16] Hue-Tam Ho Tai, 'Remembered Realms: Pierre Nora and French National Memory', *American Historical Review*, 106 3 (2001), 906–22, esp. 915–16.

[17] John Gillis, 'Memory and Identity: The History of a Relationship', in *idem* (ed.), *Commemorations: The Politics of National Identity* (Princeton: Princeton University Press, 1994), 3–26, esp. 14.

MEMOIRS, DRAMAS, AND COMEDIES

The first popular memorialization of domestic service can be located in a new publishing genre of working-class autobiography that flourished from the 1950s to 1970s, inspired by the focus on social histories 'from below'. Memoirs of former servants such as Jean Rennie, Margaret Powell, and Winifred Foley were published, televised, or serialized on the radio, and were full of tales of poverty, bitterness, and thwarted aspirations.[18] They found a ready audience at a moment when family history was increasingly popular. Interest in family members of the recent past who had been domestic servants has been enormously significant in fuelling the popular interest in domestic service. The repeated mention of mothers, sisters, and grandmothers who had been servants permeates popular history. Family history can motivate an inclusive narrative of sympathy and empathy with the lives of servants, and this was presented to popular audiences, in, for example, Frank Huggett's 1977 illustrated collection of memories, *Life Below Stairs*. Huggett offered the conventional narrative that Chapter 1 has suggested was prominent in British social history: 'Good mistresses seem to have been exceptional... Domestic service could provide only slender benefits, and far less rarely some affection, in a world of seemingly unbridgeable social and economic differences.'[19] These popular narratives tended to seek responses of guilt, shame, and pity, and such responses can indeed be found in media commentaries; as one colour supplement put it in 1968, 'We feel such humiliation on behalf of Victorian servants.' This led Sybil Hahoe to comment with some frustration on how her employment as a Norfolk general maid was imagined by younger generations, when interviewed for an oral history collection in 1975:

With all that work, I felt like a lady, after living at home with all those children. Yes, I felt like a lady. My children can't make that out, to think that I had to work so hard, and I was a lady! You dress with a nice white apron on, you see, White cap. Oh, it was ever so smart![20]

Cultural memories of domestic service were already deeply shaped by the popular televisual representations of it. *Upstairs, Downstairs* was conceived in the late 1960s by actresses Jean Marsh and Eileen Atkins as depicting the servants' view of the upper-class home, in response to the neglect of 'below stairs' in the BBC dramatization of the *Forsyte Saga* in 1967. For Marsh, this was a political project, borne not of nostalgia, but of social history, and motivated by a personal sense of anger

---

[18] Winifred Foley, *A Child in the Forest* (London: Futura, 1974); Margaret Powell, *Below Stairs* (London: Pan Books, 1968); Jean Rennie, *Every Other Sunday: The Autobiography of a Kitchenmaid* (London: Barker, [1955] 1978).

[19] Frank E. Huggett, *Life Below Stairs: Domestic Servants in England from Victorian Times* (London: Book Club Associates, 1977), 173.

[20] Maggie Angeloglou, 'Life Below Stairs', *Sunday Times Magazine*, Feb 25, 1968, 37; Mrs Hahoe, quoted in Mary Chamberlain, *Fenwomen: A Portrait of Women in an English Village* (London: Virago, 1975), 97.

generated by her own and Atkins' family origins: 'Neither of us have quite got the chips off our shoulders... we wanted to show that, for the servants, it was freezing in their attic bedrooms and boiling hot in the kitchen. We wanted to see servants as people.'[21] Marsh envisaged the series as a drama, and was wary of hackneyed comic servants. The original selling document put together by the production company, however, took a contrasting line. The series was pitched in more melodramatic terms as exploring acute social contrasts: 'in every large London house there were two worlds, two households, races apart but dependent on each other, each with its own rituals, rules and disciplines.' The comic-erotic mode was to the fore: 'with a preponderance of frustrated females below stairs, jealousy and emotional scenes were the order of the day and love affairs of every sort were unrestrained.'[22] The title of the series was adopted explicitly to connote the nursery rhyme sexual innuendo: 'Upstairs, Downstairs, | In my lady's chamber'.[23]

Enormously successful, *Upstairs, Downstairs* ran for five series between 1971 and 1975, was exported around the world, and produced countless heritage industry spin-offs (cookery books, fiction, music, gifts), as well as a copy-cat American series, *Beacon Hill*. It is clear that there were from the outset competing narratives or themes that the series could be associated with. While some felt that it was a vehicle for social history, and a means of giving dignity to servants, for others, it remained comic-erotic, in keeping with the *Carry On* genre of British cinema. The series was described by its sometime scriptwriter Fay Weldon as 'quite a joke of an idea. Kind of frilly knickers on the stairs and oo-ers all over the place!'[24] The comic servant certainly still had considerable cultural resonance alongside the sexualized servant in the 1970s, and the *Carry On* producers exploited this with their 1978 spoof of a soft porn film, *Carry On Emmanuelle*, which foregrounded the erotic lives of domestic servants.

For some cast members, *Upstairs, Downstairs* inspired critical attention to contemporary practices of domestic labour. Lesley-Ann Downs commented on the irony of having to scrub the concrete stairs in her London flat while daily performing as 'Miss Georgina', an upstairs debutante.[25] However, a more common reception of the series was nostalgia, set against a sense of late-twentieth-century social disintegration. Many of the viewers and participants of the series regarded it as a positive depiction of past times. One of the main actors, David Langton, felt that the popularity of the show was due to the sense it engendered of everyone 'knowing their place': 'it was ordered, disciplined, and people knew where they stood. There was shape.' For the chief scriptwriter, Alfred Shaughnessy, viewers 'like to look back from our confused world, where there is no automatic discipline

---

[21] Marsh, quoted in Richard Marson, *Inside Updown—The Story of Upstairs Downstairs* (Bristol: Kaleidoscope, 2001), 3.
[22] 'Below Stairs', Jan 1970, cited ibid. 10–11.
[23] While the erotic elements were eventually toned down, the viability of the theme as a vehicle for sexual antics is suggested by the pornographic spoof version made in 1980, *Downstairs, Upstairs*, starring the 'sex crazed' Bunn family.
[24] Marson, *Inside Updown*, xx.
[25] Ibid. 280–1.

or rank, to a well-ordered house like the Bellamy's, which was a microcosm of the real world.' For John Whitney, a director of the production company, *Upstairs, Downstairs* succeeded in attracting very large audiences because 'everybody could either identify with the upstairs people or the downstairs people.' There was no automatic assumption that viewers would identify more with the servants' lives from motives of sympathy. Repeatedly in these interpretations, the stress is on the comfort and belonging for all in the early twentieth-century servant-keeping household, placed in negative contrast with late-twentieth-century Britain. This was a reading of the series that worked against the intention of the original vision of Edwardian Britain as a time of uncertainty and flux, with 'similarity to our own times'.[26] Understood against the grain, *Upstairs, Downstairs* seemed to provide a warm and welcoming narrative of servant-keeping between 1914 and 1930, set starkly against 1970s Britain.

Domestic service might thus be understood as of a piece with other representations of the past, such as the repackaged Edith Holden's *Country Diary of an Edwardian Lady*, and the rustic interior design and Laura Ashley fabrics that flourished in the 1970s and 1980s. The colour supplements and magazines such as *Country Life* had indeed been evoking such nostalgia since the 1960s, ironically from roughly the same moment when traumatized sensations of being 'servantless' were finally fading from domestic columns in the middlebrow press. Rather than the exploitation of labour and social gulfs between servants and employers, the media stressed the comedies of snobberies amongst servants. Domestic service was depicted as a good job, and readers were reminded not to 'forget how the rest of the working-class were living.'[27] Advertisers drew on similar cultural scripts, though ethnicity was sometimes evoked in place of class in their visual repertoire of smart, cheerful, and deferential servants. A cruise company drew on empire nostalgia in its full-page advertisement in the 1968 *Sunday Times Magazine*, depicting a well-heeled white couple greeting their non-Anglo-Saxon servants, with the tagline: 'Remember the days of lady's maids? Re-live them on the sea route to South Africa' (Figure 18).[28] Those who had kept servants frequently looked back to that phase of their life with deep nostalgia, as one mistress noted in the late 1970s: 'In all the senseless class and clamour of today when there is no peace, no standards, and apparently no aim in life, and certainly little happiness and no contentment however much people "have," one looks back with great contentment, thankfulness

---

[26] Ibid. 241, 80, 78, xx.
[27] Angeloglou, 'Life below Stairs', 37. See also 'In Which We Serve', *Observer*, July 30, 1967, 4–12; 'The Dying Reign of the Pantry', *Daily Telegraph Magazine*, July 6, 1973, 14–19.
[28] Union-Castle Safmarine advertisement, *Sunday Times Magazine*, Feb 25, 1968, 38. This nostalgic appeal was based on a still viable association of South Africa under the National Party in 1968 with stable and deferential race relations. While servants in Britain were almost universally remembered as ethnically white, there was nonetheless a small but significant mid-twentieth-century phenomenon of Southern European or Afro-Caribbean immigrant women entering domestic service on arrival in the United Kingdom. Service was viewed by officials as a good job for these recent arrivals, though immigrant groups themselves resisted this attempt to confine them to a niche in the labour market. For a rare depiction of such workers, see *Observer*, July 30, 1967, 4–12.

214 *Knowing Their Place*

> # Remember the days of lady's maids? Re-live them on the sea route to South Africa
>
> If you fancy tea at three in the morning, or need a stitch in your evening dress—just say the word. On a Union-Castle ship there is someone to give you smiling service all day and all night. It takes eleven idyllic days to Cape Town, through blue seas and golden weather. You'll grow younger as you live them. See your travel agent, or post the coupon in the right-hand column.   **UNION-CASTLE SAFMARINE**

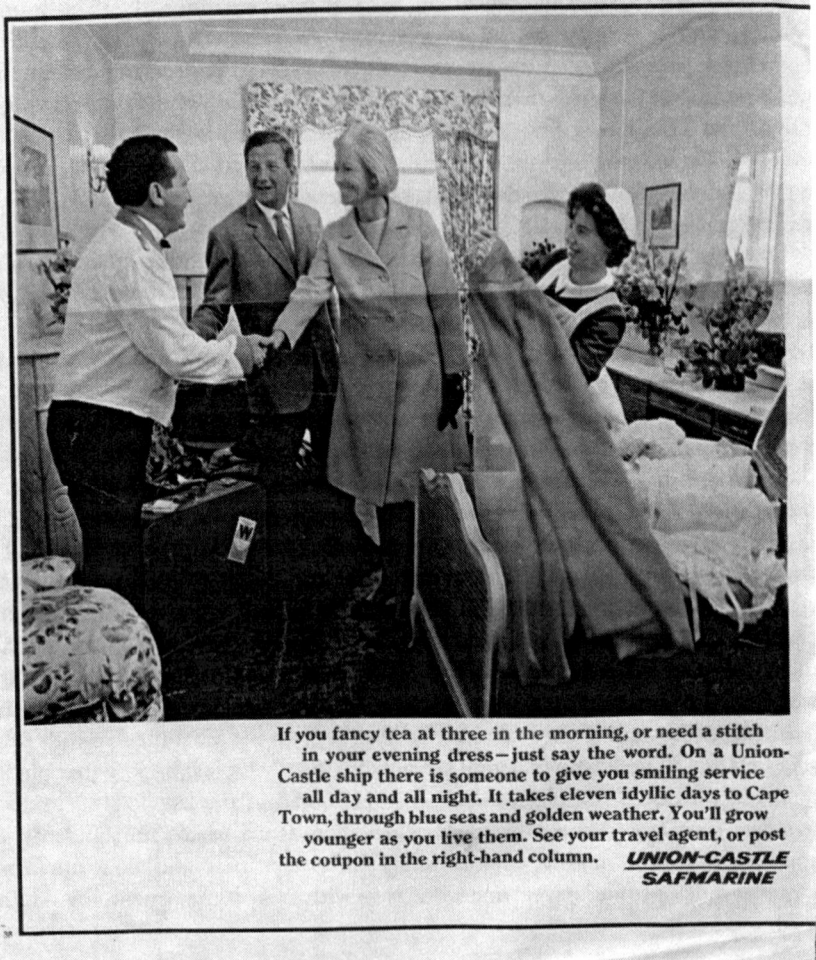

Figure 18. Union-Castle Safmarine advertisement, *Sunday Times Magazine*, February 25, 1968, 38.

and happiness to a so much more worthwhile life.'[29] Despite the evident material comforts of servant-keeping houses, domestic service was able to stand in for a less materialistic world, in which individuals at all social levels were committed to

---

[29] Frank V. Dawes, *Not in Front of the Servants: Domestic Service in England 1850–1939* (London: Wayland, 1973), 167.

service and duty. There were, then, many possible readings of what had been a social history-inspired recuperation of marginalized voices.

Upstairs, Downstairs did not exhaust the potential for domestic service to act as a comic, nostalgic, or critical vehicle to convey past times in Britain. In the 1980s, service continued to feature prominently in British televisual culture. Politically and culturally, two historical moments became prominent sites of memory in late-twentieth-century Britain—the Victorian period, as an imagined site of moral certainty, and the interwar years, as a period conveying imperial greatness, social order, and resurgent traditional values. In the imagining of both these periods, domestic service has been foregrounded as a highly visible and significant social institution, perceived as being at either its peak or 'swansong'. It is no surprise that these periods are commonly evoked in many of the productions of the 1980s. *You Rang, M'Lord*, for example, was a pastiche of *Upstairs, Downstairs*, which ran from 1988 to 1993, set in the 1920s, and which relied heavily upon the comic servant. *The Victorian Kitchen*, a BBC series produced in 1989, was narrated mainly by a former cook, Ruth Mott, who portrayed her work as a domestic servant as a site of hard work, pranks, comforting traditions, and culinary satisfaction. There seems to be a deep divide between the academic history generated during this decade, much of it based on oral histories, which stressed exploitation, and the televisual histories that preferred to see service as a warm, caring institution.

The televisual depictions of servant-keeping of subsequent years were more ambivalent. Jo Littler and Roshi Naidoo describe the post-Thatcher years as much less oriented to heritage than the 1980s, characterized by more forward-looking representations of 'young Britain'.[30] Nonetheless, there appeared to be no diminution of interest in servant-keeping. The Kazuo Ishiguro novel, *The Remains of the Day*, won the Booker Prize in 1989, was adapted into a film in 1993, and proved enormously successful with audiences. It portrayed a much darker world of 'above and below stairs' in the late 1930s, where the employers are seen as helpless and dependent, but also insulting and patronizing towards servants. The servants of the film are depicted as profoundly shaped, or scarred, by their class encounters, and they find it hard to sustain lives and identities outside of their service jobs.[31] In both book and film, all associated with service seem emotionally stunted and are 'victims' in psychologically complex ways. Nonetheless, the directors were clearly also influenced by country house nostalgia. Film critic Geoffrey McNab accused the film version of undermining its potential critique of the social institutions of the upper classes through its clichéd depiction of 'baying hounds, cheery cooks in the conservatory, soriées in the drawing room, rustic pubs and lots of English autumnal scenes'. The 'sheer visual relish' of this nostalgic evocation of country house living produced an 'ambivalent' film that, in his reading, could not succeed in

---

[30] J. Littler and R. Naidoo, 'White Past, Multicultural Present: Heritage and National Stories', in H. Brocklehurst and R. Phillips (eds), *History, Nationhood and the Question of Britain* (Basingstoke: Macmillan, 2004).

[31] Baxendale and Pawling, 'A Feeling for Tradition and Discipline'.

its 'few floundering, satirical slaps at the class system'.[32] Viewers, readers, and commentators were indeed quite resistant to the darker interpretation of domestic service that could be read into *The Remains of the Day*. *The Times* portrayed the central butler figure as a slightly comic 'Jeeves' character, starring in what it termed a 'melancholy and humorous love story'.[33] With an apparent absence of irony, a London hotel took its employees to see the film, hoping to inculcate more deferential behaviour. One of the staff commented 'It was so gracious the way the staff worked together... The butler was so at ease with himself, so professional. It does make you think you want to be like that.'[34]

The Remains of the Day was widely read nostalgically, portraying a society ordered by class that offered dignity to all. McNab was, however, far more positive about the critical potential of another 'country house' film also set in the 1930s, *Gosford Park*, directed by Robert Altman and released in 2002. This film took the *Upstairs, Downstairs* attempt to foreground the servants' viewpoint to an extreme, allowing the camera to film the 'upstairs' cast only when a servant was present: 'If a servant leaves the room, so does the camera... the story is transmitted through downstairs gossip, through what the servants know.' But there is no heavy-handed message of nostalgia or sympathy. Altman himself commented that great house service was a good job; McNab noted: 'Altman is far too subtle and insightful a film-maker simply to dismiss the aristocrats as contemptible and to idealise the servants. Each world provides a distorted reflection of the other. Strangely, the servants cling to the rules of behaviour as stubbornly as their employers.'[35] The commercial success of the film suggests the continuing fascination with domestic service in British society, still interpreted by some participants through the lens of family history. Helen Mirren, playing a housekeeper, commented that 'My mother came from that upstairs downstairs world... She narrowly escaped domestic service and I wanted to do the film to show the world of upstairs through the eyes of downstairs.' She sought, however, to deny that the film was 'a political comment on Britain, or the English class system'.[36] There was a lingering unwillingness to judge servant-keeping.

The reality TV and costume drama productions of the early twenty-first century have, like cinema productions, found domestic service to remain a powerful draw, through its psychologically and physically demanding nature, and its possibilities of dramatic juxtaposition. In contemporary popular memory, a detached sense of service as 'just one job amongst many' does not figure; it is seen as a realm of confrontations and dramatic, powerful emotions that lend themselves to television. The heavy concentration of British series based on service (*The 1900 House* (1999), *The Edwardian Country House* (2003), *Servants* (2003), *What the Butler Saw* (2004), *Downton Abbey* (2010)) suggests that recent television producers have

---

[32] Geoffrey McNab, 'The Remains of the Day', *Sight and Sound*, Dec 1993, 51/12.
[33] Philip Howard, 'A Butler's Tale...', *The Times*, Oct 27, 1989.
[34] 'Film School', *The Evening Standard*, Mar 9, 1994.
[35] Robert Altman, quoted in 'You Rang, Mr Altman?', *Daily Telegraph*, Sept 1, 2001, A7; Geoffrey McNab, 'Gosford Park', *Sight and Sound*, Feb 2002, 46/2.
[36] Helen Mirren, quoted in *The Belfast Newsletter*, Jan 29, 2002.

been obsessed with exploiting this cultural motif. Indeed, *Upstairs Downstairs* was revived for a new run in late 2010, with one critic greeting it as an escapist form of 'servant porn'.[37]

The 1900 House production was a nine-part reality TV series screened by Channel Four in 1999, and showed the efforts of the 'real-life' Bowler family to place themselves back into a late-Victorian domestic setting. The production company aimed to highlight the historical distance between 1900 and 1999, commenting: 'Although it's within living memory, it will be as alien as a Roman encampment.'[38] The house the Bowlers inhabited in south-east London was a four-bedroom middle-class suburban villa ('a sort of Barratt home of the period'[39]), and the family was portrayed by the producers as a newly prosperous lower-middle-class household. Though this was a comfortably off family, the issue of domestic service was not raised until some way into the series, when the endless and exhausting cleaning of the house was felt by Mrs Bowler to be stopping her from experiencing anything of the Victorian era other than housework. Accompanied by enormous media interest, which was deliberately amplified by the production company, a local, live-out maid-of-all-work was hired, named Elizabeth Lillington.

The experiment with servant-keeping was uncomfortable and unsustainable. Mr Bowler commented: 'I tried to be masterful, complaining about the staff, and it didn't really work.'[40] Mrs Bowler found her interactions with Elizabeth to be painful, eliciting self-conscious performances of class. Mrs Bowler stated to Elizabeth on her first day, 'we'll do the girls room first,' then corrected herself with a nervous laugh, 'you'll do the girls room, I'm not doing it.' Having ended the conversation, she commented, 'Off I go to be middle-class'—there's a powerful feeling of role play around mistresshood that did not characterize other attempts by the Bowlers to 'be Victorian'.[41] Fairly swiftly, Mrs Bowler decided to 'let Elizabeth go', with the slightly laboured justification that her feminist commitment to the right of all women to be liberated from the domestic grind made it impossible to employ someone else to do her housework. She declared: 'I'm liberating Elizabeth. I'm setting her off free into the world to find her own way and do her own thing. I just can't have someone else coming in and cleaning up my house.'[42] She communicated this to Elizabeth by letter, apparently unable to face her in the flesh.

Ironically, it was feminism that was positioned as explaining why servant-keeping had become impossible for a twenty-first-century family, though many earlier feminists had been slow to acknowledge the claims of domestic servants within their movement. Mrs Bowler's feminist explanation for sacking her servant

---

[37] Kathryn Hughes, 'Upstairs, Downstairs, and Servant Porn', *Guardian*, Dec 27, 2010, 28.
[38] *Daily Mail*, Sept 18, 1999.
[39] Daru Rooke, quoted in 'Victorian Values', *The Press* (York), Oct 1999.
[40] Paul Bowler, *Sunday Times*, Aug 15, 1999, 4.
[41] 'A Woman's Place', *The 1900 House* (Wall to Wall Media, 1999). For other forms of role play associated with domestic service, see Lucy Delap, 'Campaigns of Curiosity: Class Crossing and Role Reversal in British Domestic Service, c.1890–1950', *Left History*, 12 2 (2007).
[42] 'The End of an Era', *The 1900 House*.

was not commented on by the media, and it was the servant who was perceived as the feminist agent. The *Radio Times* noted that 'Working from nine 'til nine, it takes a single day to turn [Elizabeth] into a committed feminist.'[43] In the mainstream media, feminism was understood to make domestic service impossible to sustain because it gave working-class women alternative aspirations; it was presented to twenty-first-century viewers as a form of class resentment, rather than providing any analysis of the gendered divisions of labour and authority in the household.

For Elizabeth, being a day servant was given significance by her sense of personal family history—her mother, grandmother, and great-grandmother had all been 'cleaners'. Family history remains the most cited motive for the broad public interest in domestic service in recent decades. Elizabeth talked of her astonishment at the hard work and low pay of her role, and the camera dwelt on her sore, red hands in close-up. A narrative of the hard physical work of domestic servants was foregrounded, alongside the social snobbery that added to the unpleasantness of the job. There is little trace of earlier narratives of belonging and stability within the servant-keeping home that seemed so important to audiences and producers in the 1970s and 1980s, and rather, a mixture of class and gender oppression. For Elizabeth herself, it was not exactly oppression, but rather her sense of the loss of script that made the experience difficult: 'the hardest thing about it was going to the house and knowing that Mrs Bowler was embarrassed at having a maid. 'Cos I always felt like I was in her way.'[44] The failures of authority discussed in Chapter 2, and the sense of invasion of privacy discussed in Chapter 3, were still genuine components of the relationship between a twenty-first-century domestic worker and her employers. Though the *1900 House* aimed to re-create the otherness of past times, there was little role play in this sense of embarrassment and lack of script between the Bowlers and Elizabeth, and their enactment of 'the servant problem' seemed vividly contemporary.

Domestic service emerged as an emotive and divisive issue, both within the *1900 House* re-enactment and amongst viewers. The viewer feedback suggested a loss of sympathy with Mrs Bowler when she became a mistress, and media reports stressed that she was treating Elizabeth 'like dirt' and paying her 'next to nothing' for her hard physical work.[45] Journalists were sympathetic to Elizabeth, describing her through the persistent cultural trope of being a 'Mrs Mopp' or a 'poor skivvy', and celebrating her powers to resist the Bowlers.[46] Narratives of exploitation and class defiance proved to have deep social resonance with British audiences and the media. The *1900 House* tried to offer a complex narrative of empathy with both mistress and servant, but this was not reflected in the public response. Media commentators found it easy to centre on the servant as the victim of both gender and class

---

[43] *Radio Times* Oct 16, 1999.
[44] *1900 House—A Year to Remember*. Documentary (Wall to Wall Media, 1999).
[45] *Bath Chronicle*, Oct 16, 1999.
[46] 'My Brush with the Life of a Victorian Mrs Mopp', *The Sun*, Oct 22, 1999, 56; *The Scotsman*, Oct 21, 1999.

discrimination, and preferred to highlight Elizabeth's physical exploitation rather than her own identification of social uncertainty as the chief problem.[47]

A reality TV production that similarly placed domestic service centre stage, *The Edwardian Country House*, was produced and screened by Channel Four in 2002. Set in 1905, in an aristocratic house employing at least ten domestic staff, the first comment of the show was given to Mr Edgar, the role-playing butler, who noted: 'Everyone knew whether they were upstairs or downstairs. I believe it may have made for an easier life.' The producers of this programme offered viewers deliberately controversial statements on the role of domestic service, foregrounded at the start of each episode. The master of the house, Sir John Oliff-Cooper, for example, opined: 'I would have enjoyed the clarity of the system in 1905. It seemed to work. I can understand that the inequalities must gall. But the poor are always with us. Jesus said it, I'm sure that's right.' The nostalgic sentiments prompted by *Upstairs, Downstairs* in the 1970s were here being presented in a detached, ironic manner, held up for critical examination by audiences. As the re-enactment progressed, servants talked of the loneliness and hard work, as well as their feelings of social antagonism, though they were clearly following established and clichéd cultural scripts in doing so. One commented: 'It was completely upstairs downstairs the minute they walked in through the door. They're the enemy, sort of thing.'[48]

The series charted a disenchantment with the early statements of complacent nostalgia for the certainties of servant-keeping, for both employers and servants. The mistress, Lady Oliff-Cooper, reflected on the problematic nature of service: 'I feel cosseted, pampered, and curiously child-like again... everything is designed to make me feel smaller as a human being.' Even the master acknowledged the painful constraints of etiquette and propriety upon the employers of servants. And most poignantly, Mr Edgar commented: 'The more you do, the more they seem to want, and the more you give, the less they seem to appreciate it.'[49] This depiction of the Edwardian upper-class servant-keeping household dwelt with relish on the tensions and misunderstandings between employers and staff. Overall, viewers were offered a negative assessment of Edwardian society, which was positioned as problematic for raising children, emotionally stunted for all participants, physically damaging for servants, and highly confining for upper-class women.

As for the *1900 House*, the past was physically and vividly re-enacted in *The Edwardian Country House*, but seemed deliberately distanced, with most participants commenting upon its alien nature and astonishing foreignness. Only Mr Edgar commented that the atmosphere and rules of 'below stairs' were similar to those of his own childhood; but this link to a more recent past marked him out from the rest of the household, and he appeared a living relic, out of touch with his own age. The preferred reading being offered is of the past as an entertaining respite from the present, without any particular relevance for or influence upon today.

---

[47] For some progress narratives, see *The Times*, Sept 23, 1999, 45; Kathryn Flett, *The Observer*, Sept 26, 1999.
[48] Eva Morrison, Ladies Maid, Episode 1, *The Edwardian Country House* (Channel 4, 2002).
[49] Mr Edgar, Episode 4, *The Edwardian Country House*.

These twenty-first-century televisual depictions of service as belonging to the past offer the satisfaction of historical termination—historian David Lowenthal identifies this as a pleasure of being able to sum up and summarize the past in ways not available for accounts of the present.[50] This is a stance that deliberately ignores the long-standing and contemporary presence of domestic service in Britain.

'BELOW STAIRS' IN THE 'GREAT HOUSE'

Domestic service has sustained depictions of exploitation, comedy, and belonging in televisual productions that have consistently drawn large audiences over the past forty years. The more critical accounts of 'heritage' see no difference between heritage productions in the museums sector and those of the television and cinema. However, though the two sectors are linked, homogenization misses the diversity of popular history and memory.

'Living history' and social history interpretations became more influential amongst curators of stately homes from the 1960s, displacing the architectural and design issues that had dominated the interpretation of great homes earlier in the twentieth century.[51] Revised interpretations focused upon the social relations of the properties, and on the 'untold stories' of those who became perceived as truly integral to the houses—the servants and estate staff. Since the 1990s, there has been a wave of restorations and major interpretive projects of 'below stairs'. 'Below stairs' experience attractions create a dramatic link between the material, spatial, and social orders—status and privilege are laid out in the decorative contrasts, the light and headroom available above and below stairs, and the multiple routes through the house that governed social interactions. The artefacts of below stairs—kitchen ranges and implements, laundries with dollies and mangles, pantries and sculleries—have been recovered and restored. The 'heritage performances' of domestic service frequently operate through engagement with tangible, material objects used by servants. Material objects have proved highly evocative in conveying the 'reality' of the lives of servants—they have come to serve as 'storied objects' or 'biographical objects',[52] and many heritage performances are based upon them. At Wimpole Hall in Cambridgeshire, for example, staff comment that above all, 'it is the artefacts that people can relate to'.[53]

Until recently, these artefacts were mostly understood as 'speaking for' servants, telling a mute tale of hard work and disparities of labour. However, in the past decade, the histories of servants themselves have been foregrounded in interpretations, alongside the material culture of service. Oral histories began to be taken

---

[50] Lowenthal, *The Past Is a Foreign Country*, 62.
[51] Samuel, *Theatres of Memory*, 169–202.
[52] Janet Hoskins, *Biographical Objects: How Things Tell the Stories of People's Lives* (New York: Routledge, 1998). See also Adrian Forty, *Objects of Desire: Design and Society, 1750–1980* (London: Thames and Hudson, 1986).
[53] Interview by the author with Sophie Brown, Education Officer, Wimpole Hall, Cambridgeshire, Aug 20, 2008.

from servants in the 1960s, and while initially these primarily focused on the decorative aspects of the house, social details were also recorded and became seen as significant in their own right. There is a repeated, sometimes melodramatic insistence amongst those involved with below stairs heritage performances that domestic service is an 'untold story'. Descriptions and tags, such as 'Blenheim Palace: The Untold Story', or 'Ickworth's hidden staircases and passages', convey the sense that this is 'a story that otherwise wouldn't be told': 'Visitors to the Audley End estate can now wander through a world that was never intended to be seen ... [servants'] voices have not been heard in the stories of the House—we want to change that.'[54] The kind of physical labour undertaken by servants frequently dealt with tabooed areas of physical existence, to do with the management of dirt and disorder. As tasks not normally done in public, this adds to the appeal of domestic service as a site of 'untold stories'.

The increasing interest in and knowledge of the untold stories of real historical individuals has encouraged a turn towards 'live interpretation' of below stairs—in other words, the employment of actors or volunteers who talk, often using the first person, about what it was to be a servant at a particular historical moment.[55] At Audley End House in Essex, the aim of English Heritage has been to restore the servants to history as full characters, rather than appendages of their employers: 'At Audley End visitors can see the real people who worked as servants here, with their personalities, aspirations, friendships and feuds.'[56] The performative element of being a servant—the rituals, front- and back-stage delineations—clearly lend themselves well to live interpretation. Its use has gathered pace, as more properties have opened up service rooms, and visitors came to expect and demand this aspect of the 'heritage experience'. Domestic service is thus extensively re-enacted within countless 'great houses', making it available to much wider circles than the dedicated devotees of military re-enactment that have tended to dominate historians' commentary on re-enactment. Commercial motives have reinforced historiographical trends inviting histories 'from below'. The new attention to servants has extended to the 'heritage' products sold to visitors; representations of domestic service are available for purchase in many forms, ranging from the reissued household manuals that advise how to manage the presence or absence of servants to the reproduction of 'domestic service humour' featured on greetings cards.[57]

Like the televisual productions, the great house re-enactments have tended to focus on quite a narrow historical period, mostly late Victorian and early twentieth century. The strong preference for the recent rather than the distant past is

---

[54] Andrew Hann, Audley End House publicity, available at http://www.english-heritage.org.uk/server/show/nav.19026, accessed July 10, 2009.

[55] Tivers, 'Performing Heritage'; C. Wilks and C. Kelly, 'Fact, Fiction and Nostalgia: As Assessment of Heritage Interpretation at Living Musuems', *International Journal of Intangible Heritage*, 3 (2008), 127–43, assess the potential of 'live interpretation'.

[56] Audley End House publicity, http://www.english-heritage.org.uk/server/show/nav.19024, accessed July 10, 2009.

[57] See, for example, the National Trust's 'Rules for Servants' tea towel, or the cards illustrated by *Punch* 'servant jokes' by the company At Your Service, and marketed by English Heritage.

motivated by the sense of familiarity and empathy that are consciously looked for within these narrations of domestic service. This contrasts to the 'Roman encampment' distancing approach of most televisual approaches, even where they deal with the relatively recent past. The 'when' of the great house or country house productions is also often dependent upon specific historical events, the contingent discovery of objects, or available oral histories. Many homes depict a specific date—such as the census year of 1871 at Shugborough Hall in Staffordshire—though others simply evoke a decade or even an era. At Wimpole Hall, the costumed servant-volunteers are simply Victorians 'in a very general sense', without the accuracy of a more specific production.[58] This more generalized approach is partly motivated by a sense pervading popular history that domestic service was a realm of ossified social relationships, often described as feudal, which were not subject to historical change. There are echoes of Tess Durbeyfield's relentless, historically static 'long row' of domestic servants in Frank Huggett's comments to a popular readership in the 1970s: 'the fundamental pattern of domestic service was so uniform from early Victorian times to the outbreak of the Second World War, that [servants'] remarks and reminiscences might often equally well come from the lips or pens of maidservants who had been born a century earlier.'[59]

Visitors to great houses are commonly invited to imagine themselves in the servants' roles. Their ability to make this imaginative leap is aided by the prominence of domestic service both in the British 'mediascape' and within contemporary family history. Many visitors identify with below stairs because their own family history includes servants, often in very recent generations; they comment, 'this is the basement where I belong.'[60] For some heritage properties, the production of family history and spaces for reminiscence are intimately incorporated into the learning programme; they keep records and help visitors initiate searches. Below stairs interpretations elicit and incorporate letters and evaluations that talk of visitors' own memories of using the artefacts displayed, or of relatives who had been in service. The links made to the present are powerful, and objects such as recipe books are foregrounded, to suggest the continuity in cooking and cleaning practices that stretches from the past to the present. Mike Sutherill of the National Trust, for example, deliberately used the local accents of servants in live interpretations to evoke familiarity and recognition amongst local visitors to Blickling Hall in Norfolk, avoiding the dramatic distances looked for by television producers.[61]

Part of the attraction of offering service as a key site of physical and emotional engagement with the past is practical; the artefacts of domestic service are cheap, and can be handled without much fear of damage. Stone hot water bottles, dolly sticks, and kitchen implements are not *objets d'art*. Frances Bailey, curator of Castle

---

[58] Brown interview, Aug 20, 2008.
[59] Huggett, *Life below Stairs*, 168.
[60] Brown interview, Aug 20, 2008.
[61] According to Mike Sutherill, the appeal of below stairs lies in the scale of the rooms and familiarity of the objects—these spaces are more like visitors' homes than anything in the grand 'upstairs'. Interview by the author with Mike Sutherill, Curator for the East of England, National Trust, Sept 12, 2008.

Figure 19. Ironing, Audley End House, English Heritage.

Coole in Northern Ireland, describes the kitchen there as 'a more robust space, one can be slightly more relaxed about how people use those spaces.'[62] And the daily activities of servants can be re-enacted by visitors in a way that the more elaborate activities of their employers cannot. However, curators are also motivated by a desire to promote empathy with the experiences and lives of below stairs historical characters through physical and sensual engagement. Empathic identification is sought through the 'hands-on' nature of the domestic service artefacts and the lack of barrier ropes in service rooms. Visitors are encouraged to imagine themselves in the servants' roles: 'there are artefacts just waiting to be handled. Are you strong enough to lift a fully laden housemaid's coalscuttle?', declares the publicity for the Below Stairs collection at Harewood House near Leeds.[63] The divides of servant-keeping households can be physically experienced by interaction with artefacts of service, and their associated physical tasks of scrubbing, mopping, food preparation, and washing clothes—experiences that many visitors will themselves have experienced in their everyday lives. The displays at Audley End House, for example, are motivated by a fascination with the physical aspects of servants' labour conveyed by the objects (Figure 19). Visitors are invited to:

Wander the kitchen and view the vast array of utensils used to prepare feasts for the Braybrooke family; see the intricate rope and pulley systems in the dry laundry, a vast

---

[62] Interview by the author with Frances Bailey, National Trust Curator, Northern Ireland, Oct 9, 2008.
[63] Publicity for Harewood House's Below Stairs collection, Leeds, available at http://www.culture24.org.uk/places+to+go/yorkshire/leeds/art23843, accessed June 10, 2009.

space with plenty of room for hanging freshly-scrubbed clothes; marvel at the authentic butter churn which would have given the dairy maid a regular morning workout, brought back to life and ready for a bit of elbow grease.[64]

Physical stimulation is also deliberately extended to other senses. Curators aim to offer tastes as a part of the heritage experience of kitchen spaces.[65] Smells are also reproduced; the Shugborough Estate website proclaims: 'The real smell of history can be experienced outside too, and we advise that you don't wander too close to the Servant's Latrine in the courtyard unless you have a laundry peg on your nose!!'[66] Domestic service has long been linked to the senses—particularly to noise and smell—and this has persisted in the greater attention to smells and tastes below stairs. As George Orwell has noted, smell has long evoked working classness in Britain, and it is foregrounded alongside the physical presence of bodies in live interpretation.[67] Visitors mention their fascination with the sweat of the actor-servants, and clearly the physicality of domestic service lends itself well to this kind of interpretation.[68]

In the main, the emotional tenor of these interpretations is positive, stressing belonging rather than exploitation. Most curators and performers rightly note that domestic service in a large house was a relatively good job. The hard physical labour and social inequalities are portrayed, but without a strong interpretive steer that these things were negative. Inequalities in dress, food, and modes of interaction are of course evident, and act as reminders of how pervasive the material expression of inequality was; nonetheless, they are rarely presented as scandalous or degrading. The interpretation at Audley End, for example, offers impressive detail on the lives of individual servants, and stresses both the hard work and the relatively high wages and good nutrition for great house servants. The financial independence of long-serving upper servants, and their ability eventually to employ their own servants, is highlighted. This nuances the clichéd, melodramatic presentation of the social gulf of domestic service that tends to dominate in television and cinema.

Despite these strengths, critics of live interpretation and living history have argued that these approaches tend to refuse the possibility of interpreting the past from the standpoint of the present. Historian Catherine Belsey regards attempts to make popular audiences 'participants' in history as curtailing critical historical interpretation. Live interpretation, she fears, provides 'experience' at the expense of 'meaning'. The empathy sought within the heritage sector can also erase the

---

[64] Audley End House publicity, available at http://www.english-heritage.org.uk/server/show/nav.19026, accessed July 10, 2009. Gaynor Bagnall's research has described how physical sensations are deeply connected to the emotional and imaginative responses to heritage presentations of the past (Bagnall, 'Performance and Performativity at Heritage Sites').

[65] Interview by the author with Colin MacConnachie, Head of Learning Services, National Trust for Scotland, Oct 3, 2008.

[66] Shugborough Estate publicity, available at http://shugborough.cmhosts.net/SQMAINRUSS-132, accessed Oct 15, 2008.

[67] On the relationship of smell to the past, see Janice Carlisle, 'The Smell of Class: British Novels of the 1860s', *Victorian Literature and Culture*, 29 1 (2002), 1–19; Constance Classen, David Howes, and Anthony Synnott, *Aroma: The Cultural History of Smell* (London: Routledge, 1994).

[68] Brown interview, Aug 20, 2008.

otherness of past times.[69] As Alexander Cook similarly points out, historical re-enactments can 'end up misrepresenting the past by implying that it is so easy to recapture.'[70] Perhaps in response, there is a foregrounding of the fallibility or partiality of sources in many of the heritage performances of domestic service. The question 'How do we know?' is publicly asked, disrupting the sensation of a total immersion in experience, and reminding the visitor of their location in the present.[71] Some curators opt to conserve rather than restore abandoned kitchens or service rooms, to show the passage of time, as at Newhailes House in Musselborough, or Castle Coole in Co. Fermanagh. Other below stairs interpretations are deliberately established as an unfinished historical project, to which visitors themselves can contribute. For Anna Forrest of the National Trust, the redevelopment of the basement of the Suffolk stately home Ickworth Hall is premised on the interpretation of being conjectural and evolving: 'we are hoping to stress that we haven't got all the answers... We'll say to people, "can you help, did your family work here, have you lived in the area a long time?"' The opening of service rooms has demonstrated the potential for a much more active, two-way engagement with visitors, who are seen as being able to interpret and comment in their own right, rather than simply be educated. Indeed, Anna Forrest points out that below stairs projects are leading to a rethink of the interpretation of other areas of heritage properties, and to interactivity and creativity spreading to the 'upstairs' areas.[72] The reflexivity of family history, drawing as it does on cultural and personal memory, sits comfortably with efforts to make the process of interpretation more overt.

However, the stress on fallibility can run counter to the strong emphasis on entertainment and fun, the joke of 'time travel', both as a historical feature of servants' lives and in the mode of presentation. One costumed interpreter commented: 'I don't think we're "hard done by servants" when we're doing things down there... We're here for entertainment value... I don't think they want to see chapped hands and steam and dirt and grot and what not.'[73] As for many televisual productions, it is more commonly the servant-keepers who are depicted as stifled by the social norms in which they lived: 'we mustn't assume that life below stairs was necessarily miserable... but upstairs could be far more miserable than downstairs.'[74] This emphasis on fun does, of course, run the risk of idealizing the social relations of service; it is not easy to portray relationships of conflict in what is

---

[69] Catherine Belsey, 'Reading Cultural History', in Tamsin Spargo (ed.), *Reading the Past: Literature and History* (Basingstoke: Macmillan, 2000), 103–17.

[70] Alexander Cook, 'Sailing on the Ship: Re-Enactment and the Quest for Popular History', *History Workshop Journal*, 57 (2004), 247–55.

[71] Shugborough, for example, has developed a 'Knowing Their Place' exhibition in 2006 to complement their live interpretation, which explains what kind of records were used in developing the below stairs experience attractions. Interview with Helen Johnson, Museum Development Officer, Staffordshire Arts and Museums Service, Oct 2, 2008. In the Audley End interpretation, curators have emphasized the snapshots of information provided by the census, actively engaging visitors in the flaws and resources of the research process.

[72] Interview by the author with Anna Forrest, Curator (Interiors) for the National Trust East of England, Sept 12, 2008.

[73] Brown interview, Aug 20, 2008.

[74] Sutherill interview, Sept 12, 2008.

intended to be an entertaining as well as educational experience. Instead, it is the familiar comic servant who provides the script that seems to work best; at Shugborough, the publicity declares: 'We can guarantee that the answers you get will surprise you, that the banter they spout will make you smile.'[75] Though the jokes made about servants as ill-educated and snobbish that predominated for much of the twentieth century are no longer resonant, the servant is still presented as a jester character, able to comment humorously and with license on the doings of their employers.

The comic servant, however, points to a danger that below stairs live interpretations treat servants as 'colourful', and fail to place them into history, in contrast to the treatment of employers who have been seen as meriting more accurate historical research and characterization (or indeed are saved from the indignity of characterization). Below stairs is occasionally seen as a realm where historical accuracy is, while desirable, not strictly necessary, and where anyone can don the cap and apron. As one educational officer commented:

It's . . . somehow easier to do it down there, you don't have to be quite as . . . accurate in the portrayal whereas if you were doing something upstairs in the house it's very much, you know, an above stairs domain, you've got your upper class people and the details would have to be . . really spot on.

When it came to impersonating servants, 'we're here for entertainment value rather than an accurate portrayal of the sort of life and times of servants, it's something for people to do hands on.'[76]

The employers of servants are rarely represented through live interpretation or oral histories. At Wimpole Hall, educationists foreground the class divisions associated with servant-keeping, though they admit, 'we don't actually do the other side of the coin, we don't really do the upstairs.'[77] In many cases this is because the house only became public after the death of the employer, so their voices are unavoidably absent from the oral histories that inform much of the recent live interpretation. In other cases, however, where the 'upstairs' family or visitors to the house survive, they frequently do not remember much about the domestic workings of the house, or had not encountered many servants, and so can play little part in the below stairs turn informing heritage interpretations. Domestic service at the higher social levels was designed to be invisible, and it was a license granted to employers that they need not notice or remember who waited on them at table.[78] As one child of a servant-keeping family put it, the servants 'don't seem to have left any kind of impression on me very much, they were there . . . but not.'[79] Many

[75] Shugborough Estate publicity, available at http://www.shugborough.org.uk/meet-the-characters-191, accessed Oct 15, 2008.
[76] Brown interview, Aug. 20, 2008.
[77] Ibid.
[78] My thanks to Bob Carter, National Trust consultant on the Blickling Hall below stairs oral histories, interviewed by the author on Aug 14, 2008, for this insight.
[79] Mrs West (b. 1899), Interview 6, in P. Thompson, *Family Life and Work Experience before 1918, Middle and Upper Class Families in the Early 20th Century, 1870–1977* [computer file], 2nd edn, Colchester, Essex: UK Data Archive [distributor].

servants in great houses saw their employers very rarely, and for lower servants, their social relationships were almost exclusively with other servants. Yet while social history aims to dignify 'neglected lives', there is a contrasting kind of dignity being offered to the aristocratic owners of these houses—they are usually represented through their formal portraits, their 'legacies' of public achievements, or through artefacts associated with public life. Visitors are not invited to smell their toilets, or project themselves into their physical being, though employers had toilets and bodies as much as servants did. By implication, their presence 'in history' is secure, and seems to need no re-enactment or empathy. Curators are sometimes sensitive to this; Frances Bailey of the National Trust in Northern Ireland comments that in recent years, social history has become a less significant influence on her work. She argues that 'history from below' has its own areas of neglect, and has limited the ability of the heritage sector to depict the employers of servants as 'ordinary people' too.[80]

Overall, interpretations of domestic service in great houses range widely in the 'memory work' they undertake and the responses looked for. While domestic service has been an ingredient of the 'cult of the country house' associated with conservative constructions of heritage of the 1970s and 1980s, the heritage performances of domestic service since the 1990s display a wider and more ambiguous set of engagements with the past. Heritage, clearly, is not simply a commodification of the past. As Raphael Samuel has argued, heritage has the potential to initiate open-ended conversations between the present and the past, and can engage the knowledge of both audiences and 'experts'. At best, heritage performances of domestic service can give us grounds to critically interrogate the historical basis for all kinds of nostalgia for the past. They can offer a reflexive, responsive realm in which visitors can engage physically and emotionally with an area of the past, and can make the past 'their own' through bringing personal memories and biographies to bear on the interpretation. Less productively, domestic service is sometimes a vehicle for melodrama, with its stereotypical scripts of villains and victims. It can be used as a realm of light entertainment in which the usual concerns about accuracy and authenticity can be suspended, fulfilling Raphael Samuel's fears that re-enactment 'invites us to play games with the past and to pretend we are at home in it, ignoring the limitations of time and space by reincarnating it in the here-and-now.' However, wholesale condemnations of heritage and nostalgia cannot distinguish the many ways in which these cultural resources can embody different kinds of 'memory work'.[81]

---

[80] Bailey interview, Oct 9, 2008. Her critical assessment of the promises and pitfalls of social history resonates with the recent critiques that stress the nostalgic impulses of social history. Frank Mort, for example, notes that social history 'has striven to lift the veil of darkness on ordinary lives. In doing so it has held out the hope that that which is gone, that which is so obviously lost, that which is past time, can be resurrected and conjured up before our eyes.' It therefore offers 'consolations of memory' that are not dissimilar from the re-enactments of the heritage sector (Frank Mort, 'Social and Symbolic Fathers and Sons in Postwar Britain', *Journal of British Studies*, 38 3 (1999), 353–84, esp. 359).

[81] See Samuel, *Theatres of Memory*, 195–6; Stuart Tannock, 'Nostalgia Critique', *Cultural Studies*, 9 3 (1995), 453–64.

NOSTALGIA AND 'UNTOLD STORIES'

If domestic service is 'good to think with', as Carolyn Steedman has suggested, it does not lend itself to any one narrative, but to many.[82] Domestic service conveys stories that are broadly organized around social class, but its narratives tend to be complex and capable of many interpretations. A narrative of working-class labour exploitation is often emphasized, accompanied by a sense of relief that the hard domestic labour of the past is no longer with us. Initially, it was this narrative of exploitation, pivoting on a sense of servants as socially, and sometimes sexually, victimized, that I expected to encounter most often in the course of this research. Sympathy and shame are, however, not the only emotions elicited. The narrative options in representing and enacting domestic service have proved unexpectedly diverse, and the emotional responses of the British public have been unpredictable. Nostalgia for a more organic community has been repeatedly evoked. In the 1960s and 1970s, in response to what historians have identified as the challenges of a more interventionist welfare state and public bureaucracy, a nostalgic past as 'a realm of imagined personal choice' became more actively deployed, both politically and in popular opinion.[83] It seems surprising that domestic service should feature within such nostalgia, standing for community and belonging, given its associations with constraint and exploitation. Yet somehow these different dimensions have been compatible; servants' memoirs could be read 'against the grain', to evoke intimacy and certainty. To some degree, former servants themselves were also equivocal, talking of their happiness and pleasure in their work alongside their sense of bitterness and loneliness. Elizabeth Young, for example, described her first job as a 'between maid' in Woking in 1919, aged 13, in heart-breaking terms: 'I hated it so much that a few times I scrubbed my arms with the wire brush used for cleaning pans, till they bled, hoping they would send me home. No such luck! A bit of Vaseline and a clean rag and that was that.' Yet she stayed in service all her working life, and looked back on her first jobs with affection, perhaps aiming to achieve personal composure through such memories: 'Happy days! I think I must have been one of the happiest teenagers alive.'[84] Reflecting this ambivalence, *The Guardian* commented in an editorial of 1971 on a sense of unease felt about domestic service, founded upon an awareness of exploitation in tandem with

---

[82] Carolyn Steedman, *Master and Servant: Love and Labour in the English Industrial Age* (Cambridge: Cambridge University Press, 2007).

[83] For Chris Waters, 'if modernity entails both dislocation and a rupture in historical consciousness, then one of its byproducts is nostalgia for older, presumably more settled ways of life—and for the places in which past lives were lived' ('Representations of Everyday Life: L.S. Lowry and the Landscape of Memory in Postwar Britain', *Representations*, 6 (1999), 121–50, esp. 138).

[84] Elizabeth Young, *Bessie Remembers* (Braunton: Merlin, 1989), 11–12. Oral histories are, of course, affected by the passage of time: 'The "voice of the past" is also inescapably the voice of the present too,' and memories can become organized retrospectively around nostalgia, or a sense of grievance, felt later in life (John Tosh, *The Pursuit of History: Aims, Methods and New Directions in the Study of Modern History*, Rev. 3rd edn (London: Longman, 2002), 199.

a 'sneaking guilty nostalgia for how things "below stairs" were always supposed to be'.[85]

The heritage performances of domestic service are perhaps best characterized not as a single site of memory, but through James Young's concept of 'collected memory'—the 'discrete and conflicting memories brought to converge in a common space' without necessarily resolving into a single story.[86] In keeping with other forms of popular history, they offer 'a number of suppressed meanings and narratives within stories which audiences can recover if they resonate.'[87] The emotions that accompany domestic service encompass pity, guilt, humiliation, titillation, laughter, and empathy. Comedy persists, and an association between domestic servants and a deep connection to physical bodies and smells, which is sometimes eroticized. There is a surprisingly subdued critique of domestic service within heritage performances and a strong sense throughout recent decades of attachment to service as an institution.

Ironically, though domestic service is commonly tagged as an untold story, its depiction is far from marginal in contemporary British society, and might be described as an overloaded site of memory. Yet within its heritage performances, certain narratives and lines of interpretation *are* relatively invisible. Nostalgia always requires a degree of forgetting and obfuscation in order to gain discursive purchase.[88] In the great houses, a feminist or women's history analysis, for example, seems curiously underplayed. This is partly explained by the continuing employment in great houses of men and boys, long after they had departed from smaller houses. Nonetheless, there was a preponderance of female servants even in stately homes. Female servants worked longer hours, and had their movements more strictly controlled. Men in service were more upwardly mobile than women, and tended to dominate the higher status or better paid roles. Where a parlourmaid was substituted for a footman, though very similar tasks would be carried out by these individuals, the wages paid would be reduced. The shift to a female staff was seen as a loss of status for an employer, motivated by economy.

There is a clear feminist dimension to acknowledging the burdens of domestic work that some women took on and others relinquished. This, however, is a narrative that has barely emerged within great house interpretations of service, even though men and women experienced service very differently. Some curators label feminism a dogmatic or factionalist approach, despite their awareness of the gender differences influencing how visitors interacted with a heritage display; one noted: 'it's grannies and mums who recognise the objects.' Yet he commented on feminism: 'I don't think in that way because I don't think of a difference between men and women...I'm not telling a particular factional story.'[89] The heritage

[85] *Guardian*, Feb 15, 1971.
[86] James E. Young, *The Texture of Memory: Holocaust Memorials and Meaning* (New Haven, CT: Yale University Press, 1993), xi.
[87] David Glassberg, 'Public History and the Study of Memory', *The Public Historian*, 18 2 (1996), 7–23, esp. 15.
[88] Tannock, 'Nostalgia Critique', 457.
[89] Sutherill interview, Sept 12, 2008.

interpretations since the 1970s have tended to focus on memories and legacies of class inequalities, rather than gender, despite the growing depiction of women's experiences and occupations within the 'everyday' heritage experience attraction.[90] Television producers have proved more willing to bring in a feminist dimension, aware of its dramatic potential and appeal to some audiences. However, speculation along these lines within programmes such as *The 1900 House* and the *Edwardian Country House* tended to be reinterpreted by audiences and the media, who found it hard to sympathize with Mrs Bowler or Lady Oliff-Cooper, and preferred to see servants as the 'victim' of social hierarchies, without gender differentiation. They also relished the humour of the servants' playful pranks and sexual banter, in contrast to the 'stifling formality' of upstairs.[91] Feminist historians have been attentive to the relations women of all social classes sustained amongst themselves, and the ability of some women to exert authority over others, but this has largely been a conversation amongst academic historians, and has rarely extended to public history. A feminist reading is hampered by its apparent inability to determine the clear-cut victim looked for within popular heritage performances.

Other aspects of service have also been downplayed within these performances, sometimes for practical reasons. In stately homes, the day and night nurseries in which children were raised tended to be on the upper floors of houses, and many of these floors are not open to the public because of safety restrictions and limited budgets. However, there is perhaps another motive for avoiding the nurseries, applicable to both TV and heritage houses, which is that the 'us and them' narrative of 'upstairs, downstairs' is made more complicated by the existence of other cross-cutting relationships. Previous chapters have suggested that the relationship between children and domestic servants is more emotionally and socially complex in contrast to the more straightforward authority of employers over employees. While the children of servant-keeping households were clearly regarded as socially superior to their servants, nannies and nursery maids also exercised authority. Emotional ties of love, dependency, and dislike, even shading into disgust, were perhaps most intensely felt between servants and children. The cross-cutting divides around age that were so important in social experiences of domestic service are hard to fit into overall narratives that tend to stress disparities of class or wealth.

Finally, middle- or lower-middle-class servant-keeping is also downplayed, and working-class servant-keeping is entirely absent. The nostalgic certainties of authority and belonging of *Upstairs, Downstairs* are not compatible with the status uncertainties, shared labour, and lack of delineation of roles in lower-middle-class households. The Bowler family of the *1900 House* was a rare exception; their servant-keeping in a Victorian suburban terraced house was an unusual reminder to many viewers still inhabiting such houses that servant-keeping may have been enacted in their own domestic spaces. It was, however, depicted as a failed experiment for the Bowlers. Revealingly, they attempted to establish styles of authority out of keeping with a lower-middle-class suburban family. There was no historical

---

[90] Littler and Naidoo, 'White Past, Multicultural Present'.
[91] See, for example, 'Time Travel: UPSTAIRS DOWNSTAIRS', *Sunday Mirror*, Apr 14, 2002.

awareness that mistresses of single-handed day servants commonly cleaned and cooked alongside their servants, and may have taken their meals together. The Bowlers joked about 'the staff', attempted to set up elaborate status differentials, and clearly lacked a script when interacting with Elizabeth. Lower-middle-class servant-keeping could not be enacted within the established framework of heritage performances of service, perhaps because it most closely resembles the contemporary employment of cleaners and nannies, and thus can be historically distanced less successfully.

CONCLUSIONS

The remembering of domestic service can shed light on contemporary uses of nostalgia, and to what ends narratives of the past are invoked in British society. It also helps us to move on from the sterility of the negative assessments historians have made of heritage and popular history, and points to some positive achievements in the representations and enactments of heritage. As Alexander Cook argues, the physical immediacy of living history and live interpretation can add to the understanding of the working lives of servants, and can potentially appeal to broad audiences through its 'visceral, emotional engagement with the past'. It is valuable to reconstruct past *mentalités* through engagement with physical spaces, material culture, and embodied experiences.

As an intimate site of memory, domestic service rarely stands in for larger entities such as a nation, but rather serves to cement individuals' and families' sense of heritage and the past. It is used as a means of projecting the self into a personal past through a physical and embodied medium of history; Shugborough's publicity asks the visitor to 'Look at the chores involved in the kitchen and laundry—would you have been suitable to be a maid or servant?'[92] This style of popular memory lends itself to the processes of individualization in contemporary society. A relationship to the past is established through individual or family perspectives, and in a domestic, intimate location, rather than through collective memory at the level of the nation or some other community. Looking at service usefully extends the literature on 'sites of memory' to these more intimate spaces. Family history seems to lend itself to the promotion of dialogue between past and present, since its trajectories must always end in the contemporary existence of the researcher. The exploration of domestic service within family histories can be an active, productive, and historically sensitive process of shaping personal identity and social belonging. Indeed, it seems more likely to serve this role than to offer, as some critics have feared, the satisfaction of a fantasized 'second identity', safely located in 'distant times' and perceived to be extraordinarily different from the twenty-first century.[93]

---

[92] Shugborough Estate publicity, available at http://shugborough.cmhosts.net/AdultGroupsPAGE2RUSS-150, accessed Oct 15, 2008.
[93] Samuel, *Theatres of Memory*, 247, 30.

These positive dimensions, however, are accompanied by less productive tendencies. Cook acknowledges that the empathy public history inspires obscures a critical distance from the past: 'it is extremely difficult to employ sympathy as a universal mode of engagement with the past. . . . a sympathetic identification with one group of people almost inevitably entails taking a critical distance from the perspective of some other group.'[94] Sympathy also tends to give a unidimensional view of complex social institutions. Other troubling dimensions to the heritage performances of domestic service include the persistence of somewhat tired scripts of sexual innuendo and comic banter, which probably add little to popular understanding of domestic service.[95] This problem is exacerbated by the tendency for all forms of heritage performance to base themselves not on the past, but on a dominant cultural representation—in other words, for all subsequent re-enactments of domestic service to be based primarily on televisual productions. Curators comment that for many people, *Upstairs, Downstairs*, or to a lesser extent, *The Remains of the Day*, remain the interpretative frames that mediate visitors' perceptions of heritage properties. This is unsurprising in a contemporary world of cultural literacy, and this phenomenon does not only affect heritage performances, but also oral histories and memoirs of servants themselves, and accounts of contemporary paid domestic work. Edith Baxter, for example, recalled during an interview conducted in 1998: 'Although we were only maids we were never treated like—you know. When I hear stories in books, I mean, I read stories and books about how people were treated years ago, even that "Upstairs, Downstairs." Our people were never treated like that.'[96] As Pierre Nora points out, memory has become 'powerfully televisual' in contemporary society, and he acknowledges that his *lieux de mémoire* tend to be self-referential rather than deeply rooted in 'reality'.[97] Media discussions of the rise of domestic employment in the 1980s and 1990s invariably used *Upstairs, Downstairs* as a cultural frame of reference, and illustrated their articles with cast photographs.[98] Heritage can sometimes become a discourse of 'hyper-reality', through the self-referential convergence of the different genres of heritage performance, which become less and less clearly demarcated, and

---

[94] Alexander Cook, 'The Use and Abuse of Historical Reenactment: Thoughts on Recent Trends in Public History', *Criticism*, 46 3 (2004), 487–96, esp. 490.
[95] One cultural production that suggests how these influences are received and interpreted is a youth film-making project, *Monument to Folly*, of Ickworth Hall in Suffolk, 2007. What emerges from this project is a primarily negative view of service and the social relations it set up; the servants emerge as both comic and authoritarian, prone to gossip and flirting, and competitive over questions of social status. The employers seem socially awkward and frivolous. The film's plot is based on an 'impossible love' between a servant and employer, using again the familiar cultural script of erotic impulses that cross class barriers in domestic service. There is a great deal of cultural cliché here, and the project very much follows in the steps of *Upstairs, Downstairs* in seeing servants as colourful, comic, sexualized characters.
[96] Edith Maude Baxter, City of Westminster Archives Centre, *Upstairs Downstairs* Collection.
[97] Nora, 'Between Memory and History', 17, 18.
[98] See, for example, 'The Spirit of *Upstairs Downstairs* Is Alive and Kicking in 21st Century Britain', *Birmingham Post*, Jan 20, 2007; 'Upstairs Downstairs', *Daily Mail*, Aug 12, 2004; 'The World of *Upstairs, Downstairs* Is Making a Comeback', *Sunday Telegraph*, Sept 10, 2000.

less grounded in either historical research or lived experiences.[99] It has been argued by many scholars that the past always exceeds our representations of it; in the case of domestic service, it seems that the representations of certain aspects may come to exceed the past.

Examining re-enactments of domestic service allows for some speculative thoughts about the relationships between past and present enabled by heritage performances. Public history, and particularly re-enactment and other forms of nostalgic history, has been accused of typically offering 'refined' or processed versions of public history, which aim to make the means of processing and interpretation invisible, and shed little light on the present.[100] Raymond Williams suspected that whatever the political valency of nostalgia, it could lead to forms of retreat, indifference, and 'withdrawal from any full response to an existing society'. However, its proponents insist that re-enactment can 'denaturalise the present' and promote dialogue between past and present. As Stuart Tannock argues, nostalgia can work to 'retrieve the past for support in building the future'.[101] Of course, the impact of popular history cannot easily be generalized, and is mediated by individual circumstances and reception. However, at least some heritage performances of domestic service have deliberately offered interpretative agency to audiences. I have suggested that the most promising element of the live interpretations offered by actor-servants or re-enactors perhaps lies in how well their performances lend themselves to attempts to make domestic service an ongoing story, connected to the present through family histories, contemporary domestic work, and the persistence of material artefacts or housework practices. More specifically, it seems helpful to ask to what extent do heritage performances of domestic service allow individuals to engage with contemporary issues of class identity? And do these performances encourage reflection on who undertakes domestic labour and under what conditions? Much of the evidence here must be fairly speculative, but I will look at these related aspects in turn.

Raphael Samuel speculates that heritage offers an escape from class—all can re-enact working- or upper-class pursuits and roles at will.[102] However, the compulsive interest in domestic service also suggests a continuing need to evoke and explain class amongst contemporary Britons. Class remains a persistent central concern of contemporary British socio-cultural life, yet one that is curiously opaque and elusive, operating 'through an almost unconsciously known and operated set of signals'. Widely heralded as being transcended in the decades of affluence after World War II, it nonetheless retains enormous resonance and emotive power in the fashioning of personal subjectivities and biographies. As Richard Hoggart described Britons in 1995: 'we are still branded on the tongue ... those who cannot instantly decipher your class from your clothes or bearing tend to assume you are a kind of

---

[99] Samuel, *Theatres of Memory*, 243.
[100] Jordanova, *History in Practice*.
[101] Tannock, 'Nostalgia Critique', 459; Raymond Williams, *The Country and the City* (Oxford: Oxford University Press, 1973), 140; Cook, 'Use and Abuse of Historical Reenactment'; Tivers, 'Performing Heritage', 198.
[102] Samuel, *Theatres of Memory*, 246.

nondescript. Then, because they are at that point compassless, they are likely to respond in a cagily indifferent manner, until they have found a bearing.'[103] Class, understood variously as a binary, tripartite, or complex gradation of social status, is conceived of as operating both historically and in contemporary British society; as David Cannadine points out, 'Britons are always thinking about who they are, what kind of society they belong to, and where they themselves belong in it.'[104]

Domestic service helps to locate 'class' in specific settings, and render it tangible in domestic furnishings, objects, and décor. The heritage performances of domestic service seem predominantly backward-looking, and locate the social institutions of the past as distant or foreign. Mrs Bowler's self-conscious performance of 'being middle-class' suggests its embarrassment and psychic discomfort. Tangible identities of class are not easily incorporated into contemporary subjectivities, or at least not openly. The comments of some of the participants of *The Edwardian Country House* re-enactments are also revealing. Most role-playing servants talked of the disparity between their current lifestyles and the 'distant past' of domestic service. Only one participant spoke of her own contemporary sense of class, and linked this back to domestic service. As a police control-room operator, Antonia Dawson reported to the *Sunday Telegraph*: 'A woman of my class would almost certainly have been in service and I would like to know what that meant.'[105] Though these kinds of links are made fairly sporadically, their presence suggests that domestic service has potential to supply historical insights for those navigating the personal and social imaginaries of contemporary class.

The unevenly distributed affluence of the 1980s and 1990s enabled the rise of employment of modern-day domestic servants, now renamed domestic workers—nannies, au pairs, gardeners, cleaners, and housekeepers, as previous chapters have discussed. Margaret Thatcher endorsed the return of middle-class employment of paid domestic workers in 1990, calling for modern career women to acquire what she termed (in nostalgic 1950s style) 'a treasure'—but this term deliberately left vague the nature of such arrangements, and whether they were to be undertaken for love or money.[106] In 1998, the *Birmingham Evening Post* estimated that 'almost every household in the West Midlands' buys in domestic services of some sort, from window cleaning to dog walking.[107] In the same year, the *Which? Guide to Domestic Help* estimated that the domestic service industry was as big as it had been before 1939, with 38 per cent of Britons employing some kind of help. Twenty-first-century estimates of the amount spent annually on domestic workers range from £4 to 9 billion, and around nine-tenths of this money was probably paid as 'cash in

---

[103] Richard Hoggart, *The Way We Live Now* (London: Chatto and Windus, 1995), 212, 199.
[104] David Cannadine, *Class in Britain* (New Haven, CT: Yale University Press, 1998), 23.
[105] Oliver Poole, 'Volunteers Join Real Life "Upstairs, Downstairs"', *Sunday Telegraph*, Aug 26, 2001.
[106] Margaret Thatcher, July 18, 1990, Pankhurst lecture to the 300 Group in 1990, available at http://www.margaretthatcher.org/speeches/displaydocument.asp?docid=108156, accessed May 5, 2009.
[107] 'Why Housework is Out of Fashion', *Birmingham Evening Post*, Oct 22, 1998.

hand'.[108] These social developments have added to the cultural fascination with domestic service, though in a mostly muted and unacknowledged fashion. It is perhaps this growth in domestic workers that motivated the setting of the 2004 Channel Four television series *What the Butler Saw* in the present, rather than making it a historical re-enactment. Yet there is little acknowledgement of contemporary experiences of domestic labour, paid or unpaid, in what have mostly been backward-looking heritage performances—they are, in Hochschild's terms, 'culturally light'. Where the cultural weight of the past is acknowledged, this is sometimes only to comment on the positive aspects of cleaning. Journalist Hannah Betts, for example, undertook a range of domestic service tasks as a 'maid for a day' at Audley End, and reported her experiences in a 2008 colour feature in *The Times Magazine*. She stressed the physical toil of the jobs she undertook, though also noted that 'for a woman who has not deigned to clean her own home for several years, it proves a curiously satisfying experience.'[109] Betts chose not to name the individual who cleans her house. Domestic service and modern domestic work both emerge in her account as hard work, but also avenues of social advancement or even pleasure; there is little acknowledgement of the structural inequalities facing either a single-handed servant or a contemporary cleaner.

Overall, few have wanted to draw links between contemporary domestic workers and servants of the heritage past. The retreat from the present perhaps makes it possible to employ, or be employed as, cleaners and nannies under informal, low-pay conditions that resemble aspects of early-twentieth-century domestic service, but which can be reconciled as egalitarian, friendly 'fictive' familial relations.[110] An employer of a nanny emphasized in *The Times* in 1967, 'Employing a servant doesn't fit in with my generation's way of life and attitudes. Janice Macmillan, my nanny, is more like a younger sister.'[111] The conditions of the most intimate and necessary labour that supports the reproduction of society is only engaged with as a feature of the past, and outside of feminist scholarship, is rarely debated or represented in the present, or even as relevant to the present. Heritage performances have preferred the pleasures of a 'terminated' past to the challenge of linking past and present experiences of paid domestic work in Britain.

---

[108] Lynn Brittney, *The Which? Guide to Domestic Help* (London: Which?, 1998); *Twenty-First Century Housekeeping* (Norwich Union, 2000), quoted in Alison Gray, 'Servant Culture Has New Look', *Scotsman*, Sept 13, 2000.

[109] Hochschild, *The Commercialization of Intimate Life*; Hannah Betts, 'Maid for a Day', *The Times Magazine*, June 21, 2008, 39.

[110] The study by Gregson and Lowe of 1980s paid domestic labour suggested the very widespread use of these strategies of 'fictive kinship', particularly in the care of children (*Servicing the Middle Classes: Class, Gender and Waged Domestic Labour in Contemporary Britain* (London: Routledge, 1994), 57). See also Rosie Cox, *The Servant Problem: Domestic Employment in a Global Economy* (London: I. B. Tauris, 2006).

[111] Ruth Miller, 'Wanted: New Image for an Old Profession', *The Times*, Dec 6, 1967, 9.

Conclusion

Knowing Their Place has argued that domestic service was central to core elements of twentieth-century British society—to the class, ethnicity, and gender elements of personal subjectivities and identities, to the expectations or aspirations of children and the sense of generational difference, to what was erotic or funny, and to what it was to make or inhabit a home. Domestic service has been understood as a form of knowledge, a site of self-fashioning, as well as an employment relationship and a site of physical and emotional labour. It formed 'an extensive ensemble of sites, practices, and occasions that mediate across the frontiers of the putative public/private divide.'[1] As a 'place' of self-fashioning and emotional investment, it was indeterminate, challenging, and mobile.

It is these qualities that have led the British media, in print, audio, and visual forms, to show a deep fascination with the relationships of domestic service, whether conveying laughter, lust, belonging, exclusion, or pathos. Domestic service emerges as a fetishized object for the late twentieth and early twenty-first centuries, a subject to which British socio-cultural life and individuals have compulsively returned. Mrs Peel, for example, was incensed (and fascinated) by the trappings of affluence displayed by her char in the 1930s:

When moving into our present house I employed a charwoman whose miserable appearance excited pity. I saw to it that she had milk to drink and tried to persuade her to have her teeth put in proper order. One afternoon her sixteen-year-old daughter appeared 'to help mother,' in reality to see what our house was like. She was dressed in a smart coat with a fur collar, a modish little hat, silk stockings, patent leather shoes, carried a *chic* handbag and umbrella, and was liberally powdered and lipsticked. Her clothes might have been worn by any young girl, but her face was not only common but vulgar, and further disfigured by two large strips of sticking plaster. I learned afterwards that my poverty-stricken looking charwoman was the wife of a man who earned £4 a week... The collective wage of the family was £8 16s. a week in money and something in kind, and the whole family, including two more children still at school, lived together in two rooms and a kitchen. They had a piano, which none of them could play, and an expensive wireless set, both bought on the hire purchase system. They proposed to buy a motor car on the same system.[2]

---

[1] I borrow here from Peter Bailey's description of the licensed public house, a site with interesting parallels to the 'public house' of servant-keeping: Peter Bailey, *Popular Culture and Performance in the Victorian City* (Cambridge: Cambridge University Press, 1998).

[2] Mrs C. S. Peel, *Life's Enchanted Cup: An Autobiography (1872–1933)* (London: Lane, 1933), 258–9.

There's disgust here, and an insistence on the embodied nature of class—the vulgar face that the smart clothes cannot disguise. The empty pretensions of the piano, the hedonism and eroticization of the fur collar, powder, and lipstick, all convey Mrs Peel's sense of a corrupted, disordered social world. Domestic work—the care of bodies and objects—has been widely imagined as a realm of disgust and erotic sensation. The near-constant revisiting of domestic service can be read as an attempt to assimilate and make pleasurable or titillating that which disgusts, which threatens to transgress boundaries, and to render its subjects vulnerable. In Sara Ahmed's perceptive analysis of the emotion of disgust, the compulsive return revolves around the need to 'achieve mastery' over that which disgusts.[3]

Yet this study has made clear that to associate service exclusively with disgust would be an impoverished reading. There is also anger in Mrs Peel's account at her pity proving misplaced, and a painful awareness of the power of the nosy servant to surveil the servant-keeping house (though her own nosings into her char's domestic circumstances and income went uncommented on). Mrs Peel experienced what it was to imagine herself through the eyes of others—the 'double consciousness' of domestic service. Buried slightly deeper is Mrs Peel's fear that her gift of milk and interest in her charwoman's teeth might have been found comic.

Though Mrs Peel was sure that fine clothes could not disguise the essential vulgarity of her char's daughter, her text is imbued with fear that the social differences domestic service had dramatized were no longer operative. Like many servant-keepers, she feared the eroding boundaries of social authority and hierarchy—the inapplicability of a sense of 'place'. As Homi Bhabha has written, 'all the affect, anxiety, disavowal comes not at the point at which differences can be binarized or polarized [but where] differences are . . . very small.'[4] This lack of social distance became particularly acute as the twentieth century progressed, though fictive kinship, or refusals of intimacy, allowed domestic workers to be retained in many upper- and middle-class homes. It has been a central argument of this study that domestic service did not only epitomize fears of the disintegration of class, but had a much broader role in dramatizing forms of otherness and social differentiation. Cross-cutting factors of religion/ethnicity, age, region, and gender set class in a complex social landscape. Service offered a multifaceted way of conveying social distinctions, observed in the dress, naming, speech, physical characteristics, morals, and emotional character of servants, masters, and mistresses.

Domestic service was also crucial to how it became possible to imagine forms of 'modernity' in the twentieth century. Associations between servant-keeping and forms of feudal or 'outdated' social relationships began to be made in the late nineteenth century. In the twentieth, it became increasingly possible to see 'modernity' as embodied in the middle-class labour-saving house and its linoleum floors, or in the private and intense emotional relationships advocated between

---

[3] Sara Ahmed, *The Cultural Politics of Emotion* (Edinburgh: Edinburgh University Press, 2004), 95.
[4] Gary Hall and Simon Wortham, 'Rethinking Authority: Interview with Homi K. Bhabha', *Angelaki: A New Journal in Philosophy, Literature, and the Social Sciences*, 2 2 (1996), 59–63, quoted in Beverley Skeggs, *Class, Self, Culture* (London: Routledge, 2004), 96.

mother and child and the intimacies of companionate marriage. Servants became intrusive in this reworked domestic realm, and seemed incompatible with secular, egalitarian, and democratic versions of the modern. Yet servant-keeping was more integrated into the imagining of twentieth-century modernities than previous histories have allowed. The material objects of modern lifestyles were frequently presented and understood through the prism of servant-keeping. The iconic telephone, symbolic of twentieth-century modernity, for example, was featured in *Good Housekeeping* as 'the month's selected appliance' for January 1930, and enthusiastically presented as ideal 'for room to room communication': 'the voice of the mistress can be clearly heard by the maid, who transmits her reply by telephone'.[5]

Domestic service was sometimes foregrounded by twentieth-century Britons with brazen optimism and validation, or with ironic laughter, but more often was silently or uneasily interwoven with a sense of personal and collective 'place'. It became harder to name servants, and polite euphemisms, jokes, or endearments predominated. Margaret Thatcher talked of 'reliable help' or 'a treasure'; Claire Smith, who worked for a retired doctor and his wife in Cambridgeshire in the early 1970s, was responsible for cleaning, cooking, answering the telephone, laying out her mistress's clothes, and care of the pet poodles. She called her employers 'Sir' and 'Madam', and termed herself (with irony) a 'general dogsbody'.[6]

The persistence of domestic service, whether named or not, was due in part to its practical role in enabling the claims that could be made to be modern and trendsetting, 'busy and useful' amongst the middle classes. Particularly for women, their self-identity rested on the ability to undertake creative or civic work. As the feminist writer Naomi Mitchison argued in *Good Housekeeping* in 1934,

> If a woman can do interesting and valuable work which humanity needs, either immediately or in the future, then it is obviously wrong that she should be prevented from doing this work and forced instead to spend her time mending and washing and cleaning-up, the kind of work which is peculiarly heart-breaking for the creative woman, because it has to be done over and over again and its result is not positive but only, at best, preventive.[7]

Housework was always viewed ambivalently, being simultaneously presented as modern and rewarding, yet dull and repetitive; middle-class women proved resistant to the 'modern' science and efficiency connotations of 'labour-saving' or 'servantless' forms of housework. 'The modern woman, whether she is a mistress or a maid-servant, is no longer content to spend the whole day cooking, washing-up, and chasing dirt from the home,' declared one domestic manual in 1930.[8] Yet

---

[5] 'A micro-telephone', *Good Housekeeping*, Jan 1930, 56.
[6] Margaret Thatcher, July 18, 1990, Pankhurst lecture to the 300 Group in 1990, available at http://www.margaretthatcher.org/speeches/displaydocument.asp?docid=108156, accessed May 5, 2009.; Mrs Claire Smith (b. 1946), interview with the author, Apr 19, 2007.
[7] Naomi Mitchison, 'Motherhood', *Good Housekeeping*, Jan 1935, 33–6, esp. 34.
[8] Mrs Robert Noble, *Labour-Saving in the Home: A Complete Guide for the Modern Housewife* (London: Macmillan, 1930), 8.

for all the apparent willingness to see commonalities between servant and mistress, 'the modern woman' was rarely imagined as anything other than a woman who delegated her housework to other women. There was a deep reluctance to renounce the cultural capital and material comforts of servant-keeping, though 'mistress', like 'servant', became an unattractive and rarely named social position.

A sense of status (or 'place') was a product of what has been termed the 'double consciousness' of domestic service, that imagining of oneself through the eyes of others. In later popular historical re-enactments this has become a process of imagining oneself in the *place* of others. Domestic service has long had a role in evoking fantasized pasts. This has played a part in the refusal to acknowledge contemporary tensions in domestic work relationships, or even their existence, preferring to locate these in a comfortably distant past. The fantasized servants and employers of the past are predominantly locked into scripted, historically inadequate relationships, variously imagined as exploitative, sexually charged, or comfortably secure. There are few resources to think about the shared work of the suburban house, or the intimacies or petty conflicts of the day servant working for neighbours or kin. The relationships of domestic service were intensely intimate, without necessarily being marked by disgust and otherness. Mrs Lilley, for example, was a general maid to Edwardian employers she called 'Mrs' and 'Mr'. They were probably of a similar background to her, and she recalled that they took a daily bottle of stout at 11am: 'I well remember they used to leave me a drop in the bottom of one of their glasses.' Their generosity amused rather than disgusted her, and suggests the potential intimacy of the relationship: 'I still have some of the presents they gave me. They always kept writing to me.'[9]

Servants did not passively internalize the many representations of their work as comic, erotic, degrading, or comforting. Their active participation in shaping these representations suggests the diversity of their own emotional responses. Some did deploy the cultural clichés of the dirty or sluttish servant, but often did so in ways that asserted their own difference and respectability. Others reversed the discourses, and accused their employers of gross, disgusting behaviour. Others simply did not identify their work as disgusting, and presented dignified narratives of satisfying labour, or even of glamour, despite the structural inequalities built into their employment: 'I was thrilled at the idea of wearing long print dresses and a mob cap,' recalled Miss Gearl, a former London 'tweeny'.[10] The interwar period witnessed change in experiences of domestic service, but there were also strong continuities with previous decades. Perhaps because of the renewed experiences of poverty for some young women and the constraints this imposed on them, the period has been read as one of *more* intense exploitation of servants, particularly as the state took measures to compel unemployed women into domestic service through training, emigration policies, and refusals to pay unemployment benefit to women who

---

[9] Mrs E. N. Lilley, AC 'My First Job' (1961), ERO T/Z 25/324.
[10] Miss E. Gearl, AC 'My First Job' (1961), ERO T/Z 25/304.

rejected domestic service employment.[11] However, some young women continued to choose domestic service in some circumstances, and those choices must be investigated and not simply seen as compulsion. The sense of career progress, of 'bettering oneself', continued to be important to some servants, whose aspirations were not simply thwarted by becoming servants. The interwar years were a period of increasing autonomy in negotiating interviews, references, agencies, and working conditions in service. Servants themselves had a clear sense that these decades were distinctively different. Mrs Sturgeon, working through the 1930s in various service jobs, reflected on her luck in serving 'at the end of that time, when servants were harder to get'.[12] Servants increasingly treated service as integrated with the rest of the labour market, or as a building block to a number of other occupations. Domestic service was not, as it has been portrayed, necessarily an intolerable job, only taken as a last resort and experienced as a realm of continuing girlish dependence; instead, it was a broad sector, employing very large numbers, with regional variations and internal stratification.

Nonetheless, the broad pattern of dislike to domestic service was clear. During periods of full employment, or where war service offered other opportunities, young women were quick to take other employment. Domestic service was particularly onerous in terms of the hours worked, the unpleasant and physically demanding nature of many of its tasks, and its constraints on dress, courtship, and leisure. Depictions of service as a modernized, dignified, pleasurable occupation were available—such as the National Union of Domestic Workers 1938 'Something Nice' (Figure 20), or the 1963 pamphlet *Service in the Sixties*, which promised opportunities to travel, and 'the fascination of seeing in real life the people you have read about in the newspapers and seen on television.'[13] For most young women, these were unconvincing depictions of a modern, servant-keeping lifestyle. Yet as Chapters 2 and 3 argued, servant-keeping continued to imbue some versions of modernity, even in the absence of traditional forms of domestic service.

Though great change can be seen across the twentieth century, the continuities in domestic service are worth dwelling on. Across the entire period, there were continuities in the types of tasks undertaken—despite the vast changes we might associate with the aftermath of World War I, the actual tasks undertaken in homes changed little. As Chapter 3 noted, labour-saving devices were available as mass-market commodities too late to be widely integrated with residential domestic service, and the hard work of scrubbing, scouring, minding children, and cooking persisted. Throughout the century, those working as servants found various strategies for dealing with the tensions of their socially complex and ambiguous role in middle-class homes. Some cathected with material objects, others found privacy and beauty in marginal spaces such as the sparsely furnished attics they occupied. Most simply

---

[11] Roy Lewis and Angus Maude, *The English Middle Classes* (Bath: Cedric Chivers, 1973 [1949]), 253; Lucy Noakes, 'From War Service to Domestic Service: Ex-Servicewomen and the Free Passage Scheme, 1919–22', *Twentieth Century British History*, 22, 1, 1–27.

[12] Interview with Mrs Sturgeon (b.1917), George Ewart Evans collection.

[13] 'Few British Girls Attracted to Domestic Work', *The Times*, Mar 26, 1963.

THERE IS MORE TO BE DONE

FIRST, the National Union of Domestic Workers is trying to make sure that every domestic worker in Britain gets these conditions at the very least.

SECOND, the Union's aim is to see that every domestic worker gets the chance to qualify for the guaranteed wage now being paid to the trained worker.

THIRD, the Union will work for better living accommodation for domestic workers.

FOURTH, the Union is giving free legal advice, accident benefit, holiday benefit and social activities to its members.

FIFTH, the next step is up to you—please turn over.

Figure 20. National Union of Domestic Workers pamphlet, 'Something Nice', 1938.

changed their jobs rapidly. Servants also found ways of working that resisted employers—the covert strategies of sullenness, clumsiness, or feigned stupidity. However, throughout this period we find these coexisting with more overt resistances amongst those young women, aware of their improving labour market position and stronger cultural and social resources. The 'long' first half of the twentieth century, from 1890 to the temporary residualization of service in the 1950s, reveals no passive acquiescence in domestic service as a total or all-consuming institution.

The aspirations of young women workers show change across the twentieth century, though poverty and state policies continued to constrain their choices and direct them towards domestic service. However, later generations of young working-class women simply opted for other kinds of work. There were clearly economic motives at play in this decision—the pay of domestic servants was less than in other occupations, and in some regions of Britain, the benefits in kind it brought had become less valuable as rehousing programmes and secure employment brought greater material affluence. The hours had always been excessive in comparison to factory or retail work, and Selina Todd has argued that young women withdrew their labour without regrets. However, the decision was also based on an assessment of status, and this incorporates more than simply an economic calculation, but a reshaping of the self. Young women welcomed their broader opportunities to establish their own domestic independence through marriage and motherhood, and thus to establish a competing vision of themselves as agents of domestic, or suburban modernity, as Judy Giles has argued.[14] This study does not try to trace which of these alternative 'modernities' became dominant; the triumph of suburban, affluent, egalitarian (yet often patriarchal) modern lifestyles seemed inevitable to sociologists of the 1970s, yet is clearly challenged by the inegalitarian, servant-keeping closing decades of the twentieth century. It seems more productive, however, to see twentieth-century modernity as being about the irresolvable, ongoing encounter between these competing, conflicting claims, dramatized throughout the century by domestic service.[15] Their encounter was always subject to nostalgic revisions, and as this study has shown, undertaken through resources of culture and memory. It is their irresolvable tensions that gives domestic service its compelling presence and contemporary cultural weight.

---

[14] Judy Giles, *The Parlour and the Suburb: Domestic Identities, Class, Femininity and Modernity* (Oxford: Berg, 2004). Wendy Webster's critical account of how these domestic identities were created through discourses of ethnicity is relevant here, and has influenced my own work: Wendy Webster, *Imagining Home* (London: UCL Press, 1998).

[15] As Georg Simmel has argued, conflict (and emotions like disgust) function in productive and constitutive ways—Simmel suggests the Indian caste system as emblematic of this process, but the competing modernities evoked by domestic service seem an equally good candidate. Simmel argues that 'it is hardly to be expected that there should be any social unity in which the converging tendencies of the elements are not incessantly shot through with elements of divergence' (Georg Simmel, 'The Sociology of Conflict: I', *American Journal of Sociology*, 9 (1903), 490–525, esp. 491). I am grateful to Christopher Clark for this insight and reference.

Private domestic service employment in Britain became much less widespread from around the 1950s, though it continued to provoke unresolved controversy as an absence that could not be forgotten in what were uncomfortably termed 'servantless' homes. Service continued to organize post-war middle-class domesticity, to entertain in popular and elite culture, and to fuel various kinds of fantasies. And in practical terms, the employment of non-residential or casual workers, or new arrangements such as the 'family guest' au pair, continued to supply domestic labour in large numbers of British homes. Issues of ethnicity and refugee status had always inflected the domestic service relationship, and continued to do so in more recent decades. The poet and writer Kate Clancy observed her early twenty-first-century relationship with her Kosovan cleaner with honesty and insight: 'Having someone clean my house makes me feel powerfully guilty and obliged. When I am typing upstairs...and Antigona is cleaning downstairs, each bang of the broom makes me blush.' Clanchy acknowledged that her resistance to employing a cleaner had been very easily overcome by a lingering sense of entitlement. She dealt with her guilty emotional response by helping Antigona with her immigration and welfare claims, perceiving that 'I liked the sense of so powerfully obliging someone, tying them close to me with gratitude.'[16] Yet rarely were such emotions and practices set in the context of the long-standing set of discourses around the employment of servants in British homes, since all parties had an investment in distancing these forms of workers from the indignities and conflicts associated with domestic service. This study has placed these late-twentieth- and early-twenty-first-century relationships into a longer narrative, linking them through the persistent cultural, emotional, and material presence of domestic service, and demonstrating the many ways in which this site of labour has shaped how British society is imagined and 'placed' in historical time.

---

[16] Kate Clanchy, *Antigona and Me* (Basingstoke: Picador, 2009), 24, 31.

Bibliography

PRIMARY SOURCES

*******, Right Hon. the Countess of, *Mixing in Society. A Complete Manual of Manners* (London/New York: Routledge, 1870).
A Member of the Aristocracy, *The Management of Servants: A Practical Guide to the Routine of Domestic Service* (London: Warne, 1880).
A Mistress and a Mother, *At Home* (London: Macintosh, 1874).
Adcock, Arthur St John, *Wonderful London*, (London: Amalgamated Press, 1926).
An Engineer and his Wife, *The Ideal Servant-Saving House* (London: Chambers, 1918).
Association for Trained Charwomen, 'Annual Report 1904–5' (London: Women's Industrial Council, 1905).
Banks, Elizabeth, *Autobiography of a Newspaper Girl* (London: Methuen, 1902).
Beerbohm, Max, *Servants* (1918).
Belcher, George, *Potted Char and Other Delicacies* (London: Methuen, 1933).
Black, Clementina, *A New Way of Housekeeping* (London: Collins, 1918).
Bloom, Ursula, *Mrs Bunthorpe's Respects: A Chronicle of Cooks* (London: Hutchinson, 1963).
Booth, Charles, *Life and Labour of the People in London* (London: Macmillan, 1902).
Boumphrey, Geoffrey Maxwell, *Your House and Mine* (London: Allen and Unwin, 1938).
Brandt, Bill, *The English at Home* (London: B. T. Batsford, 1936).
Breese, Charlotte, and Hilaire Gomer, *The Good Nanny Guide: The Complete Handbook on Nannies, Au-Pairs, Mother's Helps and Childminders* (London: Century, 1991).
Brereton, Mrs M. A. Cloudesley, *Domestic Service as a Career for Educated Women: How the Substitution of Gas for Coal Affects the Domestic Service Problem* (London: National Gas Congress and Exhibition, 1913).
'British Weekly' Commissioners, The (eds), *Toilers in London, or, Inquiries Concerning Female Labour in the Metropolis*, ed. John Law (London: Hodder and Stoughton, 1889).
Brittain, Vera, *Testament of Youth: An Autobiographical Study of the Years 1900–1925* (London: Victor Gollancz, 1933).
Brittney, Lynn, *The Which? Guide to Domestic Help* (London: Which?, 1998).
Brown, Pam, *Mutterings of a Char* (Watford: Exley, 1984).
Burnham, Dorothy, *Through Dooms of Love* (London: Chatto and Windus, 1969).
Butler, C. V., *Domestic Service: An Enquiry by the Women's Industrial Council* (London: Bell, 1916).
Caddy, Florence, *Household Organization* (London: Chapman and Hall, 1877).
Census of England and Wales 1931, *General Report* (London: HMSO, 1950).
Census of England and Wales 1951, *Occupation Tables* (London: HMSO, 1956).
——, *General Report* (London: HMSO, 1958).
Census of Scotland 1921, vol. II (Edinburgh: HMSO, 1923).
Census of Scotland 1951, *Occupations and Industries*, vol. IV (Edinburgh: HMSO, 1956).
Chamberlain, Mary, *Fenwomen: A Portrait of Women in an English Village* (London: Virago, 1975).
Chesterton, Ada, *Women of the Underworld* (London: Stanley Paul, 1928).

Clifford, Henry Dalton, *Country Life Book of Houses for Today* (London: Country Life, 1963).
Cooper, Lettice, *The New House* (London: Virago, 1987 [1936]).
Daily Mail Ideal Labour-Saving Home (London: Associated Newspapers, 1920).
Davies, Agnes Maud, *A Book with Seven Seals: A Victorian Childhood* (London: Chatto and Windus, 1974).
Delafield, E. M., *Diary of a Provincial Lady* (London: The Folio Society, 1979).
Dewan, K., *The Girl* (London: Bell, 1921).
Dickens, Monica, *One Pair of Hands* (London: Joseph, 1939).
Eaton, Constance, 'The Gordian Knot of Domestic Service', *Good Housekeeping* (1930), 48–9.
Ellis, Havelock, *Studies in the Psychology of Sex* (Philadelphia: Davies, 1897).
Emmott, Gertrude, *Report of the Women's Advisory Committee of the Ministry of Reconstruction on the Domestic Service Problem* (London: HMSO Cmd. 67, 1919).
Evans, Joan, *Prelude and Fugue* (New York: Museum Press, 1964).
Findlater, Mary, and Jane Helen Findlater, *Content with Flies* (London: Smith, Elder, 1916).
Firth, Violet M., *The Psychology of the Servant Problem: A Study in Social Relationships* (London: Daniel, 1925).
Foley, Winifred, *A Child in the Forest* (London: Futura, 1974).
Frazer, Mrs J. G., *First Aid to the Servantless* (Cambridge: Heffers, 1913).
Frederick, Christine, *The New Housekeeping: Efficiency Studies in Home Management* (Garden City, NY: Doubleday, Page, 1913).
Fremlin, Celia, *The Seven Chars of Chelsea* (London: Methuen, 1940).
Gavron, Hannah, *The Captive Wife: Conflicts of Housebound Mothers* (London: Routledge & Keagan Paul, 1966).
General Register Office, *1951 Census of England and Wales, General Report* (London: HMSO, 1958).
Gibbs, Rose, *In Service: Rose Gibbs Remembers* (Bassingbourn: Archives for Bassingbourn and Comberton Village Colleges, 1981).
Gilman, Charlotte Perkins, *The Home: It's Work and Influence* (New York, 1903).
Gloag, John, and Leslie Mansfield, *The House We Ought to Live In* (London: Duckworth, 1923).
Graves, Robert, *Goodbye to All That* (London: Penguin, 1976 [1929]).
Gray, N., *The Worst of Times: An Oral History of the Great Depression in Britain* (London: Wildwood House, 1985).
Greer, Germaine, *The Female Eunuch* (London: Flamingo, 1993).
Greig, Cicely, *Ivy Compton-Burnett: A Memoir* (London: Garnstone Press, 1972).
Grigson, Geoffrey, *The Crest on the Silver* (London: Cresset Press, 1950).
Hamilton, Peggy, *Three Years or the Duration: The Memoirs of a Munition Worker, 1914–1918* (Wellington: Reed, 1978).
Hammond, Paul, *French Undressing: Naughty Postcards from 1900 to 1920* (London: Jupiter Books, 1976).
Hardy, Thomas, *Tess of the D'Urbervilles* (London: Vintage Classic, 2008).
Harrison, Rosina, *Rose: My Life in Service* (London: Cassell, 1975).
Hartnell, Norman, *The Complete Housewife* (London: Evans, 1960).
Haweis, Olive, *Four to Fourteen* (London: Robert Hale, 1939).
Hendry, Morrison, *Planning Your Home for Tomorrow* (London: Faber, 1950).
Hobbs, May, *Born to Struggle* (London: Quartet Books, 1973).

Hughes, M. Vivian, *A London Family between the Wars* (Oxford: Oxford University Press, 1940).
Inchfawn, Fay, *Homely Talks of a Homely Woman* (London: Ward, Lock, 1923).
Ingham, Mary, *Now We Are Thirty: Women of the Breakthrough Generation* (London: Eyre Methuen, 1981).
James, John, *The Memoirs of a House Steward* (London: Bury, Holt, 1949).
Johnson, Mrs, *The Bride Elect* (London: Hand and Heart, 1878).
Joyce, James, *Dubliners* (London: Penguin, 1996).
Keppel, Sonia, *Edwardian Daughter* (London: Hamilton, 1958).
Kilvert, Adelaide Sophia, *Home Discipline; or, Thoughts on the Origin and Exercise of Domestic Authority. By a Mother, and Mistress of a Family* (London, 1841).
King, Aileen, *Better Home Management* (London: Mills and Boon, 1961).
L., A. E. L., *How She Managed without a Servant* (Liverpool: J. Burniston, 1883).
L'Estrange, A. G., *A History of English Humour* (New York: Burt Franklin, 1970).
Leverton, Edith Waldemar, *Housekeeping Made Easy: A Handbook of Household Management Appealing Chiefly to the Middle-Class Housekeeper* (London: George Newnes, 1910).
Lewis, Roy, and Angus Maude, *The English Middle Classes* (Bath: Cedric Chivers, 1973 [1949]).
Linton, Eliza Lynn, *Ourselves. A Series of Essays on Women* (London: Chatto and Windus, 1884).
London, Jack, *The People of the Abyss* (London: Isbister, 1903).
Macrae, Mrs. Stuart, *Cassell's Household Guide: A Complete Cyclop'Dia of Domestic Economy* (London: Waverly Book, 1912).
Markham, Violet, *Return Passage* (Oxford: Oxford University Press, 1953).
——, and Florence Hancock, *Report on the Organisation of Private Domestic Employment* (London: HMSO, 1944).
Masterman, C[harles]. F[rederick]. G., *The Condition of England* (London: Methuen, 1960 [1909]).
——, *England after War. A Study* (London: Hodder and Stoughton, 1922).
Mitchison, Naomi, *The Home and a Changing Civilisation* (London: John Lane, 1934).
Mortimer, Geoffrey, *The Blight of Respectability. An Anatomy of the Disease and a Theory of Curative Treatment* (London: University Press, 1897).
Mullins, Samuel and Gareth Griffiths, *Cap and Apron: An Oral History of Domestic Service in the Shires, 1880–1950* (Leicester: Leicestershire Museums, 1986).
Noakes, Daisy, *The Town Bee-Hive: A Young Girl's Lot in Brighton, 1910–1934* (Brighton: QueenSpark Books, 1975).
Noble, Mrs. Robert, *Labour-Saving in the Home: A Complete Guide for the Modern House-wife* (London: Macmillan, 1930).
Norton, Margaret, *Jam Tomorrow: Portrait of a Daily Help* (London: Victor Gollancz, 1962).
Oliver, Kathlyn, *Domestic Servants and Citizenship* (London: People's Suffrage Federation, 1911).
Orwell, George, *The Road to Wigan Pier*, in Davison (ed.), *Orwell's England* (London: Penguin, 2001).
Panton, J. E., *From Kitchen to Garret Hints for Yong Householders* (London: Ward and Downey, 1888).
——, *A Gentlewoman's Home* (London: Gentlewoman Offices, 1896).
Peck, Winifred, *Home for the Holidays* (London: Faber and Faber, 1955).
——, *House-Bound* (London: Persephone Books, 2007 [1942]).
Peel, Mrs C. S., *The Labour Saving House* (London: John Lane, 1917).
——, *Life's Enchanted Cup: An Autobiography (1872–1933)* (London: John Lane, 1933).
Porter, N., *Webster's Revised Unabridged Dictionary* (Springfield, MA: Merriam, 1913).
Powell, Margaret, *Below Stairs* (London: Pan Books, 1969).

——, *My Mother and I* (London: Joseph, 1972).
Praga, Mrs., *How to Keep House on £200 a Year* (London: Arthur Pearson, 1904).
Raverat, Gwen, *Period Piece: A Cambridge Childhood* (London: Faber and Faber, 1952).
Rennie, Jean, *Every Other Sunday: The Autobiography of a Kitchenmaid* (London: Barker, 1978 [1955]).
Reynolds, Stephen, *A Poor Man's House* (Oxford: Oxford University Press, 1982).
Roberts, Nickie, *The Front Line* (London: Grafton Books, 1986).
Rowntree, Seebhom, *Poverty: A Study of Town Life* (London: Macmillan, 1902).
Royden, A. Maude, *Downward Paths: An Inquiry into the Causes Which Contribute to the Making of the Prostitute* (London: G. Bell, 1916).
Sanders, Deidre, and Jane Reed, *Kitchen Sink, or Swim? Women in the Eighties—The Choices* (Harmondsworth: Penguin, 1982).
Schreiner, Olive, *Woman and Labour* (London: Virago, 1978 [1911]).
Scott Moncrieff, M. C., *Yes Ma'am! Glimpses of Domestic Service, 1901–51* (Edinburgh: Albyn Press, 1984).
Segal, Lore, *Other People's Houses* (London: Bodley Head, 1974 [1965]).
Sims, George, *Living London* (London: Cassell, 1901).
Smith, H. Llewellyn, *The New Survey of London Life and Labour* (London: King, 1929).
Storey, Joan, *Running a Home: A Guide to Efficient Household Management* (London: Faber and Faber, 1968).
Strachey, Ray, *The Cause: A Short History of the Women's Movement in Great Britain* (London: Virago, 1928).
——, *Our Freedom and Its Results* (London: Hogarth Press, 1936).
Todd, Dorothy, and Raymond Mortimer, *The New Interior Decoration: An Introduction to Its Principles, and International Survey of Its Methods* (London: Batsford, 1929).
Wallace, Mrs Agatha Willoughby, *Woman's Kingdom: Containing Suggestions as to Furnishing, Decorating, and Economically Managing the Home for People of Limited Means* (London: Archibald Constable, 1905).
Walter, *My Secret Life* (Wordsworth editions, 1996).
Wayne, Jenifer, *Brown Bread and Butter in the Basement: A 'Twenties Childhood* (London: Victor Gollancz, 1973).
White, Florence, *A Fire in the Kitchen: The Autobiography of a Cook* (London, 1938).
Williams, Sheila, and F. D. Flower, *Foreign Girls in Hendon: a Survey* (London: Hendon Overseas Friendship Association, 1961).
Wilson, Amrit, *Finding a Voice: Asian Women in Britain* (London: Virago, 1978).
Wood, E. M., *Report to the Committee Appointed to Enquire into the Present Conditions as to the Supply of Female Domestic Servants by the Ministry of Labour* (London: HMSO, 1923).
Wortley, Richard, *Skin Deep in Soho* (London: Jarrolds, 1969).
Wylde, Mary, *A Housewife in Kensington* (London: Longmans, Green, 1937).
Young, Elizabeth, *Bessie Remembers* (Braunton: Merlin, 1989).

SECONDARY SOURCES

Adonis, Andrew and Stephen Pollard, *A Class Act: The Myth of Britain's Classless Society* (London: Penguin, 1997).
Ahmed, Sara, *The Cultural Politics of Emotion* (Edinburgh: Edinburgh University Press, 2004).

Aiken, Diane, *The Central Committee on Women's Training and Employment: Tackling the Servant Problem, 1914–1945* (Oxford: Oxford Brookes University, 2002).

Anderson, Benedict, *Imagined Communities: Reflections on the Origins and Rise of Nationalism* (London: Verso, 1982).

Anderson, Gregory, *The White Blouse Revolution: Female Office Workers since 1870* (Manchester: Manchester University Press, 1988).

Ashplant, T. G. and Gerry Smyth, *Explorations in Cultural History* (London: Pluto, 2001).

Assmann, Jan, 'Collective Memory and Cultural Identity', *New German Critique*, 65 (1995), 125–33.

Attfield, Judy and Pat Kirkham, *A View from the Interior: Feminism, Women and Design History* (London: Women's Press, 1989).

Bagnall, Gaynor, 'Performance and Performativity at Heritage Sites', *Museum and Society*, 1 2 (2003), 87–103.

Bakhtin, Mikhail, *Rabelais and His World* (Bloomington: Indiana University Press, 2008 [1968]).

Bailey, Jenna, *Can Any Mother Help Me?* (London: Faber and Faber, 2007).

Bailey, Peter, 'Ally Sloper's Half Holiday: Comic Art in the 1880s', *History Workshop*, 16 (1983), 4–31.

——, 'Conspiracies of Meaning: Music-Hall and the Knowingness of Popular Culture', *Past and Present*, 144 (1994), 138–70.

——, *Popular Culture and Performance in the Victorian City* (Cambridge: Cambridge University Press, 1998).

Banerjee, Swapna M., *Men, Women, and Domestics: Articulating Middle-Class Identity in Colonial Bengal* (New Delhi/Oxford: Oxford University Press, 2004).

Barthes, Roland *Mythologies* (London: Cape, 1972).

Baxendale, John and Christopher Pawling, *A Feeling for Tradition and Discipline: Conservatism and the Thirties in Remains of the Day* (Basingstoke: Macmillan, 1996).

Beaumont, Caitriona, 'Citizens Not Feminists: The Boundary Negotiated between Citizenship and Feminism by Mainstream Women's Organisations in England, 1928–39', *Women's History Review*, 9 2 (2000), 411–29.

Beddoe, Deirdre, *Munitionettes, Maids and Mams: Women in Wales, 1914–1939* (Cardiff: University of Wales Press, 1991).

Bingham, Adrian, *Gender, Modernity, and the Popular Press in Inter-War Britain* (Oxford: Clarendon Press, 2004).

——, *Family Newspapers?: Sex, Private Life, and the British Popular Press 1918–1978* (Oxford: Oxford University Press, 2009).

Bonnell, Victoria E., Lynn Avery Hunt, and Richard Biernacki, *Beyond the Cultural Turn: New Directions in the Study of Society and Culture* (Berkeley: University of California Press, 1999).

Bourdieu, Pierre, *Pascalian Meditations* (Stanford: Stanford University Press, 1997).

Bourke, Joanna, *Housewifery in Working-Class England, 1860–1914* (London: Arnold, 1998).

Bowden, Sue M., 'The Consumer Durables Revolution in England 1932–1938: A Regional Analysis', *Explorations in Economic History*, 25 1 (1988), 42–59.

—— and Paul Turner, 'The Demand for Consumer Durables in the United Kingdom in the Interwar Period', *Journal of Economic History*, 53 2 (1993), 244–58.

Boxer, Marilyn J., *Rethinking the Socialist Construction and International Career of the Concept 'Bourgeois Feminism'* (London: Routledge, 2010).

Branca, Patricia, *Silent Sisterhood: Middle Class Women in the Victorian Home* (London: Croom Helm, 1975).
Breitenbach, E., *The World Is Ill-Divided: Women's Work in Scotland in the Nineteenth and Early Twentieth Centuries* (Edinburgh: Edinburgh University Press, 1990).
Bremmer, J., *A Cultural History of Humour: From Antiquity to the Present Day* (Cambridge: Polity Press, 1997).
Brooke, Stephen, 'Gender and Working Class Identity in Britain During the 1950s', *Journal of Social History*, 34 4 (2001), 773–96.
Broughton, Trev Lynn and Ruth Symes, *The Governess: An Anthology* (Stroud: Sutton, 1997).
Brown, Simon, 'Early Cinema in Britain and the Smoking Concert Film', *Early Popular Visual Culture*, 3 2 (2005), 165–78.
Buettner, Elizabeth, *Empire Families: Britons and Late Imperial India*, (Oxford: Oxford University Press, 2004).
Burke, Peter, *What Is Cultural History?* (Cambridge: Polity Press, 2004).
Burrell, Kathy, *Polish Migration to the UK in the 'New' European Union: After 2004* (Farnham: Ashgate, 2009).
Cabrera, M. A., *Postsocial History: An Introduction* (Lanham, MD: Lexington Books, 2004).
Cannadine, David, *Class in Britain* (New Haven, CT: Yale University Press, 1998).
Carlisle, Janice, 'The Smell of Class: British Novels of the 1860s', *Victorian Literature and Culture*, 29 1 (2002), 1–19.
Castoriadis, Cornelius, *The Imaginary Institution of Society* (Cambridge: Polity Press, 1987).
Clanchy, Kate, *Antigona and Me* (Basingstoke: Picador, 2009).
Clapson, Mark, 'Working-Class Women's Experiences of Moving to New Housing Estates in England since 1919', *Twentieth Century British History*, 10 3 (1999), 345–65.
Clark, Anna, *Scandal: The Sexual Politics of the British Constitution* (Princeton: Princeton University Press, 2004).
Classen, Constance, David Howes, and Anthony Synnott, *Aroma: The Cultural History of Smell* (London: Routledge, 1994).
Cocks, H[arry]. G., 'Saucy Stories: Pornography, Sexology and the Marketing of Sexual Knowledge in Britain, c. 1918–70', *Social History*, 29 4 (2004), 465–84.
——, 'Modernity and the Self in the History of Sexuality', *Historical Journal*, 49 4 (2006), 1211–28.
Cohen, Deborah, *Household Gods: The British and Their Possessions* (New Haven, CT: Yale University Press, 2006).
Colligan, Collette, *The Traffic in Obscenity from Byron to Beardsley: Sexuality and Exoticism in Nineteenth Century Print Culture* (Basingstoke: Palgrave, 2006).
Collins, Marcus, *Modern Love: An Intimate History of Men and Women in Twentieth-Century Britain* (London: Atlantic Books, 2003).
Cook, Alexander, 'Sailing on the Ship: Re-Enactment and the Quest for Popular History', *History Workshop Journal*, 57 (2004), 247–55.
——, 'The Use and Abuse of Historical Reenactment: Thoughts on Recent Trends in Public History', *Criticism*, 46 3 (2004), 487–96.
Cook, Hera, *The Long Sexual Revolution: English Women, Sex and Contraception, 1800–1975* (Oxford: Oxford University Press, 2004).
Coser, Lewis A., 'Servants: The Obsolescence of an Occupational Role', *Social Forces*, 52 1 (1973), 31–40.
Cowan, Ruth Schwartz, *More Work for Mother: The Ironies of Household Technology from the Open Hearth to the Microwave* (New York: Basic Books, 1983).

Cowman, Krista and Louise Jackson, *Introduction: Women's Work, a Cultural History* (Aldershot: Ashgate, 2005).
Cox, Rosie, *The Servant Problem: Domestic Employment in a Global Economy* (London: I. B. Tauris, 2006).
——, 'The Au Pair Body: Sex Object, Sister or Student?', *European Journal of Women's Studies*, 14 3 (2007), 281–96.
Crossick, Geoffrey, *The Lower Middle Class in Britain* (London: Croom Helm, 1977).
Darnton, Robert, *Workers Revolt: The Great Cat Massacre of the Rue Saint-Severin* (London: Penguin, 2001).
Davidoff, Leonore, *Where the Stranger Begins: The Question of Siblings in Historical Analysis* (New York: Routledge, 1995).
——, *Worlds Between: Historical Perspectives on Class and Gender* (New York: Routledge, 1995).
—— and Catherine Hall, *Family Fortunes: Men and Women of the English Middle Class, 1780–1850* (London: Hutchinson, 1987).
——, Megan Doolittle, Janet Fink, and Katherine Holden, *The Family Story: Blood, Contract and Intimacy, 1830–1960* (London: Longman, 1999).
Davidson, Caroline, *A Woman's Work Is Never Done. A History of Housework in the British Isles, 1650–1950* (London: Chatto and Windus, 1982).
Davies, Christie, *Jokes and Their Relation to Society* (New York: Mouton de Gruyter, 1988).
Davin, Anna, *Growing up Poor: Home, House and Street in London* (London: Rivers Oram Press, 1996).
Davis, Tracy C., *The Actress in Victorian Pornography* (Athens: Ohio University Press, 1992).
Dawes, Frank V., *Not in Front of the Servants: Domestic Service in England 1850–1939* (London: Wayland, 1973).
Dean, Carolyn, *The Frail Social Body: Pornography, Homosexuality, and Other Fantasies in Interwar France* (Berkeley: University of California Press, 2000).
Delaney, Enda, *The Irish in Post-War Britain* (Oxford: Oxford University Press, 2007).
Delap, Lucy, 'Campaigns of Curiosity: Class Crossing and Role Reversal in British Domestic Service, c.1890–1950', *Left History*, 12 2 (2007), 33–63.
——, Abigail Wills, and Ben Griffin (eds), *The Politics of Domestic Authority in Britain since 1800* (Basingstoke: Palgrave Macmillan, 2009).
Dickson, Tony and James H. Treble, *People and Society in Scotland. 3, 1914–1990* (Edinburgh: John Donald, 1992).
Douglas, Mary, *Purity and Danger: An Analysis of the Concept of Pollution and Taboo* (London: Routledge, 2002).
Du Bois, W. E. B., *The Souls of Black Folk* (Oxford: Oxford University Press, 2008 [1897]).
Dudden, Faye, 'Experts and Servants: The National Council on Household Employment and the Decline of Domestic Service in the Twentieth Century', *Journal of Social History*, 20 (1986), 269–89.
Dyhouse, C., 'Graduates, Mothers and Graduate Mothers: Family Investment in Higher Education in Twentieth-Century England', *Gender and Education*, 14 5 (2002), 325–36.
Eco, Umberto, *The Frames of Comic Freedom* (Berlin: Mouton, 1984).
Edwards, Arthur M., *The Design of Suburbia* (London: Pembridge Press, 1981).
Eley, Geoff and Keith Nield, *The Future of Class in History: What's Left of the Social?* (Ann Arbor: University of Michigan Press, 2007).

Fairchilds, C., *Domestic Enemies: Servants and Their Masters in Old Regime France* (Baltimore: Johns Hopkins University Press, 1984).

Fisher, Kate, *Birth Control, Sex and Marriage in Britain 1918–1960* (Oxford: Oxford University Press, 2006).

—— and Simon Szreter, '"She Was Quite Satisfied with the Arrangements I Made": Gender and Birth Control in Britain 1920–1950', *Past and Present*, 169 (2000), 161–93.

Forty, Adrian, *Objects of Desire: Design and Society, 1750–1980* (London: Thames and Hudson, 1986).

Freedman, Jesse, '"To Feel Fiercely": Tradition, Heritage, and Nostalgia in English History', *The History Teacher*, 39 1 (2005), 107–15.

Freeman, June, *The Making of the Modern Kitchen: A Cultural History* (Oxford: Berg, 2003).

Gathorne-Hardy, Jonathan, *The Rise and Fall of the British Nanny* (London: Hodder and Stoughton, 1972).

Gatrell, Vic, *City of Laughter: Sex and Satire in Eighteenth-Century London* (London: Atlantic Books, 2006).

Giddens, Anthony, *The Transformation of Intimacy: Love, Sexuality and Eroticism in Modern Societies* (Cambridge: Polity Press, 1993).

Giles, Judy, *Women, Identity and Private Life in Britain* (London: MacMillan, 1995).

——, 'Help for Housewives: Domestic Service and the Reconstruction of Domesticity in Britain, 1940–50', *Women's History Review*, 10 2 (2001), 299–323.

——, *The Parlour and the Suburb: Domestic Identities, Class, Femininity and Modernity* (Oxford: Berg, 2004).

——, *Good Housekeeping: Professionalising the Housewife, 1920–50* (Aldershot: Ashgate, 2005).

Gillis, John R., 'Servants, Sexual Relations, and the Risks of Illegitimacy in London, 1801–1900', *Feminist Studies*, 5 (1979), 142–73.

——, *Memory and Identity: The History of a Relationship* (Princeton: Princeton University Press, 1994).

Gilroy, Paul, *The Black Atlantic: Modernity and Double Consciousness* (London: Verso, 1993).

Glassberg, David, 'Public History and the Study of Memory', *Public Historian* 18 2 (1996), 7–23.

Glenn, Evelyn Nakano, *Issei, Nisei, War Bride: Three Generations of Japanese American Women in Domestic Service* (Philadelphia: Temple University Press, 1986).

Glucksmann, Mirriam, *Women Assemble: Women Workers and the New Industries in Inter-War Britain* (London: Routledge, 1990).

Gordon, Eleanor and Gwyneth Nair, *Public Lives: Women, Family and Society in Victorian Britain*, (New Haven, CT/London: Yale University Press, 2003).

Gordon, Sarah, *Humour and Household Relationships: Servants in Late Medieval and Sixteenth-Century French Farce* (Basingstoke: Palgrave, 2008).

Graves, Robert and Alan Hodge, *The Long Weekend: A Social History of Great Britain 1918–1939* (Manchester: Carcanet, 2006).

Gregson, N. and M. Lowe, *Servicing the Middle Classes: Class, Gender and Waged Domestic Labour in Contemporary Britain* (London: Routledge, 1994).

Grossmith, George and Weedon Grossmith, *The Diary of a Nobody* (London: Collector's Library, 2008).

Halbwachs, Maurice, *On Collective Memory* (Chicago: University of Chicago Press, 1992 [1950]).

Hall, Gary and Simon Wortham, 'Rethinking Authority: Interview with Homi K. Bhabha', *Angelaki: A New Journal in Philosophy, Literature, and the Social Sciences*, 2 2 (1996), 59–63.

Hamlett, Jane, *Material Relations: Domestic Interiors and Middle-Class Families in England 1850–1910* (Manchester: Manchester University Press, 2011).

Hammerton, A. James, 'Pooterism or Partnership? Marriage and Masculine Identity in the Lower Middle Class, 1870–1920', *Journal of British Studies*, 38 3 (1991), 291–321.

——, 'The Perils of Mrs Pooter: Satire, Modernity and Motherhood in the Lower Middle-Class, England, 1870–1920', *Women's History Review*, 8 2 (1999), 261–76.

Hansen, Karen Tranberg, *Distant Companions: Servants and Employers in Zambia, 1900–1985* (Ithaca, NY: Cornell University Press, 1989).

Hardyment, Christine, *From Mangle to Microwave: The Mechanisation of Household Work* (Cambridge: Polity Press, 1988).

Harrison, Brian, 'For Church, Queen and Family: The Girls' Friendly Society, 1874–1920', *Past and Present*, 61 (1973), 107–38.

Harrison, Mary, 'Domestic Service between the Wars: The Experiences of Two Rural Women', *Oral History*, 16 1 (1988), 48–54.

Hart, Marjolein 't and Dennis Bos, *Humour and Social Protest* (Cambridge: Cambridge University Press, 2007).

Hearn, Mona, *Below Stairs: Domestic Service Remembered in Dublin and Beyond, 1880–1922* (Dublin: Lilliput Press, 1993).

Hegstrom, Jane, 'Reminiscences of Below Stairs: English Female Domestic Servants between the Two World Wars', *Women's Studies*, 36 1 (2007), 15–33.

Hewison, Robert, *The Heritage Industry: Britain in a Climate of Decline* (London: Methuen, 1987).

Heynen, Hilde and Gülsüm Baydar, *Negotiating Domesticity: Spatial Productions of Gender in Modern Architecture* (London: Routledge, 2005).

Higgs, Edward, 'Victorian Domestic Service', *Social History*, 8 (1983), 201–10.

Higman, B. W., *Domestic Service in Australia* (Melbourne: Melbourne University Press, 2002).

Hilton, Matthew, *Consumerism in Twentieth-Century Britain: The Search for a Historical Movement* (Cambridge: Cambridge University Press, 2003).

Hinton, James, *Women, Social Leadership, and the Second World War: Continuities of Class* (Oxford: Oxford University Press, 2002).

Hochschild, Arlie Russell, *The Commercialization of Intimate Life: Notes from Home and Work* (Berkeley: University of California Press, 2003).

Hoggart, Richard, *The Way We Live Now* (London: Chatto and Windus, 1995).

Holden, Katherine, *The Shadow of Marriage: Singleness in England, 1914–60* (Manchester: Manchester University Press, 2007).

Horn, Pamela, *The Rise and Fall of the Victorian Servant* (Gloucs: Alan Sutton, 1990).

——, *Life below Stairs in the Twentieth Century* (Stroud: Sutton, 2001).

Hoskins, Janet, *Biographical Objects: How Things Tell the Stories of People's Lives* (New York: Routledge, 1998).

Howkins, Alun and Nicola Verdon, 'Adaptable and Sustainable? Male Farm Service and the Agricultural Labour Force in Midland and Southern England, c.1850–1925', *Economic History Review*, 61 2 (2008), 467–95.

Huggett, Frank E., *Life below Stairs: Domestic Servants in England from Victorian Times* (London: Book Club Associates, 1977).

Hutber, Patrick, *The Decline and Fall of the Middle Class, and How It Can Fight Back* (Harmondsworth: Penguin, 1977).
Hyam, Ronald, *Empire and Sexuality: The British Experience* (Manchester: Manchester University Press, 1990).
Jackson, Alan, *The Middle Classes 1900–1950* (Nairn: Daivd St John Thomas, 1991).
Jamieson, Lynn, *Limited Resources and Limiting Conventions: Working-Class Mothers and Daughters in Urban Scotland, c. 1890–1925* (Oxford: Blackwell, 1986).
Jeremiah, David, *Architecture and Design for the Family in Britain, 1900–70* (Manchester: Manchester University Press, 2000).
Johnson, Paul, *Saving and Spending: The Working-Class Economy in Britain 1870–1939* (Oxford: Clarendon Press, 1985).
Joyce, Patrick, *Visions of the People: Industrial England and the Question of Class, 1848–1914* (Cambridge: Cambridge University Press, 1991).
Katzman, David M., *Seven Days a Week: Women and Domestic Service in Industrializing America* (New York: Oxford University Press, 1978).
Kearney, Patrick J., *The Private Case: An Annotated Bibliography of the Private Case Erotica Collection in the British (Museum) Library* (London: Jay Landesman, 1981).
Kidd, Alan and David Nicholls, *Gender, Civic Culture and Consumerism: Middle-Class Identity in Britain, 1800–1940* (Manchester: Manchester University Press, 1999).
Koch, Gertrude, 'On Pornographic Cinema', *Jump Cut: A Review of Contemporary Media*, 35 (1990), 17–29.
Kushner, Tony (1991), 'An Alien Occupation—Jewish Refugees and Domestic Service in Britain, 1933–1948', in Werner E. Mosse (ed.), *Second Chance: Two Generations of German-Speaking Jews in the United Kingdom* (Tubingen: JCB Mohr), 553–78.
Langhamer, Claire, *Women's Leisure in England 1920–1960* (Manchester: Manchester University Press, 2000).
——, 'The Meanings of Home in Postwar Britain', *Journal of Contemporary History*, 40 (2005), 341–62.
Last, Nella, Patricia E. Malcolmson, and Robert W. Malcolmson, *Nella Last's Peace: The Post-War Diaries of Housewife, 49* (London: Profile, 2008).
Behlmer, George K. and Fred M. Leventhal, *Singular Continuities: Tradition, Nostalgia and Identity in Modern British Culture* (Stanford: Stanford University Press, 2000).
Light, Alison, *Forever England: Femininity, Literature and Conservatism between the Wars* (London: Routledge, 1991).
——, *Mrs Woolf and the Servants: The Hidden Heart of Domestic Service* (London: Penguin, 2007).
Littler, J. and R. Naidoo, *White Past, Multicultural Present: Heritage and National Stories* (Basingstoke: Macmillan, 2004).
Lockwood, David, 'Sources of Variation in Working Class Images of Society', *Sociological Review*, 14 (1966), 248–67.
Long, Helen, *The Edwardian House* (Manchester: Manchester University Press, 1993).
Lowenthal, David, *The Past Is a Foreign Country* (Cambridge: Cambridge University Press, 1985).
McBride, Theresa, *The Domestic Revolution* (London: Croom Helm, 1976).
McKibbin, Ross, *Classes and Cultures: England 1918–1951* (Oxford: Oxford University Press, 1998).
McLaren, Angus, *The Trials of Masculinity: Policing Sexual Boundaries 1870–1930* (Chicago: University of Chicago Press, 1997).

Mandler, Peter, *The Fall and Rise of the Stately Home* (New Haven, CT: Yale University Press, 1997).
——, 'Problems in Cultural History', *Cultural and Social History*, 1 (2004), 94–117.
Marcus, Steven, *The Other Victorians: A Study of Sexuality and Pornography in Mid-Nineteenth Century England* (London: Weidenfeld and Nicolson, 1966).
Marson, Richard, *Inside Updown—The Story of Upstairs Downstairs* (Bristol: Kaleidoscope, 2001).
Meacham, Standish, *A Life Apart: The English Working Class 1890–1914* (London: Thames and Hudson, 1977).
Medhurst, Andy, *A National Joke: Popular Comedy and English Cultural Identities* (Abingdon: Routledge, 2007).
Meldrum, Tim, *Domestic Service and Gender, 1660–1750: Life and Work in the London Household* (Harlow: Longman, 2000).
Melman, Billie, *Women and the Popular Imagination in the Twenties* (London: Macmillan, 1988).
Momsen, Janet Henshall, *Gender, Migration and Domestic Service* (London: Routledge, 1999).
Mort, Frank, 'Social and Symbolic Fathers and Sons in Postwar Britain', *Journal of British Studies*, 38 3 (1999), 353–84.
——, 'Striptease: The Erotic Female Body and Live Sexual Entertainment in Mid-Twentieth-Century London', *Social History*, 32 1 (2007), 27–53.
Moyse, Cordelia, *A History of the Mothers' Union Women, Anglicanism and Globalisation, 1876–2008* (Woodbridge: Boydell Press, 2009).
Muggeridge, K., *Beatrice Webb: A Life* (London: Secker and Warburg, 1967).
Nash, Walter, *The Language of Humour: Style and Technique in Comic Discourse* (London: Longman, 1985).
Nava, Mica, *Modernity's Disavowal: Women, the City and the Department Store* (London: Routledge, 1996).
Nazarieff, Serge, *The Stereoscopic Nude 1850–1930* (Cologne: Benedikt Taschen, 1993).
Nead, Lynda, 'Strip: Moving Bodies in the 1890s', *Early Popular Visual Culture*, 3 2 (2005), 135–50.
Nelson, Margaret K., *'I Saw Your Nanny': Gossip and Shame in the Surveillance of Child Care* (Nashville: Vanderbilt University Press, 2009).
Newby, Howard, *The Deferential Worker* (London: Allen Lane, 1977).
Noakes, Lucy, 'From War Service to Domestic Service: Ex-Servicewomen and the Free Passage Scheme, 1919– 22', *Twentieth Century British History*, 22, 1, 1–27.
Nora, Pierre, 'Between Memory and History: Les Lieux De Memoire', *Representations*, 26 (1989), 7–24.
——, *Realms of Memory: Rethinking the French Past* (New York: Columbia University Press, 1996).
Offer, Avner, *The Challenge of Affluence: Self-Control and Well-Being in the United States and Britain since 1950* (Oxford: Oxford University Press, 2006).
Oliver, Paul, Ian Bentley, and Ian Davis, *Dunroamin': The Suburban Semi and Its Enemies* (London: Barrie and Jenkins, 1994).
Palmer, Phyllis, *Domesticity and Dirt: Housewives and Domestic Servants in the United States, 1920–1945* (Philadelphia: Temple University Press, 1989).
Pearsall, Ronald, *Collapse of Stout Party: Victorian Wit and Humour* (London: Weidenfeld and Nicolson, 1975).
Perkin, Harold, *The Rise of Professional Society: England since 1880* (London: Routledge, 1989).

Philips, Deborah and Ian Haywood, *Brave New Causes: Women in British Postwar Fictions* (London: Leicester University Press, 1998).

Pooley, Siân, 'Domestic Servants and Their Urban Employers: A Case Study of Lancaster, 1880–1914', *Economic History Review*, 62 2 (2009), 405–29.

Popular Memory Group, 'Popular Memory: Theory, Politics, Method', in G. McLennan, R. Johnson, B. Schwarz, and D. Sutton (eds), *Making Histories: Studies in History-Writing and Politics* (London: Hutchinson, 1982), 205–52.

Ravetz, Alison, with Richard Turkington, *The Place of Home: English Domestic Environments, 1914–2000* (London: SPON, 1995).

Redclift, Nanneke and Enzo Mingione, *Beyond Employment: Household, Gender and Subsistence* (Oxford: Blackwell, 1985).

Robbins, Bruce, *The Servant's Hand: English Fiction from Below* (New York: Columbia University Press, 1986).

Roberts, E., *A Woman's Place: An Oral History of Working-Class Women 1890–1940* (Oxford: Blackwell, 1995).

Romain, Gemma, *Connecting Histories: A Comparative Exploration of African-Caribbean and Jewish History and Memory in Modern Britain* (London: Kegan Paul, 2006).

Roper, Lyndal, *Oedipus and the Devil: Witchcraft, Sexuality, and Religion in Early Modern Europe* (London: Taylor and Francis, 1994).

Roper, Michael, 'Slipping out of View: Subjectivity and Emotion in Gender History', *History Workshop Journal*, 59 (2005), 57–72.

——, *The Secret Battle: Emotional Survival in the Great War* (Manchester: Manchester University Press, 2009).

Rosenman, Ellen B., *Unauthorized Pleasures: Accounts of Victorian Sexual Experience* (Ithaca, NY: Cornell University Press, 2003).

Ross, Duncan M., ' "Penny Banks" in Glasgow, 1850–1914', *Financial History Review*, 9 1 (2002), 21–39.

Rowbotham, Shelia, 'Cleaners' Organizing in Britain from the 1970s: A Personal Account', *Antipode*, 38 3 (2002), 608–25.

Ruger, Jan, 'Laughter and War in Berlin', *History Workshop Journal*, 67 1 (2009), 23–43.

Russell, Dave, *Popular Music in England, 1840–1914: A Social History* (London: St Martin's Press, 1997).

Rutherford, Janice Williams, *Selling Mrs. Consumer: Christine Frederick and the Rise of Household Efficiency* (Athens: University of Georgia Press, 2003).

Ryan, Louise, 'Family Matters: (E)Migration, Familial Networks and Irish Women in Britain', *Sociological Review*, 52 3 (2004), 351–70.

Sa'ar, Amalia, 'Postcolonial Feminism, the Politics of Identification, and the Liberal Bargain', *Gender and Society*, 19 5 (2005), 680–700.

Sambrook, Pamela, *Keeping Their Place: Domestic Service in the Country House* (Stroud: Sutton, 2005).

Samuel, Raphael, *Theatres of Memory: Past and Present in Contemporary Culture* (London: Verso, 1994).

Sarti, Raffaella, 'All Masters Discourage the Marrying of Their Male Servants, and Admit Not by Any Means the Marriage of the Female': Domestic Service and Celibacy in Western Europe from the Sixteenth to the Nineteenth Century', *European History Quarterly*, 38 3 (2008), 417–49.

Schwarz, Laura, *Gender, Education and Community: The Experience of St Hugh's College 1886–2011* (London: Profile Books, 2011).

Schwarz, Leonard, 'English Servants and Their Employers during the Eighteenth and Nineteenth Centuries', *Economic History Review*, 52 2 (1999), 236–56.

Scott, James C., *Weapons of the Weak: Everyday Forms of Peasant Resistance* (New Haven, CT: Yale University Press, 1985).

——, *Domination and the Arts of Resistance: Hidden Transcripts* (New Haven, CT: Yale University Press, 1990).

Scott, Joan W., 'The "Class" We Have Lost', *International Labor and Working-Class History*, 57 (2000), 69–75.

Seizer, Susan, 'Jokes, Gender, and Discursive Distance on the Tamil Popular Stage', *American Ethnologist*, 24 1 (1997), 62–90.

Sigel, Lisa Z., 'Name Your Pleasure: The Transformation of Sexual Language in Nineteenth-Century British Pornography', *Journal of the History of Sexuality*, 9 4 (2000), 395–419.

——, *Governing Pleasures: Pornography and Social Change in England, 1815–1914* (New Brunswick: Rutgers University Press, 2002).

——, *International Exposure: Perspectives on Modern European Pornography, 1800–2000* (London: Rutgers University Press, 2005).

Simmel, Georg, 'The Sociology of Conflict: I', *American Journal of Sociology*, 9 (1903), 490–525.

Skeggs, Beverley, *Formations of Class and Gender: Becoming Respectable* (London: Sage, 1997).

——, *Class, Self, Culture* (London: Routledge, 2004).

Smallshaw, Kay, *How to Run Your Home without Help* (London: Persephone Books, 2005).

Smith, Clarissa, *A Perfectly British Business: Stagnation, Continuities, and Changes on the Top Shelf* (London: Rutgers University Press, 2005).

Smith, Sidonie and Julia Watson, *Women, Autobiography, Theory: A Reader* (Madison: University of Wisconsin Press, 1998).

Spargo, Tamsin, *Reading the Past: Literature and History* (Basingstoke: Macmillan, 2000).

Stedman Jones, Gareth, *Languages of Class: Studies in English Working Class History 1832–1982* (Cambridge: Cambridge University Press, 1982).

——, *Outcast London: A Study in the Relationship between Classes in Victorian Society* (Oxford: Clarendon Press, 1991).

Steedman, Carolyn, *Landscape for a Good Woman: A Story of Two Lives* (London: Virago, 1986).

——, 'Lord Mansfield's Women', *Past and Present*, 176 1 (2002), 105–43.

——, 'Servants and Their Relationship to the Unconscious', *Journal of British Studies*, 42 (2003), 316–50.

——, 'Poetical Maids and Cooks Who Wrote', *Eighteenth-Century Studies*, 39 9 (2005), 1–17.

——, *Master and Servant: Love and Labour in the English Industrial Age* (Cambridge: Cambridge University Press, 2007).

——, *Labours Lost: Domestic Service and the Making of Modern England* (Cambridge: Cambridge University Press, 2009).

Straub, Kristina, *Domestic Affairs: Intimacy, Eroticism, and Violence between Servants and Masters in Eighteenth-Century Britain* (Baltimore: Johns Hopkins University Press, 2009).

Streatfeild, Noel (ed.), *The Day before Yesterday: Firsthand Stories of Fifty Years Ago* (London: Collins, 1956).

Summerfield, Penny, 'Culture and Composure: Creating Narratives of the Gendered Self in Oral History Interviews', *Cultural and Social History*, 1 1 (2004), 65–93.

Sutherland, Daniel E., *Americans and Their Servants: Domestic Service in the United States from 1800 to 1920* (Baton Rouge/London: Louisiana State University Press, 1981).

Szreter, Simon and R. M. Smith, *Fertility, Class, and Gender in Britain, 1860–1940:* (Cambridge: Cambridge University Press, 1996).

Tai, Hue-Tam Ho, 'Remembered Realms: Pierre Nora and French National Memory', *American Historical Review*, 106 3 (2001), 906–22.

Tang, Isabel, *Pornography: The Secret History of Civilisation* (London: Channel Four Books, 1999).

Tannock, Stuart, 'Nostalgia Critique', *Cultural Studies*, 9 3 (1995), 453–64.

Taylor, Pam, *Daughters and Mothers—Maids and Mistresses: Domestic Service between the Wars* (London: Hutchinson, 1979).

Thaddeus, Jane, 'Swift's Directions to Servants', *Studies in Eighteenth-Century Culture*, 16 (1986), 107–23.

Thompson, Paul, *The Edwardians: The Remaking of British Society* (London: Routledge, 1992).

Tivers, J., 'Performing Heritage: The Use of "Live" Actors in Heritage Presentations', *Leisure Studies*, 21 3 (2002), 187–200.

Todd, Selina, 'Poverty and Aspiration: Young Women's Entry to Employment in Inter-War England', *Twentieth Century British History*, 15 2 (2004), 119–42.

——, *Young Women, Work and Family in England, 1918–1950* (Oxford: Oxford University Press, 2005).

——, 'Domestic Service and Class Relations in Britain 1900–1950' *Past and Present*, 203 (2009), 181–204.

Tosh, John, *A Man's Place: Masculinity and the Middle-Class Home in Victorian England* (New Haven, CT/London: Yale University Press, 1999).

——, *The Pursuit of History: Aims, Methods and New Directions in the Study of Modern History* (London: Longman, 2002).

——, *Manliness and Masculinities in Nineteenth-Century Britain: Essays on Gender, Family, and Empire* (Harlow: Pearson Longman, 2005).

Toulalan, Sarah, *Imagining Sex: Pornography and Bodies in Seventeenth-Century England* (Oxford: Oxford University Press, 2007).

Turner, E. S., *What the Butler Saw* (London: Penguin, 2001).

Urban, Andrew, 'Irish Domestic Servants, "Biddy" and Rebellion in the American Home, 1850–1900', *Gender and History*, 21 2 (2009), 263–86.

Vigne, Thea, 'Parents and Children 1890–1918: Distance and Dependence', *Oral History*, 3 1 (1975), 5–13.

Wahrman, Dror, *Imagining the Middle Class: The Political Representation of Class in Britain, c.1780–1840* (Cambridge: Cambridge University Press, 1995).

Walter, Bronwen, *Irish Domestic Servants and English National Identity* (Bern: Peter Lang, 2004).

——, 'Strangers on the Inside: Irish Women Servants in England, 1881', *Immigrants and Minorities*, 27 2 (2009), 279–99.

Waterfield, Giles, *Below Stairs: 400 Years of Servants' Portraits* (London: National Portrait Gallery, 2004).

Waters, Chris, 'Representations of Everyday Life: L.S. Lowry and the Landscape of Memory in Postwar Britain', *Representations*, 6 (1999), 121–50.

Waterson, Merlin, *The Servants' Hall: A Domestic History of Erdigg* (London: Routledge, 1980).
Webster, Wendy, *Imagining Home* (London: UCL Press, 1998).
Weeks, Jeffrey, *The World We Have Won: The Remaking of Erotic and Intimate Life* (London: Routledge, 2007).
White, Jerry, *Rothschild Buildings: Life in an East End Tenement Bock, 1887–1920* (London: Routledge & Keagan Paul, 1980).
Whitehorn, Katharine, *Selective Memory* (London: Virago, 2007).
Wilks, C. and C. Kelly, 'Fact, Fiction and Nostalgia: As Assessment of Heritage Interpretation at Living Musuems', *International Journal of Intangible Heritage*, 3 (2008), 127–43.
Williams, Linda, *Hard Core: Power, Pleasure and the 'Frenzy of the Visible'* (Berkeley: University of California Press, 1989).
Williams, Raymond, *The Country and the City* (Oxford: Oxford University Press, 1973).
Willis, Paul E., *Learning to Labour: How Working Class Kids Get Working Class Jobs* (Farnborough: Saxon House, 1978).
Wills, Abigail, 'Delinquency, Masculinity and Citizenship in England 1950–1970', *Past and Present*, 187 (2005), 157–85.
Wolf, Nicholas, 'Scéal Grinn? Jokes, Puns, and the Shaping of Bilingualism in Nineteenth-Century Ireland', *Journal of British Studies*, 48 1 (2009), 51–75.
Wolff, Janet, 'The Invisible Flaneuse. Women and the Literature of Modernity', *Theory, Culture and Society*, 2 3 (1985), 37–46.
Wright, Patrick, *On Living in an Old Country: The National Past in Contemporary Britain* (London: Verso, 1985).
—— and Michael Bommes, *'Charms of Residence': The Public and the Past* (London: Hutchinson 1982).
Young, James E., *The Texture of Memory: Holocaust Memorials and Meaning* (New Haven, CT: Yale University Press, 1993).

Index

Association of Trained Charwomen 37

Banks, E. 147–8
Bateman, H. M. 166–7
Beerbohm, M. 85, 145, 148
Belcher, G. 154
Bevin, E. 90
Black, C. 99, 100, 128
Brandt, B. 5, 9
British Broadcasting Corporation (BBC) 123, 131, 156, 211, 215
Brittain, V. 1, 11

Chesterton, A. 37, 39
cinema 44, 149, 177–8, 186, 212, 215–16
class 18–20, 29, 60–2, 74, 205, 226–7, 233–4
   lower-middle 65, 69–70, 100, 146–7, 149, 163–5, 217, 230–1
   middle 64–6, 69–70, 96–7, 105, 136, 163–4, 217
   working 6, 19, 29–30, 40, 80–2, 99, 146, 184, 211, 242
comics 141, 151–2, 155, 156, 186–7, 190–1
Compton-Burnett, I. 159
Cooper, L. 18, 66
Craig, E. 116
cultural history 6–7

Darwin, E. 2, 147
David, E. 130
Davidoff, L. 29, 92, 145, 179, 180
Dickens, M. 121, 155, 159, 163, 166
domestic service
   'characters' and references 33, 52, 75, 91
   and children 10, 51, 76, 93–6, 109, 158–9, 180, 230
   emotions 9–11, 44–6, 48, 74, 94–5, 109, 134, 156, 228–9, 239–40
   erotics 96, 133–4, 173–5, 180–6, 189–90, 201–5, 212
   farm service 6, 32, 34, 50, 77
   gift-giving 50, 53, 75–6, 237
   'great house' service 5, 33, 68, 93, 182, 205, 216, 220–7
   jokes 83, 140, 142, 146, 147, 157–9, 163, 166–8, 186–8, 226
   law 87–8
   'living in' 39–41
   naming 17, 49, 78–9, 108, 134–5, 174, 238
   wages 52–3, 55–6, 75, 108, 134, 137
domestic servants
   au pairs 55, 110, 127, 133–5, 192

chars and 'dailies' 32, 35–9, 40–1, 50, 83, 101, 135–7, 151, 154, 156, 192, 236–7
cleaners 8, 14, 28, 35–7, 43–5, 72, 78, 80, 137, 218, 235
cooks 92–3, 125–6, 130, 151, 215
disabled 15, 42–3, 86
Irish 16, 18, 37–8, 77–8, 145
   see also Ireland
Jewish 17, 78–9, 135, 167–8
lady helps 105–9
memoirs of 23, 211
mother's helps 109–10, 132, 134
mothers of 29–30, 33–4, 48, 52–3, 56–9
male 14–16, 85–6, 153, 160–2, 193–4, 202, 203, 229
migrants 13, 14, 16, 78–80, 86, 90, 243
portraits 54–5
siblings of 34, 48–9
'single-handed' and maids-of-all-work 48, 66, 73, 178
smell 159, 170, 180, 224
step-girls and steps 36–7, 45, 62
Welsh 38, 57
   see also Wales
DWU, *see* National Union of Domestic Workers

Edwardian Country House (television series) 219–20, 230, 233
electricity 41 n. 66, 115, 117, 119, 123, 129
empire, British 17, 79 n. 77, 101 n. 10, 181
employers
   female 46, 51, 67–74, 85–6, 124–5
   male 16, 83–8
   working-class 80–2
   unmarried 82, 85
employment exchanges 42
ethnicity 17–18, 33, 61, 78–81, 145, 167–8, 181, 199, 213–14, 243

factory work 32, 33, 44, 53
family history 211, 216, 218, 222, 225, 231
feminism 8, 63, 71, 91, 103–4, 120, 131, 217–18, 229–30
Firth, V. 36, 37
Foley, W. 31, 32–3, 43, 68 n. 23, 183, 203
Frederick, C. 111–12, 121
Fremlin, C. 19, 155 n. 52, 165, 192

gas 98 n. 1, 114–15, 117
Gavron, H. 131
generational divides 48–9, 82–3
Giles, J. 6, 160, 242

Gilman, C. P. 2, 71
governesses 178
Gosford Park (film) 216
Graves, R. 69, 95, 103, 124, 179
Greer, G. 131

Hancock, F. 128, 155
Hardy, T. 207
Harrison, R. 10, 27, 49, 93
heritage 207–9, 213–15, 220–8, 232–3
Holden, U. 159, 165, 188
home helps 14, 36, 40, 129, 133, 156
housewives 99, 115, 116, 119–20, 126, 131–3, 136, 138–9, 170–1
humour 142–5, 147–9, 150, 157, 169–72, 187

Institute of Home Help Organisers 156
institutional care 33–5, 36, 52
Ireland 12, 15, 77, 79 n. 77, 89, 223

Joyce, J. 185

kitchens 116, 121–6

labour-saving 102–3, 110–15, 116–20
Lancashire 12, 37
Last, N. 43
laughter 140–2, 145–6, 156–62, 164–5, 166, 168–9, 186–9
Light, A. 51, 65, 92
London, J. 5

Markham, V. 95, 128, 155
Mass Observation 36, 43, 135
Masterman, C. 65, 70
material culture 45, 220–1, 222–4
memory 207, 209–10, 227–32
Ministry of Labour 12, 14, 90, 128, 154, 161
Mitchison, N. 120, 238
modernity 3, 120, 129, 139, 237–8, 242
music hall 144, 148–51, 155, 170, 186–7

1900 House (television series) 217–19, 230
National Institute of Houseworkers 128–9, 135
National Union of Domestic Workers 39, 90, 108, 129, 240–1
nannies 10, 73, 93–5, 108–10, 134, 160, 235
New Survey of London Life and Labour, 39, 120
Noakes, D. 26, 53, 54–5

Oliver, K. 8, 26, 104, 160
oral history 23–5, 27, 30, 211

orphans, *see* institutional care
Orwell, G. 146, 170, 224

Panton, J. E. 76, 85, 101
Peck, W. 124–5
Peel, C. S. 19, 63, 71, 108, 115, 121–2, 123, 236–7
Pooter, C. 163–4
pornography 175–8, 194–201
Powell, M. 50, 161, 163, 165, 183, 184, 192, 193, 203
Priestley, J. B. 2, 4, 103

Raverat, G. 104, 193
refugees 13, 17, 78, 81, 86, 90, 131, 132
religion 33, 38, 135
Remains of the Day (book and film) 215–16, 232
Rennie, J. 57, 72, 75, 92, 183
Reynolds, S. 173–4, 180
Roper, M. 10, 85, 95, 141

Scotland 12, 15 n. 56, 16, 44, 46–7, 72, 84, 105, 193
Schreiner, O. 71
servantlessness 98, 100–5, 111, 126–7, 132–3, 136–9
Sherriff, R. C. 45, 83
Steedman, C. 4, 28, 157, 228
Sturgeon (née Powley), H. 7, 48, 166, 188
Strachey, R. 13

Taylor, P. 29, 57
Thatcher, M. 234
Todd, S. 33, 56, 60–1, 242
Tosh, J. 84

Upstairs, Downstairs (television series) 170, 211–13, 230, 232
unions, 40, 88–92, 163
 see also National Union of Domestic Workers

Wales 11, 33, 57, 77, 82
Webb, B. 95–6
Whitehorn, K. 1, 132, 133, 139
Wodehouse, P. G. 153
Women's Industrial Council 12, 58
Woolf, V. 51, 124
workhouse, *see* institutional care
World War I 1, 10, 11, 12, 15, 84–5, 96, 102, 103, 116–17
World War II 14, 41, 79, 99, 125, 127, 130

Lightning Source UK Ltd.
Milton Keynes UK
UKOW04f0853190614

233701UK00002B/3/P